Soldiers and Civilians, Transport and Provisions

Early Modern Military Logistics and Supply Systems during The British Civil Wars, 1638–1653

Glenn W. Price

'This is the Century of the Soldier', Fulvio Testi, Poet, 1641

Helion & Company Limited
Unit 8 Amherst Business Centre
Budbrooke Road
Warwick
CV34 5WE
England
Tel. 01926 499 619
Email: info@helion.co.uk
Website: www.helion.co.uk
Twitter: @helionbooks
Visit our blog http://blog.helion.co.uk/

Published by Helion & Company 2023
Designed and typeset by Mary Woolley (www.battlefield-design.co.uk)
Cover designed by Paul Hewitt, Battlefield Design (www.battlefield-design.co.uk)

Text © Glenn W. Price 2023
Illustrations as individually credited
Maps by George Anderson © Helion & Company 2023

Every reasonable effort has been made to trace copyright holders and to obtain their permission for the use of copyright material. The author and publisher apologize for any errors or omissions in this work and would be grateful if notified of any corrections that should be incorporated in future reprints or editions of this book.

ISBN 978-1-804513-52-1

British Library Cataloguing-in-Publication Data.
A catalogue record for this book is available from the British Library.

All rights reserved. No part of this publication may be reproduced, stored in a retrieval system, or transmitted, in any form, or by any means, electronic, mechanical, photocopying, recording or otherwise, without the express written consent of Helion & Company Limited.

For details of other military history titles published by Helion & Company Limited contact the above address or visit our website: http://www.helion.co.uk.

We always welcome receiving book proposals from prospective authors.

Contents

Acknowledgements iv
Conventions and Notes v
Abbreviations vi
Introduction vii

1 Land Transportation 27
2 Water Transportation 75
3 Recruitment 110
4 Provisioning 179
Conclusion 230

Bibliography 237

Acknowledgements

I would like to thank my PhD supervisory team of Ian Atherton, Siobhan Talbott, and Andrew Sargent for their support throughout the project on which much of this book is based. I am also deeply grateful to the numerous academics, researchers, archivists, examiners, and others whose assistance and encouragement helped further refine this topic with particular thanks to Christopher Harrison, Gavin Robinson, Stuart Peachey, Anne Hughes, and Martyn Bennett.

I want to thank the team at Helion, especially Charles Singleton for this opportunity to share my research with a wider audience. Also, profuse thanks to Stephen Ede-Borrett, my (very patient) editor whose suggestions, insight, care, and handling made this book a reality.

I want to also thank those friends who gave their unwavering support, encouragement, and (where necessary) distractions; Jules Odams, Bethan Casinelli, Carl Monaghan, and Charles Anderson. Particular thanks go to Ben Odams, who never tired of hearing or talking about it.

To my parents John and Pam, to whom I owe so much, but not least for the nurturing of my fascination with history from an early age.

However, my most heartfelt thanks go to my wife Sophia because without her continued love, patience, and support, in all areas and in all things, nothing is achievable. This one is for you.

Conventions and Notes

Regarding dates, the year has been taken to begin on 1 January, rather than 25 March. Quotations from manuscript sources have not been adjusted for spelling although square brackets have been used for clarification purposes. The quotations from printed sources have been given as they appear in the printed source.

The monetary values in this book are in the contemporary English coinage of pounds, shillings, and pence. One pound (£1) was worth 20 shillings, and each shilling was worth 12 pence or pennies.

Abbreviations

BL – The British Library, London
CJ – *Journals of the House of Commons*
CSPD – *Calendar of State Papers, Domestic*
CSPI – *Calendar of State Papers, relating to Ireland*
CSPV – *Calendar of State Papers, Venetian*
HMC – Reports of the Royal Commission on Historical Manuscripts
LJ – *Journals of the House of Lords*
NRS – National Records of Scotland, Edinburgh
SA – Shropshire Archives, Shrewsbury
TNA – The National Archives, Kew
WSL – William Salt Library, Stafford

Introduction

Military logistics and supply systems are fundamental to the successful prosecution of any war. This has been true throughout the history of warfare, from earliest antiquity through to the modern age. The Chinese general and military strategist Sun Tzu, writing in the fifth century BC, claimed 'we may take it then that an army without its baggage-train is lost; without provisions it is lost; without bases of supply it is lost.'[1] No general in history could hope to defeat the enemy if his own army lacked sufficient numbers of soldiers, the weapons to equip them, the provisions to sustain them on campaign, or the means of transportation necessary to move these essentials with the army.

This was no less the case for the series of interconnected conflicts that raged across the British Isles (then including the Kingdom of Ireland) from 1639–1653. These conflicts include the First and Second Bishops' Wars (1639–1640), the Irish Rebellion (1641), the wars of the Irish Confederation (1641–1653), the English Civil Wars (1642–1651), and the Cromwellian Conquest of Scotland and Ireland (1649–1653). For brevity, and to reflect the interconnected nature of these conflicts, the British Civil Wars will be used as an umbrella term throughout this book when referring to these interconnected conflicts. The initial outbreak of these wars followed decades of internal peace, at least relative to the contemporary European experience, during which there were no substantial standing armies, merely some small garrisons and militia companies scattered around the British Isles. Subsequently, any military logistics and supply systems for these new armies had to be created from very little pre-existing structure. The progress of these wars, and the concurrent increase in the numbers and size of armies across the British Isles, provides a clear path for the historian to trace the creation, implementation, and development of military logistics and supply systems. These conflicts allow for the study of a variety of logistical and supply systems used by the various factions involved, and they provide clear evidence of differing methods, practice, and proficiency, the potential of which were often influenced by the regional capacity or

---

1   Sun Tzu, *The Art of War* (Minneapolis: Filiquarian Publishing, 2006), Chapter VII, p.38.

capabilities. The use of 'British' for these various civil wars also reflects the turn in scholarship towards a more integrated, three kingdoms, approach to the conflicts as opposed to traditional scholarship that considered the wars, and their causes, independent of one another.[2] Despite the many studies of the military history of these wars and the numerous studies on their political, economic, religious, and social ramifications, we still know surprisingly little about precisely how warfare at this time was prosecuted at an operational level, particularly in regards to how armies were moved, and supplied, both on campaign and in garrison. This book investigates and provides a detailed analysis on the logistics and supply systems of the British Civil Wars, outlining not only how they functioned but also emphasising the role and importance of military logistics in early modern warfare. This work will demonstrate how an understanding of these systems is an important contribution to wider historical debates, and one not limited to a more narrowly defined military historiography.

The terms 'logistics' and 'supply' are worth dwelling on briefly, as clarity in their definitions is understandably necessary for this study. The word 'logistics' postdates the period under study, with the word itself emerging during the development of military science as a field of theoretical analysis during the early nineteenth century. However, it is used in this work to indicate the collection and transport of supplies because not only are modern audiences more familiar with the term, but it also serves to differentiate between the transport itself and the materials being transported. These materials are usually those meant when talking about 'supplies' in modern terms. Military officers in the early modern period were generally less clear on this division, referring to the procurement, transport, distribution, and the materials themselves by the same all-encompassing word of 'supply'. This was used by contemporaries when discussing all the necessaries of campaign, be it pay, food, ammunition, or other materials. For an officer of the period, to be 'in supply' was to have access to whatever the officer needed for his forces, which included the procurement and transport of said materials. In a study which analyses the operational nature of early modern military supply systems for a modern audience, it seems sensible to provide more clarity by making use of the word 'logistics' as well as 'supply'. This is not to state that soldiers of the period did not understand the complexities of logistics and supply, but rather that they viewed these problems differently and therefore applied different terminology.

---

2   For a selection of works which consider the wars through this context see Martyn Bennett, *The Civil Wars in Britain & Ireland, 1638–1651* (Oxford: Blackwell, 1997); James Scott Wheeler, *The Irish and British Wars 1637–1654: Triumph, Tragedy, and Failure* (London: Routledge, 2002); Allan Macinnes, *The British Revolution, 1629–1660* (Basingstoke: Palgrave Macmillan, 2005).

As the published writings of veteran officers from the period reveal, there was no dedicated and specially trained support arm for supplying frontline troops. Instead, early modern field commanders at all levels, be it company, regimental, or higher, were expected to engage in the operations of movement, transport, and even the acquisition of supplies, in addition to combat duties. This will be made clear in the main body of the book, but for now it is important to understand that contemporary officers did not have the same clear demarcation between support and combat roles, rather that all such responsibilities were part of an officer's duties.

Seventeenth century military essayists have detailed both the theoretical ideal and the realities of keeping companies, regiments, and armies supplied. Francis Markham, a veteran officer who had fought in the Low Countries, France, Ireland, and various other conflicts in Europe, wrote his *Five Decades of Epistles of War* (first published in 1622) which outlined the responsibilities and duties of officers at every level of command.[3] Sir James Turner, a Scottish professional soldier and veteran of both The Thirty Years' War and the British Civil Wars, wrote a treatise on warfare, *Pallas Armata*, in the 1670s. This attempted to outline the organisation of an army in order that his readers might 'know all that belongs to a compleat Souldier', in addition to the basic duties and responsibilities of officers.[4] In an army, those few officers assigned to particular roles which supported keeping the army in supply lacked large specialist units under their command, instead acting more as liaisons and organisers between the various regiments of an army whose own officers worked to fulfil their company's or regiment's needs. According to Turner, those officers whose responsibilities included sourcing and providing the essential supplies to an army were considered very 'necessary and useful' men, without whom an army could not function.[5] Markham stated that those officers charged with supplying the needs of the army had to be both efficient and principled and were out of necessity an 'eminent person holding a place both of great Trust, Care and Estimation.'[6]

However, it was the commanders in the field themselves who were ultimately responsible for ensuring the supply needs of their forces were met. George Monck, Duke of Albemarle who had served in Ireland, England, and Scotland during the British Civil Wars, and fought for both King and for Parliament, wrote in his own *Observations upon Military & Political Affairs* that 'A General ought to be careful before he taketh the Field with his Army, that he provide for the punctual

---

3 Francis Markham, *Five Decades of Epistles of Warre* (London: 1622).
4 James Turner, *Pallas Armata: Military Essayes of the Ancient Grecian, Roman, and Modern Art of War. Written in the Years 1670 and 1671* (London: 1683).
5 Turner, *Pallas Armata*, p.201.
6 Markham, *Five Decades of Epistles of Warre*, p.101.

supplying of his Army.'[7] While this emphasises the importance that contemporary officers placed on being properly supplied, it leaves us with a problem. The rather all-encompassing use of 'supply' to signify not just the materials they needed but also their procurement, transport, and distribution, may be too ambiguous when it comes to analysing the operational methods used, our use of the terms needs to be clearer. For Antoine-Henri Jomini, writing about the Napoleonic French army in the nineteenth century, logistics was 'the art of moving armies' that comprised 'the means and arrangements which work out the plans of strategy and tactics. Strategy decides where to act; logistics brings the troops to this point.'[8] However, Jomini focused on analysing the skills of the French army's general staff rather than detailing the systems of supply themselves, so his definition is too broad for my purposes. Prussian general and military theorist Carl von Clausewitz, also writing during the nineteenth century, claimed 'The end for which a soldier is recruited, clothed, armed, and trained, the whole objective of his sleeping, eating, drinking, and marching is simply that he should fight at the right place and the right time.'[9] Martin van Creveld, in the preface to his 1977 study *Supplying War: Logistics from Wallenstein to Patton* defines logistics as 'the practical art of moving armies and keeping them supplied.'[10] Note how van Creveld folds supply in with transportation. Geoffrey Parker, discussing a period from the beginning of the sixteenth century to the end of the eighteenth century, stated that supplying armies meant providing them with sufficient 'money, equipment and food.'[11] Earl Hess, in his work on logistics in the American Civil War (1861–1865), interpreted logistics to mean only transportation infrastructure and networks: he actively chose not to include supply in his definition.[12] If we combine all of these we can arrive at a definition for logistics and supply systems suitable for this study, this being the acquisition and movement (the logistics) of the necessaries (the supplies) for an army's survival. These necessaries include the manpower needed to fill and replenish the army, the provision of food, shelter, clothing, and footwear to sustain them, the weapons, armour, and horses to equip them, and the creation

---

7 George Monck, *Observations upon Military & Political Affairs Written by the Most Honourable George, Duke of Albemarle* (London: 1671), p.36.
8 Antoine-Henri Jomini, *The Art of War*, (ed.) Charles Messenger (London: Greenhill, 1992), p.69.
9 Carl von Clausewitz, *On War* (ed.) M. Howard and P. Paret (Princeton: Princeton University Press, 1984), chapter II, p.95.
10 Martin van Creveld, *Supplying War: Logistics from Wallenstein to Patton*, 2nd Edition (Cambridge: Cambridge University Press, 2004), p.1.
11 Geoffrey Parker, *The Military Revolution: Military Innovation and the Rise of the West, 1500–1800,* 2nd Edition (Cambridge: Cambridge University Press, 2006), p.44.
12 Earl Hess, *Civil War Logistics: A Study of Military Transportation* (Baton Rouge: Louisiana State University Press, 2017), p.9.

and maintenance of the transport links necessary to provide these supplies where they needed to be. Or more succinctly, logistics and supply are the procurement and transportation of men, equipment, and provisions necessary to maintain an army in the field and the infrastructure to support this.

Some further clarification on other nomenclature used throughout this work is also necessary. 'Strategic,' 'tactical,' and 'operational' are key terms when discussing the impacts of logistics and supply systems and are therefore worth outlining. The strategic level operates at the highest level of the three being associated with long-term policies and aims related directly to the outcome of a war or a series of campaigns within a single theatre of war. The tactical level is that at which battles, and other engagements, take place and is therefore focused on events occurring during immediate contact or proximity to the enemy. The operational level sits between the strategic and tactical levels, linking the two together. It involves the employment of military forces within a theatre of war (modern forces refer to these as theatres of operations) to achieve strategic goals. Operational levels are commonly associated with the active implementation of logistics and of supply systems.[13]

Historiography

Despite the importance of logistics and supply to military campaigns it is only comparatively recently that this topic has been studied by historians of military history. Even then, considering the vast history of military conflict, those studies that do exist on logistics and supply only graze the surface – the existing military studies of the British Civil Wars focus mainly on the tactical level. It is perhaps understandable how a factor of such importance to military strategy, encompassing how to raise, feed, equip, and move men, does not appear to be covered by many works of military history, focused as they often are in the detailed tactical layer of warfare. However, this focus on the tactical (the battle) being the most important element can lead to the exclusion of other aspects of warfare. For instance, Malcolm Wanklyn and Frank Jones, in their excellent study of the major battles of the First English Civil War, argue that the war was decided solely on the battlefield due to Royalist tactical errors rather than combined with non-tactical factors such as administration, taxation, or diplomacy.[14] Studies such as these remain heavily battle-centric and when they are placed in a wider context they take the

---

13   Lawrence Freedman, *Strategy: A History* (Oxford: Oxford University Press, 2013), pp.72–75, 202–204.
14   Malcolm Wanklyn and Frank Jones, *A Military History of the English Civil War: Strategy and Tactics* (Harlow: Pearson Education, 2005).

form of a series of linked battles within a campaign, with the history focused on the immediate events leading up to the battles, the battles themselves, and their immediate aftermath.[15] While this is perhaps natural given their tactical focus, by moving from one battle to the next for an easier reconstruction of a timeline of events much of the wider detail of the conflict is lost. At a basic level a battle is a brief period, only several hours in a campaign, which itself could last weeks or even months, with associated logistical and supply requirements needing to be tended to every day of the campaign. These requirements, met or unmet, could even influence the progress, direction, or result of the campaign itself. By focusing primarily on the battles, the overwhelming majority of the human experience across that campaign, and the accompanying impacts on local populations, is simply excised from history. This study is influenced by both strategic and tactical studies of the British Civil Wars but provides new interpretations for the locations or outcomes of battles with the aim of deepening our understanding of the period. Historians have struggled to fully comprehend the strategic reasoning of contemporaries at significant sieges such as Gloucester (*cf* chapter two) and battles such as Marston Moor (*cf* chapter four), but these are logically explicable when viewed through the lens of the relevant logistical and supply issues surrounding them. This lens, and the explanation provided, can connect us, several centuries removed from these events, to the very real pressures and problems that seventeenth century officers faced. It is also possible that, as Edward Luttwak believed, the lack of studies of logistics and supply amongst military historians is due to how battles are simply seen as more entertaining or attractive to readers, Luttwak claiming that 'whatever is dramatic easily displaces what is merely important.'[16]

This curious silence runs through the academic study of military history to this day. In his passionate defence of traditional military history, John Lynn, an expert in early modern France, made no mention of either logistics or supply in his 1997 article 'The Embattled Future of Academic Military History.'[17] Lynn was, at the time, writing in defence of traditional military histories in the face of the 'new military history' that was then emerging. Despite the turn in academia to this more encompassing approach to military history, concerning itself with the impacts of

---

15 A selection of such would include Alfred Burne, and Peter Young, *The Great Civil War: A Military History of the First Civil War, 1642–1646* (Moreton-in-Marsh: Windrush Press, 1998); Stuart Reid, *Crown, Covenant, and Cromwell: The Civil Wars in Scotland, 1639–1651* (Barnsley: Frontline Books, 2012).
16 Edward Luttwak., 'Logistics and the Aristocratic Idea of War' in John Lynn (ed.), *Feeding Mars: Logistics in Western Warfare from the Middle Ages to the Present* (Boulder: Westview Press, 1993), p.4.
17 John Lynn, 'The Embattled Future of Academic Military History', *Journal of Military History*, Vol. 61, No. 4 (1997), pp.777–89.

war rather than their narratives, the study of logistics and supply has remained minimal at best. Mark Moyar's 2007 summary of the state of military history, while arguing that the field itself went far beyond tactical analysis, mentioned only two major studies which take logistics or supply into account and these were both of nineteenth and twentieth century conflicts.[18] As recently as 2018, Gary Sheffield asserted that 'the study of supply and transportation, collectively known as logistics, has been deeply unfashionable amongst military historians.'[19] Outside this problem of disinterest, or perhaps a lack of awareness of logistics and supply, there has been a noticeable dearth in the number of new academic studies focused on the military history of the British Civil Wars more broadly. Jonathon Worton, using detailed bibliographical listings, emphasised that only 20 of the 670 articles published between 2009 and 2014 that were concerned with the Civil Wars and associated British history of the seventeenth century address their military history. Only 9 of 156 theses, in progress at UK universities in 2014 regarding seventeenth century British and Irish history, were military-focused studies of any kind.[20] In 2019 there were only 3![21] This supports Ronald Hutton's belief of a decline in the study of military-focused histories of the British Civil Wars, with instead a turn towards the causes of war and the political ramifications of warfare itself.[22]

This view is further supported by James Gratton who argues that there has been an increase in work studying philosophical, religious, political, social, and gender issues at the cost of the military study of the wars.[23] Perhaps this simply reflects the shift away from histories of strategic and tactical warfare to the study of war and societies which military history scholars such as Lynn feared over two decades ago. Yet as this work will show there is much more that can be said and that focusing on issues such as logistics and supply, which connect military history to wider historical themes, could be one way in which the field of military history might be revitalised at the same time as reinforcing its connection to concepts of war and society. If that is a possibility, then more work is needed to highlight the importance of logistics and supply to all historians and this work aims to play a

---

18 Mark Moyar, 'The Current State of Military History', *The Historical Journal*, Vol. 50, No. 1 (2007), pp.225–240.
19 Gary Sheffield, *Forgotten Victory: The First World War: Myths and Realities* (Sharpe Books, 2018), Kindle Edition, loc. 3834.
20 Jonathan Worton, *To Settle the Crown: Waging Civil War in Shropshire, 1642–1648* (Solihull: Helion, 2016), p.xxx.
21 'Theses in progress (UK)', listed in *History Online*, website of the Institute of Historical Research, www.history.ac.uk/history-online, Accessed 31 Jun 2019.
22 Ronald Hutton, *The Royalist War Effort, 1642–1646*, 2nd Edition (Abingdon: Routledge, 2003), p.xviii.
23 James Gratton, *The Parliamentarian and Royalist War Effort in Lancashire, 1642–1651* (Manchester: The Chetham Society Series III Vol. 48, 2010), p.xxvii.

part in that. This book will show the closely interconnected relationships between the military and the civilian in the British Civil Wars, and the effects that the success of these relationships could have on the battlefield.

To date, most of the existing work on logistics and supply is scattered across multiple journal articles or is confined to essay chapters within larger collected works. While these works are valuable, their limitations due to their length and their focus on specific case studies do not allow for a wider contextual approach. At the time of writing, few existing works are dedicated primarily to logistics and supply and almost all of those which consider them are concerned with warfare in the nineteenth and twentieth centuries, with fewer still concentrated on the British Isles.[24] This work aims to redress some of this disparity, both as a study of operational logistics and supply more broadly, and for an early modern and British focus more specifically.

Even Marten van Creveld's pioneering study considering the impact of logistics on strategy, *Supplying War: Logistics from Wallenstein to Patton*, spends only a little over 30 pages on the history of military logistics in Europe for the years 1560 through to 1805.[25] The early modern period is discussed only in terms of the Thirty Years' War, and primarily the campaigns of Gustav II Adolph, King of Sweden, and this more as a baseline for wars of later periods. The innovative nature of van Creveld's initial work lay in highlighting the implications that logistical needs had on military strategy and battlefield success. In the balance of his book, van Creveld used examples of logistical needs to challenge existing historical assumptions and narratives of campaigns during the Napoleonic wars and in both World Wars, most notably the Schlieffen Plan and Operation Barbarossa. *Supplying War* was largely concerned with the influence logistics had on strategy, and this study broadens that by highlighting the value that studying logistics and supply can have on more than simply military history.

---

24 Examples include Julian Thompson, *Lifeblood of War: Logistics in Armed Conflict*, (London: Brassey's, 1998); For the British experience in World War One see Ian Brown, *British Logistics on the Western Front*, (Westport, Connecticut: Praeger Publishers, 1998); For a modern look at logistics consider P. D. Foxton, *Powering War: Modern Land Force Logistics*, (London: Brassey's, 1994); For the U.S. see James Huston, *The Sinews of War: Army Logistics 1775–1953* (Washington D.C.: Office of the Chief of Military History, United States Army, 1966); Roland Ruppenthal, *Logistical Support of the Armies*, II Vols. (Washington D.C.: Office of the Chief of Military History, United States Army, 1959) provides the U.S. Army's official history of logistics during World War Two in the European Theatre.
25 van Creveld, *Supplying War*, 'The background of Two Centuries', pp.5–39. This summary of the period is not limited to van Creveld, John Lynn, giving his slightly longer timeframe of 1500 to 1815, summarises it over a total of only 8 pages, including notes. See Lynn's introduction for the section on early modern logistics, in Lynn (ed.), *Feeding Mars*, pp.101–108.

The importance logistics and supply can have on areas of study other than battlefield or campaign planning is illustrated by Geoffrey Parker's 1972 work, *The Army of Flanders and the Spanish Road*, which spends little time considering the combat effectiveness or battle record of his chosen army of interest in detail.[26] Parker focuses instead on the extensive supply needs of this force, the administration that it created, and the implications that meeting these needs had on Spain's foreign policy. Interestingly, in the second edition, issued in 1996, the chapter previously titled 'The Army of Flanders and Logistics' is renamed 'The Army of Flanders and Grand Strategy,' perhaps to reflect the efforts to supply and maintain such a large and distant army requiring the extensive use of Spain's widespread dominions alongside diplomatic agreements with multiple realms.[27] Parker's work highlights how, to paraphrase Luttwak, the undramatic yet important logistical and supply needs of an army can have an impact on state-building, international recruitment, and even diplomacy.[28] Given the nature of the British Civil Wars as a series of internal conflicts the diplomatic aspects will not be a focus in this work, although the use of internal administration, its development, and the variety of methods of recruitment will be. Army-focused studies for the British Civil Wars exist but, unlike Parker's work on the Army of Flanders, these take very little account of the logistics and supply needs of their chosen case studies. Instead, work by Peter Young and Wilfred Emberton, John Barratt, and Chris Scott and Alan Turton are more narrative rather than analytical histories of their respective forces, while Ian Gentles and Mark Kishlansky are interested more in the political influence of the New Model Army.[29] However, this study itself owes much to the research and clarity on the individual armies that these earlier works provide. While not focused on any one army, this book will show the differences in some of the forces created by factors of logistics and supply, and will highlight and explain the resulting differences in artillery train composition, recruit quality, and strategic aims and capabilities between various armies.

---

26 Geoffrey Parker, *The Army of Flanders and the Spanish Road 1567–1659: The Logistics of Spanish Victory and Defeat in the Low Countries' Wars*, 2nd Edition (Cambridge University Press, 2004).
27 Parker, *The Army of Flanders and the Spanish Road*, pp.109–117.
28 Luttwak, 'Logistics and the Aristocratic Idea of War' p.4.
29 Peter Young, and Wilfred Emberton, *The Cavalier Army: Its Organisation and Everyday Life* (London: George Allen & Unwin, 1974); John Barratt, *Cavaliers: The Royalist Army at War, 1642–1646* (Stroud: Sutton Publishing, 2000); Christopher Scott and Alan Turton, *Hey For Old Robin! The Campaigns and Armies of the Earl of Essex During the First Civil War, 1642–44* (Solihull: Helion, 2017); Ian Gentles, *The New Model Army in England, Ireland, and Scotland, 1645–1653* (Oxford: Blackwell, 1992); Mark Kishlansky, *The Rise of the New Model Army* (Cambridge University Press, 1979).

Both van Creveld's and Parker's studies, initially published in the 1970s, were perhaps aspects of the growing interest in academia during that time of the 'military revolution' debate. This debate, started by a paper delivered by Michael Roberts in 1955, has been championed, expanded, and contested over decades by historians such as Geoffrey Parker, Clifford Rogers, and Jeremy Black.[30] The academic exchanges over the early modern military revolution have moved from the initial first concepts of Roberts's argument about tactical reforms to include such elements as new styles of fortifications, dramatic changes in army size and composition, state-development and centralisation, and the changing of the actual time frame of the debate itself.[31] The element of the military revolution debate which was least contested by the contributors was the growth in army size of the early modern period, although the precise period, causal factors, and effects of this growth remain disputed. What is clear is that larger armies had dramatic impacts on the development of financial instruments, administration, even state formation and centralisation, all to meet the need to raise and maintain larger armies.[32] Cathal Nolan, in his book *Allure of Battle* which sought to highlight what he saw as history's obsession with battles, stated that warfare in the early modern period was when 'logistics became everything' as these military developments demanded ever greater need for supplies to support the military expansion.[33] Despite the importance of logistics and supply on all of the above, few academics took an interest in what might seem a natural step from discussing army growth and administration into studying the connections and implications of these to logistics and the supply needs of those forces. Those that did, such as David Parrott and Derek Croxton, highlighted the impact provisioning had on strategic objectives and noted that strategy during the Thirty Years' War was based around securing control of areas in order to extract resource from them.[34] However, neither author appears to have developed these ideas further, having directed their research into

---

30 Michael Roberts, 'The Military Revolution, 1560–1660', in Clifford Rogers (ed.), *The Military Revolution Debate, Readings on the Military Transformation of Early Modern Europe* (Boulder, Colorado: Westview, 1995), pp.13–35; Geoffrey Parker, 'The "Military Revolution," 1560–1660 – A Myth?', *The Journal of Modern History*, Vol. 48, No.2 (1976), pp.195–214; Clifford Rogers, 'The Military Revolutions of the Hundred Years' War', *The Journal of Military History*, Vol. 57, No.2 (1993), pp.241–278; Jeremy Black, *A Military Revolution? Military Change and European Society, 1550–1800* (London: Palgrave, 1991).
31 For a broad summary of the debate and its development over the first 40 years, see Clifford Rogers, (ed.), *The Military Revolution Debate, Readings on the Military Transformation of Early Modern Europe* (Boulder, Colorado: Westview, 1995).
32 See for example Parker, *The Military Revolution*, pp.45–81.
33 Parker, *The Military Revolution*, pp.75–80; Cathal Nolan, *The Allure of Battle: A History of How Wars Have Been Won and Lost* (Oxford: Oxford University Press, 2017), p.84.
34 David Parrott, 'Strategy and Tactics in the Thirty Years' War: The "Military Revolution"', *Militärgeschichtliche Mitteilungen*, Vol. 18 (1985), pp.7–25; Derek Croxton, 'A Territorial

other areas. In *Supplying War*, van Creveld attempted to estimate the quantity of provisions available to troops within a geographical area, an idea also studied by Géza Perjes's 1970 article 'Army Provisioning, Logistics and Strategy in the Second Half of the 17th Century.'[35] However, these operate at the strategic theoretical level only and assume much regarding average productivity, local capabilities, and infrastructure. Hugh Davie's more recent work delves into greater detail on the capacity of a landscape to supply horses, arguing this was the key limiting factor in the size of horse-drawn armies.[36] However, Davie's work covers a very broad period over three centuries, and does not cover the British or Irish experience of the seventeenth century in any detail. The study of military logistics and supply in the early modern period, as it stands, lacks a detailed understanding of the operational capabilities and methods of armies of that time. It is one thing to estimate the amount of population in an area, but without a sense of how armies drew upon these areas for supply any theory would be difficult to develop or support. This study's focus on the operational methods of logistics and supply systems builds on these ideas of van Creveld and others providing a necessary element to further studying the capabilities and strategies of early modern armies outside of the British Isles and their impact on local populations.

The logistical and supply needs of the armies of the British Civil Wars interacted with local administrators and officials at the operational level to a great extent in order to function. There exists a large body of work on the contribution of local elites during the English Civil War, originating in revisionist history of the war stemming from historians in the 1970s which stressed localism and the importance of the political dynamic between the counties and the central government.

These county-by-county historical studies of the war varied in their aims and conclusions. Historians were broadly spilt on whether local interests, or localism, were coerced into supporting the King's or Parliament's war effort (either local partisans or imposed from outside) or that too much emphasis is placed on localism and that a complex blend of interests both inside and outside the locality contributed to a region's support.[37] A by-product of these studies was the investigation into the

---

Imperative? The Military Revolution, Strategy and Peacemaking in the Thirty Years War', *War in History*, Vol. 5, No.3 (1998), pp.253–279.
35 van Creveld, *Supplying War*, pp.33–35; Géza Perjes, 'Army Provisioning, Logistics, and Strategy in the Second Half of the 17th Century', *Acta Historica Academiae Scientiarum Hungaricae*, Vol. 16, No. 1/2 (1970), pp.1–52.
36 Hugh Davie, 'The Economics and Logistics of Horse-drawn Armies', *British Journal for Military History*, Vol. 7.1 (2021), pp.21–45.
37 A selection includes Alan Everitt, *The Community of Kent and the Great Rebellion, 1640–60* (Leicester: Leicester University Press, 1966); David Underdown, *Somerset in the Civil War and Interregnum* (Newton Abbot: David and Charles, 1973); John Morrill, *Cheshire 1630–1660: County Government and Society During the 'English Revolution'* (Oxford:

contributions of the various counties towards the war effort and the engagement of local elites in that process. Notable examples of this include Ann Hughes's work on Warwickshire and James Gratton's work on Lancashire.[38] Growing out of this broader body of research on the local community are two works which focus on the wider war effort – Clive Holmes's work on the Parliament's Eastern Association in the English Civil War, which covers one of the supra-regional associations of Parliament, and Ronald Hutton's work on the Royalist war effort in Wales and the West Midlands during the same conflict.[39] The Parliamentarian county associations attempted to improve the administration of areas under Parliament's control, recognising that the war required a broader outlook than a county-by-county basis. This is not dissimilar to my own view on the need to understand logistics and supply by looking beyond the isolated experiences of a few English counties. As interesting as Holmes's work is it has very little to offer on the topic of logistics and supply, which is surprising if you expect it to be a treatise on the administration of the Eastern Association. However, given that Holmes wrote a history and analysis of a supra-regional organisation, and its relations to its constituent counties and to Parliament, this is understandable. In his work on the Royalist administration Hutton uses the term 'war effort' to cover the efficient administration of the country to provide men, materiel, and money to the Royalist cause. In fact, Hutton argues that the impact on civilians and their resistance to the war effort, and their eventual refusal to support, is what ultimately doomed King Charles's military efforts, causing his war effort to collapse. Subsequent work by Ian Atherton has cast some doubt on this view of a Royalist administrative collapse. Atherton, by making use of surviving Royalist accounts to examine the activities of the Royalist garrison at Lichfield, showed that Royalist military administration actually became more efficient as the war progressed, and that active and violent civilian resistance to the war effort was far from universal.[40] Although now in its second edition, the 1970s origin of the Hutton's *Royalist War Effort* is clear in its coverage of localism and neutralism prevalent in the county studies of that time. All this is not to undercut the value of Hutton's study and its approaches. Quite the opposite as this work, like Hutton's, emphasises the reliance the military had

---

Oxford University Press, 1974); Mark Stoyle, *Loyalty and Locality: Popular Allegiance in Devon During the English Civil War* (Exeter: Exeter University Press, 1994).

38 Ann Hughes, *Politics, Society, and Civil War in Warwickshire, 1620–1660* (Cambridge University Press, 1997), James Gratton, *The Parliamentarian and Royalist War Effort in Lancashire* (Manchester: The Chetham Society Series III Vol. 48, 2010).

39 Hutton, *The Royalist War Effort 1642–1646*; Clive Holmes, *The Eastern Association in the English Civil War* (London: Cambridge University Press, 1974).

40 Ian Atherton, 'Royalist Finances in the English Civil War: The Case of the Lichfield Garrison, 1643–5', *Midland History*, Vol. 33, No.1 (2008), pp.43–67.

on local civilian infrastructure and people. However, unlike the local and regional studies, I have not focused solely on England as the study compares the impacts across all the Stuart realms – England and Wales, Ireland, and Scotland.

James Wheeler's work *The Making of a World Power* is likewise associated with these ideas of a 'war effort' with an integrated history of the military, financial, and administrative developments in England during the seventeenth century.[41] Wheeler uses his study to emphasise the growth of the state in financial matters, arguing that a 'financial revolution' took place in English administration which eventually allowed and facilitated military success at home and abroad. Wheeler's work is part of a wider trend focused on taxation and administration in the war, similar to both Holmes and Hutton, and of state-building such as John Brewer and *Sinews of Power*.[42] However, although Wheeler shows how logistics and supply were financed, and the works by Holmes and of Hutton both show how the local administration which contributed might have been organised, this study is concerned with how logistics and supply worked in detail, particularly at the operational level, thereby perhaps tying works such as Wheeler's and Hutton's into a more human experience of the war.

This focus on the human experience is very much a mainstay of the 'war and society' approach which has replaced more traditional tactical histories of warfare. The focus of early modern military histories is often solely on combat while proponents of the 'new military history' increasingly focus on the impacts of war upon groups and societies rather than the traditional narratives focused on combat. For example, Barbara Donagan's work on the English Civil War focuses on issues such as military codes of conduct, military education, and atrocities in the wars while John Wroughton's work discusses the experiences of ordinary people during the war.[43] Martyn Bennett's work *The Civil Wars Experienced*, eschews as much as possible a 'grand narrative' and instead considers the profound impact the British Civil Wars had on individuals and society by highlighting the personal experiences of a wide range of people, mostly civilians, from across the British Isles.[44] These approaches have largely replaced traditional military history in academia, placing the study of warfare in history away from traditional tactical narratives towards a

---

41 James Scott Wheeler, *The Making of a World Power: War and Revolution in Seventeenth-Century England* (Stroud: Sutton Publishing, 1999), pp.v–vii.
42 John Brewer, *The Sinews of Power: War, Money, and the English State, 1688–1783* (London: Unwin Hyman, 1989).
43 Barbara Donagan, *War in England, 1642–1649* (Oxford: Oxford University Press, 2010); John Wroughton, *An Unhappy Civil War: The Experiences of Ordinary People in Gloucestershire, Somerset and Wiltshire, 1642–1646* (Bath: The Lansdown Press, 1999).
44 Martyn Bennett, *The Civil Wars Experiences: Britain and Ireland, 1638–1661* (London: Routledge, 2000).

more inclusive approach to the history of warfare. The elements necessary to create and sustain capable logistics and supply systems are deeply interwoven into areas that 'new military history' chiefly concerns itself with, these being the interactions between soldiers and civilians, or the economic and social impacts of war on civilians. This work also challenges the common preconception that civilians were simply victims of soldiers, a preconception which has likely formed due to the focus in works such as Wroughton's on the experience of civilians during war. Chapter four investigates the nature of provisioning, and sheds new light onto the other side of free quartering and billeting and shows that it was often insufficient and difficult for the soldiers involved as well.

Peter Edwards's *Dealing in Death: The Arms Trade and the British Civil Wars* provides a clear analysis of the purchase and distribution of munitions and other equipment, attempting, where possible, to do so for all sides of the various conflicts.[45] This reinforces a concept that has emerged in recent decades, which is that to understand one conflict in the British Civil Wars one needs to consider all of the conflicts in the same British context rather than a series of separate wars. According to Allan Macinnes this approach to the British angle of the civil wars, needs to 'connect and compare developments in England and Wales, Scotland, and Ireland.'[46] This has influenced my own decision to consider the logistics and supply of the British Civil Wars as a combined series of conflicts rather than focus on a specific regional conflict within them, such as the Bishops' Wars or the Irish Rebellion. Where Edwards's work is also beneficial is that, although primarily focused on the international arms trade, he has considered the local manufacturing of arms.[47]

Gavin Robinson's work on the supply of horses to Parliament's armies highlights the importance that studying supply issues can have on broader understandings of the wars.[48] In his book he uses the supply of horses as a means of re-evaluating preconceptions of the allegiance and loyalty of Parliament's supporters, while in his article it is used as an investigation into the degree of continuity between

---

45 Peter Edwards, *Dealing in Death: The Arms Trade and the British Civil Wars, 1638–52* (Stroud: Sutton Publishing, 2000); Jonathon Worton considers Edwards to be the one scholar that has 'done most to elucidate the activity of Civil War effort.' Worton, *To Settle the Crown*, p.xxxv.
46 Macinnes, *The British Revolution, 1629–1660*, p.2.
47 For Edwards's work on local arms manufacturing which uses Staffordshire as a case study see Peter Edwards, 'Turning Ploughshares into Swords: The Arms and Military Equipment Industries in Staffordshire in the First Civil War, 1642–1646', *Midland History*, Vol. 27, No.1 (2002), pp.52–79.
48 Gavin Robinson, *Horses, People and Parliament in the English Civil War: Extracting Resources and Constructing Allegiance* (Farnham: Ashgate Publishing, 2012).

the New Model Army and one of its precursor forces, the Earl of Essex's army.[49] Although there is more on the operational methods of supply in Robinson's work, the focus is on questions of allegiance and continuity rather than on the methods for meeting the demands and development of the logistics and supply systems. This work will develop and broaden these approaches while providing an analysis of other aspects of logistics and supply, rather than duplicating Edwards's work on weapons or Robinson's on horses. Edwards's, Robinson's, and Wheeler's works all show that a study of logistics and supply systems, and the implications and use of such systems, are important for research of the British Civil Wars beyond that of helping explain tactical histories. Studies on the development of financial institutions, administration, international trade, and local allegiance are all influenced by the logistical and supply demands of war.

Structure

This book not only aims to fill the gaps in existing literature on logistics and supply but also to bridge the separation between traditional military history and contemporary military history. Primarily, it illuminates the logistics and supply systems in the British Civil Wars and contributes to our understanding of those in early modern warfare more broadly. It highlights how such a study is not only useful in and of itself, but how the lens of logistics and supply can help us to improve our understanding of many areas of civil and military society. A common theme throughout the chapters of this book is how the military and civilian spheres were very much interconnected when looking at logistics and supply and that they were not as separate and distinct as we might think. However, to do all of this will require a clear understanding of the operational workings of such systems. As Martin van Creveld, in the preface to his 1977 work *Supplying War*, said:

> Before a commander can even start thinking of manoeuvring or giving battle, of marching this way and that, of penetrating, enveloping, encircling, of annihilating or wearing down … he has – or ought – to make sure of his ability to supply his soldiers with those 3,000 calories a day without which they will very soon cease to be any use as soldiers; that roads to carry them to the right place at the right time are available, and that movement along these roads will not be impeded by either a shortage or a superabundance of transport.[50]

---

49 Gavin Robinson, 'Horse Supply and the Development of the New Model Army, 1642–1646', *War in History*, Vol. 15, No. 2 (2008), pp.121–140.
50 van Creveld, *Supplying War*, p.1.

As a starting point to consider for logistics and supply this is a solid basis, although I would amend 'food' to include the provision of clothing and shelter, both as a necessity and the latter as the extensive use of quartering often blurred the line between shelter and food (*cf* chapter four). Thus, the foundations of any military supply system are forms of transport for war material; the necessary manpower to form the army, and provisions to keep these men in the field. This ties in with the definition arrived at earlier in the introduction, being that 'logistics and supply are the procurement and transportation of men, equipment, and provisions necessary to maintain an army in the field and the infrastructure to support this.' Therefore, this work is divided into a logical structure based upon transport, recruitment, and provision. Chapters one and two focus on the military transportation methods of the wars, being those on land and waterborne transport respectively. Subsequent chapters include elements of transport in their studies, so covering the transport aspects first is fundamental to their understanding and addresses the logistics element of the research question. The third chapter will cover recruitment to the armies. While there have previously been works on recruitment during the British Civil Wars these have used recruitment in an attempt to understand political or local support for the factions, or more recently in an attempt to understand the human experience of war.[51] Both are important and worthy forms of study, but as of yet no one has investigated recruitment as a facet of supply, being the gathering of sufficient numbers of men necessary to field and replenish the armies of the period. Without a substantial supply of manpower into them the armies would have simply ceased to exist. Finally, the fourth chapter will cover provisioning. This includes the necessities of food, shelter, and clothing without which soldiers would not be able to function and, in combination with recruitment, meet the supply element of the research question.

Sources

The logistics and supply systems of the Civil Wars relied heavily on the interactions, and often the cooperation, between military and civilian authorities. It will be clear at several points throughout this study how reliant the armies were on civilians and their methods, equipment, property, and production. The sources I have used in this study reflect this interconnectivity in the broad range of both military and

---

51   As an example of the use of recruitment as a tool to understand political support see Joyce Malcolm, 'A King in Search of Soldiers: Charles I in 1642', *Historical Journal*, vol. 21 (1978), pp.251–273; Joyce Malcolm, *Caesar's Due: Loyalty and King Charles, 1642–1646* (London: Swift, 1983); for the human experience of warfare see Donagan, *War in England*, pp.258–283.

civilian source material used to study the topics of each chapter and to answer the overarching research question. Some of these sources would be familiar to military historians of either the traditional or the new schools while others, or their use in this manner, are not. Examples of more commonly used military sources include SP28, the Commonwealth Exchequer Papers, in the National Archives at Kew. This extensive collection includes a wide range of material from the British Civil Wars, including Parliamentarian officers' accounts and army lists as well as accounts of Parliament's garrison commanders and records of commissary officers – those responsible for provisioning and feeding the forces they were assigned to. The National Archives also hold (in the War Office papers, or WO) a wealth of inherited documentation from the War Office precursor institutions, including the Ordnance Office. This institution, based in the Tower of London, was responsible for the receiving and issue of military stores on behalf of the English crown (and from 1642 onwards was a machine for Parliament). While most of the Ordnance Office papers in the National Archives at Kew relate to this London Ordnance Office there are a significant number of papers of the Royalist Ordnance Office created at Oxford in 1642 and initially staffed by professional officers from the London Ordnance Office who had then joined the King's cause. These papers help to build a picture of what munitions and artillery were received and redistributed by the Royalist headquarters at Oxford, and how this office functioned in the creation and running of Royalist supply and logistics needs.[52] Other sources from Oxford include the papers of Captain Henry Stevens, who was the Royalist Wagon-Master General responsible for arranging and dispatching the supply convoys the Royalist forces in the area depended on.[53] Similar to the Royalist Ordnance Papers, and those of Captain Stevens, the surviving accounts of Sir Adam Hepburn, Commissary-General of the Scottish Army of the Solemn League and Covenant for the period 1643–1647 contain many warrants and receipts related to supply.[54]

As early modern armies often drew their requirements from surrounding civilian economies and societies, this work also makes use of certain sources which may seem otherwise unusual for a topic grounded in military history. Examples include my use of carrier catalogues, written in the seventeenth century and detailing the extensive civilian carrier networks operating across England,

---

52   Ian Roy (ed.), *The Royalist Ordnance Papers, 1642–1646*, 2 Vols. (Oxford: Oxfordshire Record Society, 1963 & 1975)
53   Margaret Toynbee (ed.), *The Papers of Captain Henry Stevens Waggon-Master-General to King Charles I* (Oxford: Oxfordshire Record Society, 1962).
54   Charles Terry (ed.), *Papers Relating to the Army of the Solemn League and Covenant, 1643–1647*, 2 Vols. (Edinburgh: Edinburgh University Press for the Scottish History Society, 1917).

and into Wales and Scotland, at the time.[55] An analysis of these carrier catalogues, or cosmographies, which were originally aimed to provide customers with the locations, charges, and capabilities of the public carrier network, can be used to identify the common types of road transportation methods used during the early- and mid-seventeenth century. This type of source has not, to my knowledge, been used previously in studies of military history, although they have seen some use in economic and social studies of the period.[56]

This use of this material – unique in the context of a military history – is not solely dictated by necessity due to a lack of surviving military sources on the topic. Certainly, despite the importance placed on ready access to supplies by contemporary soldiers for their operations few, if any, overt contemporary military sources survive. However, as the military of the British Civil Wars were heavily reliant on the existing civilian infrastructure the use of civilian sources supports my investigation into the military systems. The civilian sources not only provide us with primary evidence for military use, while reinforcing both the contemporary experience of the military and civilian interconnectivity, but also highlight for the reader that the study of military logistics in the British Civil Wars is not confined to military historians of the period. It has something to offer the broader study of history of the seventeenth century as well.

While sources for England, Wales, and Scotland survive either in archival form or recorded and copied by eighteenth century historians and antiquarians, something must be said regarding the limitation of surviving Irish records. Few primary sources survive from either the initial Irish rebellion or the subsequent Confederation of Kilkenny, and the greater part of what source material may have existed regarding the Protestant Irish forces, the King's Irish supporters, and later Parliamentarian controlled Dublin were lost in the Four Courts fire of 1922. However, through surviving papers and letters from leading Anglo-Irish politicians of the time, such as the Duke of Ormonde, as well as information gleaned from the 1641 depositions held at Trinity College Dublin Library, a partial

---

55   John Taylor, *The Carriers Cosmographie or A Briefe Relation, of the Innes, Ordinaries, Hosteries, and Other Lodgings In, and Neere London...* (London, 1637); Thomas Delaune, *The Present State of London...* London: 1681).

56   The use of the carrier catalogues to analyse national and regional economic capabilities as well as economic or social studies on the state and quality of the roads in the seventeenth can be found in Dorian Gerhold, *Carriers & Coachmasters: Trade and Travel Before the Turnpikes* (Chichester: Phillimore, 2005); Stephen Porter, 'Farm Transport in Huntingdonshire, 1610–1749', *The Journal of Transport History*, vol. 3, no.1 (March 1982), pp.35–46; John Chartres, 'Road Carrying in England in the Seventeenth Century: Myth and Reality' *The Economic History Review*, Vol. 30, No. 1 (February 1977), pp.73–94; Dorian Gerhold, 'The Growth of the London Carrying Trade, 1681–1838', *The Economic History Review*, Vol. 41, No.3 (August 1988), pp.392–410.

picture of the Irish experience is possible thus allowing comparison with other forces in the British Civil Wars.

The study of military logistics and supply systems has a lot to offer historians, and not just those concerned with the military of the British Civil Wars. Such systems were far reaching and influenced military strategy, effective governance at various levels, the experience and engagement of soldiers and civilians, and much more. This work will demonstrate the value of considering logistics and supply, not just as a study conducted in isolation but as one to broaden historical understanding of the components, conclusions, and consequences of warfare. I hope that this study will provide the foundations for deepening our understanding of early modern logistics and supply, but without a strong foundation, nothing substantial can be built. The study of logistics and supply systems challenges previous preconceptions and assumptions, it answers questions which have bedevilled historians for centuries, and injects new life into old approaches, all while forging connections across multiple forms and approaches to the study of history. As essential as logistics and supply are to war, so too is their study within the history of warfare and society.

Spanish camp followers during the siege of Jülich in 1621/1622. Pieter Snayers, 1622-1650 (Rijksmuseum)

1

Land Transportation

'[M]onies, [are] the principall sinews of War' claimed King Charles I, yet the lifeblood of war: provisions, ammunition, weapons, uniforms, boots, and other essential war supplies, without which no war could be fought, were transported across land by actual sinews and muscles.[1] Seventeenth century military transportation on land was completely reliant on the muscle power of animals, in this case predominantly horses either in draught (pulling a vehicle in harness) or carrying cargo in packs on their backs. On campaign the armies of the period made use of large numbers of animal-pulled vehicles to meet their supply needs. Transportation methods for these supplies were critical to the strategic and tactical decisions of the war. How fast a force moved, where it moved, how long it could campaign, and how well it could fight a battle, were impacted by the effectiveness of its transport capabilities and the security of its supply lines.

To fully understand and appreciate military logistics and supply systems for the armies of the British Civil Wars an analysis of the methods by which the armies transported their supplies is a logical aspect on which to build the study. As will become apparent, all combatants involved in the fighting transported their supplies across land using similar, but not identical, methods. Armies operating in various theatres of the British Civil Wars, with many of these forces originating from disparate regions of the British Isles, had distinct differences in the makeup of the animals and vehicles used to meet their transportation needs. This chapter will identify and examine the methods used for land transportation during the British Civil Wars, with a consideration of these variations and of the developments of the transportation systems utilised by the forces involved. Throughout we will

---

1   Charles I, 'The Commission to the Lords and others of the privy Council concerning the present raising of money' in Thomas Fuller (ed.) *The Sovereigns Prerogative and the Subjects Priviledge Discussed Betwixt Courtiers and Patriots in Parliament...* (London, 1657), pp.229–231.

see the reliance all armies had on horse powered modes of transportation, and the difference in both form and efficiency as the factions attempted to make best use of the resources available across the conflicts. This will not be a narrative of the campaigns, although some narrative structure will be required to show the development of the military transportation at various stages of the wars and to highlight contrasting transport methods with those of earlier campaigns. The study will be more qualitative than quantitative in nature, as hard numerical data for the period has not survived and the varied and the unique source material drawn on lends itself more to a qualitative analysis than charts and tables. This chapter will begin with an outline of the different types of transport available to the armies in the British Civil Wars, highlighting regional differences on the availability of types of transport. Subsequently, the two methods used to gather these vehicles will be investigated – purchase and requisition – while emphasising how the acquisition of vehicles for the military relied on civilian interactions. A clear picture of how these transport methods were used by the military will become clear as this chapter will examine the often-overlooked role of garrisons in the creation of these transport supply systems. The chapter will conclude that different forms were being utilised by various armies due to the military dependence on civilians for its transportation needs, which in some cases were notably different to the transport systems of other forces, with differing levels of efficiency as a result. In effect, the military was beholden to pre-existing civilian networks for transport operations, with all the attendant complexities of relying upon a network based around commercial rather than military realities which impacted their military capabilities.

Despite the importance of logistics and supply in warfare, little work has been done by military historians of the Civil Wars on the operation and composition of military transport systems. Traditional military history focuses on campaign strategy and battlefield tactics without consideration of transportation despite the impacts this had on both strategic planning and on tactical outcomes. Even studies which focus on military logistics and supply make little mention of road transportation as it was used in early modern warfare.[2] Martin van Creveld argues that the accurate study of warfare and strategy cannot be separated from logistical and supply considerations without turning such a study into a simple tactical analysis of set-piece battles.[3] However, van Creveld's analysis lacks a clear focus on the importance of routes and vehicles, particularly in the early modern period. The lack of attention given to land transportation holds true for other works around

---

2   van Creveld, *Supplying War*; Lynn, J.A. (ed.), *Feeding Mars: Logistics in Western Warfare from The Middle Ages to The Present* (Boulder, Colorado: Westview Press, 1994).
3   van Creveld, *Supplying War*, pp.1–3.

the topic of supply and logistics during the British Civil Wars.[4] Peter Edwards's extensive review of the arms trade during the conflicts does make mention of transportation, but only as a brief, and broad, overview within the wider arms trading system. As Edwards's study is primarily focused on the production and purchase of military supplies, rather than the operational deployment of them, this is perhaps understandable.[5]

An army's artillery train formed a large, cohesive portion of the transport vehicles which moved with the army. Stephen Bull's work on the artillery of the English Civil Wars has a chapter devoted to logistics and supply focused solely on the manufacture and supply of artillery pieces, but making no mention of operational transport in the field despite the importance of transportation to the artillery train.[6] While it is not a study of the British Civil Wars, Geoffrey Parker's work on the Army of Flanders considers how the Spanish forces in the Low Countries were supplied and provides a near-contemporary European example. Parker's conclusions are that an extensive network of traders and merchants were quasi-officially incorporated into the Spanish army's supply network, relying on the draw of profits amongst sutlers and tradesmen to keep the soldiers' needs met.[7] However, while useful as a study of the Continental land-based experience, Parker's work tells us little about the vehicles and transport methods these sutlers would have used to bring the supplies to the troops.

Although studies of seventeenth century land conveyance in the British Isles exist, these have been written by social or economic historians which, understandably, lack any military focus.[8] For example, Dorian Gerhold's work on seventeenth century roads in England is focused on the use of pre-turnpike roads by coaches and carriers and is heavily orientated to a post-Restoration focus.[9] Gerhold's analysis of carrier networks instead provides insight into the common road vehicles which were used during the early and mid-seventeenth century. Gerhold's sources for this analysis are predominantly the contemporary publications of carrier timetables which detailed the availability of those services involved in the carrying trade. John Crofts and Joan Parkes have both written on

---

4   van Creveld, *Supplying War*, 'The background of Two Centuries', pp.5–39.
5   Edwards, *Dealing in Death*, pp.230–235.
6   Stephen Bull, *The Furie of the Ordnance: Artillery in the English Civil Wars* (Woodbridge: The Boydell Press, 2008), for his chapter on logistics pp.54–80.
7   Parker, *The Army of Flanders and the Spanish Road*.
8   See Dorian Gerhold, 'Pack Horses and Wheeled Vehicles in England, 1550–1800', *The Journal of Transport History*, Vol. 14, No.1 (March 1993), pp.1–26, and Robert Morris, *Public Transport in England and Wales, 1580–1642* (Bristol, Stuart Press, 2010).
9   Gerhold, *Carriers & Coachmasters*.

the quality, usage, and development of English roads in the seventeenth century.[10] These again, are all economic and social histories which currently add little to our understanding of the military logistics and supply systems of British Civil Wars.

Given the near total reliance that early modern armies had on vehicles and transport networks to stay supplied while moving, and to transport their necessary equipment, the absence of a detailed study of military road transportation methods until now can at least partly be explained by a lack of surviving primary source material. The evidence available to military historians is rarely concerned with details and reasoning about which type of animals or vehicles were to be used. Even the surviving papers of the Royalist Wagon-Master General, Captain Henry Stevens, are a collection of warrants and receipts which largely outline the number of vehicles Stevens was required to find for a particular task. These offer very little in the way of explanation as to why the vehicles were available or how they were used, although they are invaluable as a contemporary source for the types of vehicles Stevens had access to.[11] Other surviving sources on supply, such as the 'Contracts for the Supply of Equipment to the "New Model" Army in 1645,' are concerned with the ordering and receipt of, and payment for, equipment and not their transportation.[12] Either contemporaries in the military sphere felt little to no need to detail what must have been widely known information, or such records have simply not survived. Put simply, few officers would feel the need to explain to their peers or their subordinates the seemingly extraneous information on transport choices – either they knew it already, or it was enough that they followed orders.

However, for civilian sources more evidence has survived. This greater range of source material is likely a combination of there being a larger origin population for the material, as well as a wider contemporary audience of non-experts seeking information on civilian transport. A leading example of this type of material are the pamphlets published as carrier guides. These contemporary publications were produced for the wider civilian population detailing the carrier transport services available for hire. Authors of these works, for example John Taylor and Thomas Delaune, clearly recognised enough demand for details on transport services for

---

10   John Crofts, *Packhorse, Waggon, and Post: Land Carriage and Communications under the Tudors and Stuarts* (London: Routledge, 1967); Joan Parkes, *Travel in England in the Seventeenth Century* (London: Oxford University Press, 1925).
11   Toynbee, *The Papers of Captain Henry Stevens*…
12   Gerald Mungeam (ed.), 'Contracts for the Supply of Equipment to the "New Model" Army in 1645', *The Journal of The Arms & Armour Society*, vol. 6, no.3 (September 1968), pp.53–115.

customers to find where and when they might source carrier services.[13] These publications went into significant detail to meet these requirements, such as 'The Waggons of Bury or Berry in Suffolke, doe come every Thursday to the signe of the foure swans in bishopgate street' and 'The Waggons from Chelmsford in Essex, come on Wednesdaies to the signe of the blew Boare without Algate.'[14] The information provided by these guidebooks provides a wealth of information on the routes and the vehicles used by this carrier network. In John Taylor's 1637 *Cosmographie* alone there are more than 200 entries detailing the routes, availability, and services offered by carriers in London. Economic and social historians such as Gerhold and John Chartres have made use of these sources when writing about the road quality, road usage, and different forms of commercial traffic in early modern England.[15]

Civilian sources such as these are beneficial in the absence of military sources because they detail the non-military instruments upon which the armies of the British Civil Wars built their transport infrastructure. This interconnectivity between military and civilian in terms of transport will be evident in this chapter, but a brief explanation of why there was such a military dependence on civilian structures at the beginning of the conflicts is a useful starting point. Without a regular standing army there was no pre-existing military logistic infrastructure for effectively supplying large armies in the field. Although forces had been dispatched under Royal command against Spain and France during the 1620s these conflicts did not generate any internal British infrastructure for supplying armies. Similarly, neither did the regiments raised across the British Isles for service with foreign nations during the decades before the British Civil Wars.[16] While these and their associated conflicts, notably the fighting in the Low Countries and the Thirty Years' War, provided the Kingdoms with numbers of experienced soldiers for the Civil Wars, the nature of this fighting, being outside of the British Isles and with the majority of soldiers serving in foreign armies, meant there was very little military logistic infrastructure developed within the British Isles as a result. It should be noted that this lack of internal military infrastructure is separate from both military culture and military experience.

13   Taylor, *The Carriers Cosmographie or A Briefe Relation*; Delaune, *The present state of London*.
14   Taylor, *The Carriers Cosmographie or A Briefe Relation*, pp.7–8.
15   Gerhold centres his work on Delaune's compilation of carriers found in Delaune, *The Present State of London*, see Gerhold, *Carriers & Coachmasters*, p.xiii. Chartres makes use of both Delaune and Taylor, *The Carriers Cosmographie or A Briefe Relation*, see Chartres, 'Road Carrying in England in the Seventeenth Century: Myth and Reality', particularly pp.74–75.
16   For a study of the recruitment and supply of these two armies see Laurence Spring, *The First British Army, 1624–1628: The Army of the Duke of Buckingham* (Solihull, Helion, 2016).

The lack of a substantial pre-existing military infrastructure meant that all sides of the British Civil Wars were forced to draw heavily upon civilian methods and infrastructure by necessity to supply and equip their troops, as well as absorb many civilian vehicles and methods into their own military practices. That there was extensive and widespread experience in transportation outside of the military sphere cannot be in doubt. The early modern period saw extensive diversification and regional specialisation of production and economies, and a complex and reliable transport network was required to move the raw materials, finished products, and staples upon which the economies of the Stuart Kingdoms relied.[17] The dependency on civilian transportation methods was simply a necessity to supply large forces, which were often mobilised rapidly, and at short notice, upon the outbreak of the conflict. This reliance on civilian transportation never disappeared as the wars progressed, although changes occurred over time and across the various theatres of the wars.

The carrier network outlined was a fundamental part of this regional distribution, tying the various regions together into the wider economy of the Kingdoms. It was also these civilian transport networks which became the foundations of the various military transport systems that arose after the outbreak of war.

Transport Types

The conveyances used by the military during the British Civil Wars can be grouped into three core forms: wagons, carts and packhorses. The wagon was a large two-axle, four-wheeled vehicle pulled by a team of at least four horses and up to as many as eight if the load or circumstances demanded it. These wagons were distinct in comparison to the single axle, two-wheeled cart with the wagon being both the larger and the more substantial of the two given its two-axle construction. The accompanying image below is a contemporary engraving depicting just such a vehicle; note that the driver is not seated on the wagon, but instead moves with his team. The rearmost horse nearest the wagon appears harnessed to the vehicle between two shafts, with the rest of the team harnessed in a line ahead – the importance of the varying methods of harnessing is discussed below.

---

17   Peter Edwards, *Horse and Man in Early Modern England* (London: Continuum, 2007), pp.188–189.

A wagon and team and its driver. From: David Loggan, 'Collegium Omnium Animorum' in *Oxonia Illustrata* (Oxford, 1675) (Public Domain)

This four-wheeled configuration of wagons provided a more stable platform and larger bed (or storage area) than that provided by the contemporary two-wheeled carts. The superiority of wagons for transport and haulage is evidenced by their comparatively rapid adoption across multiple areas of society, beginning with their introduction into England during the sixteenth century, most likely from the Low Countries ('wagon' being a Dutch word).[18] The term 'wain' appears to have been applied by some contemporaries to this type of vehicle as well.[19] In England's south and east, the wagon was widely adopted by farmers, tradesmen, and professional teamsters who operated along England's carrier trade. Local businesses and farmers in these areas took to the wagon so wholly that by the late 1630s the wagon was the dominant form of road transport vehicle used in these parts of the country.[20] It was from this pool of professional carriers that the government often requisitioned wagons and teams for its use. During peacetime these carriers moved a wide variety of loads including agricultural produce, finished goods, and personal deliveries of food which included butter and cheese, as well as serving government needs for transportation between London and the ports of Chester and Bristol.[21] Considering how the guidebooks describe the carriers it is likely, as Robert Morris argues, that many were based in provincial towns or villages and ran a regular route services from their point of origin to major towns, with many travelling regularly to London.[22] On arrival in London the carriers and their

---

18 Gerhold, 'Pack Horses and Wheeled Vehicles', p.3; Edwards, *Horse and Man*, pp.195–197; John Chartres, *Internal Trade in England, 1500–1700* (London: Macmillan, 1977), p.40.
19 Robert Stuart believes that if a wagon was pulled by oxen it was referred to as a 'wain', see Robert Stuart, *Wagons, Carts, and Pack Animals, 1580–1660* (Bristol: Stuart Press, 1996), p.3.
20 Gerhold, 'Pack Horses and Wheeled Vehicles', p.5.
21 Edwards, *Horse and Man*, pp.187–189; Crofts, *Packhorse, Waggon and Post*, p.38; Morris, *Public Transport in England and Wales*, pp.4–5.
22 Morris, *Public Transport in England and Wales*, p.6.

wagons would stay overnight at an inn (or two nights if the next day was a Sunday). Curiously not all of the carriers travelling between two major towns travelled the same route. Studying the desired destinations and matching the carriers' inns and their days of availability reveal, for example, that carriers moving between Manchester and London using the 'Ax in Aldermanbury' passed through Derby, Loughborough, and Leicester, while those who stopped at the 'two neck'd Swan in Lad lane' went via Stafford.[23] This suggests that there was further business to be found through picking up and dropping off deliveries along the different routes, and an expectation of enough such work to support the regular route through these towns. It also highlights that major towns often had multiple routes to travel to them. In civilian terms this emphasises an extensive network of carriers across England, many of whom made regular weekly or fortnightly journeys to London. Militarily, this also suggests multiple choices of routes could exist for a journey, allowing different routes for troops to march along. This reinforces the importance of garrisons during the British Civil Wars, which thus had an important role in monitoring and controlling the nearby roads. Perhaps most importantly, multiple routes would have allowed for a wider range of scouting and foraging parties, able to range wider from the main line of march to secure supplies away from the main body of the army. The importance of foraging parties and their role in a marching army will be discussed later (*cf.* chapter four).

Looking at the listings of carriers detailed in the guidebooks a pattern in the spread of the use of the wagon in the carrier trade can be seen. Where possible, the published carrier guides attempted to provide information about the type of conveyance that particular carriers used. Wagons appeared most often as carrier services, although packhorses remained popular.[24] Broadly, the carriers whose origins lay in the Southeast and East of England, or at least ran carrier routes in the area, predominantly used wagons. This fits with the spread of wagons in non-carrier roles argued for by Stephen Porter.[25] The professional carriers operating along routes from the west and southwest of England, out of Wales, and from the northern parts of England, all preferred the packhorse as the main mode of transport.[26]

The use of packhorses predated the arrival of the wagon on England's shores, where the cargo was transported in panniers across the back of the animals rather than in a wheeled conveyance pulled by the horse in draught. Despite the advantages of the wagon as a vehicle, the packhorse remained a popular form of

23 Taylor, *The Carriers Cosmographie or A Briefe Relation*, pp.9–20.
24 Gerhold, *Carriers & Coachmasters*, pp.60–66; Edwards, *Horse and Man*, pp.192–195.
25 Porter, 'Farm transport in Huntingdonshire, 1610–1749', pp.38–39.
26 Stuart, *Wagons, Carts and Pack Animals, 1580–1660*, p.15; Gerhold, 'Pack Horses and Wheeled Vehicles', p.8; Edwards, *Horse and Man*, p.192.

transport amongst carriers from Wales and the western, northern, and southwestern portions of England. This raises a question as to why carriers from these areas on routes to London wanted to keep using packhorses when their compatriots and competitors on other routes did not. This is especially pertinent when we consider that wagon horses in draught conveyed nearly three times as much as a packhorse could across its back.[27] The following contemporary engraving is of a packhorse team in use and depicts how the packhorses were not always tied together, instead moving with their driver walking behind them, able to watch the entirety of the team from that position.

Packhorses.[28] (Public Domain)

The English militaries of the period certainly preferred the use of wheeled vehicles, with the packhorse used only if no alternative was available or in particular circumstances. Chartres and Gerhold both propose the possibility that the speed of packhorses was greater than that of wheeled vehicles, particularly over longer journeys.[29] In February 1644, The Committee of Both Kingdoms decided that 'the supplies to be now sent to Gloucester shall be sent by horse and not by wagon.'[30] Edwards suggests this choice was out of a necessity for speed in the relief column which ties in with studies by Gerhold comparing the speed of packhorse deliveries to wagons.[31]

Gerhold's findings when comparing wagons and packhorse deliveries along the same routes suggest that packhorses could cover between 25 to 33 miles in a day compared to 20 to 25 miles for wagons.[32] This gave packhorses a 25 to 32 percent increase in distance covered per day over wagons. Not only were packhorses likely

---

27   Chartres, 'Road Carrying in England in the Seventeenth Century: Myth and Reality', p.81;
       Edwards, *Horse and Man*, p.186; Gerhold, 'Pack Horses and Wheeled Vehicles', p.13.
28   Loggan, 'Collegium Omnium Animorum' in *Oxonia Illustrata*.
29   Chartres, 'Road Carrying in England in the Seventeenth Century: Myth and Reality',
       pp.83–84; Gerhold, 'Pack Horses and Wheeled Vehicles', pp.9–18.
30   CSPD 1644–1645, Feb. 22, Proceedings at the Committee of both Kingdoms this day, p.24.
31   Edwards, *Dealing in Death*, p.227; Gerhold, 'Pack Horses and Wheeled Vehicles', p.13.
32   Gerhold, *Carriers & Coachmasters*, pp.66–67.

to be faster than horses pulling in draught, but they could also operate better than any wheeled vehicle through rough terrain or over muddy ground.[33] It is important to note that many of these 'packhorses' were typically ponies, the same species but significantly and identifiably different to various horse breeds. Contemporaries sometimes used the term ponies, at others times referring to them as small horses 'not fit for the saddle, nor for the wars, and therefore are to be employed for the carring of burthens.'[34] Notably, ponies have a thicker coat in winter, their hooves tend to be tougher, and they are heavier built, with shorter legs in proportion to their size, than horses. They can also survive on pasture which was insufficient for a horse. Ponies are hardier, smaller, stockier, do better in cooler temperatures and on rougher ground, and survive on poorer quality grass in smaller quantities than horses.[35] Many of the areas where the packhorse carriers' point of origin can be traced to were predominantly pastoral with quite rugged terrain (shortened hereafter to 'upland'), i.e. western, northern, and southwest England and Wales. These areas stand in contrast topographically to those where the wagon was pre-eminent amongst both carriers and other users in England's Southeast and in East Anglia (hereafter 'lowland'). The topographical distribution of England and Wales can be seen in the map below, with the West, North, and Southwest of England and Wales, being substantially higher than the east and southeast.

33 Edwards, *Horse and Man*, p.186; Gerhold, 'Pack Horses and Wheeled Vehicles', p.13.
34 Edward Topsell, *The Historie of Foure-Footed Beastes Describing the True and Liuely Figure of Euery Beast, with a Discourse of Their Seuerall Names, Conditions, Kindes, Vertues* (London, 1607), p.325.
35 W.V. Lloyd, 'Montgomeryshire Horses, Cobs, and Ponies', *Collections Historical & Archaeological Relating to Montgomeryshire and its Borders*, Vol. 22 (1888), p.22; Reginald Summerhays, *The Observer's Book of Horses and* Ponies (London: Frederick Warne, 1974), pp.9–10.

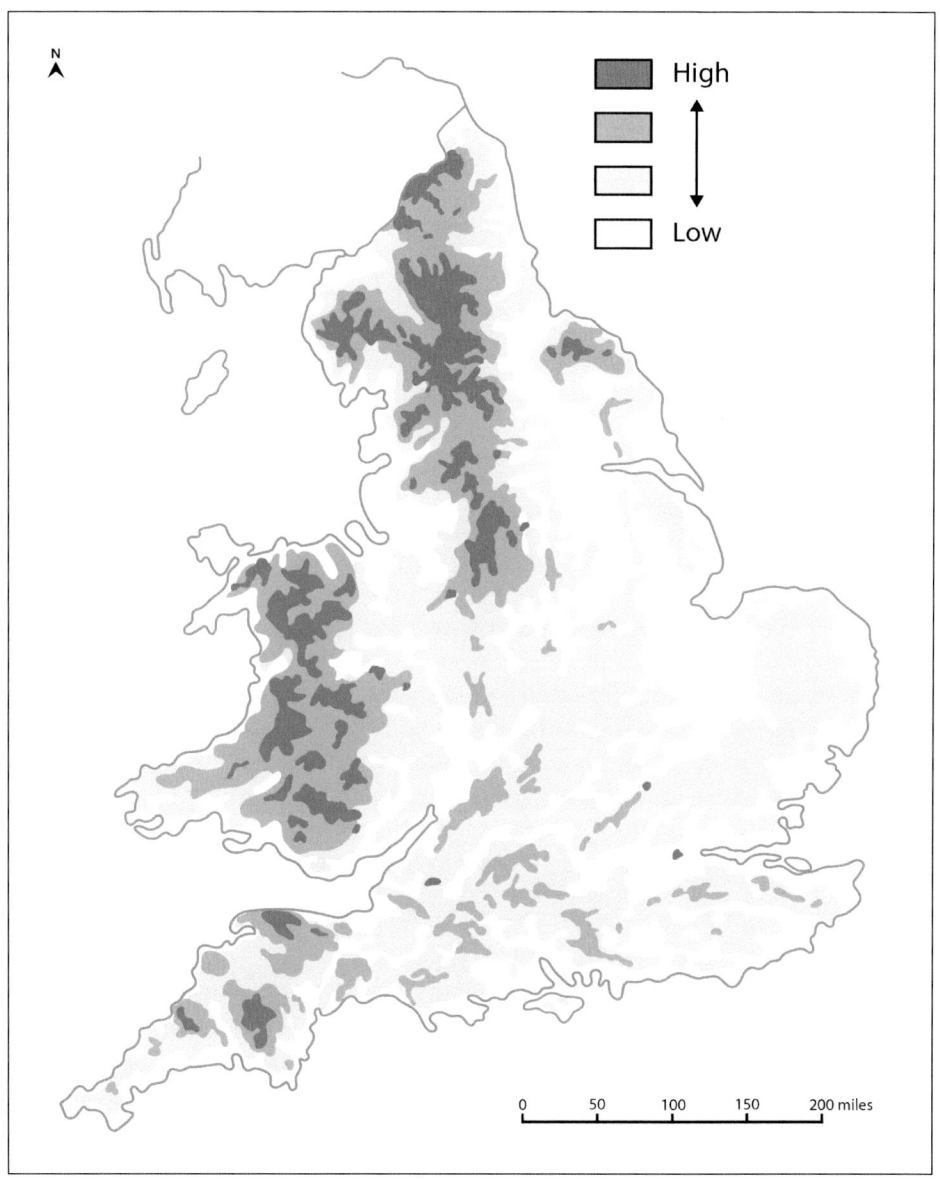

Topographical map of England and Wales.[36] (Author's artwork)

36 Compiled with information from: 'England', topographic-map.com, <https://en-gb.topographic-map.com/maps/b9/England/≥ Accessed 18 August 2020; 'United Kingdom Topographic Map', PhysicalMap.org, <https://physicalmap.org/node/45≥ Accessed 7 July 2021.

This distribution of wagons being confined to the Southeast and East of England in the seventeenth century is confirmed in work by Stephen Porter who states that while wagons rapidly became popular sights on England's roads it was not until much later, perhaps well into the 1700s, that these became common farm vehicles across the whole of England. Porter bases this on his analysis of the types of vehicles listed in surviving probate inventories from the years 1610–1749.[37] That packhorses were typically local breeds of ponies easily sourced in hilly areas, such as Galloway ponies – a common breed in both Northern England and in Scotland, is one reason they remained popular for carriers in upland areas.[38] They were also faster than wagons in traversing hills and other uneven terrain, which may be enough to explain why they remained popular with carriers originating in those areas. Wagons traversing steep and rough terrain too quickly, or in poor light, ran the risk of disaster. Parliamentarian wagons carrying supplies with the army near Prestbury Hill in 1643 found that 'our Waggons and Carriages could not get downe the hill, many of them were overthrowne and broken, it being a very craggy steep and dangerous hill, so that the rest of the Waggons durst not adventure to goe downe, but stayed all night there.'[39] The cost of feeding ponies compared to feeding large draught horses was also significantly cheaper. According to Gerhold, the costs of feeding a packhorse might have been as little as 60 percent of that of feeding a draught horse.[40] This cost was not in volume of food alone but also due to type. According to early modern sources, horses needed a daily balanced diet of grass (or hay) and a 'quantity of three pintes of good old, and drie Oats, and to put to them an handfull or two of spelted-beanes, hulls and all' whereas ponies could make do with a greater proportion of grass and fresh fodder.[41] Yet, despite all these advantages, the English military much preferred the use of vehicles pulled in draught rather than packhorses. This preference for wheeled vehicles is explained by the fact that an animal towing a vehicle could transport around three times as much as that same animal could carry across its back. This point will be expanded on later in more detail. However, in short, while a train of pack ponies might outpace a wagon, particularly on poor terrain, the wagon would carry far more.

---

37 Porter, 'Farm transport in Huntingdonshire, 1610–1749', pp.38–39; Crofts, *Packhorse, Waggon and Post,* pp.1–2
38 Gerhold, 'Pack Horses and Wheeled Vehicles', p.12.
39 Henry Foster, *A True and Exact Relation of the Marchings of the Two Regiments of the Trained-Bands of the City of London Being the Red & Blew Regiments* (London, 1643), p.7.
40 Gerhold, 'Pack Horses and Wheeled Vehicles', p.13.
41 Gervase Markham, *The Complete Farriar, or the Kings High-Way to Horsemanship* (London: 1639), p.85; Gerhold, 'Pack Horses and Wheeled Vehicles', pp.13 & 17; Gerhold, *Carriers & Couchmasters,* p.66.

In contrast to the experience of armies in England, the armies raised in Scotland in the Civil Wars seem to have relied heavily on packhorses as their pre-eminent form of transportation. If English military preference was generally for draught animals rather than pack, then the Scottish experience needs to be analysed to see why they used packhorses instead. Certainly, the Covenanter Lord General Alexander Leslie struggled to find sufficient numbers of powerful draught horses necessary to pull the Covenanter's artillery in 1639, which hampered the strategic ability to advance into England as the army had neither 'carriage, horses, nor strong enough convoyes for it.'[42] This was a problem, as almost all forms of artillery of the period required large numbers of horses to move a gun and the vehicles carrying the attendant equipment and supplies. For example, to dispatch 'one Peece of Ordnance and one Morter Peece', from Oxford on 16 May 1643, along with ammunition and other 'Materialls and other Utensills' the Royalists needed two wagons, ten carts and a total of 67 horses.[43] The topographical environment of Scotland is similar to many upland areas of England, though in many places more rugged, making packhorses the norm rather than heavy freight wagons.

In 1640 the Covenanters' invading army was equipped with up to 3,000 'carriage horses', or pack animals, conveying its baggage.[44] The Covenanters had limited numbers of large draught animals capable of pulling the artillery in 1640, which were focused on pulling their heaviest cannon, backed up by teams of men to assist. Leslie had clearly learned from the previous year as the Covenanters' artillery train contained several 'leather guns.' These artillery pieces were able to be carried by horseback, which provided Leslie with a mobile artillery train that he could campaign with and that utilised the type of transport animals he had most available to him in Scotland.[45] After occupying Newcastle, the Covenanters sent back into Scotland 'our greatest ordnance, most cumbersome to carry' replacing it with smaller captured English cannons.[46] This could have been due to the lack of horses able to pull heavy artillery in the area as described by the Marquess of Hamilton to King Charles in June 1638 stating 'for ther are non to be had ther that will be abill to draw them.'[47] A survey of the accounts of Sir Adam Hepburne, Commissary-General of the Army of the Solemn League and Covenant for

---

42 Robert Baillie (David Laing, ed.), *The Letters and Journals of Robert Baillie, 1637–1662*, I (Edinburgh: Bannatyne Club, 1841–1842), p.219.
43 TNA WO 55/458.65, ff.7–8. Warrant for equipment dispatched under the command of Price Maurice.
44 Baillie, *Letters and Journals*, I, p.256.
45 Edward Furgol, *A Regimental History of the Covenanter Armies, 1639–1651* (Edinburgh: John Donald, 1990), p.42
46 Baillie, *Letters and Journals*, I, p.259.
47 NRS GD 406/1/10491, Letter from the Marquess of Hamilton to Charles I, 25 June 1638.

1643–1647, makes no mention of wagons.[48] This lack of wagons available in Scotland is reinforced by anecdotal evidence many years after the period where the sight of wagons near Glasgow in 1723 caused widespread amazement amongst the populace.[49]

Much of the Scottish Covenanter (and later Engager) cavalry from 1639 onwards was mounted on ponies rather than horses, suggesting a prevalence of the former and shortage of the latter.[50] This is further supported by Scottish attempts to purchase English horse stock in both 1638 and 1639, which the King and his Privy Council countered by ordering that 'no horses be permitted to be carried into Scotland or any part beyond the seas without his [the King's] order.'[51] Writing to the Commissioners at York in May 1645, Leslie complained that the Covenanter army marching southwards in support of Parliament was suffering 'great impediment we find through the want of draught.'[52] On 10 February 1651 the Scottish Committee for Managing the Affairs of the Army ordered that each company of foot was to have 'three horses for carrying ammunition, and two baggage men to attend these horses.' In April of that year, the Committee ordered the Wagon-Master General's staff to 'go to the colonels of foot of the new regiments and require from them and their under officers an account of the three horses and two men ... for carrying ammunition; every company in every regiment is supposed to have them.'[53] Compare this to the New Model Army's standing requirement of two wagons and ten draught horses for each of its infantry regiments.[54] The English military appears not to have used packhorses unless circumstances demanded it. Even the Royalist Ordnance Papers have very limited mention of packhorses. An entry for 5 October 1644 of two conductors from Basing House returning into the stores: 'Pannells [pack saddles] 11, Cropwers 10, Girthes 6, Wanthes 6, Covers for Packs 6.' This would have been sufficient equipment for only six animals, although the extra cruppers and pack saddles suggest part of the necessary furniture for four or five more.[55] Packhorses may instead have been used more for individual officers' needs, such as when Captain Samuel Fawcett took one pack saddle and a pair of panniers (the packs for the saddle) 'for the he doth engage himselfe to retorne

---

48   Terry, *Papers relating to the Army of the Solemn league and covenant*, I, p.lxxviii.
49   Crofts, *Packhorse, Waggon and Post*, pp.29–33.
50   Edwards, *Dealing in Death*, p.164.
51   *CSPD 1638–1639*, p.347, Jan 22, The Council to the Vice-President and Council of York.
52   *CSPD 1644*, p.537, May 29, Alexander Leslie to the Commissioners of Parliament at York.
53   'Calendar of the Register of the Committee for Managing the Affairs of the Army, 4th April 1651, Perth' in David Stevenson (ed.) *The Government of Scotland Under the Covenanters, 1637–1651* (Edinburgh: Scottish History Society, 1981), pp.114–115, 127.
54   *CSPD 1651*, p.528, May 15, Warrants from the Council of State and Admiralty Committee.
55   Roy, *The Royalist Ordnance Papers*, I, p.142.

into the said stores.'[56] Generally, packhorses appear to have transported military supplies in areas where heavy goods vehicles were either unavailable at short notice or when speed was essential. Such appears to be the case where '80 horse loads of muskets and bandoliers' arrived at Chester at the end of September 1642 escorted by two troops of cavalry from Lancashire.[57] Both Cheshire and Lancashire would classify in the general description of upland areas and were unlikely to have had a surfeit of local wagons for the military to requisition for this convoy.

The other major form of vehicle in use at the period was the cart. Unlike the four-wheeled wagon, carts were single axle, two-wheeled vehicles. By the 1630s the wagon was the wheeled heavy goods vehicle of choice, while the cart, although it remained ubiquitous across the British Isles in other roles, was a smaller form of transportation. The image below, again a contemporary engraving, not only shows a substantially smaller two-wheeled vehicle than the previous engraving of the wagon, when compared against the accompanying drivers, but depicts also a smaller team of horses needed to pull the laden vehicle.

A cart and team with driver. Note the difference in numbers of draught animals to the above image of a wagon and team, and the size of the vehicles in comparison to the drivers. From David Loggan, 'Aula Novi Hospitii' in *Oxonia Illustrata* (Oxford, 1675) (Public Domain)

During the 1600s the smaller cart was a common vehicle for tradesmen, farmers, and others. Large carts, still on a single axle but built to a larger scale, had been supplanted by the more reliable four-wheeled wagon in the years preceding the Civil Wars.[58] Edwards argues that wagons replaced carts on the carrier trade in England at the beginning of the seventeenth century.[59] Prior to the shift to wagons amongst the national carriers, at least on London routes, these carriers

---

56   Roy, *The Royalist Ordnance Papers*, II, p.326
57   H. Beaumont, 'Events in Shropshire at the Commencement of the Great Civil War', *Transactions of the Shropshire Archaeological Society*, vol. 51, no.1 (1941), p.31.
58   Edwards, *Horse and Man*, p.201; Stuart, *Wagons, Carts and Pack Animals, 1580–1660*, p.16.
59   Edwards, *Horse and Man*, pp.195–197.

had made use of carts. These carts used by the earlier carriers before the change to wagons were significantly larger and more substantial than the smaller version of the cart in use on many farms and villages during the sixteenth and seventeenth centuries. The growing demand for transportation, and an increase in the size of loads, had likely led to the carriers relying on the scaled-up version of the old cart design before the 1600s. However, the single axle construction of these large carts meant that they were significantly inferior to the wagon. Carriers defending themselves against the Stuart government's attempt to prevent damage to roads by banning wagons in 1618 outlined why they needed to use wagons rather than other vehicles.[60] Interestingly, the carriers argued that the larger and more unwieldy carts that they had used before wagons could not be kept in good balance with the load and were difficult to manoeuvre downhill without the risk of tipping over. As a 'common carrier' was held responsible and liable for any damage or loss incurred on the goods he transported this was no small consideration.[61] The carriers also claimed that these larger carts were unsuitable for many different types of goods that were better matched to wagons.[62] Traversing through fords or flooding on the roads was far less hazardous with wagons than attempting to navigate the same in a large, and less-stable, two-wheeled cart. Finally, the carriers giving evidence claimed that older-style large carts were considerably more difficult to load than the newer wagons.[63] Despite the various attempts to limit the use of four-wheeled vehicles by the Stuart government, carriers continued to turn away from two-wheeled vehicles in favour of the more stable wagon. Rather than enforcing the earlier ban, the government responded by limiting the number of horses that carriers could use to pull their wagons, in an attempt to limit the weight of goods being transported and, they thought, limit the damage to roads from the heavier loads.[64] According to Gerhold, the last certain reference to a long-distance carrier service operating a two-wheeled vehicle of any size was in 1623.[65] By the time of the Civil Wars, the pre-eminent transport vehicle amongst the carriers along the roads of England and Wales was either the four-wheeled wagon or the packhorse.

However, the local hauliers, as surmised separately by Crofts, Gerhold, and Edwards, served a similar role to the carriers on major routes, such as those for

---

60   For proclamations against use of wagons under James I, see James Larkin and Paul Hughes (eds), *Stuart Royal Proclamations, Vol. 1: Royal Proclamations of King James I, 1603–1625* (Oxford: Oxford University Press, 1973), pp.396–397, 551–553; Gerhold includes details of this defence in Gerhold, 'Pack Horses and Wheeled Vehicles', pp.4–5, 9–10.
61   Crofts, *Packhorse, Waggon and Post*, pp.29–33.
62   Gerhold, 'Pack Horses and Wheeled Vehicles', pp.9–10.
63   Gerhold, 'Pack Horses and Wheeled Vehicles', p.10.
64   Edwards, *Horse and Man*, p.202.
65   Gerhold, 'Pack Horses and Wheeled Vehicles', p.5.

London and the other major towns and cities, but the hauliers' routes were limited to much smaller and more localised regions.⁶⁶ Local hauliers were typically parttime operators who provided ad hoc haulage services within and around their local area and rarely travelled far beyond it. Their work linked to the wider carrier network by their collation and dissemination of local produce and deliveries from, and to, staging points along the carriers' routes. Such staging points were likely the same inns that full-time carriers used along the routes to major towns and London or those at waterside landings for river-borne traffic. The wider road network itself would be tied into the waterborne transport network, with goods often partly moved by river or coastal transport eventually reaching their destination by carrier or haulier. The reverse could be true as well, with hauliers and carriers transporting goods to the waterside for further transport from there.⁶⁷

While not all local hauliers used carts, many did across all of England and Wales. Furthermore, apart from the Southeast and East of England, local and carrier uptake of the wagon was minimal by the outbreak of the Civil Wars. This left almost all remaining regions of England, as well as Ireland, Wales, and Scotland, reliant on carts for local work and primarily on packhorses for long-distance civilian transportation. Given the part-time nature of many local hauliers it would not have been economical for them to invest in a wagon when their small farm cart or a string of ponies was fit for their local purpose. The cost of a wagon and team in the 1640s was estimated at around £80, with the wagon itself costing perhaps around £12 to £13.⁶⁸ If you were a local farmer or tradesman, seeking to supplement your income with work as a local haulier, then doing so using local ponies (possibly from your own farm) was far more economical than investing in a wagon and team.⁶⁹ By the Civil Wars it was common knowledge that the cart was distinctly different to a wagon in both name and construction, with a cart being understood to be the smaller vehicle with reduced carrying capacity. When the Earl of Essex's army re-equipped after the disaster at Lostwithiel in 1644 the list of equipment requirements of the train included 'Twenty four Close Waggons. Fifteen long open waggons or 24 carts.'⁷⁰ If they were to receive carts, instead of open wagons, they would need more vehicles to make up the difference in size. The numbers outlined, 15/24 (or 62.5 percent), suggest that carts had less than two-thirds the carrying

---

66 Edwards, *Horse and Man*, pp.191–192; Gerhold, 'Pack Horses and Wheeled Vehicles', p.8.
67 Edwards, *Horse and Man*, p.187.
68 For a petition to the House of Commons regarding a wagon seized by Royalists see *Journals of the House of Commons* II, pp.736–737, Cloaths seized by E. of Northampton. See also National Archives SP 16/497, f.148r, 'Certificate on behalf of Robert Benitte, late wagoner of Exeter, to Lord General Essex'.
69 Gerhold, 'Pack Horses and Wheeled Vehicles', p.18.
70 Bodleian Tanner MS. 61, f.149.

capacity of a wagon. According to work by Gerhold, a seventeenth century wagon with a team of six horses could transport around two tons.[71] This would mean a commonly available cart and their team would be expected by contemporaries to be able to transport at most around 1.25 tons – a significant difference. The military preference for wagons as a means of transportation begins to be more apparent. For clarification, a 'close waggon' was one with an enclosed wagon bed usually under a supported canvas or similar material. These were essential for keeping the contents of the wagon as dry as possible and were primarily used for materials that would be otherwise damaged, such as gunpowder which would be rendered useless if damp. Apart from being 'close' or open, there is no evidence that the two types of wagons were substantially different in construction. Close wagons were constructed for the New Model Army in 1645, with six of them assigned to Sir Thomas Fairfax, two 'for the Major General' and another fourteen additional close wagons for the army.[72] It seems a general officer's baggage would be expected to be covered rather than exposed to the elements. These wagons cost £13 each compared to open wagons at £12 each, the difference being the work enclosing the wagon bed.[73] Apart from being 'close' or open, and the associated difference in price, there is no evidence that the two types of wagons were substantially different in construction.

Given that universal or widespread standardisation did not exist at the time, specifying the requirements of the vehicle was the only way to ensure the vehicle was fit for a particular purpose. Similarly, carts would often be called 'tumbrills' or 'tumbrill carts' on receipts and warrants, although these were not a separate type of vehicle and more a cart of a particular construction. Tumbrils were compact and sturdy carts, whose construction provided their operator particularly with the ability to load and unload the cart from the rear via a detachable back panel or moveable tailgate, making them much easier to load and unload. For these reasons they appear to have been used by civilians primarily for transporting manure, at least often enough to earn the nickname of 'muck cart' or 'dung cart'.[74] For the military these small, yet sturdy, carts appear to have been frequently used for transporting ammunition for the artillery.[75]

---

71   Gerhold, 'Pack Horses and Wheeled Vehicles', pp.12–14; Gerhold, *Carriers & Coachmasters*, p.52.
72   Mungeam, 'Contracts for the Supply of Equipment', p.114.
73   Mungeam, 'Contracts for the Supply of Equipment', p.114.
74   Randle Holme, *The Academy of Armory, or, A Storehouse of Armory and Blazon Containing the Several Variety of Created Beings, and How Born in Coats of Arms, Both Foreign and Domestick: with the Instruments Used in All Trades and Sciences* (London, 1688), p.339.
75   Roy, *The Royalist Ordnance Papers*, II, p.255 & p.284; Stuart, *Wagons, Carts and Pack Animals, 1580–1660*, p.4.

In each case the type of vehicle dictated the number of animals required in its team. Whereas animals could be added to, and removed from, a train of packhorses relatively quickly and easily this was not true for draught animals. Combined with a packhorse's greater speed in hilly terrain, this flexibility probably attracted the Committee to Both Kingdoms towards them for the Gloucester convoy in February 1644. Both carts and wagons required a minimum number of horses to effectively operate the vehicle, which would increase with the size and weight of the load being conveyed. A wagon required a minimum of four to five animals in its team when loaded, and teams of six or even eight horses were known for heavy loads for civilian use. However, civilian usage before and after the wars generally appears to be a team of five at most, in no small part because of the government's attempts to limit the amount that wagons could carry, as mentioned above.[76] A cart could make do with a smaller number of horses, with the very smallest of contemporary carts making use of only one animal. However, cart-teams could go as high as five animals if the size, load, and weight of the cart required it.

Military practice for carts at this time was between three and five horses, and for wagons between five and six. An inventory for a Royalist train of artillery of the 22 April 1643 listed the teams required for each vehicle's role within the train, but does not specify how the listed 'Carts, Waggons & Tumbrells' were distributed across these roles. All the teams are of five horses, apart from two vehicles which are listed as requiring six. As these were designated as transporting the powder it is possible these were closed wagons, and explains the slightly larger teams.[77] Horse teams for both the 'close waggons' and 'open waggons' for the New Model Army in 1645 appear to have been composed of at least five horses based on the orders of harnesses.[78] The stability of a wagon, and its size, meant it could hold more, and so needed more horses to pull the greater load. Carts, being smaller and not being able to be as heavily loaded as the four-wheeled wagon, generally needed smaller teams.

Economic historians such as Gerhold and Thomas Willan have studied the carrying capacity of packhorses and wagons. An individual packhorse could transport around 240lbs and a wagon pulled by six draught horses could move around two tons.[79] Thus a single wagon with a team of six could move as much, if not a little more, than 18 packhorses. If we place this in context with what the military judged to be the differences in carts capacity, we can estimate some

---

76 Gerhold, 'Pack Horses and Wheeled Vehicles', pp.12–13.
77 Roy, The *Royalist Ordnance Papers*, I, pp.218–219.
78 Mungeam, 'Contracts for the Supply of Equipment', pp.114–115.
79 Gerhold, 'Pack Horses and Wheeled Vehicles', pp.12–13; Thomas Willan, *The Inland Trade: Studies in English Internal Trade in the Sixteenth and Seventeenth Centuries* (Manchester: Manchester University Press, 1976), p.12.

rudimentary comparisons for the military loads of the three main forms of land transport: wagons, carts, and packhorses. Five wagons each with a team of six horses, 30 horses in total, could transport the same amount as eight carts each with a team of four or five horses, which is at least 32 horses and could be as many as 40. The transport capacity of five wagons or of eight carts would need around 55 packhorses to match. When seen in that light, it further demonstrates why the military preferred to use wagons wherever possible.

Drawing of a four-wheeled covered wagon, Isaac van Ostade c.1646–1649. Collection of the Metropolitan Museum of Art, New York. (Public Domain)

It is unclear how many men were necessary to operate the various vehicles, as firm information is not available although we can extrapolate possible numbers from the source material. At least one wagoner would be needed to control each cart or wagon, although based on contemporary drawings these men often walked or rode alongside their teams to manage them rather than sat on the vehicle. For packhorses, at least in the context of the military, it appears that at least two men were allocated for every three packhorses.[80] This could have meant that packhorses were not only a more intensive form of transport per animal compared to wheeled vehicles but also more manpower intensive needing a higher proportion of men per animal to manage them.

For pulling wagons and carts draught horses were preferred to oxen, despite the popularity of oxen in earlier centuries.[81] Formerly, oxen had been the stronger beast of burden and were able to pull greater weights than horses, although this changed as England's horse stock improved dramatically over the early modern period, particularly since laws regarding horse breeding were enacted during the reign of Henry VIII.[82] An often-perceived advantage of oxen over horses (but not ponies) was that oxen were only fed on grass. Horses required, as understood by contemporaries, a more complex and therefore more expensive diet which included oats, barley, and hay to remain in good working condition. However, this meant that a large amount of lush grassland was needed to feed oxen, whereas a horse could be fed from foods such as cereal and oats in a nosebag.[83] Feeding by nosebag was often more convenient, as the animals would not need to be dispersed into a field to graze, and it meant that feeding was less reliant on access to and quality of the grass along the route.

The horse was also much faster than the ox, which may have proven important for carrier roles and was certainly paramount for military needs. A horse or a pony was easier to shoe and thereafter far less susceptible to laming while hauling loads over uneven, frozen, or hard ground. The difficulty in shoeing oxen would mean that the animals would have struggled with their footing and in turn when pulling a load in poor conditions, due to weather and terrain. The shortage of draught horses at the outbreak of the Civil Wars did lead to some oxen being used as military draught animals to meet the initial demands by the Royalist forces for the artillery train during the period 1642–1643. Parliamentarian forces in the North of England under the command of Colonel Rigby captured a Royalist ammunition vehicle 'drawn with eight oxen' in November 1643.[84] In 1643 attempts were made by the Royalists to sell such animals and to purchase horses for the

---

80 'Calendar of the Register of the Committee for Managing the Affairs of the Army, 4th April 1651, Perth' in Stevenson, *The Government of Scotland Under the Covenanters*, pp.114–115, 127.
81 John Langdon, *Horses, Oxen and Technological Innovation: The Use of Draught Animals in English Farming from 1066 to 1500* (Cambridge: Cambridge University Press, 1986), pp.273–276.
82 Edwards, *Horse and Man*, p.184; Langdon, *Horses, Oxen*, pp.160–164.
83 Edwards, *Horse and Man*, pp.184–186.
84 John Vicars, *Gods Arke Overtopping the Worlds Waves, or the Third Part of the Parliamentary Chronicle* (London: 1646), p.80.

artillery train's use with the proceeds as soon as it was practicable to do so.[85] A year later in July 1644 the Royalist Wagon-Master General was ordered to enumerate any remaining oxen and 'make sale of all those oxen left here.'[86] In general, if an ox was found in harness in England it was far more likely to be pulling a plough across a farmer's field than a vehicle along a road, and in military usage it was far less likely to be used if horses were available.

In the less wealthy and less agriculturally developed regions of the British Isles, particularly in Wales and Ireland, oxen were a much more common sight. During the British Civil Wars oxen were used as military draught animals by all sides in Ireland.[87] This was largely due to the lack of native draught horses and such were the limited numbers of draught horses in Ireland that whole teams of English draught horses were shipped over to Ireland, with their wagons, in 1642 for use by the Protestant forces.[88] However, even this limited supply of wagons with horse teams from England was halted after fighting broke out between Royalists and Parliamentarians in England. Several of these wagons and their teams never even made it to Ireland as 'some carriage-horses and waggons which were prepared for the service of Ireland, that lay ready at Chester to be transported' were secured by the Royalists in late September.[89] This dearth of wagons and heavy horses reflected the prevalence of cattle in Ireland's predominantly pastoral farming economy that made minimal use of the draught horse, not dissimilar to the more pastoral regions of England, Wales, and Scotland of the time. However, without an extensive native draught horse breeding capability, and with a very limited ability to import more after the 1641 rebellion, Ireland had to rely on native oxen for the majority of its draught needs. Even artillery, a priority for good quality draught animals, had to be pulled by oxen in Ireland because of the lack of draught horses.[90] This state of affairs continued throughout much of the war in Ireland for all the combatants. Even years later, after the Battles of Dungan's Hill and Rathmines in 1647 and 1649 respectively, the victors willingly incorporated captured oxen-pulled artillery and

---

85   Edwards, *Dealing in Death*, p.14.
86   Toynbee, *The Papers of Captain Henry Stevens*, p.30.
87   Edwards, *Dealing in Death*, p.167.
88   TNA WO 49/72, f.96.; 'Minute Book of the Commissioners for Irish Affairs (4 April–1 June 1642)', in Vernon Snow, and Anne Young (eds), *Private Journals of the Long Parliament, 2 June to 17 September 1642* (New Haven: Yale University Press, 1987), pp.327–372.
89   Edward Hyde, *The History of the Rebellion and Civil Wars in England*, (ed.) W.D. Macray, III (Oxford: Clarendon Press, 1826), p.337
90   Pádraig Lenihan, *Confederate Catholics at War, 1641–1649* (Cork: Cork University Press, 2001). p.57.

carts into their own army following the battle.[91] At Rathmines Michael Jones's victorious forces captured seven pieces of ordnance for their artillery train as well as 'about two hundred draught Oxen for the Trayn.'[92] Ireland's wider use of oxen-pulled vehicles in both peace and war suggests a situation not unlike England of prior centuries – pre-wagon and with a reliance on oxen and packhorses.

Transport vehicles in Ireland were predominantly lighter carts capable of traversing difficult roads or terrain and as such Ireland lacked the civilian need for heavy horse haulage that was found in south-eastern England.[93] This proved particularly problematic when attempting to move artillery of any substantial size following the outbreak of rebellion in 1641. General Barry's siege cannon with which he captured most of the fortified towns in Limerick was loaded onto a jury-rigged sled towed by oxen.[94]

All this would have meant that forces operating in Ireland, with transport sourced locally, would have had several unique features. A dependence on carts and packhorses (most likely native Irish ponies), would have had a far less efficient lift capacity than an army supported by wagons. However, military preference came secondary to availability. Cromwell's initial campaigns in Ireland in 1649 and 1650 were focused on securing important ports held by Royalist or Confederate forces.[95] Cromwell's speed of movement in his campaign compared to what they had been used to in previous campaigns stunned both his Royalist and his Confederate opponents. The Parliamentarian troops were supplied from, and the artillery were often transported by, supply ships, thus negating the reliance on Irish roads and land transport methods. The Royalists and their allies under command of the Marquess of Ormond were simply unable to react swiftly enough to the Parliamentarian forces' movements.[96]

A further note on the selection of draught animals must be made. Given the wide use of mules in military transport systems in Europe at the time it is worth explaining their absence amongst the armies in the Civil Wars. Mules, the infertile offspring resulting from crossbreeding donkeys and horses, were not in common use in the British Isles. No reason for this is given in surviving source material, with the animal itself being very rarely mentioned. Likely reasons for their absence

---

91 Michael Jones, *Lieut-General Jones's Letter to the Councel of State, of a Great Victory Which it Hath Pleased God to Give the Forces in the City of Dublin Under his Command* (London: 1649), p.4; James Scott Wheeler, *Cromwell in Ireland* (Dublin: Gill & Macmillan, 1999), p.35, p.79.
92 Jones, *Lieut-General Jones's Letter to the Councel of State*, p.4.
93 Edwards, *Dealing in Death*, p.167.
94 Lenihan, *Confederate Catholics at War*, p.57.
95 Wheeler, *Cromwell in Ireland*, pp.80–100.
96 Wheeler, *Cromwell in Ireland*, pp.80–100.

in the British Isles include the dramatically growing English horse trade, the legislation regarding the breeding of horses since the Tudor period, and the private ownership preference for producing fertile herd animals.[97] The mule's advantages are in its ability to carry heavy loads on its back and its resistance to dehydration in dry or arid areas. While this made it a popular beast of burden across much of Europe, particularly around the Mediterranean, dry and arid terrain was, and is, hardly a problem in the British Isles. The development of the wagon in this period and the improvement of both horse and pony stock neatly countered the load bearing benefit of the mule – all are possible, or even probable, reasons why mules are rarely mentioned either as beasts either of burden or draught in the early modern British Isles.

Acquisition

The combination of artillery train, baggage train, and transport for other purposes such as foraging (see chapter four) meant that armies in the British Civil Wars required large numbers of vehicles and their associated horse teams. Gavin Robinson has highlighted the difficulties Parliamentarian armies had in securing sufficient horses throughout 1643, both cavalry mounts and draught horses, a problem not fully resolved until late 1645. To provide some context, in 1644 the total number of horses in the Earl of Essex's artillery train alone was 1,042. This comprised 558 horses owned by the artillery train, 179 hired to serve in it, another 50 teams (say five horses each) requisitioned on the march, and a further 55 replacements.[98] The baggage train of an army would add further large numbers of both animals and vehicles. At Naseby in 1645, when the New Model Army overran the Royalist artillery train and captured 'most of their Badgage' totalling 'about two hundred Carriages all he had, and all his Guns, being twelve in number.'[99]

The gathering of such large numbers of vehicles and their horse teams was undertaken by two methods of acquisition – purchase or requisition. Requisition is expanded upon below, but in brief it includes both the hiring and the impressment of civilian vehicles, teams, and drivers for military purposes.

---

97   Edwards, *Horse and Man*, pp.184–186; Edwards, *Dealing in Death*, pp.155–157.
98   TNA SP 28/146 f.183, Account of charges of draught horses to the Lord General's Army.
99   Thomas Fairfax and Oliver Cromwell, *Three Letters, from the Right Honourable Sir Thomas Fairfax, Lieut. Gen. Crumwell and the Committee Residing in the Army* (London: 1645), p.2, 4.

LAND TRANSPORTATION 51

An Army on the march, engraving by Stefano della Bella. The number of horses required to pull even one piece of field artillery was substantial, quite apart from those needed to draw the equipment and ammunition it needed.
(Collection of the Metropolitan Museum of Art, New York. Public Domain)

Purchasing vehicles might, at first glance, appear to be the most effective means of quickly guaranteeing the required number of vehicles. However, during the long internal peace before the outbreak of the Bishops' Wars in the late 1630s, maintaining large numbers of unemployed vehicles, horses, and drivers would have been costly and therefore to be avoided. Indeed, no armies in Europe during the early modern period kept a large pool of transport vehicles in storage. Even the Spanish 'Army of Flanders', a force in near continuous existence for almost a century, did not have a large pool of military owned transportation vehicles to supply their forces.[100] The Ordnance Office located in the Tower of London had skilled craftsmen on staff that could, theoretically, maintain and monitor a pool of transport vehicles. However, these were individuals rather than teams of artisans and they were kept busy maintaining and repairing the limited numbers of carriages, gun carriages, and other stores within the Tower and in the King's various storehouses.[101] At the outbreak of the Bishops' Wars, the Council of War in England issued purchase and construction orders to these artisans to provide '400 waggons for carriages for the use of the army.'[102] This purchase was dependent on the availability of existing vehicles for sale or those that could be constructed

---

100 Instead, the Spanish government agreed special contracts with civilian carters in Savoy and Lorraine: see Parker, *The Army of Flanders and the Spanish Road*, p.86–87.
101 Edwards, *Dealing in Death*, p.222.
102 *CSPD 1638-1639*, p.541, Mar. 7, Minutes of the proceedings of the Council of War.

in time and the Council stipulated that the order was for 'the making' of wagons rather than the securing of that number.[103] The collaborative nature of the work limited the speed of production, as several skilled craftsmen – including carpenters, blacksmiths, and wheelwrights – had to contribute time towards making the different elements of a road vehicle at the time. During the mobilisation for war many of these skills were required elsewhere which further delayed the artisans' abilities to work on vehicles. Thus the Master Wheelwright at the Ordnance Office, Thomas Bateman, had to subcontract out to other artisans to support the construction of vehicles for the army's needs in 1639, including coachmakers such as Thomas Phelps of London.[104] For all their combined efforts the vehicles were not completed in time to be taken north by road and instead needed to be sent north via ship in a disassembled state to be assembled later.[105] Despite this, various armies throughout the conflicts would continue to place orders for the purchase of transport vehicles. Thomas Bateman continued constructing vehicles at the Tower for Parliament throughout the British Civil Wars. In September 1642 Bateman supplied 10 wagons to the Earl of Essex's army and supplied wagons for Parliamentarian forces in the Midlands, in Kent, and for the New Model Army from 1645 through to 1652. According to Edwards, 20 other artisans also made over 100 new wagons for Parliament.[106] However, this centralised method of vehicle purchasing could not keep pace with either the demand or the fluctuating nature of transport needs as forces grew and command authority decentralised.

The relatively small numbers of purchased vehicles supplied were generally assigned to the artillery train of an army, rather than to other elements of the army's wider baggage train.[107] The train of artillery, despite its name, included all manner of supporting elements essential to a field army on campaign. These artillery trains were significant in size, and their composition contributed to the demand for vehicles and teams for field armies equipped with artillery. An estimate for the necessary vehicles and animals required for a train of artillery in 1639 for the Army to operate against Scotland was 'waggons and tumbrels, 208; horses, 1,080' with 360 attendant carters.[108] Officers of the artillery train such as waggonmasters, conductors, comptrollers, and commissaries of various kinds were

---

103 *CSPD 1638–1639*, p.541, Mar. 7, Minutes of the proceedings of the Council of War.
104 TNA WO 49/68, ff.33–34; TNA WO 49/76, ff.55–56.
105 Edwards, *Dealing in Death*, p.224.
106 Edwards, *Dealing in Death*, p.228.
107 The baggage train, which included the artillery train, was the general term for the whole of the transport vehicles and animals accompanying an army into the field. Turner, *Pallas Armata*, pp.275–276.
108 CSPD 1638–1639, Mar. 23, Particularly of the number of horses and waggons required for a train of 50 pieces of artillery, p.602.

employed to manage this large numbers of vehicles, and their drivers, teamsters, and animals.[109] The Royalist artillery train staff in the summer of 1643 included – over and above the officers and artillerymen of various kinds – surgeons, surgeon's mates, nearly 50 conductors, 7 armourers, 9 gunfounders, 11 smiths, 2 farriers, 12 carpenters, 12 wheelwrights, 2 collar makers, a master cooper with 2 servants, a gunsmith, a gunstock maker, a turner, a ladle maker, a chaplain, and a paymaster with his own clerk, amongst others.[110] It is easy to see why the train was deemed a priority for reliable, permanent transport vehicles, particularly as several of those skills listed, such as farriers, smiths, wheelwrights and collar makers, would have been involved in maintaining and repairing the rest of the transport moving with the army.

Unsurprisingly, the demand for vehicles grew far beyond what solely purchasing, either existing or built to order, could provide. Inevitably, despite the preference for purchased vehicles, the artillery trains at the outbreak of the Civil Wars were at least partially composed of hired vehicles and teams. On 13 October 1642, King Charles issued an order that anyone 'Whoe shall receive warrants for the bringeing, or singing in any Carts warnes, or Horses for the use of o[ur] Trayne of Artillery that they, and every of them continue w[ith] y[er] Cartes Waynes, and Horses in that o[ur] service, and not depart from thence w[ith]out o[ur] expresse pleasure declared therin upon payne of death.'[111] So, while a small core of an army's transport needs was purchased or built at the start of the Civil Wars, the overwhelming majority was filled by requisition.

As mentioned above, requisition encompasses both the hiring and the impressment of civilian vehicles, teams, and drivers for military purposes. The reason why both of these are folded into a single term lies in the problems of the surviving contemporary source material and the language used for the practice. The term 'hiring' suggests a more transactional or collaborative relationship between the carters and the army, whereas impressment suggests the opposite. Impressment was a contested term of the period, and this complicates matters when using it. It was often used as a general term for the imposed hiring of a wagon and team, and usually its drivers as well, for a fee set by the hirer for a set period of time. Typically, this was either a per mile rate or a day rate to be paid on completion of the period. This was nothing new in government service and temporary impressment of conveyances for official purposes, such as transporting the King's timber, was not unusual and could be considered, because a wage was

---

109 Bull, *The Furie of the Ordnance*, Appendix III, pp.179–180.
110 Bodleian Rawlinson Ms D 395, ff.208–9, Trayne of Artillery.
111 TNA WO 55/457/60, f.1. Proclamation of the King, 13 October 1642.

paid, to be a form of hire.[112] However, impressment was also used to describe the forcible recruitment into military service, often without compensation and recognisably a form of commandeering.

Any form of impressment was an imposition on the owners and operators of the vehicles, as they would be taken from other work which might pay better than the government rate or even be necessary for the owner's livelihood, such as farm work. The problem lies in how the surviving sources themselves describe the impressment. Taking the King's proclamation of 13 October 1642 there is no way of knowing if the majority of these vehicles referred to were hired or impressed before that date as the warrants do not survive. However, we know that Parliament hired carriers to work in the Earl of Essex's artillery train and that at least some of these men felt they were pressed into service. For instance Robert Bennet, a carrier from Exeter delivering Devonshire cloth to London in September 1642, was 'pressed to go in the Parliament's service in the train of artillery.'[113] While in this role Bennet 'lost his waggon and horses worth £82 at least, being his whole livelihood' at the Battle of Edgehill.[114] Several carriers stayed in the Parliament's service for years such as Isaac Peare who, with his wagon and team, served in the Earl of Essex's artillery train from November 1642 until September 1644 when the artillery train was captured by the Royalists at Lostwithiel.[115] The convoluted nature of terminology surrounding this area, and the ambiguity of the surviving evidence, distracts from the operational elements of transport with which this chapter concerns itself.

The militaries were notoriously bad at returning vehicles and teams to their owners, as well as reimbursing them. According to Edwards, in September 1641, the counties of Lincolnshire and Huntingdonshire were still awaiting the return of the horses they had sent north for service with the armies the previous year.[116] The only surviving sources we have for final repayment of service come from

---

112 This practice of making local counties responsible for transporting timber continued throughout the 1630s according to various entries in the *Calendars of State Papers (Domestic)*. For example, on 1 March 1633, Justices of the Peace in Surrey were asking to be excused the responsibility of pressing and paying for carriage of timber, see *CSPD 1631–1633*, p.553. In 1638 timber carriage in Kent was paid at 5d per mile, *CSPD 1637–1638*, pp.479–480, May 31. In July representatives from Kent requested to be excused from transporting timber through other counties partly because 'This county having also been of late much charged [to transport timber]', p.550.
113 TNA SP 16/497, f.148r, Certificate on behalf of Robert Benitte, late wagoner of Exeter, to Lord General Essex; *CSPD 1641–1643*, p.459, May 10, Petition of Robert Bennet.
114 TNA SP 16/497, f.148r, Certificate on behalf of Robert Benitte, late wagoner of Exeter, to Lord General Essex; *CSPD 1641–1643*, p.459, May 10, Petition of Robert Bennet.
115 Gavin Robinson, 'Horse Supply in the English Civil War, 1642–1646', PhD thesis, (University of Reading, 2001), pp.79–82
116 Edwards, *Dealing in Death*, p.159.

Parliament, and there is little to no surviving evidence of repayment to those who served in the trains of the defeated forces. Even amongst waggoneers working for Parliament, many had to wait years for repayment with money not forthcoming until at least 1647 when an Ordinance was passed that 'all such Waggoners that have Arrears owing them for Service done with their Carts and Waggons for the Commonwealth; and what shall appear to them to be justly owing them, to give Warrant to the said Treasurers for maimed Soldiers to make proportionable Payments thereof, as the said Money shall come in, till their said Debts are fully satisfied.'[117]

Perhaps the most advantageous aspect of requisition, for the military, was that it allowed local commanders the ability to fulfil their transport needs more quickly and easily than would otherwise be the case. The decentralised nature of much of the military authority with the distance and time in communications separating many commanders from their central authority, and the distances between allied forces meant that this method of gathering transport locally would be far more responsive to a local commander's needs. It meant commanders were not reliant on the pace of construction for new vehicles. According to Edwards, commanders 'tended to requisition horses and carts when they needed them.'[118] Four teams of horses were impressed from Padbury parish in Buckinghamshire and served in the Earl of Essex's artillery train for 17 days.[119] A cart worth £5 was requisitioned from a Jeffery Bampton of Walton in Aylesbury.[120] Mentmore parish in Buckinghamshire 'lost four horses and harness' to Essex's army.[121] As a result of this practice of requisitioning, as well as a reliance on civilian construction for militarily used vehicles, the vehicles and teams of the military were the same design and build, in fact often the same vehicles themselves, as civilians used.

The commanders of armies also attempted to limit the amount of what might be termed as unnecessary vehicles accompanying the forces. To provide some earlier context, the Council of War's February 1639 planned allowance of horses and vehicles for the officers of the English army was 'for the Officers of the Army, besides those for the carriage of the tents for the foot and likewise for the train of artillery. Total 481 waggons.'[122] Restricting the number of officer's baggage vehicles

---

117 LJ, IX, 21 July 1647, pp.341–343. This was distinct from losses which occurred while in service to an opposing force, such as the aforementioned Robert Bennet, whose petition for relief was granted on 26 May 1643, see *CSPD 1641–1643*, p.459, Article 82, Section II.
118 Edwards, *Horse and Man*, p.167.
119 TNA SP 28/150 part I, f.108. Padbury Parish Accounts. I am indebted to Dr Gavin Robinson for pointing me towards the Buckinghamshire parish accounts.
120 TNA SP28/219, unfol. Walton Parish Accounts.
121 TNA SP28/221 unfol. Mentmore Parish Accounts.
122 *CSPD 1638–1639*, p.421, Feb. 3, List of the carriages appointed.

was seen as necessary to reduce the overall size of the baggage train, as otherwise officers were often willing to 'provide waggons for themselves with all speed.'[123] Such private vehicles were kept for the sole use of the officers' baggage and his comfort. The number of vehicles allocated to an officer was a reflection of his rank and status. At the establishment of the New Model Army, Sir Thomas Fairfax as overall commander was allowed six baggage wagons, whereas the Sergeant-Major General, in overall command of the infantry, was allowed only two. There were several reasons to limit the numbers of vehicles with the army, including concerns that large numbers of vehicles slowed an army and unnecessary vehicles could exacerbate this. Further concerns likely existed for the maintenance of such vehicles, and quite possibly the limited availability of vehicles that could otherwise be used for other purposes.

These limits placed on officers' baggage transport were separate from the regimental or company transport vehicles which were for the use of the regimental supply needs, such regimental vehicles themselves formed part of the wider baggage train of the army. These regimental vehicles were seen as necessary to the effectiveness of the regiments to which they were assigned, fulfilling a variety of tasks which the regiments needed such as transporting provisions, ammunition, wounded and sick men, tents, and other necessaries. However, even these vehicles were not spared from the general trend in reducing the size of baggage trains. Regimental vehicles gradually reduced in number throughout the course of the wars. For the English forces in 1639 there were at least 10 draught vehicles allocated for each infantry regiment as 'every colonel is to speak with his captains to provide themselves with a wagon or cart for the company's accommodation, for which the King will give allowance.'[124] This was reduced down to the two wagons total allowed for each of the infantry regiments of the New Model Army in 1645. General Monck wrote in 1667 claiming army regiments needed 'two waggons, four waggoneers, and ten horses' in the face of planned government economies in the military due to the wagons usefulness in transporting food, ammunition, and other stores between regiments and garrisons.[125] From the evidence it appears that there may well have been an increase in the proportion of government-owned wagons in the New Model Army at its formation. Thomas Bateman, Master Wheelwright at the Ordnance Office, was again ordered to produce wagons for these forces producing both close and open wagons.[126] Almost certainly, the consolidation of

---

123 *CSPD 1638–1639*, p.387, Jan. 30, Capt. Anthony Thelwall.
124 *CSPD 1638–1639*, pp.179–180, Dec. 19, the King to Sir Thomas Morton.
125 George Monck, *Reasons for the Continuance of Certain Officers*, (1667), cited in Charles Firth, *Cromwell's Army: A History of the English Soldiers During the Civil Wars, the Commonwealth and the Protectorate* (London: Methuen, 1902), p.423.
126 Mungeam, 'Contracts for the Supply of Equipment', p.114.

the supply trains of the Earl of Essex's army, and those of the Southern and the Eastern Association Armies would have yielded a number of government-owned wagons already operating with those forces.[127] These, together with the ones being produced by Bateman, could suggest that the need for civilian-owned and operated wagons was at least partly reduced for the smaller needs of the New Model Army. It is perfectly reasonable, although only supposition, that after several years of warfare there were simply fewer civilian carriers operating and therefore fewer available for requisition by late 1644. With the war interrupting civilian transport routes those civilian waggoneers who used them risked being requisitioned into military service and suffering financial loss as a result, many civilian carriers may thus have avoided operating under such circumstances. If this is the case, relying solely on government-owned wagons and horses for the New Model Army could have been a blend of financial security, propitious reorganisation, and necessity forced on them by scarcity amongst available civilian wagons.

Regional Variation

The First Civil War serves as a strong example of the regional variation in vehicles and how this affected the collection of suitable vehicles for the military. Leaving aside contested areas, the geographical divide between the varying upland and lowland usage of civilian vehicles is roughly similar to the general pattern of Royalist and Parliamentarian controlled areas in the early, and even middle years of the First Civil War, the Royalists (roughly) in the west, southwest, and the north, and Parliament (again loosely) in the east, and southeast. The accompanying map outlines the areas of support between the opposing Royalist and Parliament factions during late 1642. If we compare this to the topographical map, discussed above, we can see a rough but clear separation in the topographical distribution between the factions, with most of the upland areas of England and Wales controlled by the Royalists and with almost all the lowland areas of England under Parliamentarian control.

---

127 See Gentles, *The New Model Army in England, Ireland and Scotland*, pp.31–33.

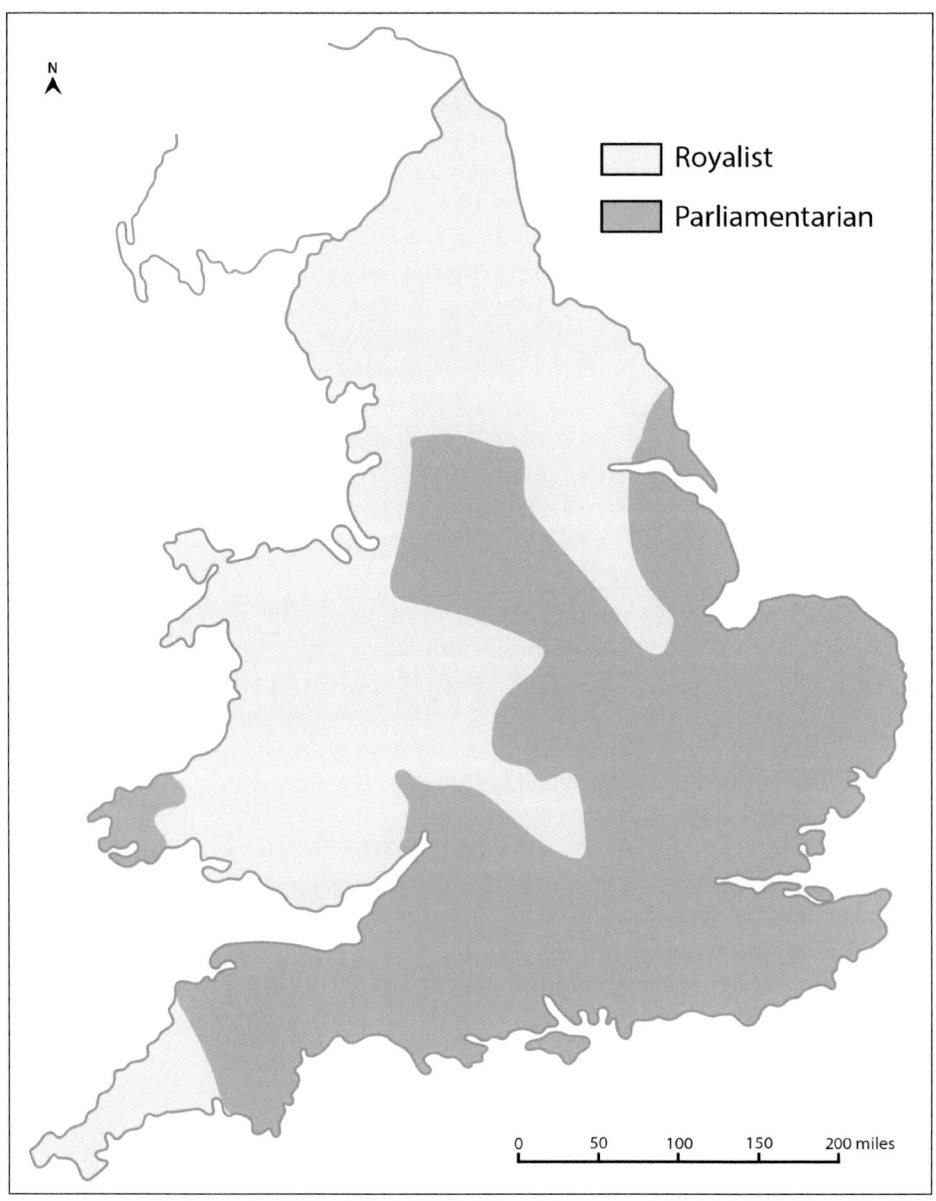

1642 map of support. This map shows the areas of support for the Royalists and Parliamentarians across England and Wales in late 1642.[128] (Author's drawing)

128 Compiled with information from: Peter Newman, *Atlas of the English Civil War* (London: Routledge, 1998), p.32; Peter Young & Richard Holmes, *The English Civil War* (Ware: Wordsworth editions, 2000), p.109; Nick Lipscombe, *The English Civil War: An Atlas and Concise History of the Wars of the Three Kingdoms, 1639–51* (Oxford: Osprey, 2020), p.101.

In late 1642, the outbreak of armed conflict in England disrupted large parts of the carrier network. During the Edgehill campaign, conceived as it was as a short season of fighting to decide the war, little organised thought or preparation was given to preparing supply trains, with both Royalist and Parliamentarian soldiers suffering from hunger for days at a time. Edward Hyde, later Earl of Clarendon, claimed that 'when they came to Edge-hill, that there were very many companies of the common soldiers, who had scarce eaten bread in eight and forty hours before.'[129] As evidenced earlier, field officers appear to have secured whatever transport they could for their artillery or regiments from wherever they could, throughout the wars. Therefore, at the outbreak of civil war in England the various armies' trains were filled with largely locally sourced means of transportation. The control of the different regions would have led to very different types of local vehicle available. For the first part of the English Civil War, contested areas left aside, this meant that the Royalists were far more reliant on sourcing road transportation from areas that had far fewer wagons. As discussed, even major carriers to London originating in these Royalist controlled areas tended to rely on packhorses. Local hauliers and other local vehicles in these pastoral regions again tended to be the lighter two-wheeled cart. Parliament, however, could draw their vehicles for their forces from areas where much of the civilian transport vehicles were the larger wagons. Carts certainly appear more often in Royalist Ordnance Office accounts than wagons. In Oxford on 21 January 1643 a train of artillery for Prince Rupert listed one 'waggon cov'ed' and five carts.[130] On 3 May 1643 'a marching Trayne of 4 peeces of Ordenance' included ten carts and one wagon.[131]

This would have given the Royalist forces the advantage of a train of supply that could have been capable of moving faster on poorer roads, and across rougher terrain, by using the lighter carts, but would have been less efficient in terms of lift capability per vehicle. To transport the same amount took more carts than wagons, as well as an increase in the number of horses overall, as analysed above. A Parliamentarian convoy would be able to carry the same amount of bulk cargo in fewer wagons with fewer horses than the Royalists could manage with their lighter carts. This is without factoring in the food necessary to keep the extra horses and carters that the Royalists would have needed. A military equipped primarily with wagons would have had fewer vehicles, and more supplies shipped where available, than a similarly equipped foe using mostly carts. The size and capabilities of the wagon as a transport vehicle gave Parliament a far more efficient transport system, allowing them to transport more goods per horse (and vehicle)

---

129 Hyde, *The History of the Rebellion and Civil Wars in England*, pp.359–360.
130 Roy, *The Royalist Ordnance Papers*, I, p.191.
131 Roy, *The Royalist Ordnance Papers*, I, pp.222–223

than the Royalists. As being economically viable is not the same as militarily viable it is likely that Parliament would not have suffered from taking these wagons into the upland areas on campaign and would not have had to 'downgrade' to lighter carts as civilian carriers might have had to. With the addition of an artillery train the movement speed of any large force would have been reduced to that of the towed guns. In 1644, the Earl of Essex claimed that Sir William Waller's army was better suited to pursue the withdrawing Royalist force rather than his own army, which was substantially slower due to the extensive artillery train.[132] This is also important for what it tells us of the road quality of the period, because while packhorses might be suitable for paths and tracks, large four-wheeled vehicles such as wagons with a team of horses needed a more substantial road.

Roads

The roads of the British Isles formed an essential link in the communications and trade network of the Kingdoms. Yet it is important to note that there is very little surviving evidence on the state of the roads and highways of the British Isles during the seventeenth century. Much of the quality and capability of the road network must be deduced from the limited evidence we do have: the types of vehicles used, how they were used in peacetime, and what military records and accounts can tell us of the operational nature of armies along the roads. Taking what we know about the vehicles and animals used across the British Isles, and in conjunction with other sources, we can begin to establish a picture of what the road network was like. Earlier historians have generally assumed that the roads were in terrible condition.[133] According to the letters and journals of early modern travellers on which they based this appraisal, even roads from major ports were not passable all year round, sometimes being unable to take any form of traffic beyond foot or packhorse.[134] The historian Charles Wilson summed up the roads in England in the seventeenth century as 'everywhere deplorable and getting steadily worse. In many places they were little more than grassy tracks tracing a wayward and fitful

---

132 Wheeler, *The Irish and British Wars, 1637–1654*, p.105. According to Scott and Turton, this was Essex's reasoning for leaving the pursuit of the Royalist forces to Waller, see Scott and Turton, *Hey For Old Robin!*, p.226.
133 Chartres, 'Road Carrying in England in the Seventeenth Century: Myth and Reality', pp.74–75; Parkes, *Travel in England in the Seventeenth Century*; Crofts, *Packhorse, Waggon and Post*, p.16.
134 Crofts, *Packhorse, Waggon and Post*, p.2, For counterarguments see Gerhold, 'Pack Horses and Wheeled Vehicles', and Chartres., 'Road Carrying in England in the Seventeenth Century: Myth and Reality', although Gerhold thinks the increase in trade was not as explosive as Chartres argued.

passage through open fields.'[135] Yet, as Edwards mentions, there was increasing regional agricultural and industrial specialisations occurring across England in this period.[136] In order for this to occur, and for regions to export their specialised produce to others that needed it, this strongly implies that an increasing number of goods had to traverse the Stuart realms by road as not all areas could be served by river or coastal transportation. This would require a road network able to support the increase in traffic. If the roads and highways nearer London were sufficient to manage large and growing numbers of carriers of various kinds, then the roads themselves had to be at least passable and useable.[137]

Legislation beginning in the Tudor period required parishes to be responsible for the roads in their neighbourhood.[138] The Stuarts continued with this policy requiring local authorities and leading local landowners to pay towards parish funds for the maintaining and, in some cases, improving local roads. A list of people who were refusing 'to pay towards mending the highways' in 1626 included 'the Duke of Buckingham, the Earls of Suffolk, Salisbury, Rutland, Denbigh, Holland, and Berkshire, the Countess of Derby, Viscount Wallingford, Lords Grandison and Conway,' and several other nobles and 'well-known persons.'[139]

In 1633 Sir Edward Duncombe wrote to Secretary of State Sir Francis Windebank proclaiming his innocence to the charges of neglect of the roads in his care, claiming that he 'intends to lay yearly on [the road between Hockley and Woburn] 400 loads of gravel and stone.' He also complained he was already out of pocket for repairs to two other major roads in the parish of Battlesden.[140] Examples such as this, while admittedly placing responsibility onto local people, do indicate attempts to organise road maintenance and repair. Parish surveyors were assigned and given permission to take gravel and stone for road repair, and to improve and extend drainage of the roads.[141] These powers suggest that the common problems that occurred included flooding, substantial surface damage, and possibly even subsidence of the road, and were due to heavy use and poor maintenance following bad weather. One of the reasons the shod horse was favoured over the oxen in pulling the carriers' and others' wagons along the roads was its superiority in pulling over frozen ground. This itself indicates that some roads were passable by wagon when heavy frost, or even ice, was on the ground.

---

135 Charles Wilson, *England's Apprenticeship, 1603–1769* (London: Longman, 1965), p.43.
136 Edwards, *Horse and Man*, pp.188–189.
137 Chartres, 'Road Carrying in England in the Seventeenth Century: Myth and Reality', pp.82–84.
138 Willan, *The Inland Trade*, p.3.
139 *CSPD 1625–1626*, p.392, July, Article 112. List sent to the Earl of Dorset.
140 *CSPD 1633–1634*, April 6, Sir Edward Duncombe to Sec. Windebank, p.6.
141 Willan, *The Inland Trade*, p.3.

This could mean that certain routes at least were passable well into late autumn and even early spring, and very possibly winter in some areas, provided one had a sufficient team of suitable animals to manage it.

We know that local upland hauliers preferred the use of lighter vehicles and packhorses because they served better in those areas than larger wagons. Croft argues that some roads and areas were particularly bad, generally getting worse the further west or north from London that you went, which also ties into Chartres's claims.[142] Yet these areas included the major western ports of Bristol and Chester, and it seems very unlikely that roads around these centres of import and export, not to mention the Stuart government's links to Ireland, would be impassable by all significant wheeled traffic. Upland rural areas certainly saw less economic traffic and roads there were only of a sufficient standard for local hauliers, packhorses, and carts as a minimum. We do know that, if necessary, these more rural 'upland' roads could support heavily laden wagons. A typical upland area would be the Devon and Cornwall peninsular. During the British Civil Wars, the Earl of Essex's army was driven by multiple Royalist armies towards the sea at Lostwithiel and Fowey. Here, running low on food, Essex's army was forced to surrender along with its attendant baggage and artillery.[143] The roads in this upland area had to have been sufficient for Essex's army of at least 16 infantry regiments and nine cavalry regiments to march along, with the roads in enough repair and wide enough to take multiple sizes of cannon and the wagons of his artillery train which together with the army's baggage was over 350 vehicles.[144] Overall, the ability of the army to move so far into a rural, upland area is a strong case *against* the 'impassable' picture of roads presented by earlier historians.

In more rural areas during peacetime the roads would have had less traffic moving between villages and farms and would therefore have needed less maintenance in the eyes of the locals. Roads in upland regions of England were often based on drovers' routes following the pastures of the hills and valleys down to the local market towns.[145] The experience was almost certainly akin to much of Ireland and Scotland, given the similarity in topography and pastoral farming regions to these those areas of England. These roads, carved by the passage of livestock over generations, meandered down the lines of least resistance and followed water courses for the driven animals – these roads not necessarily created for vehicular needs. Widening or levelling these routes would have been seen as prohibitively

---

142 Crofts, *Packhorse, Waggon and Post*, pp.19–20; Chartres, 'Road Carrying in England in the Seventeenth Century: Myth and Reality', pp.82–84.
143 Scott and Turton, *Hey For Old Robin!*, pp.137–143.
144 Scott and Turton, *Hey for Old Robin!*, p.139, pp.151–152.
145 Gillian Hutton, 'Roads and Routeways in County Durham: 1530–1730', PhD Thesis (University of Durham, 2011), pp.161–167.

expensive as well as unnecessary given the types of traffic which made use of them. The roads only needed to be maintained for the purposes of rugged, light vehicles and packhorses, so they were kept in a state necessary only to take this lighter traffic. The fact that the packhorse remained economically viable for so long strongly argues that the western and northern areas contained roads less suitable for wagons.

Even upland roads at the extreme edge of the English mainland were able to handle, at least in late summer, heavy wagons, artillery, and all their draught horses, not to mention substantial foot traffic of infantry and cavalry. Wagon use would continue to grow in popularity as the eighteenth century approached, in tandem with the improving roads under the turnpike system, with wagons becoming more economically viable when roads were of higher quality in both upland or lowland areas.[146] Eric Pawson argues that the system of relying on parish funds and labour for local road maintenance was adequate for local roads but not for the principal highways.[147] This ties in with Crofts's belief that communities in rural areas would work to maintain a road, but not improve it.[148] The roads of this period were routes linking towns and villages areas together, not highways linking two distant points, bypassing the towns and villages in between. Even the Great North Road was more a collection of sequential roads that meandered northwards from London linking town to town until York, with alternative routes between towns and continuing similarly towards Edinburgh through Durham. This is further supported by the competing carriers' different transport routes which indicate that there was often more than one route between towns.

I would suggest then that the roads in England were therefore not as universally bad as historians such as Parkes or Crofts have claimed. Certainly, in some parts of the country the roads were not wide and level enough to make wagon use economically practicable, although perhaps sufficient for military needs, but they remained useable for other forms of transportation such as carts and packhorses. These economic practicalities impacting on civilian transport availability would have an impact on military operations.

---

146 Edwards, *Horse and Man*, p.187.
147 Eric Pawson, *Transport and Economy: the Turnpike Roads of Eighteenth Century England* (London: Academic Press, 1977), pp.70–71; Crofts, *Packhorse, Waggon and Post*, p.18.
148 Crofts, *Packhorse, Waggon and Post*, p.14.

Operational Realities

The realities of the system of requisition as a means of supplying transport for an army had one fundamental requirement in order to work. It needed vehicles to be available that could be requisitioned. Edwards has stated that the King and many of his advisers in 1639 were 'oblivious of the time it took to produce goods on such a scale.'[149] This is confirmed from the example given above of the order for constructing wagons, which came so late that these wagons were not ready in time for the campaign. It appears this also applies to the time it took to gather reluctant people's property for government service. The North of England, as already stated, simply lacked large numbers of heavy goods vehicles since the terrain was often unsuitable for them, and parts of the countryside were considered incapable of supporting an army's needs. The King's Council of War could not have been in ignorance of this as the Deputy Lieutenants of Westmoreland reported on 31 January 1639 that 'for waggons there is no passage, in respect of the mountains' and that 'this county being so mountainous and remote … they know not how provision will be got thither for the sustenance of an army.'[150] However, the initial orders to the various regions of England on preparations for the raising of an army appear to have been dispatched the previous November. A letter from the Council dated November 1638 informed the Deputy Lieutenants of Staffordshire to dispatch warrants including, amongst other things, 'that carts be in readiness.'[151] Notable is that Staffordshire, in the Western Midlands, was only able to provide carts, with no mention of wagons. However, the numbers gathered proved to be insufficient when the army began mustering, so a new round of requisitions 'for providing of able horses and carters for the train of artillery, to be ready at Newcastle-upon-Tyne by the 15th of June next' was issued on 17 March 1639 to the various County Lord Lieutenants.[152] It was only on 16 April that a Deputy Lieutenant of Lincolnshire, Sir Anthony Irby, was able to report that they were 'providing of 60 horse and 20 carts, which we have sent to Newcastle-upon-Tyne.'[153] Again, note the lack of wagons being sourced in this north-eastern county. However, the intervening lack of transport capacity was already making itself felt amongst the army in operational terms. In May, reports were emerging of hungry soldiers in the North stealing food from civilians while large amounts of food sat

---

149 Edwards, *Dealing in Death*, p.20.
150 *CSPD 1638–1639*, pp.397–398, Jan. 31, Answers of the Deputy Lieutenants of Westmoreland.
151 *CSPD 1638–1639*, pp.416–417, Feb. 2, Deputy Lieutenants of co. Stafford to the Lord Lieutenant.
152 *CSPD 1639*, p.100, April, The same to [the Lords Lieutenants of the several counties].
153 *CSPD 1639*, p.49, April 16, Sir Anthony Ibry, late sheriff of co. Lincoln.

unused at Newcastle, so Charles decided to delay the general rendezvous of the regiments until June.[154] At the beginning of June the lack of available transport in Northumberland grew even more dire as 'many of our arms are left behind at Alnwick for want of carts, the country bringing in none, for indeed they have them not.'[155] The army sent into Yorkshire for '150 carts to attend the army' but it seems resistance to the increasing demand for transport was growing amongst the general population.[156] On 12 June it was reported that men were 'refusing to pay their contribution towards the charge of sending fifty horses and seventeen carters out of Northamptonshire to Newcastle, for the train of artillery and carriage of ammunition and other provisions for his Majesty's army.'[157]

At the beginning of May in 1639 the Lieutenant of the Ordnance, Sir John Heydon, wrote to the Master General of the Ordnance regarding the lack of available horse harness in the north. It appears that the Council of War had also erroneously assumed that the North of England was 'as plentifully furnished with cart ware as other countries through which his Majesty has made his yearly progresses' and had instead found 'a want of harness for their waggons and carts.'[158] The Ordnance Office had 'neither received any money, made any demand for, or ever did provide horse harness for carts or wagons, which upon all services hitherto were taken up with the horses of the country.'[159] As discussed above, military practice for carts at this time was between three and five horses, and for wagons between five and six.

However, civilian use was perhaps as few as two or even a single animal for carts and perhaps four horses for wagons. Before the cart could meet military transportation requirements the number of animals, and thus the number or amount of harness, generally needed to be increased. The problem appears to be that, when the wagons and carts arrived in the north with their teams, from the previous order in November 1638, the civilians had naturally sent only the existing teams with the vehicles, and not any additional animals and harness. As the government then sent out more requisitions for horses in the April of 1639, it appears the civilians had not sent extra harnesses with these new horses. The Ordnance Office had not previously had to worry about providing harnesses according to Heydon's letter, as they were usually 'taken up with the horses of the country.'[160]

---

154 *CSPD 1639*, p.148, May 10, The Council to the Lords Lieutenant of the several counties.
155 *CSPD 1639*, pp.281–282, June 5, Edward Norgate to [Robert Read].
156 *CSPD 1639*, pp.281–282, June 5, Edward Norgate to [Robert Read]
157 *CSPD 1639*, p.303, June 12, William Earl of Exeter to Thomas Meautys.
158 *CSPD 1639*, p.121, May 5, Sir John Heydon, Lieutenant of the Ordnance.
159 *CSPD 1639, p.121,* May 5, Sir John Heydon, Lieutenant of the Ordnance.
160 *CSPD 1639*, p.121, May 5, Sir John Heydon, Lieutenant of the Ordnance.

Simply ordering extra harness would not have been an easy solution, as they would take time to make, and not all harnesses would have fitted all vehicles. The type of harness used was influenced by the design of cart or wagon and the role of the animal in the team, with at least three different forms of harness in common use at this time: the thill, the cope, and the trace. Each vehicle required one of these harnesses to be able to increase the team as required depending on the harness design of the rearmost animal. For a thill harness the rearmost animal was harnessed between the two shafts (or thills) of the vehicle, whose weight it supported on a special saddle on its back, with the animals in front either in single line or pairs in a trace harness. For a cope harness the rear of the team of animals was a pair, either side of a central shaft, with the rest of the team harnessed in front accordingly – again in a trace.[161] Carts primarily made use of the thill harness, being smaller vehicles designed for smaller teams, whereas wagons could be either. When horse harnesses were supplied to the New Model Army in 1645, alongside other orders for wagons (but no carts), it was stipulated that 'every fifth harness to be a Thill horse harness' which suggests that these wagons were of thill design.[162] In the spring of 1639, to misquote an old maxim, perhaps a war was lost for want of a harness, rather than for want of a nail.

The methods of supplying forces sent to counter the Irish rebellion stand as a sharp contrast to the English attempts during the Bishops' Wars. For the English regiments dispatched to Ireland (the recruitment and provision of which is covered below) there was no need for the creation and operation of extensive military logistics supply trains of hundreds of wagons and thousands of horses. Instead, the regiments were mustered to the north-western and western ports of Chester and Bristol with the supplies being shipped over to Ireland, often from those same ports, as soon as they became available. This was strikingly similar to the methods used for supplying regiments mustering for Royal service against Spain and France in the 1620s, and for those raised for volunteer service in Europe.[163] This approach required less of a reliance on forming new systems and instead made much use of existing civilian infrastructure.

During the winter of 1641–1642, in response to the initial uprising, the English Ordnance Office appears to have requisitioned carriers to be able to quickly move large amounts of weapons to the western ports for shipping to Ireland. Thirty vehicles were requisitioned by Ordnance Office officials to transport weapons to Chester from London in a single large convoy.[164] Later, supplies such as uniforms,

---

161 Stuart, *Wagons, Carts and Pack Animals, 1580–1660*, pp.10–15.
162 Mungeam, 'Contracts for the Supply of Equipment', p.114.
163 See Spring, *First British Army*.
164 TNA WO 49/72, f.96, Warrant of Nicholas Cox.

clothing, hats, boots, and food were transported from London to the ports in quite a different manner for the regiments being formed in England and in Ireland. Instead of requisitioning vehicles and teams to supply these regiments, the government representatives made use of the civilian carrier network to transport these supplies from London and then westward across England to ports such as Bristol and Chester. Many of the shipments were paid for by weight, not by wagon, suggesting they were taken as part of a carrier's wagon load on his route rather than requisitioned for a single journey paid by a per diem rate.[165] George Wood, Commissary for the clothing of the soldiers in Ireland, appears to have used the carrier network to send supplies to Ireland as he was reimbursed for 'package and carriage of divers particulars' and at 'reasonable rates'.[166] Official pressure appears to have been applied to carriers in the event of such important deliveries, such as when William Pennoyer was employed to transport to 'Bristoll six hundred barrells of gunpowder, forty tonn of match, and other necessaries.' Pennoyer was to employ all 'Bristoll and Westerne wagons [as] now or shallbe in towene [London] within theis five daies' and pay them 'the usuall rates'. Although the carriers were 'required to yeild obedience hereunto as they will answer the contrary' it appears they stopped short of requisitioning them, relying instead on Pennoyer employing them as carriers rather than requisitioned transport.[167]

The cost of carriage, although fronted by monies raised by the Committee of Irish Adventurers, was to ultimately rest on the soldiers who were thus equipped 'with the prices they cost heere and the charges of carriage, that defalcacian [defalcation, deduction] may be made thereof out of the souldiers pay.'[168]

The difference in the two approaches to using the carrier network shows a balance between urgency and availability. For example, the shipment of arms urgently needed in Ireland in the winter of 1641–1642 was dispatched in a large convoy and likely represented stores from the Ordnance Office itself. Similarly, the Commissaries' remits of food, clothing, boots, et cetera, would have been dispatched when a sufficiently large amount of those orders placed had been completed to warrant a delivery. In other words, the form the deliveries took were based on the amounts being sent. After the first bulk shipment of equipment from the Ordnance Office was moved in the large convoy, this would have drawn down most of the available material in the stores and hence the subsequent new orders

---

165 Morris, *Public Transport in England and Wales*, p.4.
166 Bodleian Rawlinson Ms A 110, ff.44, 45v, Wood £214 13s 7d for sending away of provisions.
167 Bodleian Rawlinson Ms A 110, f.8, 'Mr. Pennoyer for wagons to carry powder and match to Bristoll'.
168 Bodleian Rawlinson Ms A 110, f.13,' Provisions for Athlone'.

for equipment. These would appear to have then been shipped as and when they became available along the civilian carrier network.

As the conflict between King and Parliament gathered pace in the autumn of 1642, Parliament was still attempting to send supplies to the western ports for service in Ireland. However, the unescorted civilian carriers carrying military stores proved tempting targets for the growing numbers of Royalist patrols. Carriers rapidly learned that using the increasingly contested roads for civilian traffic meant they could fall victim to seizure and confiscation. In August 1643, William Whittacre, who had been hired to carry uniforms destined for Ireland, encountered Royalist troops under the Earl of Northampton who 'seized upon his Waggon, Eight Horses; and all the Cloaths; and said, They should serve the King's Soldiers.'[169] Several wagons were requisitioned by the Royalists in Shropshire for transporting arms and armour to Shrewsbury. Given the lack of native wagons in an area where carts were the popular vehicle it is safe to suggest these were carrier wagons, perhaps on route to the port at Chester. These vehicles were then kept for use in the Royalists' growing artillery train rather than being released.[170]

Garrison Operations

The reliance that all forces had on land transport during the British Civil Wars meant that control of the roads themselves was essential to ensure an army's supply lines were secure. In England, Ireland, and Wales, at various points in the wars garrisoned towns were important strategic targets for the warring factions. Several important battles resulted when one side was attempting to relieve a threatened garrison, or to destroy a threat to besiege one, such as First Newbury 1643 (Gloucester), Nantwich 1644, Marston Moor 1644 (York), or Rathmines 1649 (Dublin).[171] Most of the ports in Ireland were attacked in the early stages of the rebellion, and when the English Parliamentary forces invaded Ireland in order to defeat the Royalist and Confederate forces there, the initial focus of the Parliamentarian campaign was the ports garrisoned by the enemy.[172] Following the English conquest of both Ireland and Scotland, garrisons were the instruments in retaining control of the occupied territories.[173] However, this is not the focus of

---

169 *CJ*, II, pp.736–737, Cloaths seized by E. of Northampton
170 Roy, *The Royalist Ordnance Papers,* I, p.16, fn.8.
171 Jon Day, *Gloucester & Newbury 1643: The Turning Point of the Civil War* (Barnsley: Pen & Sword Books, 2007), pp.177–178; Lipscombe, *The English Civil War: An Atlas and Concise History*, pp.133–142, 153–155, 167–178, 296–298
172 Wheeler, *Cromwell in Ireland*, pp.64–89.
173 Gentles, *The New Model Army in England, Ireland and Scotland*, pp.380–381; Keith Roberts, *Cromwell's War Machine: The New Model Army, 1645–1660* (Barnsley: Pen &

this study which is instead the consideration of the role of garrisons in logistics and supply. Garrisons across the British Isles were more than strongholds that simply dominated the landscape to extort food, money, and other supplies from the locality. The garrisons often had a myriad of functions including, but not limited to, securing and controlling the local area (particularly major towns) tax collection, magazines, waystations, and recruitment hubs.[174] A particularly good case study for garrisons and their role in land transportation is that of the Midlands during the period 1642–1646.

From almost the beginning of the Civil War, the Midlands was an important strategic location for both sides and much of it was heavily contested – the area adjoined Wales which provided so many soldiers for the Royalist armies that it was referred to as 'the nursery of the King's infantry.'[175] The Midlands was therefore a route through which to bring these Welsh recruits, and later English veterans from Ireland, to the Royalist forces fighting in England. It was through the Midlands that large parts of what Hutton termed the 'Cavalier Corridor' ran, connecting the King's capital at Oxford with Wales, and the Midlands linked both Wales and Oxford with other Royalist areas in the Southwest of England and in the North.[176] The Queen's convoys of imported supplies and troops to arm and equip the King's Oxford field army passed down this corridor in 1643 on their way south after landing at Bridlington in Yorkshire.[177] In 1644, Prince Rupert's army marched through the same area gathering troops as they continued towards the relief of York and subsequently the Battle of Marston Moor.[178] The local forces in the Midlands also served as a defence-in-depth to the Royalist base at Oxford, providing a series of strongpoints that guarded the main ways and approaches to the capital. For Parliament the Midlands held important routes between their support base of London and the Northwest, particularly Manchester. The area

Sword Military, 2009), pp.193–197.
174 For literature on garrisons more generally see Ronald Hutton, and Wylie Reeves, 'Sieges and Fortifications' in John Kenyon, and Jane Ohlmeyer, (eds), *The Civil Wars: A Military History of England Scotland and Ireland, 1638–1660* (Oxford: Oxford University Press, 1998), pp.195–233; Atherton, 'Royalist Finances in the English Civil War: The Case of Lichfield Garrison, 1643–5', pp.43–67; Elias Kupfermann, 'The Role of Windsor Castle During the English Civil Wars, 1642–1650', MPhil diss. (University of Leicester, 2019).
175 Thomas Carte (ed.), *A Collection of Original Letters and Papers, Concerning the Affairs of England, from the Year 1641 to 1660. Found Among the Duke of Ormonde's papers*, I (London, 1739), p.89; Mark Stoyle, *Soldiers & Strangers: An Ethnic History of the English Civil War* (New Haven: Yale University Press, 2005), p.11.
176 Hutton, *The Royalist War Effort 1642–1646*, pp.54 & 79.
177 Roy Sherwood, *The Civil War in the Midlands, 1642–1651*, 2nd Edition (Stroud: Alan Sutton, 1997), pp.44–46.
178 A short narrative summary of the war in the Midlands can be found in Sherwood, *The Civil War in the Midlands, 1642–1651*.

therefore offered both sides opportunities to hinder or damage their opponent's war efforts by applying pressure to the territory. To these ends, forces from both sides established garrisons in the area in an attempt to secure the region for their side, or at very least to deny it to the enemy. Gloucester's garrison was critical to Parliament in part because of its ability to threaten Royalist supply lines between Bristol (after the Royalists captured the port in July 1643) and Worcester, along the Welsh borders, into the Severn valley.

One of the most important aspects of a garrison's existence was that of the logistical nexus. As many garrisons were stationed at or near major roads in the area they functioned as key links in a logistics chain that connected and tied the region together. At a basic level, the mere existence of a garrison forced the opposing side to protect and patrol their own lines of communication and supply that ran near it. While every garrison had its own magazine for arms and ammunition, rarely did a commander ever feel it was sufficient. Supplies came into the localities from outside and were distributed by the regional authorities to the local forces and garrisons. With the main field armies claiming the lion's share of the war materiel produced at the major centres of industry, garrison commanders needed to source ammunition and weapons in their locality to supply their forces. In April 1643, Colonel John Lane, garrisoned at Stafford, requested supplies of powder from Sir Henry Hastings, commander of Tutbury Castle. Lane assured Hastings that if Stafford could be supplied with powder then they could supply the rest of their 'wants either at Shrewsbury or elsewhere'.[179] Later in the wars, after it had been secured by Parliament, the County Committee at Stafford tended to source the weapons for Stafford and other local Parliamentarian garrisons nearby from Manchester rather than rely on supplies from London.[180] While for some garrison commanders these attempts to source sufficient ammunition or weapons meant purchasing from suppliers as close as possible to their area, for others there were attempts to create local arms industries on-site. The Royalist garrison at Lichfield was able to produce gunpowder and possibly some small cannon.[181] The Parliamentarian garrison of Stafford was able to secure the services of an expert gunpowder manufacturer from Derbyshire, much to the frustration and annoyance of the Derbyshire Parliamentarian Sir John Gell.[182] Mostly the amounts were small and likely only proved able to make such garrisons self-sufficient for their everyday

---

179 *Report on the Manuscripts of the Late Reginald Rawdon Hastings, Esq. Of the Manor House, Ashby-de-la-Zouch*, II, (London: HMSO, 1930), p.98.
180 Donald Pennington and Ivan Roots (eds), *The Committee at Stafford, 1643–1645: The Order Book of the Staffordshire County Committee* (Manchester: Manchester University Press, 1957), p.82, p.319; Edwards, *Dealing in Death*, p.238
181 Edwards, *Dealing in Death*, p.53.
182 Edwards, 'Turning Ploughshares into Swords', p.61.

needs. However, some of the larger towns appear to have been capable of quite substantial local manufacturing. Apparently, Bristol was expected to produce up to 200 muskets a week by August 1643, and these numbers increased along with other types of weapons, powder, and other equipment throughout 1644.[183] Sir Francis Ottley was managing the production of small arms in Shrewsbury in April 1643, following attempts to centralise Shropshire's arms industry in the town.[184] Letters from Oxford imply production was underway and Ottley was asked by Edward Hyde to 'make what shift you can for I assure you it will be the greatest service you can to his Majesty if you could help him to 1000 arms.'[185]

Extensive fighting or being placed under siege would rapidly exceed the ability of these garrison industries to support themselves, dependent as they were on the raw materials coming in from outside. These raw materials heading to the garrisons also contributed to the traffic that wound its way between strongholds. For example, even something as simple and common as the wood ash necessary for the refinement of nitrogenous soil had to be bought and conveyed to Stafford for the production of gunpowder.[186]

Sometimes convoys moved between garrisons as local officers redistributed scarce resources where possible, in an attempt to mutually support their colleague's military efforts or simply expand and improve the magazines of their own garrisons. Parliamentarian-held Stafford in 1644 sent out supplies to the garrison at Carswell on 18 March 1645 as the garrison there was 'at a grate want both of provision of victuals and ammunition.'[187]

Garrisons appear to have been expected to supply elements of the field armies operating nearby. In April 1643 the Royalist Colonel Arthur Trevor had to order the civilian authorities of Shrewsbury to arrange a convoy of ammunition to Prince Rupert's forces, then besieging Lichfield Cathedral close in Staffordshire, writing 'I awakened the foggy burghers of the place to set the ammunition going towards your close work at Lichfield.'[188] In early 1644, it was reported that 'saltpetre is very plentiful at Lychfield' and Hastings was offered 'half a ton' of gunpowder from Oxford in exchange for the same weight of saltpetre from Lichfield.[189] This

---

183 Roy, *The Royalist Ordnance Papers*, I, p.38
184 W. Phillips (ed.), 'The Ottley Papers Relating to the Civil War', *Transactions of the Shropshire Archaeological and Natural History Society*, 2nd Series, Vols. 6 (1894), p.72.; Staffordshire Archives (hereafter SA) 6000/13292 Propositions for the security of Shrewsbury.
185 Phillips, 'Ottley Papers', p.71.
186 TNA SP 28/134/12, ff.353–355, 'Stafford Garrison Accounts'.
187 Pennington and Roots, *The Committee at Stafford, 1643–1645*, p.274.
188 WSL SMS 600, Letter from Col. Arthur Trevor addressed Dear Wm.
189 *HMC Report on the Manuscripts of the Late Reginald Rawdon Hastings,* II, p.119 Ja[mes] Du Port to Lord Loughborough.

La maraude (The raid) from The Miseries and Misfortunes of War, Jacques Callot (Rijksmuseum, Amsterdam)

responsibility of garrison commanders to ensure either supplies or convoys were successfully moved through their territory formed a large part of their duties. In February 1643 Colonel Henry Hastings claimed he was able to escort an arms convoy from Oxford, or at least 'may it be brought forth to Wolverhampton … from there will convoy it.'[190] This suggests a distinct convoy moving through his territory, with the garrison commander held responsible for the convoy's safety while under his jurisdiction. Similarly in early 1644 the Royalists reported that a Parliamentarian convoy of '1,000 muskets' with an escort 'of about sevenscore' was moving from Leicester to Nantwich via Nottingham and then Derby.[191] Again this suggests a distinct convoy, moving between the shelter of friendly garrisons and in this case, attempting to avoid patrols from the Royalist garrisons of Ashby, Tutbury, and Lichfield. In other cases, the practice seems to have been that the garrisons themselves were held responsible for assembling transport to move supplies onto the next stronghold. Jonathan Worton has reconstructed one of these convoys using surviving Royalist ordnance papers. Leaving Oxford on the 29 September 1643, the convoy changed horses at Enstone and continued onto Worcester where, on the 2 October, they were met by replacement carts and horses sent from Shropshire. From Worcester the convoy continued onto Ludlow where more requisitioned carts and horse teams awaited them.[192] This suggests that

190 WSL, SMS 550/10 Letter from Henry Hastings to Prince Rupert, 9 February 1642 [1643].
191 HMC *Report on the Manuscripts of the Late Reginald Rawdon Hastings,* II, p.119, Ja[mes] Du Port to Lord Loughborough.
192 Worton, *To Settle the Crown, p.196.*

convoys in the Midlands might take one of two forms. The first taking the form of a large, distinct, assembled convoy using garrisons as 'waystations' with transport assigned to it for the length of its journey. At each garrison, the commander and the troops there would be responsible for ensuring the convoy reached the next garrison along the route, handing the convoy, and their escort role, off in turn to their comrades. The other form of convoy was, in effect, a series of staggered, individual convoys. Here the supplies were offloaded at every garrison and the local commander had to find sufficient transport to move the supplies safely onward to the next garrison. Almost all the transport used in this second type of convoy was recruited locally and was therefore civilian.

In 1644, the village of Yarnfield had to supply transport and men to move supplies between Parliamentarian Eccleshall Hall and Wem.[193] Not only did this mean that the drivers, the horses, and their vehicles had to face the dangerous risks of becoming part of an early modern war effort, but that these vehicles and horses were taken out of the local civilian economy temporarily – or permanently. In 1643, Parliament's garrison commander at Caverswall Hall was authorised by its regional representatives to impress horse teams for transport having 'power to call for and command Teames and Horses for carriages.' He was also to have 'an espetiall care to prevent the carrying of salt or other provision to any of the Enemies Garisons.'[194] In 1644, the Royalist Colonel Bagot at Lichfield claimed he could not seize any more horses in the vicinity of Lichfield despite orders to do so, as there were none left.[195]

Convoys appear to be the contemporary term for either a large delivery, or perhaps an escorted one. Sir Arthur Gorges dispatched a small delivery of powder from Oxford northwards to Sir Henry Hastings, and in a letter discussing a later shipment of arms being readied wrote that 'I hope the last powder came safe unto you, though it had no convoy, but the arms shall not move with my consent without.'[196] So deliveries could be made in small amounts, but doing so did not 'countervail the charge and trouble' of doing so.[197] Despite all efforts, there were no guarantees with either convoy system as either could still be intercepted and captured or simply destroyed by enemy forces. Sometimes convoys had the misfortune of encountering elements of one of the local field armies, such as when Parliament's Sir William Brereton captured a supply of cannonballs as it made its way to Royalist Lichfield.[198]

---

193 Pennington and Roots, *The Committee at Stafford, 1643–1645*, p.281.
194 Pennington and Roots, *The Committee at Stafford, 1643–1645*, pp.19–20.
195 WSL, SMS 479 Letter from Colonel Bagot at Lichfield to Prince Rupert.
196 *HMC, Report on the Manuscripts of the Late Reginald Rawdon Hastings*, II, pp.121–122.
197 *HMC, Report on the Manuscripts of the Late Reginald Rawdon Hastings*, II, pp.121–122.
198 Hutton, *The Royalist War Effort 1642–1646*, p.76.

Conclusion

There were three main forms of cargo transportation over land, these being the wagon, the cart, and the packhorse, where the wagon was the larger and more efficient form of bulk transport. Where possible the military, certainly the English military, preferred to use wagons but were often forced to rely on what vehicles were available to them in the local area. However, in the case of the Bishops' Wars, the failings of the English army to recognise the limited availability of local vehicles, and the differences between how civilians used their vehicles, and how the army wished to use them, most notably in size of teams, led to structural failings in the attempts by the English to provide for their men. Even though large amounts of provisions were available at coastal magazines, the confusions over vehicle availability, number of horses, and even the availability of horse harness led to many English soldiers starving and falling ill. In comparison, their Scottish adversaries constructed not just a supply train, but also a strategic plan to account for both the advantages and limitations of the Scottish army having to largely rely on a transport system based on packhorses.

While hard data is unavailable, it is clear that land transportation had a fundamental impact upon the operation of early modern military forces. The type of region where an army was raised and from where it drew its transportation had an impact on the types of animals and vehicles it used, affecting the army commander's choices in terms of movements, the speed of that movement, and how it could conduct operations. English armies raised in different parts of the country could have very different supply vehicles to each other based on the local civilian equipment. This civilian equipment was based around the needs of the local civilians, and not military needs which had to adapt to fit what was available. The situation was similar in Scotland and Ireland where overall strategy was influenced by the native forms of transportation available. Perhaps the most important element running through this chapter is the interconnectivity between the military and civilians when it came to land transportation for their forces. The military needed to acquire its vehicles from civilian stocks, by purchase, hiring, or impressment and often the operators of the vehicles in military hands were impressed or hired civilians. Even the types of vehicles available to the armies were due to the difference in local civilians' needs.

2

Water Transportation

As established above, all armies in the British Isles were heavily reliant on land transport, though the methods and applications varied geographically and between factions, often noticeably so. However, transportation by water was as important as transport types across land in the early modern period. Similar to the experience of military transport systems on land, these river and coastal transport systems made use of vehicles, routes, and civilian infrastructure already in operation before the wars. Much like road transport the differences and limitations across different regions of the British Isles greatly impacted operational decisions and approaches and with water transport we can clearly see the impact it had on strategic decision making. Water transportation, however, was not fully incorporated into the armies, instead being hired or impressed on a short-term basis from civilians. The two methods of waterborne transportation utilised by the armies – coastal and river – combined with roads, were already highly interconnected for the purposes of internal communications and transportation within the British Isles before the outbreak of the wars. For example, cargo may have been moved from its point of origin by road to a river where it could then be transported by river barge to a port, and there loaded onto a coastal vessel to be shipped to another port and, if necessary, distributed by land and/or river to its final destination. There were, however, notable differences in available coastal transport amongst military operators as the Civil Wars spread across the British Isles.

The choice of the term 'coastal' in this context is a deliberate one. The transport vessels which plied the coasts of the British Isles were a vital part of the transport and logistics networks of the British Isles. Although coastal vessels frequently travelled far from the shore, the term 'coastal' is used to describe the British Isles' internal trade and communication networks operating upon the surrounding bodies of saltwater; more specifically, where the vessel journeyed between two points within the British Isles and did not detour to an external location along its journey. This could otherwise be confusing as many ships sailing from London to

Edinburgh for example, sailed out into the North Sea and often out of sight of the coast before making landfall nearer their destination. The Irish Sea varies from 12 miles at its narrowest section to 120 miles at its widest. Even on a fine and clear day a small trading vessel operating from coast to coast could be out of sight of both Ireland and England.

These coastal vessels rarely travelled as close to shore as the name suggests if they could possibly avoid doing so, as changeable winds, tides, or other threats meant any vessel dependent on sails for propulsion required enough sea-room to manoeuvre without fear of the rocks, shoals, sandbars, and other common hazards found around the coastlines. Often the size of the vessel in question would dictate the amount of sea-room needed. Larger vessels amongst those operating coastal routes would typically have had a much deeper draught than smaller ships thus needing a greater depth of water than many close-in coastal areas could safely provide. Using the determiner of a journey, with departure and destination within the bounds of the British Isles, one can therefore include routes out to sea within the term of coastal. So, while coastal is an imperfect word, it serves to describe shipping that operated between two points of the British Isles along a coast, even if sometimes via the open sea. To differentiate between the lighter and smaller ships that plied the coastal trade, transporting cargoes between ports, and the more substantial vessels that were capable of crossing oceans (the latter engaged in international trade) I have used the terms 'trader' and 'merchantman' respectively. This choice of terminology is simply to clarify when a ship is a coastal vessel, and when it is not. The exception to this rule is the larger form of coastal trader dedicated to the Newcastle-London coal route. These vessels, which are discussed later, were referred to as 'Newcastle colliers' or just 'colliers' and I have used this term to differentiate them from other types of coastal trading vessels.

The focus of this chapter is river and coastal transport, and is not be concerned with the transportation of supplies into the British Isles from outside, primarily because the chapter's focus is on operational, water-based transport for the armies of the British Civil Wars rather than the arms trade. Furthermore, by focusing on the internal British system of transportation this encapsulates the means of distribution to the armies of those supplies coming in from abroad. Peter Edwards's work, *Dealing in Death: The Arms Trade and the British Civil Wars* details this arms trade and highlights that as the wars continued, the internal production of war material became more important.[1] This reinforces the need to understand the internal transportation systems for the armies within the British Isles and builds on Edwards's work.

---

1   Edwards, *Dealing in Death*.

Studying the water-based logistical and supply aspects of the Civil Wars requires the use of a much wider and more varied range of sources than has previously been used in more traditional military history. This use of a broader source base in turn provides a clearer understanding of logistics and supply because of the military reliance on civilian methods and vehicles to supply the armies – emphasising the interconnected nature of early modern militaries and societies which is often lost in traditional military studies of the British Civil Wars.

This difficulty in locating more exact, and perhaps more traditional, military source material is a potential reason for the absence of studies on waterborne transport and logistical systems of the armies involved in the Civil Wars. Another possibility for this absence of study is that 'water transport', particularly the coastal aspect, may have been seen as coming more under the purview of naval history rather than that of the armies. Yet traditional naval history of the wars focus on sea battles or political loyalties in the navy, specifically the Ship Money fleet, rather than operational logistics.[2] Only more recently have studies considered the role of the navy as anything other than a battle fleet. The most prominent of recent works are those by Elaine Murphy, both independently and in collaboration with Richard Blakemore, which consider the role of naval contributions to land actions and the impact that extensive privateering campaigns had on the wider war effort. While these works primarily focus on the deployment and actions of warships, they also emphasise the importance of supplying and equipping fleets on all sides and provide evidence for the impact naval military operations had on local coastal trade.[3] Blakemore and Murphy's work not only provides an effective summary of naval actions, but reiterates the importance of civilian transport vessels being seconded to military requirements.[4] However, these works are not focused on the operational supply of armies by water. Fundamentally the study of water-based transport systems for the armies has been lost somewhere between land-based military histories and sea-based naval histories.

More valuable than existing military history studies for the study of water-carried army logistics are works by economic historians of the early modern period. These studies consider the coastal and river trades in an attempt to establish histories of economic development and the interconnectivity of regional economies. Economic historians such as Willan have studied these connections between land,

---

2   See John Powell, *The Navy in the English Civil War* (London: Archon Books, 1962); Nicholas Rodger, *The Safeguard of the Sea: A Naval History of Britain, Vol. 1, 1660–1649* (London: Harper Collins, 1997).

3   Richard Blakemore and Elaine Murphy, *The British Civil Wars at Sea, 1638–1653* (Woodbridge: Boydell & Brewer, 2018); Elaine Murphy, *Ireland and the War at Sea, 1641–1653* (Woodbridge, The Boydell Press, 2012).

4   Blakemore and Murphy, *The British Civil Wars at Sea, 1638–1653*, pp.35–37, 186–189.

river, and coastal trading networks, establishing their reliance on each other as parts of a wider, interwoven transport economy. Although his work is somewhat dated, much of it published in the middle of the last century, he made extensive use of a variety of contemporary sources in highlighting the co-dependency of seventeenth century transport networks.[5] Matthew Greenhall's much more recent work on Anglo-Scottish trade considers trading across land borders and along the coast. This work also emphasises the nuanced and complex interconnectivity between these two modes of transport.[6] Other economic studies have examined what types of cargo, and in what amounts, were shipped along the coastal ports – these accentuating the importance of the coastal trade for the early modern economy of the British Isles, and in establishing ideas of the regional economic diversification of the period.[7] These studies are further supplemented by work rebuilding historical coastal routes, using advances in computer software-based statistics and database manipulation, to analyse the speed and efficiency of coastal transportation of the period.[8] While this field of research is growing, many studies focus on the eighteenth century and later where there is more widespread source material. Oliver Dunn, writing in *The Journal of Transport History* as recently in 2020, stated that 'Coastal shipping, despite its historical prominence, appears to

---

5   Thomas Willan, *River Navigation in England, 1600–1750* (London: Oxford University Press, 1936); Willan, *The Inland Trade*.
6   Matthew Greenhall, 'The Evolution of the British Economy: Anglo-Scottish Trade and Political Union, an Inter-regional Perspective, 1580–1750', PhD Thesis (University of Durham, 2011).
7   Thomas Willan, *The English Coasting Trade, 1600–1750* (Manchester: Manchester University Press, 1938); John Armstrong, J., and Philip Bagwell, 'Coastal Shipping,' in Derek Aldcroft and Michael Freeman (eds), *Transport in the Industrial Revolution* (Manchester University Press, 1983), pp.142–161; Rosalin Barker, *The Rise of an Early Modern Shipping Industry, Whitby's Golden Fleet, 1620–1750* (Woodbridge: Boydell & Brewer, 2011); Mark Matthews, 'Shipping and Local Enterprise in the Early Eighteenth Century', *Journal of Transport History*, vol. 24, no.2 (2003), pp.139–153; Bronwen Cook, '"A True, Faire, and Just Account": Charles Huggett and the Content of Maldon in the English Coastal Shipping Trade, 1679–1684', *The Journal of Transport History*, vol. 26, No.1 (2005), pp.1–18; Peter Skidmore, 'Vessels and Networks: Shipowning in North-West England's Coasting Trade in the Late Eighteenth and Early Nineteenth Centuries', *The Mariner's Mirror*, vol. 99, no.2 (April 2013), pp.153–170; Malcolm Wanklyn, 'The Impact of Water Transport Facilities on the Economies of English River Ports, c.1660–c.1760', *The Economic History Review*, vol. 49, no.1 (1996), pp.20–34.
8   D. Bogart, O. Dunn, E. J. Alvarez-Palau and L. Shaw-Taylor, 'Speedier Delivery: Coastal Shipping Times and Speeds During the Age of Sail', *The Economic History Review Website*, 04 August 2020, <https://onlinelibrary.wiley.com/doi/abs/10.1111/ehr.13004≥ Accessed 16 August 2020.

be under-researched'.[9] Furthermore, none of these works directly contribute to the study of military transport networks.

Military historians have focused little on the strategic impact rivers played in the wars, although works such as Ian Roy's article 'England turned Germany' uses the fighting for control of the Severn Valley as a case study for the violence of the war, and his article clearly highlights the importance both sides placed on controlling the region.[10] The study of the operational use of rivers for logistics and supply, and the impact they may have had in determining wider military strategy remains understudied.

Given the geographic nature of the British Isles and how most of the major islands within this 'Atlantic Archipelago' saw fighting during the British Civil Wars, coastal forms of military transport were often essential to military operations, impacting on the decision to embark on, and supply, many significant military ventures.[11] Coastal transportation links played an essential role in the economy of the Kingdoms, with such transport for bulk goods being more cost effective than both road and river transportation. The efficiency of coastal shipping for transporting bulk produce meant it was often used in preference to road for such cargo. Examples of bulky produce included foodstuffs, coal, iron ore, and other heavy goods. Contemporaries certainly believed that sea transport was substantially cheaper than land; Sir Robert Southwell stated in a paper to the Royal Society in 1675 that 'the ordinary proportion between ship and wheel-carriage is about one to twenty.'[12] The Stuart government's preferred location in London in the South-East of England meant that coastal communications were necessary for the routes between London and the Irish Government in Dublin, at least in part via land across England, and then from the port of Chester. Coastal communications along the east coast of England and Scotland linked the Privy Council in Edinburgh with London as well. That military commanders of the period might be unaware of the importance and benefit that secure coastal or river transportation could have on their operations is frankly absurd, not least because so many had seen service in the Low Countries and Germany where such transport was paramount, yet military historians have seemingly left such transportation considerations of

---

9   Oliver Dunn, 'A Sea of Troubles? Journey Times and Coastal Shipping Routes in Seventeenth-Century England and Wales', *The Journal of Transport History*, vol. 41, no.2 (January 2020), p.186.
10 Ian Roy, 'England Turned Germany? The Aftermath of the Civil War in Its European Context', *Transactions of the Royal Historical Society*, 5th Series, vol. 28 (1978), pp.127–144.
11 John Pocock, *The Discovery of Islands* (Cambridge: Cambridge University Press, 2006) pp.29–30.
12 Sir Robert Southwell, 'Concerning Water' delivered 8 April 1675 in Thomas Birch (ed.), *The History of the Royal Society*, III (London, 1756) p.208; Chartres, *Internal Trade in England 1500–1700*, p.42.

the armies unstudied and unappreciated, particularly so pertaining to coastal vessels.[13]

Acquisition of Coastal Transport

In a distinct departure from the situation with land transportation, coastal vessels for military transport purposes do not appear to have been either purpose-built or directly purchased by the armies. Instead, ships were 'taken up' as and when they were needed for military purposes. Following an official decision, which would outline the port where shipping would be needed, orders would be sent to an assigned official to start collecting sufficient shipping either through impressment or hiring. As is often the case in this period, the lines between impressment and hiring appear to be somewhat blurred, and we cannot always be certain which was used – not least because of the ambiguous terminology sometimes used in the sources such as 'taken up'. In 1638, Captain George Bagg and his command of soldiers and gunners were to be transported, possibly to Ireland, in 'one of his Majesty's lesser ships, or a ship taken up at Plymouth.'[14] Sir Nicholas Slanning, Captain of Falmouth Fort, was ordered in February 1639 'to take up shipping for transporting' a company of his men and some artillery to Cumberland.[15] On 31 January 1643 the phrase was still commonly in use, as when the Commissioners of the Navy were ordered 'to take up a ketch of twenty tons in the Thames to transport provisions.'[16] None of these earlier sources make clear if the ship was to be hired or impressed for service, possibly suggesting that the final decision between impressing or hiring would be situational.

The official assigned to secure the necessary shipping could be the officers in charge of the expedition, such as Sir Nicholas Slanning, or they could be a local authority such as the port's mayor. In early 1642, the Lord Admiral of England ordered the mayor of Bristol to contract 'for the hire of 2 ships'.[17] On other occasions it would be someone selected for their experience in shipping. Alexander Bence MP was chosen by the Commission for Irish Affairs on 19 July 1642 to secure

---

13 For a brief selection of examples of officers with European experience see Donagan, *War in England*, p.233; Christopher Scott, Alan Turton and Eric von Arni, *Edgehill, The Battle Reinterpreted* (Barnsley: Pen & Sword, 2005), pp.40–43; Steve Murdoch and Alexia Grosjean, *Alexander Leslie and the Scottish Generals of the Thirty Years' War, 1618–1648* (London: Pickering & Chatto, 2014), pp.119–140.
14 *CSPD 1638–1639*, pp.237–238, Undated, 1638, Account of a proportion of ordnance stores.
15 *CSPD 1638–1639*, pp.503–504, Feb. 25, Instructions [of the King] to Sir Nicholas Slanning.
16 *CSPD 1641–1643*, p.556, Jan. 31, Letters and Papers relating to the Navy.
17 'Minute Book of the Commissioners for Irish Affairs' in Snow and Young, *The Private Journals of the Long Parliament: 2 June to 17 September 1642*, p.419.

'400 ton of shipping or thereabouts in two ships' for transporting 'ordnance, arms, ammunition, and materials'.[18] Bence was a London merchant with interests in shipping, along with financial stakes in several merchant vessels, and in September of 1643 would be selected by Parliament as a Commissioner of the Navy.[19]

It is important to clarify here that 'impressment' here refers to the coercion of a ship and its crew into service as a transport, rather than the forced recruitment of individual sailors into military service aboard warships. Hiring costs would be dependent on a number of factors, not only the number of vessels currently available and the willingness of a ship's master (or owners) to have the vessel's trading runs postponed until their government service had been completed, but also the wider circumstance. The appointed agent to acquire shipping usually negotiated for costs based on weight of cargo, per soldier if transporting troops, or at an agreed rate of pay on a weekly or monthly basis. At Bristol in June 1649, in preparation for sending reinforcements to Ireland, James Powell was ordered 'to stay all ships in the ports of Bristol, Minehead, Barnstaple, and Appledore, fit for transportation of horse and foot for Dublin, agree with them … by the month of freight, and order them to Milford Haven, where the horse and men are to be shipped.'[20]

The problem with impressment, which extended to using it as a threat to impact hiring prices, was that it required the active and willing participation of those in authority over the port. Without this, any official attempting to secure shipping encountered greater expenses. Such was the case of the Norfolk Deputy Lieutenants and Justices of the Peace charged with dispatching the Norfolk levies from the port of Harwich, Essex, during the First Bishops' War. They reported that their 'charges and trouble in getting boats to ship the men and other occasions did rise much higher, for we were in another county, and could neither command nor get any help from the mayor of the town or other officers.'[21] In contrast, where such cooperation was possible the threat of impressment could be explicitly used as a lever to obtain lower hiring prices. John Powell, continuing to act as shipping agent in Bristol was told in March 1650 that,

---

18 'Minute Book of the Commissioners for Irish Affairs' in Snow and Young, *The Private Journals of the Long Parliament: 2 June to 17 September 1642*), p.408.
19 Mary Keeler, *The Long Parliament, 1640–1641: A Biographical Study of its Members* (Philadelphia: American Philosophical Society, 1954), p.106; 'September 1642: Ordinance appointing Commissioners of the Navy', in *Acts and Ordinances of the Interregnum, 1642–1660*, Charles Firth, and Robert Rait, *Acts and Ordinances of the Interregnum, 1642–1660*, I (London: His Majesty's Stationery Office, 1911) pp.27–29.
20 *CSPD 1649–1650*, p.210, June 27, Council of State to James Powell, at Bristol.
21 *CSPD 1639*, p.55, April 17, The Justices of the Peace and Deputy Lieutenants of Norfolk.

the rates paid by you last winter, for transportation of foot and horse to Munster, are excessively dear, considering what is paid from Chester to Dublin, which about the same distance Bristol is from Youghall, the State paying by 2s. 6d. for every footman and 10s. for every horseman from Chester; let them [the ship captains] speedily understand the lowest rates for the transportation of each foot and horse soldier to Munster, advising with the governor and mayor of Bristol, and such others as you shall think fit; and upon return of the rates, you shall receive orders to press any vessel for the service that refuses to go upon these terms.[22]

Note that Powell was informed he would have the assistance of not just the civil but also the military authorities in order to have the powers to impress a ship. A military governor of a port had both the means and the will to enforce such compulsory service out of military necessity regardless of the effect on the owners. Parliamentarian Colonel Nathaniel Fiennes, Governor of Bristol, impressed a local merchant vessel, *Reformation,* several times in 1642 for duties ranging from guard ship to the transportation of supplies to Ireland, with the owner of the ship, Richard Locke, being responsible to 'victuall and man the saide Shipps with all things necessarie' for which Locke was never reimbursed.[23] After Bristol's capture by the Royalists in 1643, the same ship was also impressed by the Royalists 'for a voiadge to bee made to Leverpoole to transport Souldiers unto Dubline and did then force the saide Lock to sett forth the saide Shipp to sea uppon his owne accompt.'[24] Locke's refusal led to his arrest and temporary imprisonment as well as the impressment of his vessel. Locke would not have the *Reformation* released from military use until 1644, whereupon during its return from its first profitable sailing in three years it was lost when taken as a prize by Lord Inchiquin while it was anchored in the port of Kinsale.[25] The example of Lord Inchiquin taking the ship as a prize might suggest that this was another method for the securing of transport vessels. However, the *Reformation* was considered a warship, or used as one, due to its armaments. What happened to captured merchant vessels or coastal traders is not fully clear and may warrant further research, but I suspect it would be difficult

22 *CSPD 1650*, pp.62–62, March 27, Council of State to James Powell at Bristol.
23 'The Misfortunes of Richard Locke in the Civil War', in Patrick McGrath (ed.) *Merchants and Merchandise in Seventeenth-Century Bristol* (Bristol: Bristol Record Society, 1955), p.150.
24 'The Misfortunes of Richard Locke in the Civil War', p.151.
25 'The Misfortunes of Richard Locke in the Civil War', p.152. This then is almost certainly the same vessel *Reformation* listed as belonging to Lord Inchiquin in the Appendix 6 'Prominent Parliamentary Shipowners on the Irish Coast', in Murphy's *Ireland and the War at Sea, 1641–1653*, p.221.

to answer the question without sufficient surviving administrative sources that would detail the methods and records of the condemning and reselling of ships captured during the Civil Wars. Murphy's research into the topic of shipping losses is based on various reports from newsbooks and from the surviving testimonies of captured enemy captains. While this provides a picture for when and where a ship was taken, it does not show the process of what happened to the vessels afterward.

For military transportation purposes the size of the vessel was of key importance, with a single large vessel preferred since this could perform the work of several smaller vessels. The likelihood that a vessel had some form of defensive armaments appears substantially related to size, as the larger the vessel the greater the likelihood of it being equipped with at least some ordnance.[26] Because of a lack of naval vessels, in 1643 the authorities in Dublin hired several merchantmen to perform military duties. These included the *William of London*, of eight guns 'for the better guard of St. George's Channel' as well as to 'carry provisions to the fort of Duncannon.' They also hired the *Constance of Yarmouth* 'to attend this harbour and coast' and act as an escort for 'several vessels laden with provisions' from which we can infer that the *Constance* was also armed.[27] The ships secured by the Dublin authorities appear, from their names and size, to be merchantmen originating from English east coast ports rather than local to Dublin. Finding such suitable vessels locally was not always possible as another key element of both impressment and hiring was the availability of shipping in the port when the required transport was being gathered. This caveat would have had a significant impact on the available transport vessel capabilities for the different sides of the British Civil Wars. As the wars progressed, and particularly as the threat of warships (real or perceived) grew around the British Isles, the dynamic changed towards impressment. Owners and masters became less willing to risk their vessels and so would charge either extortionate rates or would refuse the hire outright, in which case impressment of the vessel became a necessity. A growing lack of available money, or at least hard currency, as the wars progressed resulting in delays and a complete lack of payment would have removed any pretence of the vessel being 'hired'. The number of suitable vessels available to be 'taken up' in a port was typically dependent on the location and importance of the port and there were distinct regional differences in the size and uses of coastal vessels in operation around the coasts.

---

26 Blakemore and Murphy, *The British Civil Wars at Sea, 1638–1653*, p.13.
27 HMC, *Calendar of the Manuscripts of the Marquess of Ormonde, K. P., Preserved at Kilkenny Castle*, II (London: HMSO, 1903) pp.266, 291–292.

Regional Disparity of Coastal Transport

We do not have much information as to the exact design of the coastal trading vessels of the seventeenth century. While later periods – particularly from the later eighteenth century onwards – have much clearer and more uniform definitions and descriptions of ship types, the same is not true of the seventeenth century.[28] In this latter period of study descriptions of a ship's size are often in terms of the vessel's carrying capacity rather than its design which itself was based on its role rather than a classification. Even when descriptive terms for the ships were used these descriptions were varied and often vague, thus making any judgement not solely based on the recorded tonnage difficult. For example, 'collier' for a ship engaged in transporting coal regardless of its tonnage or number of masts, 'bark' as a type of general small vessel, or 'frigate' for a swift and well armed vessel engaged in hunting other ships – contemporary frigates being of varying size, armament, and crew.

However, knowledge of ships' tonnage does allow us to identify a clear disparity in the size of vessels engaged in the coastal trade operating around the British Isles. The largest coastal vessels in common use were the Newcastle colliers operating along England's eastern coast. Built to meet London's ongoing and growing demand for coal, these vessels were substantially larger than other contemporary coastal trading vessels as they were built to transport a high-demand yet cheap and bulky cargo.[29] Drawing on surviving port books, detailing coastal trading ships' cargo and tonnage, John Nef established that the colliers operating along England's east coast had an average size of around 140 tons.[30] It is not unreasonable to surmise that under most circumstances these colliers were capable of greater speeds than their smaller counterparts. Simply put, a larger vessel could support larger masts and sails, with potentially a larger crew to operate them, therefore generating greater speed before the wind. Meanwhile, according to Willan, the coastal traders operating along the coasts of Western England and Wales, and in the Irish Sea, had an average vessel size at around 20 tons.[31] This is supported by studying the port books of Chester for the seventeenth century. From the 25 December 1622 to the 25 December 1623 the average size vessels identifiably

---

28 Skidmore, 'Vessels and Networks: Shipowning in North-West England's Coasting Trade in the Late Eighteenth and Early Nineteenth Centuries', p.162.
29 Willan, *The English Coasting Trade, 1600–1750*, pp.13–14.
30 John Nef, *The Rise of the British Coal Industry*, I, (Oxford: Frank Cass, 1932), pp.390–391.
31 Willan, *The English Coasting Trade, 1600–1750*, pp.12–1. These findings are further supported as part of Dunn's analytical study into the speed of coastal trading vessels, which considers the size and tonnage of these vessels, see Dunn, 'A Sea of Troubles? Journey Times and Coastal Shipping Routes in Seventeenth-Century England and Wales', p.91.

engaged in the coastal trade was a little over 11 tons.[32] For the port of Liverpool, the average size of similar vessels was 10 tons.

As such, when shipping was needed for military transportation, suitably large vessels were often difficult to find on short notice in western ports as the only appropriate vessels would be larger merchantmen. This held up deployment of English troops being sent to Ireland in order to suppress the Irish rebellion in early 1642. The Earl of Leicester's regiment, under its Lieutenant-Colonel George Monck, was delayed almost a month waiting for sufficient shipping, with the regiment arriving at Chester by road in late January from where they were then unable to sail for Ireland until late February.[33] This 'want of sufficient shipping' also impacted the transport of four cavalry troops under Sir Richard Grenville, who were forced to leave '20 Horse and 60 Foote' behind on the 20 or 21 February 1642.[34] Weeks later in the spring of 1642, as more troops were converging at Chester to embark for transport to Ireland, the Lord Admiral stated his belief that 'the shipping at Chester and in the ports adjacent might not be sufficient for that purpose.'[35] In response to this lack of shipping in these ports the Commissioners for Irish Affairs ordered that 'the lord admiral be desired to cause two or three ships of what burden his lordship shall think fit to be sent from Bristol, Plymouth, or Dartmouth with all convenient speed to the port of West Chester for the service aforesaid.'[36] Bristol was the largest trading port on the west coast making it the most likely port near Chester to find suitably large merchantmen in 1642, although Bristol was not itself a centre for shipbuilding.[37] The map below shows the 10 largest ports in England and Wales in the 1600s, and only two, Bristol and Chester, are on the west coast of England.

32 TNA E 190/1333/1, ff.1–8 The Port of Chester. Port: Chester Official. The average across the 57 identifiable coastal traders departing from the port at Chester across the eight folios is 11.4 tons; E 190/1333/8, ff.1–5 The Port of Chester. Port: Liverpool Official The average of the 31 vessels in the period from 25 December 1626 to 25 December 1627 is 10.3 tons.
33 *CSPD 1641–1643*, pp.287–288, Feb. 19, Sec. Nicholas to Sir Thomas Rowe.
34 *A Relation Touching the Present State and Condition of Ireland. Collected by a Committee of the House of Commons,* (London: 1642), p.2; *Fifth Report, Part I: Report and Appendix* (London: HMSO, 1876), pp.349–350.
35 'Minute Book of the Commissioners for Irish Affairs' in Vernon Snow and Anne Young (eds), *The Private Journals of the Long Parliament: 7 March to 1 June 1642* (New Haven: Yale University Press, 1992), p.432.
36 'Minute Book of the Commissioners for Irish Affairs' in Snow and Young, *The Private Journals of the Long Parliament: 7 March to 1 June 1642*, p.432.
37 John Lynch, *Bristol and the Civil War: For King and Parliament* (Stroud: Sutton, 1999), pp.117–118.

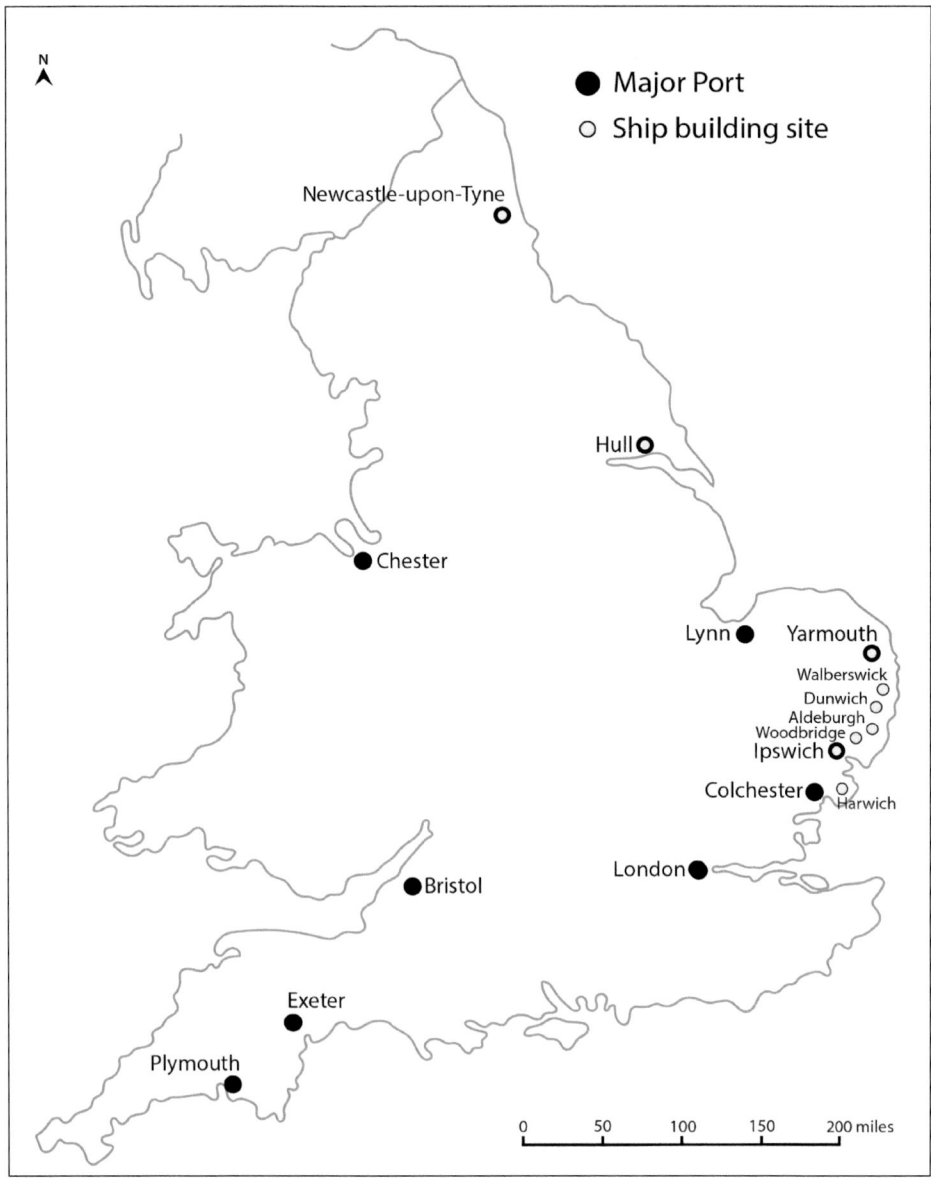

Map showing the locations of the ten largest ports in England and Wales during the period, along with other centres of major shipbuilding.[38] (Author's drawing)

38   Drawn from information from: 'James the Second, 1685: An Act to encourage the Building of Shipps in England. [Chapter XVIII. Rot. Parl. nu. 18.]', in Raithby, J. (ed.), *Statutes of the Realm: Vol. 6, 1685–94* (London: Great Britain Record Commission, 1819), pp.20–21; Table 12.1 in David Sacks, and Michael Lynch, 'Ports 1540–1700' in Peter Clark (ed.)

This is in stark contrast to ports on the east and the channel coasts of England where both colliers and merchantmen were plentiful.

An Act of 1685 contained a list of towns which had previously been important centres of shipbuilding, particularly of large collier vessels:

> Whereas for some yeares past ... there hath beene observed a more than ordinary Decay in Building Shipps in England and particularly in New Castle [Newcastle-upon-Tyne], Hull, Yarmouth, Ipswich, Alborough [Aldebourgh], Dunwich, Walderswick [Walberswick], Woodbridge, and Harwich where many stout Shipps were yearely built for the Coale and other Trade which were of great use to his Majestie in time of Warr and a Nursery for able Seamen[39]

All of the shipbuilding centres listed in the Act were located along England's eastern coastline (*cf.* the preceding map, with the major centres of shipbuilding listed in the Act highlighted). Given the focus of major civilian ship building here, and the smaller comparative size of coastal vessels elsewhere in the British Isles, the east coast Newcastle collier was clearly an anomaly in the size of coastal trading vessels, although one admirably suited for military transport purposes. During the Bishops' Wars it was colliers that moved supplies from London northwards along the coast to Hull. They were also used as troop transports for the war, with the Marquess of Hamilton's invasion force of spring 1639 being moved by 20 colliers, under escort, from the southeast of England to the Firth of Forth.[40] The capacity of English east coast colliers compared to that of local coasting vessels in Scotland is illustrated by the expedition of Captain Hill against the Covenanter forces in the spring of 1639 while detached from Hamilton's larger force. The collier accompanying Captain Hill was used to transport soldiers, men he employed in coastal raids such as when he 'sent in [his] long boat... with two boats more with soldiers' and captured a Scottish coasting vessel loaded with 'five demi-culverins in her' sheltering in Aberdeen road, shortly after he had captured another such vessel carrying '7 demi-culverins, of iron, and 24 pikes'.[41] The collier, in addition to serving as both troop transport and a supply vessel carrying stores

---

The Cambridge Urban History of Britain Volume II 1540–1840, (Cambridge: Cambridge University Press, 2000), p.384.

39 'James the Second, 1685: An Act to Encourage the Building of Shipps in England. [Chapter XVIII. Rot. Parl. nu. 18.]', in Raithby, *Statutes of the Realm: Volume 6, 1685–94*, pp.20–21.

40 SP 16/419, Spring 1639 Indentures; *CSPD 1639*, p.68, April 21, Article 33, p.68; p.127, May 7, Henry de Vic to Secretary Windebank; p.225, May 24, Newsletter; Blakemore and Murphy, *The British Civil Wars at Sea, 1638–1653*, p.39.

41 *CSPD 1639*, pp.278–279, June 4, Captain Philip Hill to Sir John Pennington.

for Hill's forces, was obviously also able to hold the cannon captured from both these Scottish vessels since Hill 'put the 12 pieces into the collier's ship for more security'.[42]

Colliers were the transport vessel of choice for military purposes by whomever held control of the east coast of England. After King Charles made his attempt to seize the arsenal at Hull in the spring of 1642, which was still filled with stores of supplies from the Second Bishops' War, Parliament ordered the magazine there be transported to London. Warships acting under Parliament's orders escorted the colliers to Hull where they loaded the stores from the stockpile and shipped them back to London. Just four colliers were used to transport '49 peices of brass ordnance, 40 carriages with shod wheels, 8 shod wheels, 105 grenadoes, 1,170 great cannon shotte, 1066 other cannon shotte, 118 ladles, sponges and worms, 20 veals [wheeled water carriers], 1 mortar peice, 17 petards' as well as 200 vats each containing four tents, 906 barrels of powder, and a large number of small arms.[43] Based on comparative cargo capacity, to move such an amount as that drawn from the Hull magazine in non-collier coasting vessels from elsewhere in the British Isles would have taken a fleet of 25 or more ships. The capacity of a Newcastle collier compared to other contemporary coastal trading vessels was clearly substantial.

This lift capacity was also not their only advantage as they seem to have been relatively easy to find in the ports along the eastern coast. As mentioned this is probably due to the numbers of such vessels engaged in the coal trade operating along the coast. There were at least 200 ships involved in the Newcastle-London coal trade in 1615. In 1699 there were more than three times that number.[44] At Ipswich in December 1638 bad weather had caused substantial numbers of colliers to gather quickly with 'ten or twelve sail of ships laden with coals' waiting for only fair weather to continue on to London, with a further '40 and 50 sail sent to Newcastle about three weeks since' and 'four or five and twenty sail which suffered damage in the late tempestuous weather' awaiting repairs.[45] The large numbers of Newcastle colliers, and the fact that at any time significant numbers could be expected in eastern England ports, made them ideal for the taking up of transport shipping as needed, at least for those seeking shipping on the east coast of England.

---

42 *CSPD 1639*, pp.278–279, June 4, Captain Philip Hill to Sir John Pennington.
43 *LJ*, V, pp.3–5, for removing the Magazine from Hull; *LJ*, V, pp.22–27, Sir John Hotham to take up Ships at Hull, for sending away the Magazine; *CJ*, II, pp.540–541, Transporting Hull Magazine; *CJ*, II, pp.593–595, Removing Magazine from Hull; TNA SP 16/490/77, *Equipment Transferred from Hull to London in 1642*.
44 Nef, *The Rise of the British Coal Industry*, I, pp.390–91.
45 *CSPD 1638–1639*, p.173, Dec. 17 William Moysey and John Barb, bailiffs of Ipswich, to the Council.

This combined with their transport capacity helps explain their use for military transport for any combatant that could obtain them.

According to Ben Coates, the First Civil War caused extensive disruption to the Newcastle-London coal trade, with the scarcity of coal causing its doubling in price.[46] Such was the demand for coal in June of 1644 that, according to the Venetian ambassador, Royalist disruption of the coal trade meant 'London may feel the miss of it [coal], which will be unbearable next winter, as they have felled most of the trees in the neighbourhood.'[47] Such a shortage of coal and extensive disruptions of its supply would argue for a large pool of collier vessels which had formally been dependent on the trade for employment, but were now available for military work due to a surfeit of ships for the smaller volume of the coal trade.

The use of low capacity coastal transport vessels in the west continued throughout the wars. As mentioned above, the west coast of England, as well as Ireland, lacked the readily available heavy transport vessels which regularly worked England's eastern coastline. Even those vessels engaged in the transport of coal along the west coast of England and Wales were substantially smaller than their east coast counterparts, with coal ships on the west coast weighing in at around 30 tons compared to the average of 140 tons of the east coast coal ships.[48]

Additionally, there was an overall lack of infrastructure of local shipbuilding on the coasts of the Irish Sea at the outbreak of the British Civil Wars, in comparison to the earlier established east coast situation. When Randal MacDonnell, the Irish Earl of Antrim, offered to raise an invasion force against the Covenanters he had to build vessels able to tackle even the narrow crossing between North-Eastern Ireland and Western Scotland. According to Mark Fissel, Antrim's attempts were ultimately unsuccessful, largely due to the inexperience of his carpenters.[49] If this is true, and they did lack the skills and practical knowledge of those carpenters and shipwrights producing the larger transport vessels along England's east coast, perhaps the reason lies in the types or sizes of vessels Antrim was attempting to build and that the local carpenters were not used to building transport vessels sufficiently large for Antrim's military purposes. This could be a situation unique to Eastern Ireland; however, the Scottish Covenanters attempts to supply their army in Ulster also supports the idea of a lack of shipping infrastructure on their west coast. During the period 1642–1644, the Covenanters struggled to supply

---

46 Ben Coates, 'The Impact of the English Civil War on the Economy of London, 1642–1650', PhD Thesis (University of Leicester, 1997) pp.161–162.
47 *CSPV 1643–1647*, p.106, June 10, 1644, Gerolamo Agostini, Venetian Secretary in England, to the Doge and Senate.
48 Willan, *The English Coasting Trade, 1600–1750*, p.12.
49 Mark Fissel, *The Bishops' Wars: Charles I's Campaigns Against Scotland, 1638–1640* (Cambridge: Cambridge University Press, 1994), p.168.

their forces in Ulster from Western Scotland. It appears that Irish Confederate privateers (by then recruited from the Continent rather than using Irish-built ships) were largely able to operate with impunity in the seas between Ireland and Scotland, preventing supplies being shipped. The Covenanter Government in Edinburgh attempted to get the English Parliament to fulfil its naval obligations under the Treaty of 1642 to provide coastal patrol vessels off Ulster, although these obligations were not met.[50] This implies a lack of facilities and infrastructure on the Scots west coast that could readily convert suitable vessels into warships, as well as a lack of ports suitable to sustain large, armed allied vessels – it also suggests that local vessels, and by inference the ports available to them, were of a smaller type. We have seen how Covenanting forces on the eastern coast of Scotland near Aberdeen had been forced to transport artillery pieces in small coastal barks which then ran afoul of Captain Hill's force. Taken together I believe that this argues against there being a large pool of readily available armed transport vessels operating along Scotland's coastlines in sufficient quantities to be readily available for military purposes.

In comparison, when the Royalists captured Bristol in July 1643 several merchant ships then in Bristol's harbour were large enough, and sufficiently well armed with cannon, to be considered welcome additions to the nascent Royalist Navy, as the bulk of the 'regular' Fleet remained under Parliament's control. Given that west coast trading vessels were substantially smaller than most military requirements it would seem likely that the vessels at Bristol were ocean-going merchantmen, built and equipped along much more substantial lines than those of coastal traders. The idea that they were larger ocean-going vessels is supported in their descriptions of being armed merchantmen.[51] Such vessels situated at Bristol, the largest port on the west coast of England, would not have been unusual. The decision the previous year by the Committee for Irish Affairs to try to source ships suitable to transport troops from Bristol rather than Chester suggests Bristol's busier port regularly saw larger and more substantial shipping than was usual on the west coast.

The activities of privateers in the Irish Sea appear to have dramatically impacted the availability of vessels suitable for military transport purposes later in the war. In comparison to a claim made in October 1638, that 'the harbours there have a great many good ships,' less than five years later, in order to move English veterans over to England for service with the King following the 1643 Cessation of Arms,

---

50 'Article 3, Summary of the Treaty for sending a Scottish Army to Ireland', reprinted in David Stevenson, *Scottish Covenanters and Irish Confederates: Scottish-Irish Relations in the Mid-Seventeenth Century* (Belfast: Ulster Historical Foundation, 1981), p.315.
51 Blakemore and Murphy, *The British Civil Wars at Sea, 1638–1653*, pp.117–118.

the Marquess of Ormond struggled to find suitable ships claiming on 19 October that:

> The maine difficulty I find in the worke is shipping, to transport and safely convay them to that port of Chester, whether, by the King's command, I am directed. This want is much increased, and our supply thereof made almost impossible, by the coming hether and lying heere certene parlyament shipps, who hinder the coming in of vessells, and the releefe they would bring us, not only to the difficultting of his service, but to the destruction of his majestie's protestant subjects heere. Which foreseeing might happen, I humbly besought his majestie, in two former dispatches, and doe now againe renue it, that he would imediately comand hether some shipps of force, for the security of this harbour, and the wastage of that part of his army.[52]

The limited amount of shipping available to Ormond meant that he had to send troops over in whatever vessels he could find, as soon as they became available, often without escort. This was not an immediate concern as the Cessation of Arms, a ceasefire between Irish Confederates and Royalists, had denied the Parliamentarian navy access to Protestant-controlled ports on the Irish coast.[53] However, the return of Parliamentarian warships during 1644 forced Ormond to slow the transport of troops when Parliamentarian naval forces executed 70 Irishmen captured on an unnamed vessel in April. The relatively small number of troops could suggest a small coastal trader, but equally it could have been the Irish contingent amongst a larger number of Royalist troops on a large merchantmen vessel.[54] Whether coastal trader or merchantman, the need to operate between ports left unescorted transports susceptible to enemy warships patrolling near their destination.

---

52   CSPD 1638–1639, pp.63–64, Oct 20, Memorandum endorsed by Secretary Windebank; Thomas Carte (ed.), *The Life of James, Duke of Ormond*, V (Oxford: Oxford University Press, 1851), p.478.
53   Bennett, *The Civil Wars in Britain & Ireland 1638–1651*, pp.157–159; Trevor Royle, *Civil War: The Wars of the Three Kingdoms, 1638–1660* (London: Abacus, 2005), p.212.
54   *Mercurius Aulicus, Communicating the Intelligence and Affaires of the Court, to the Rest of the Kingdome. The Eighteenth Weeke, Ending May 4 1644* (Oxford: 1644), p.965 states that 'some small vessels coming from Ireland' were captured, which could indicate a number of coasting vessels pressed into service as transports. See also Elaine Murphy, 'Atrocities at Sea and the Treatment of Prisoners of War by the Parliamentary Navy in Ireland, 1641–1649', *The Historical Journal*, vol. 53, no.1 (March 2010), pp.21–23.; Blakemore and Murphy, *The British Civil Wars at Sea, 1638–1653*, p.67.

Operational Use of Coastal Vessels

Coastal vessels were expected to trade between recognised ports and such vessels were invariably sail-powered, reliant on the winds for motive power rather than muscle power. For coastal traders a port was desirable for multiple reasons, not least as it was both the safest and most efficient method of loading and unloading a vessel. Most ports had been built, or developed, around navigable harbours providing a sheltered anchorage, with any hazards of tide and geography often common enough knowledge to represent little threat to the coastal trading vessels plying these familiar routes. On sailing into the harbour, the vessel might be brought to the wharf (or quay) side for unloading. This would necessitate the towing of the vessel further into the port by oared boats, though some smaller vessels may have been able to move slightly further in using sweeps (long oars) themselves.

More commonly, 'lighters' (flat-bottomed barges) were used by 'lightermen' to load and offload cargo between a ship at anchor and the port.[55] Without such facilities the amount of produce that could be moved from sea to land, or vice versa, was minimal. A ship could load or unload some cargo to a small fishing village or an open beach, but the process would be protracted, dangerous, and onerous. Without the protection of a sheltered anchorage, the process of loading or unloading a large amount of supply from ship to shore would expose the ship to the hazards of the coast and the weather. The vessel would be reliant on its own ship's boats to transport to an open beach, each one of these over-burdened and at risk of spilling its cargo and rowers into the surf. Without a harbour in which to anchor, ships would also have to stay quite far out from shore to avoid running aground. This extended distance out to sea would further complicate attempting to load and unload cargo, exhausting the boats' crews. Consequently, large numbers of lighters were needed to shift supplies from ship to shore to keep an army supplied if the harbours were unsuitable or unavailable. At the siege of Lyme Regis between April and June 1644, the Royalist besiegers placed batteries to cover the harbour, forcing the Parliamentarian naval forces to anchor further out. This almost succeeded in cutting the Parliamentarian garrison off from supplies brought by the Parliamentarian navy, particularly after a Royalist raiding party managed to burn most of the harbour's barges, dramatically slowing the amount of supplies which could be unloaded over the increased distance.[56]

---

55   Willan, *The English Coasting Trade, 1600–1750*, pp.35–37, pp.40–42.
56   John Powell, 'Blake and the Defence of Lyme Regis', *The Mariner's Mirror*, vol. 20, no.4 (1934), pp.463–464.

On 9 December 1650 the English Council of State ordered 'flat boats to be built at Newcastle'; these were apparently constructed for the specific aim of aiding in the supply of English forces in Scotland from coastal shipping, ensuring that the necessary supplies were landed quickly when required.[57] Until now the focus on these boats has been their role on 17 July 1651 when they were utilised to transport soldiers across the Firth of Forth in a flanking manoeuvre against the Scottish forces north of Edinburgh which resulted in the Battle of Inverkeithing.[58]

The importance to sailing vessels of a safe port cannot be overstated. Their reliance on a safe harbour in foul weather, or a secure anchorage to operate effectively, is what allowed military authorities the opportunity to impress ships at need. Sailing vessels of all kinds would rather avoid bad weather in the protected anchorage of the port than face it out to sea if at all possible. Indeed, during the wars sailing ships would often be driven into enemy-held ports rather than face the weather at sea. In December 1642 merchant ships bound for London were forced into the safety of Royalist held Falmouth by winter storms where they were then seized by the Royalists.[59] When the 1641 rebellion began in Ireland almost every major port in the country was either taken, or at least besieged, in the early stages of the rebellion. After 1643 all substantial ports in the British Isles 'enjoyed' some form of military presence or garrison. Of the eleven recognised major ports in England during this period, other than London (if we also include York with access to the sea via the Ouse), ten of these – Lynn, Bristol, Gloucester, Hull, Exeter, Plymouth, Newcastle, York, Chester, and Colchester – were all placed under siege at least once during the course of the English Civil Wars.[60]

Any vessels operating from, or anchored in, such a port would have been extremely susceptible to pressure from the local military commander. They would have also been vulnerable in the event of the port falling into enemy hands. This vulnerability was in no small part due to the effort required to leave the harbour. The process of leaving a port was difficult and time-consuming even in ideal

---

57   *CSPD 1650*, p.464 Dec. 9, Irish and Scotch Committee Day's Proceedings; *CSPD 1651*, pp.558, 568, 574–575, 582, various warrants for building flat boats at Newcastle for the army in Scotland; Wheeler, 'The Logistics of the Cromwellian Conquest of Scotland 1650–1651', *War & Society* vol. 10, no.1 (May 1992), p.12.
58   Peter Reese, *Cromwell's Masterstroke: The Battle of Dunbar 1650* (Barnsley: Pen & Sword, 2006), p.115; Stuart Reid, *Dunbar 1650: Cromwell's Most Famous Victory* (Oxford: Osprey, 2008), pp.85–86. Malcolm Wanklyn, 'Cromwell's Generalship and the Conquest of Scotland 1650–1651' in *Cromwelliana*, series 3, no.4 (2015), pp.36–50.
59   Coates, 'The Impact of the English Civil War on the Economy of London, 1642–1650', p.145.
60   List of ports drawn from Table 12.1 in Sacks and Lynch *Ports 1540–1700*, p.384, and sieges from Lipscombe, *The English Civil War: An Atlas and Concise History*, pp.39, 112, 121–124, 129–131, 149, 170, 234, 239, 283.

weather conditions which – unless the wind and tide were favourable – usually required the vessel to be towed out by boats or, often, by warping.[61] This latter process required the ship's anchor and its cable to be carried forward in a boat 'to lay it out towards that part or place whither they would have the Ship to go' and drop the anchor overboard ahead of the ship.[62] Once the anchor was settled on the seabed the ship's crew used their own muscle strength to haul in the cable attached to the anchor. This effectively pulled the ship towards the settled anchor until the ship was close enough to it to raise it from the seabed. This process might have been repeated several times to clear the harbour, making for slow, exhausting work until wind and tide combined were sufficient to carry the ship out to sea.[63] These necessary methods to clear the harbour of a port meant that a ship could not simply sail out of a port to avoid the authorities, and further explains why ships in port were often at the mercy of impressment if those in charge of the port needed vessels.

As seen earlier, transporting soldiers safely in large numbers required significantly more substantial vessels than non-collier coastal traders. While local trading vessels were occasionally used to transport supplies when no other vessels were available, this was a rare occurrence. The plan for Ormond's campaign against the Confederate-held port of New Ross in 1643, based out of Dublin, required ships to sail close to Ormond's marching army to keep them supplied. Ormond hired a merchantman in Dublin harbour whose captain, perhaps for lack of other suitable shipping, was able to negotiate favourable terms with Dublin's Lord Justices earning himself 'one hundred and thirteen pounds per month', but even then was delayed for almost a week due to poor weather.[64] Ormond's subordinate, Lord Esmond, in response to the deteriorating supply situation, pressed further vessels into use from his command at Duncannon Fort, including ' a little ship, then in the river by Duncannon' to dispatch to Ormond loaded with supplies.[65] Of the four transports eventually used to provide supplies at various points during this campaign, three were substantial merchantmen rather than local coastal traders. This further supports the idea that the small coasting trading vessels were not commonly used for military transport if the larger, and often

---

61 Nathaniel Boteler, *Six Dialogues About Sea-Services Between An High-Admiral and A Captain At Sea* (London, 1685), p.197.
62 Boteler, *Six Dialogues About Sea-Services Between An High-Admiral and A Captain At Sea*, p.197.
63 Boteler, *Six Dialogues About Sea-Services Between An High-Admiral and A Captain At Sea*, p.197.
64 Carte, *The Life of James, Duke of Ormond*, II, p.429.
65 Carte, *The Life of James, Duke of Ormond*, II, p.429; Murphy, *Ireland and the War at Sea*, p.30.

armed, merchantmen were available. Even in areas where a lack of large carrying capacity was a problem, such as a limited availability of large ships available along the western coasts of England and Scotland, the coastal vessels were deemed either incapable or unsuitable for the task. What made the coastal traders unsuitable in the eyes of army commanders for even accompanying transport capacity is unclear, although they evidently were – except in an emergency, such as Esmond's use of a small craft to send badly needed supplies to Ormond's army.

Years of warfare did eventually develop shipbuilding capacity and supporting infrastructure, at least in Ireland, but this appears to have been focused on the construction and support of military vessels, mostly privateers, rather than military transport vessels. In September 1642, the town of Wexford (held by the rebels) was described by the Lord Justices and Council at Dublin as 'a place plentiful in ships and seamen' although for military vessels the port had to rely on a European privateer, 'a ship of Dunkirk of good strength'.[66] Over the course of the next seven years, Wexford developed its shipbuilding capacity quite substantially. When Parliamentarian forces captured the town in October 1649, this included the capture of several substantial frigates which were either under construction or undergoing substantial repairs with 'one of them of thirty-four guns, which a week's time would fit the sea; there is another of about twenty guns, very near ready likewise. And one other frigate of twenty guns, upon the stocks; made for sailing: which is built up to the uppermost deck.'[67] Described as 'on stocks' and 'near ready', the terminology used suggests ships undergoing extensive work. Stocks were wooden frameworks built around a ship's hull which were used to support a ship while out of the water, providing access to the full exterior of the vessel. This allowed work to be done, not only on the parts of the vessel normally submerged by water, but to sections of the ship which would be difficult or hazardous to work on when afloat such as the inner hull of the lower decks, or the extreme ends of the masts. The fact that Wexford had substantial shipbuilding and repair facilities in 1649, capable of working on multiple military frigate-sized ships at a time, suggests a dramatic development of the shipbuilding industry in Ireland over the course of the conflicts.

Most of the east coast of England, and many of its major ports, would remain in Parliament's hands throughout most of the war. This indicates that most of the Newcastle collier fleet remained in Parliamentarian controlled areas, giving Parliament a substantially improved seaborne carrying and transport capacity compared to that which their enemies had access to. While Royalist and Irish

---

66   John Gilbert, (ed.), *History of the Irish Confederation,* I, (Dublin, 1882), p.lvi.
67   Oliver Cromwell to William Lenthall, Dublin, 14 October 1649, in T. Carlyle, (ed.) *Oliver Cromwell's Letters and Speeches with Elucidations*, II (London, 1850), pp.220–221.

privateers operated all around the British Isles, the east coast of England saw much greater Parliamentarian naval dominance at its ports with its relative proximity to London and the Royal Navy Fleet.[68] Having access to the collier fleet not only meant a greater coastal carrying capacity but, as they were larger and more substantial vessels, it meant there was a greater pool of naval transport capacity overall with less need to impress or contract merchantmen away from trade routes to be redirected towards military purposes. This could have had the added advantage of making such trade appear less prone to disruption for merchants due to a reduced likelihood of impressment of their particular vessels and therefore making investment worthwhile.

The ability of the side which controlled England's east coast to hire or impress sufficient coastal transport shipping is highlighted by the English invasion of Scotland in 1650. During the summer of 1650, in preparation for a war against Scotland, Parliament began gathering an army in Northern England. In response, the Scottish forces repeated their actions which had worked so well for them during the Bishops' Wars of 1639 and 1640 and stripped the areas of Scotland near the border of provisions and livestock so there would be 'no relief to the English Army'.[69] This, similar to what had happened to the King's armies a decade previously, prevented the English army from foraging for supplies in the immediate area. However, the English Council of State, the executive appointed by Parliament in 1649, had been preparing supply magazines in the northern English towns of Berwick and Newcastle, close to the border with Scotland, since the spring of 1650.[70] A further '400,000lbs of biscuit, 180 tons of cheese and 2,000 quarters of oats' were ordered to be shipped north to Berwick on 26 July 1650 and £100,000 was provided to send more materials to these magazines in August.[71] When the English army did cross the border and invade Scotland they had already established a month's supply of food to accompany the army.[72] The English strategy was to advance along the coast, capturing Scottish ports which then allowed them to be reliant on the 'provisions come in the ships from London and Newcastle' as the Scots had denuded the area of ready provisions.[73]

---

68   Blakemore and Murphy, *The British Civil Wars at Sea, 1638–1653*, chapter 4.
69   *A Briefe Relation of Some Affaires and Transactions, Civill and Military, Both Forraigne and Domestique*, 48 (16–23 July 1650), pp.735–736.
70   *CSPD 1650*, p.210, June 20, Council of State Day's Proceedings.
71   *CSPD 1650*, p.254, July 26, Irish Committee Day's Proceedings; Aug 7, Council of State Day's Proceedings, p.275.
72   *A Briefe Relation of Some Affaires and Transactions, Civill and Military, Both Forraigne and Domestique*, 48 (16–23 July 1650), pp.735–736.
73   *True Intelligence From the Head-Quarters, or, The Daily Motions and Proceedings of the Parliaments Army*, 2 (23–30 July 1650), p.13.

The amount of provisions shipped along the coast to support the army in Scotland are impressive, with surviving pay warrants stating that from September 1650 to July 1651 this coastal supply line shipped a total of over 2,500 tons of biscuit, over 3,300 tons of wheat, and at least 1,900 tons of cheese in addition to other provisions.[74] Many of the 140 ships used for this supply line were registered in east coast towns important to the collier trade, such as Aldebourgh, Yarmouth, and Newcastle.[75] While there is no certainty that these were east coast colliers rather than merchantmen registered in those towns, it still emphasises the availability of substantially sized vessels to whosoever controlled these ports and close review of the warrants of pay and the amounts shipped by them suggests none of these ships were smaller than 100 tons.[76] The fact such shipping was available allowed Parliament to plan for this form of supply for their invasion force. In this case the pre-existing civilian transportation was able to be adapted into an efficient military logistical and supply system.

Further evidence from port books suggests that the peacetime coastal trade was based around large numbers of small vessels performing a similarly large number of regular journeys between particular ports.[77] Particular vessels plying regular journeys between particular ports is not unlike that seen by the land carriers and hauliers, many of whom had a set route and schedule. Some of these local coastal traders were certainly still active during the wars, as occasionally one would be taken by privateers despite their small size. While the armies may have had little time for the carrying capacity of coastal traders, clearly there was enough value in them to make them worth the effort of privateers.[78] Even so, according to a detailed listing by Murphy of the prizes taken by Confederate privateers, it seems the overwhelming number of prizes Murphy identified were not local coastal traders. More than 400 out of the almost 500 vessels lost were identifiably either merchantmen or other types of larger vessels.[79] Almost three-quarters of those captured ships identified as small coastal vessels, 55 out of approximately 75, were taken in the years after 1646 when Parliament had secured the western coastal ports and were able to send an increasing number of warships into the Irish

---

74   *CSPD 1650*, pp.570–598, Warrants by the Council of State; *CSPD 1651*, pp.536–588, Warrants by the Council of State.
75   *CSPD 1650*, p.585, Warrants by the Council of State; *CSPD 1651*, p.544, Warrants by the Council of State; Wheeler, 'The Cromwellian Conquest of Scotland', p.12
76   CSPD 1650, Warrants by the Council of State, pp.570–598; CSPD 1651, Warrants by the Council of State, pp.536–88.
77   Willan, *The English Coasting Trade, 1600–1750*, pp.xiv, 2–3, 104–105.
78   See appendices 3 and 4 in Murphy's, *Ireland and the War at* Sea, pp.179–218 for extensive lists of captured vessels.
79   Murphy, *Ireland and the War at Sea*, Appendix 4. Confederate and Irish prizes, pp.201–218.

Sea.[80] The preference for merchantmen as targets by privateers rather than coastal traders could be due to traders being either less valuable, less likely to be engaged by enemy forces for transportation tasks, or simply smaller, lighter, and operated too close in to the coast for a privateer's captain to risk his own ship pursuing. The increasing number of coastal vessels falling to Irish warships after 1646 could be explained by the increased numbers of Parliamentarian warships patrolling and escorting the Irish Sea, forcing the privateers to look for other unescorted prey.

What can be shown – and which we can be reasonably certain of given the evidence from port books, pay warrants, and other records – is that the smaller coasting traders were not often used for direct military transportation purposes unless there was simply no other vessel more suitable to the task available. Instead, those that did continue to operate during the wars mostly continued to operate as trading vessels. In this way they continued their peacetime role of providing essential carrying capacity for local economies, tied in with river and road methods that existed alongside them. Before the outbreak of the British Civil Wars the King's forces, and then Parliament's forces after 1643, benefitted from having almost unchallenged access to a large, and effective merchant fleet for military transport purposes in the shape of the Newcastle collier. The impact of coastal shipping on supplying armies could be profound, but so too could transportation by river.

River Transport

The connection between coastal and river shipping was often blurred, with ports like Bristol, Gloucester, and to a degree York, accessible from both the sea and by river. The major ports in the British Isles all lie at an estuary where a navigable (or at least partly navigable) tidal river met the sea.[81] Economists studying the movement of goods and the trade patterns of the period have argued that coastal and river trade were so interconnected that to make any separation of the two is meaningless.[82] In locations which neither river nor coastal vessels could access, roads made up the difference. Joan Thirsk outlines how the various regions of England and Wales had very different agricultural specialisations ranging from pastoral through to extensively arable.[83] A diverse range of products needed to move between regions with butter, cheese, and cereal crops requiring transport that

---

80   Murphy, *Ireland and the War at Sea*, Appendix 4. Confederate and Irish prizes, pp.201–218.
81   Sacks and Lynch, 'Ports 1540–1700', pp.379–380.
82   Willan, *River Navigation in England, 1600–1750*, pp.4–5.
83   Joan Thirsk, *The Agrarian History of England and Wales Volume 5 Part 1 Regional Farming Systems*, (Cambridge: Cambridge University Press, 1984) p.xx.

was capable of shifting heavy, bulk loads. This existing interconnectivity between river, coastal and land, meant that the military logistics and supply systems of the British Civil Wars inevitably made use of river transportation.

Transport by river for civilian purposes before, and after, the Civil Wars was cheaper for those wanting to move goods than by road.[84] It is possible that a larger transport capacity allowed relatively cheaper costs for journeys, or that the route of the river, not always the most direct, may have demanded lower prices for a slower delivery as river craft suffered restrictions which land transport did not. The peak speed of the ship itself was dictated by the wind and at its slowest was limited by the strength of men towing a barge upstream against the current. The length of its journey was defined by the meandering path of the navigable stretches of the river. During the Civil Wars river transport was used to move heavy, bulky items which would be difficult to move by road. According to Jonathon Worton, the improvement of Shrewsbury's earthwork fortifications in September 1643 was facilitated by a hired Severn barge transporting earth and turf over several days around the town from the surrounding fields.[85] In Shropshire, in 1643, where navigable stretches of the River Severn were secure from enemy action, the transport of heavy items was taken along the Severn wherever possible. Musket ammunition was moved from the foundry at Leighton, along the River to Shrewsbury by boat.[86]

To appreciate the impact of river transport and its operational role in logistics and supply, we need to understand more about the capacity of river barges, and why they were so useful. In order to answer these questions, we again need to turn to civilian sources. There are unfortunately no contemporary surviving images of river barges from the mid-seventeenth century, but there are surviving images of vessels drawn at the close of the seventeenth and first half of the eighteenth centuries. Willan, whose research on internal shipping routes included studying the shipping volumes and tonnage of these craft, believed that while the later eighteenth century vessels may have been slightly larger in overall size compared to our period, there was little substantive difference in their design, build, and construction beyond this.[87] These craft that traversed the rivers were largely what we would refer to as barges – flat-bottomed boats with shallow draught.[88] Their

---

84 Chartres, *Internal Trade in England 1500–1700*, p.42.
85 Worton, *To Settle the Crown*, p.191.
86 SA, 6000/13314, Receipt signed by Gyles Parys, to a boatman for 900 bullets delivered by him, 8 June 1643.
87 Willan, *River Navigation in England, 1600–1750*, pp.97–99.
88 Samuel Buck and Nathaniel Buck, *Buck's Antiquities; Or Venerable Remains of Above Four Hundred Castles, Monasteries, Palaces, &c. &c. in England and Wales*, I (London, 1774), 'The South-West View of Sion Abbey'; Charles Deering, *Nottinghamia Vetus Et Nova: Or,*

design was a balance between needing to avoid running aground in rivers and providing the maximum cargo space possible. Without the risk of rough seas, or squalls, the deep keel required by sea vessels to keep them stable was unnecessary and would only prove a hindrance and even a risk in the shallower water of rivers.

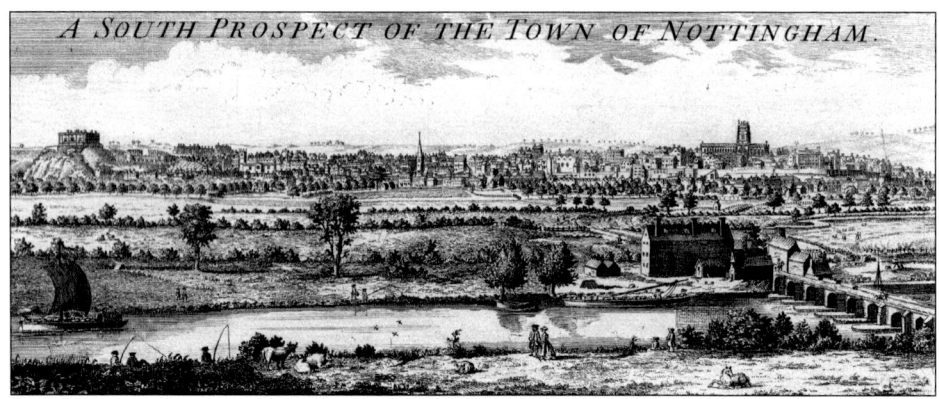

A river barge similar to those operating during the British Civil Wars. 'A South Prospect of Nottingham', Charles Deering, *Nottinghamia Vetus Et Nova: Or, An Historical Account of the Ancient and Present State of the Town of Nottingham* (London, 1751) (Public Domain)

These river vessels were built on or near the rivers they used and subsequently to a draught that the sections of the rivers could take, with vessels decreasing in size the shallower the river they operated on.[89] The cargo was placed on an open deck covered with tarpaulins and netting for security. The lack of a substantial keel meant little to no cargo space below the waterline. If there was any shelter, such as a cabin or canvas, then this was for the crew or passengers.[90] River vessels had a single mast for a large sail, but the large crew (in comparison to a sea going vessel of similar size) was there for when the wind dropped and the vessel needed to be moved with 'much strain, force and pains, the vessels being hauled by strength

An Historical Account of the Ancient and Present State of the Town of Nottingham (London, 1751), 'A South Prospect of the Town of Nottingham'; William Stukeley, *Itinerarium Curiosum, Or, An Account of the Antiquities, and Remarkable Curiosities in Nature Or Art, Observed in Travels Through Great Britain* (London, 1776), plate of Boston.

89   Wanklyn believes Severn barges at least had removable draught boards to allow them to sail in the Severn estuary, see Malcolm Wanklyn, 'The Severn Navigation in the Seventeenth Century: Long-Distance Trade of Shrewsbury Boats', p.35

90   Willan, *River Navigation in England, 1600–1750*, p.97.

of men against the stream.'[91] It may seem odd that men were used rather than horses, particularly given the preference for horses as draught animals in land transport. However, horses needed a reasonably good towpath to pull a large load while men were not only better at towing over rough ground but could remain on the boat when towing was not required and perform other tasks, e.g. sail handling, loading, unloading, or rowing. The river barges' reliance on manpower, as opposed to horsepower would have benefits in the military applications as well, where transport by river placed less demand on a limited supply of horses which would be needed for various other military roles, such as with cavalry, dragoons, or towing artillery.

Control of the Rivers

The extensive use of rivers as military supply routes and as a means to transport heavy siege artillery was well established in Europe by the time of the outbreak of the British Civil Wars, and contemporaries would not have had to look far back into history in order to find examples. The Swedish King Gustav II Adolph's campaigns in the summer of 1630 lay along the paths of the major rivers of northern Europe from the Oder, the Spree, the Havel, the Elbe, the Saal, et cetera.[92] Military commanders in the British Isles were aware of the use and importance of the rivers of the country, and much of the fighting in the English Civil Wars can be at least partially traced to one side or the other being determined to prevent total dominance of a stretch of river by their opponents.

The fighting for control of the River Severn is perhaps the most illustrative example of the importance of rivers to military strategy. One of the longest rivers in the British Isles, the Severn rises in the highlands of mid-Wales, running through Wales and England before reaching the sea at the Bristol channel, with its tributary rivers reaching even further into both England and Wales. Many of those areas which the navigable lengths of the Severn and its tributaries ran through were, in 1643, either directly under Royalist control or were within or near the contested areas of the front lines. The entirety of the Severn itself was not fully navigable, but in the seventeenth century from Bristol the Severn was 'navigable for these kind of vessels [barges] to Shrewsbury and further'.[93]

---

91   William Brereton (E. Hawkins, ed.), *Travels in Holland, the United Provinces, England, Scotland, and Ireland, 1634–1635*, (London: Chetham Society, 1844), p.187.
92   van Creveld, *Supplying War*, p.15.
93   HMC, *Thirteenth Report, Appendix, The Manuscripts of his Grace the Duke of Portland, Preserved at Welback Abbey*, II (London: HMSO, 1893), p.291; Brereton, *Travels in Holland, the United Provinces, England, Scotland, and Ireland*, p.187.

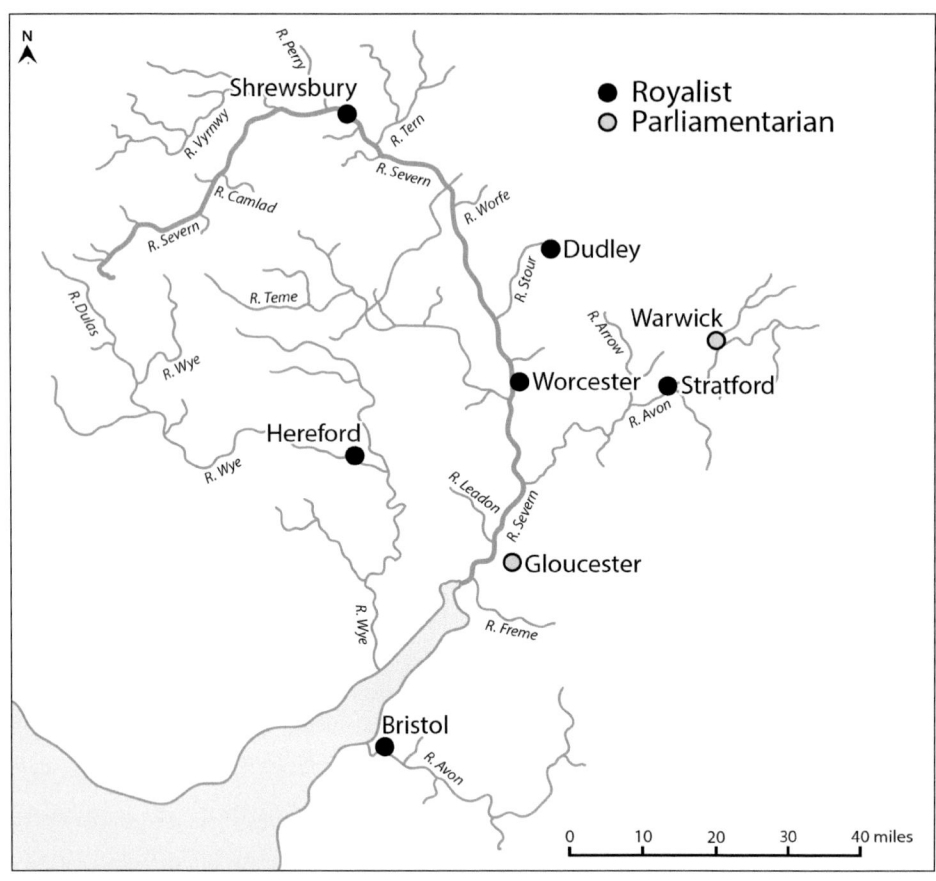

The River Severn and nearby rivers, and the major towns and garrisons under Royalist and Parliamentarian control by August 1643. (Author's drawing)[94]

94 Compiled with information from: Hutton, *The Royalist War Effort 1642–1646*; Sherwood, *The Civil War in the Midlands, 1642–1651*; Wanklyn, 'The Severn Navigation in the Seventeenth Century: Long-Distance Trade of Shrewsbury Boats', pp.34–58; Thomas Willan, 'The River Navigation and Trade of the Severn Valley, 1600–1750', *The Economic History Review*, vol. 8, no.1 (November 1937), pp.68–79.

The major Royalist garrisons of Shrewsbury and Worcester lay along the Severn. After July 1643 Prince Rupert's capture of Bristol gave the Royalists not only control of the major port of Western England, but also the possibility of a link between their Welsh and Marcher heartlands, via the Bristol channel, with their Cornish support bases. The Parliamentarian garrison at Gloucester, also on the Severn, hampered this possibility and was a major strategic concern for both Royalists and Parliamentarians precisely because of its position along the river preventing its use by the Royalist along its entire navigable length. The strategic import of Gloucester is highlighted in the accompanying map of the Severn and its garrisons, which outlines the strategic situation in August 1643. Note how Gloucester sits on the Severn, interrupting the connections between several major Royalist towns and garrisons along the river.

Historians have often failed to consider the Severn's logistical importance in Charles I's decision to besiege Gloucester in August 1643.[95] For the historian Samuel Gardiner, the siege was a 'desperate folly' as part of an overly ambitious push on London, while for recent historians, for example John Barratt, Gloucester was besieged simply as a design to draw the Earl of Essex's field army into open battle.[96] Without considering the full implications of the town's position in relation to the Severn and the impact on Royalist logistics, the decision to besiege Gloucester could look odd and so instead historians appear to have sought a rationale that made sense to them. However, the route of the Severn gives a more obvious explanation, as Gloucester, by August 1643, was also the last major Parliamentarian garrison on the River. The town's garrison prevented the full use of the river as a transport artery, requiring Royalist forces to laboriously tranship supplies around Gloucester by land. The capture of Gloucester would not only have removed this obstruction but would have secured the Severn as a highway from Parliamentarian assaults and further stabilised the Royalist hinterlands. Parliamentarian officers recognised the danger of a Royalist controlled Severn, with the Parliamentarian erstwhile Governor of Bristol, Nathanial Fiennes, claiming that if the Royalists took Gloucester the King would:

> become master of all that tract between Shrewsbury and the Lizard's Point in Cornwall. He will become master of all the traffic of that inland sea the Severn; and make all the shipping of the Welsh and English coasts

---

95   Wanklyn and Jones, *A Military History of the English Civil War*, p.114.
96   See Samuel Gardner, *History of the Great Civil War, Volume I: 1642–44* (London: The Windrush Press, 1987), p.197, and Barratt, *Cavaliers: The Royalist Army at War*, p.84.

his own. His neighbourhood to Wales will from time to time supply him with a body of foot.[97]

Contemporary civilians also saw the military need for the King's forces to reduce Gloucester, with some of the town's leading civilians wanting to come to terms with the Royalists following Prince Rupert's recent capture of Bristol in order to save Gloucester from siege and storm. However, the wishes of the townsfolk were ignored by Gloucester's Governor, Edward Massey, who was determined to hold the town.[98]

Unfortunately, given the subsequent First Battle of Newbury where the Royalists clashed with the Earl of Essex's army following the latter's relief of Gloucester, the reasoning for the Royalists initiating the siege itself was subsumed for years by the traditional military historian's obsession with battles. Yet the Severn's principal potential as a major highway of Royalist supply cannot be overstated, particularly when considering its transport capabilities. The river barges operating on the Severn (and on the Thames) were on average much larger than those operating on other rivers in the British Isles, with a freight capacity to match all but the largest of the non-collier coastal trading vessels. Some of the Severn barges of the period are estimated to have been able to hold upwards of 30 tons of cargo.[99] Compare this to the average tonnage of most coastal vessels (excluding coal ships) whose average was around 20 tons. Despite this size, and the fact that there were many smaller vessels operating on the river, these large river barges were seen to be able to make the journey upriver as far as Shrewsbury 'tow'd up by strength of men 6 or 8 at a tyme'.[100] Given the flat-bottomed nature of the barges they must have been sizeable vessels, as previously established they would have lacked the depth of keel in which sea vessels were able to store much of their cargo below the waterline. According to Malcolm Wanklyn, in his study of the navigation of the Severn, both Gloucester and Bristol civil authorities attempted to incorporate some of the larger barges and smaller ships that moved between the Severn estuary and Gloucester in their port books on the basis that they could be importing from abroad rather than engaged in local trading. However, while Wanklyn admits such records are not useful as a guide to Severn traffic these attempts do highlight that the Severn was navigable enough for some sea-going shipping beyond Bristol as far upstream

---

97   Elliot Warburton, *Memoirs of Prince Rupert, and the Cavaliers: Including Their Private Correspondence, Now First Published from the Original MSS*, II (London: R. Bentley, 1849), p.263.
98   Hutton, *Royalist War Effort*, p.54
99   Willan, *River Navigation in England, 1600–1750*, p.97.
100 Celia Fiennes (E. Griffiths ed.), *Through England on a Side Saddle in the time of William and Mary, Being the Diary of Celia Fiennes*, (London: The Leadenhall Press, 1888), p.196.

as Gloucester.[101] By any measure, the control of the Severn for its entire length would have provided the Royalist war effort with a transport and lift capacity both up and down stream that could have had a major impact on their war effort. For the rest of the war, Gloucester threatened the Royalist supply lines which ran along and near that stretch of the Severn which the town commanded, forcing longer and more inefficient land transport to be utilised, under increasingly heavy guard, and according to Roy heavily impacting the supply route to Oxford.[102] The failure to capture Gloucester and to secure the whole of the Severn was a severe blow to the Royalist strategy of 1643 with Hopton later referring to it as that 'fatale siege of Gloucester.'[103]

The length of the Thames from London to Windsor Castle was of major importance to Parliament. The castle's position upstream from London made it the ideal location to be converted into the main headquarters and supply magazine for the army of the Earl of Essex from the winter of 1642–1643. According to Elias Kupfermann's study of the role of Windsor Castle during the period 1642–1650, the traffic along the Thames helped contribute to make the castle a major distribution and supply centre.[104] Most of this traffic was transported by water, from London, to Windsor, and then from there to other Parliamentarian garrisons.[105] The barges on the Thames were no less in size than those on the Severn, each capable of transporting entire teams of horses.[106] The regiment, which occupied Windsor Castle in October 1642 was transported, along with all of their weapons, horses, ammunition, and supplies to the castle in 'botes and barges'.[107] In 1644, in an attempt to stop them from deserting, pressed men from Kent were transported under guard, along the Thames to the army at Windsor, by barge.[108]

From both the Severn and the Thames examples, it appears that river craft, much like coastal transport, were primarily hired for use by the armies, rather than being requisitioned for extended periods.[109] To what degree this hiring was compulsory the surviving sources do not reveal. However, it suggests that the skill

---

101 Wanklyn, 'The Severn Navigation in the Seventeenth Century: Long-Distance Trade of Shrewsbury Boats', p.37.
102 Roy, *Royalist Ordnance Papers*, I, pp.46–47
103 Ralph Hopton (C. Chadwyck-Healey, ed.), *Bellum Civile: Hopton's Narrative of his Campaign in the West (1642–1644) and Other Papers*, (Taunton: Somerset Record Society, 1902), p.60.
104 Kupfermann, 'The Role of Windsor Castle During the English Civil Wars', p.10.
105 Kupfermann, 'The Role of Windsor Castle During the English Civil Wars', p.58.
106 TNA SP 28/147, II, f.359.
107 TNA SP 28/34, II, f.171; Kupfermann, 'The Role of Windsor Castle During the English Civil Wars', pp.64–65.
108 Gentles, *The New Model Army in England, Ireland and Scotland*, p.32.
109 Kupfermann, 'The Role of Windsor Castle During the English Civil Wars', p.65.

and experience of the crews may have been something not easily replaced, similar to the situation with coastal vessels. Furthermore, unlike land transport which could always find a use with the army, when the army moved away from rivers, the need for a seized barge would disappear. This intermittent need for river transport could explain the more contractual nature of the military use of river craft as opposed to the way in which land transportation was often continuously retained.

The importance of rivers as communication and transport routes was such that it influenced strategy at the highest level. The senior Royalist commander in the North Midlands, Henry Hastings, was deeply concerned that successful control of the river Trent by Parliament in 1643 would mean that the river could be used to arm and equip all of the 'rebbells in this part of [the] kingdom with all necessaries from Hull'.[110] To that end, Hastings spent much time and effort maintaining several garrisons along the line of the river in an attempt to hold the more navigable lengths for the King and prevent any use by Parliament.[111] Including the major garrison at Newark, Hastings and his subordinates established and supported a series of smaller garrisons along the line of the River Trent at King's Mills, Wilne Ferry, Shelford, and Thurgarton, in an attempt to not just control the route of the Trent but also its major crossings.[112]

No less than three major campaigns were fought in the Thames valley area alone between 1642 and 1644, in no small part due to the relative ease the river offered in supplying armies marching on London as well as connecting towns and garrisons along its course.[113] In the winter of 1642–1643, to ensure no supplies went to Royalist Oxford or Reading along the Thames and to guard the approaches to London, the Committee for Ordering the Militia in the City of London placed a river guard under the command of John Taylor who was employed 'for guarding and securing the River Thames'. Taylor maintained an armed pinnace, and a wherry or rowing boat, 'above the bridge of the Thames' to stop and search vessels travelling on the river.[114]

For towns and garrisons along a river's length, the river could offer a route of resupply when the town was besieged. When Reading was under siege by the Parliamentarians in the spring of 1643, the Royalists resupplied the town from

---

110 WSL SMS 550/10, 9 Feb 1642/3, Letter from Colonel Henry Hastings, Ashby, to Prince Rupert.
111 Martyn Bennett, 'Henry Hastings and the Flying Army of Ashby-de-la-Zouch', *Transactions of the Leicestershire Archaeological and Historical Society*, vol. 56 (1980–81), p.63.
112 For an overall coverage of these garrisons see Martyn Bennet, 'The Royalist War Effort in the North Midlands, 1642–1646', PhD Thesis (University of Loughborough, 1986).
113 Wanklyn and Jones, *A Military History of the English Civil War*, pp.vii–viii, 56, 82, 157.
114 CSPD 1641–1643, Jan 26, The Committee for Safety of the Kingdom to the Lord Mayor of London, p.440.

Le pillage (Pillaging a house) from The Miseries and Misfortunes of War, Jacques Callot (Rijksmuseum, Amsterdam)

Oxford using barges along the river, including transporting dangerous loads of gunpowder.[115] During the second siege of Worcester in 1646, the besieging forces failed to completely cut access to the Severn and sorties from the garrison used this route in search for both provisions and hostages when '60 firelocks, and 40 Horse' from the Worcester garrison attempted a night attack on the Parliamentary quarters at Kempsey, 'the foot went by Barge'.[116] River transport also appears to have been the preferred method of transporting cargoes of gunpowder wherever possible, largely due to its bulk and volatile nature. There would be less jostling of the highly explosive substance than might occur along rough roads and a reduced risk of accidents caused by startled horses or lost wheels. This preference for using river transportation also held true when both powder and large amounts of equipment needed to be moved. When the Royalists established a substantial magazine at Reading in early 1644 at least 100 barrels of powder, 'six Iron peeces' of artillery and all the gun crews, along with several hundred muskets, ammunition, bandoliers, match, hundreds of other weapons, and numerous other equipment were 'repaire[d] by water to Redding' and all were moved in less than a week.[117] To move the same by road would have required a substantial series of land-based convoys. For instance, in January 1643 in order to transport just 20 barrels of

---

115 Roy, *The Royalist Ordnance Papers*, I, p.22.
116 Henry Townsend, (J. W. Willis Bund ed.), *Diary of Henry Townshend of Elmley Lovett, 1640–1663*, (London: Worcestershire Historical Society, 1920), p.164.
117 Roy, *The Royalist Ordnance Papers*, II, pp. 332–334.

powder and the equipment for only four pieces of ordnance the Royalists needed five carts, one wagon, and well over 40 horses.[118] A road convoy to move the amount sent by water to Reading might have needed as many as 12 carts, and 60 horses for the powder alone. Supplies of various sorts were regularly sent from the Royalist headquarters at Oxford by river to garrisons such as Abingdon and Wallingford, and river barges on the Thames helped keep the Parliamentarian forces of the Earl of Essex, and later the New Model Army, supplied by shipping regular deliveries of biscuit (well baked bread).[119]

The situation in Ireland is less clear. As already mentioned, the paucity of surviving Irish sources makes assessment difficult. However, the limited number of local horses in Ireland and the poor quality of the roads in comparison to the rest of the British Isles would suggest that rivers would have been used wherever possible. The Confederates built a magazine at Athlone because of its location on the Shannon River (incidentally, the longest river in the whole of the British Isles) as use of the river meant 'much trobill of land Carriadg may be saved'.[120] Even so, the Confederates themselves suffered from a lack of any substantial siege artillery and an almost total reliance on imports of powder, and their methods of provisioning by making use of large herds of livestock moving with the army (discussed in chapter four below) meant that their armies lacked the requirements of large bulk cargoes that was seen in the fighting elsewhere in the British Isles.

Conclusion

Water transportation, both coastal and river, formed a key link in the logistics chain upon which the armies of the British Civil Wars depended. The ability to transport bulk loads across distances more quickly, and more easily, and with less reliance on long wagon trains, often made it the first choice when possible. Unlike land transport which, again where possible, was hired or impressed for extended periods of times – even for years – water transport appears to have been predominantly hired and only pressed into service for a limited duration out of military necessity.

The dependence that water transport had on ports to operate, particularly coastal transport, was both a strength and a weakness for the armies when locating available ships. If the port authorities were supportive, and there was shipping

---

118 Roy, *The Royalist Ordnance Papers*, I, pp, 190–191.
119 Aryeh Nusbacher, 'Civil Supply in the Civil War: Supply of Victuals to the New Model Army on the Naseby Campaign, 1–14 June 1645', *The English Historical Review*, vol. 115, no.460 (February 2000), p.152; Kupfermann, 'The Role of Windsor Castle During the English Civil Wars', pp.58–74.
120 Bodleian Carte Ms 10, f.718.

available, securing it could be simple and quick. However, enemy naval action as well as the size and location of the port itself could mean that there were very few suitable vessels available, forcing the military to wait, to look elsewhere, or even to try and make use of unsuitable shipping that was available in an attempt to move their supplies. Curiously, throughout the wars, merchant captains and traders appear to have been able to negotiate in their hiring with some degree of strength, risking outright impressment only when intransigent to the negotiating agents.

Merchantmen and colliers were the transport vessels of choice and the preponderance of the latter in the ports on the east coast of England gave a superior lift capacity and transport availability to whomever controlled that region. Again, the pattern of regional differences in lift capacity is interesting with the east coast collier revealed to be a key instrument, much like the wagon, being readily available and able to provide larger, and more efficient lift capacity to the forces of Parliament than the options available to the Royalists. While it is perhaps a stretch to suggest these were war-winning factors, both the wagon and the collier provided Parliament's logistic and support systems with superior transport capabilities. For the Royalists, and post 1647 the Scots, as the availability of shipping was impacted by enemy naval action and loss of ports to the enemy, the ability to secure suitable transport shipping collapsed.

The impact the control of rivers and their courses had on military strategy has long been ignored and it is clear that the ability to move large amounts of heavy goods, that otherwise would require large numbers of wagons and horses, was a major reason for the military seeking control of the rivers. Quite apart from being topographical barriers, rivers were fought over for their use as highways and, more importantly, to deny their use to the enemy. It was not simply that the military logistics systems were so closely tied to pre-existing civilian transport infrastructure, but that this meant, in the case of water transport particularly, that the militaries often had to base their campaign strategies around accommodating the geographic and practical realities of those pre-existing civilian systems. Because the military could not avoid using the civilian structures, they also had to fight to control them. The progress of the wars meant that the total control of a major river in England was not achieved by either side until the rapid advances of Parliamentarian forces in 1646 and afterwards, and as such, the opportunity to study their military implications is not as strong as that of coastal shipping. The use of water transportation in contributing to the logistic and supply needs of the armies was important, regardless of being smaller in the overall number of vehicles than was the case with land transportation.

3

Recruitment

The above has established the transportation capabilities and methods for the armies of the British Civil Wars, hopefully providing a clear understanding of the operational realities of transporting military supplies.

The first and the most essential supply requirement of an army is that of manpower. Armies can be provided with all the weapons, equipment, and carts that their commanding generals could hope for but without men to fill the regiments no war could be even fought, let alone won. The armies of the British Civil Wars had a continual and compelling need for fresh recruits in order to keep their regiments in the field. The absolute necessity to obtain replacement soldiers was a major preoccupation of all officers, from company and field officers through to commanding generals. However, all armies of the period struggled to recruit sufficient men for their needs. David Parrott describes recruitment for early modern armies as the intermittent tap attempting to keep a bath filled with water when the bath's plug is left out.[1] Once the recruitment stops, the army rapidly runs out of manpower as illness, battlefield casualties, non-battlefield deaths, and desertion take their toll. While at Limerick in Ireland in July 1651, Edmund Ludlow was pleased to be strengthened by 'a reinforcement from England of between three and four thousand foot, whose arrival was very seasonable and welcome to us, having lost many men by hard service, change of food, and alteration of the climate.'[2]

Unlike the subject of transportation, recruitment is one that has been covered quite extensively by historians of the Civil Wars. However, these studies have not been focused on recruitment as a facet of supply but rather as a tool for

---

1   David Parrott, *Richelieu's Army: War, Government and Society in France, 1624–42* (Cambridge: Cambridge University Press, 2008), p.178.
2   Charles Firth, *The Memoirs of Edmund Ludlow Lieutenant-General of the House in the Army of the Commonwealth of England, 1625–1672*, I (Oxford: Clarendon Press, 1894), p.278.

understanding another chosen topic of the author entirely. Joyce Lee Malcolm's study of Royalist recruitment in 1642 is more a study on the nature of Royalist loyalties and the effectiveness of early Royalist propaganda.³ Mark Stoyle's excellent work on the varying ethnic spread of the armies of the English Civil War does cover the recruitment of, for example, Cornish or Welsh troops but it is not the focus of the work itself. Instead Stoyle's work uses the recruitment of Welsh, Cornish, and foreign troops as a method to better understand the wars as an ethnic conflict.⁴ Andrew Hopper's *Turncoats and Renegadoes* studies side-changers amongst the English forces, focusing primarily on significant individuals, which contributes to the debate on allegiances during the English Civil Wars.⁵ When a work has focused on the recruitment or enlistment of soldiers, and their dispersal amongst the armies, these are invariably about the officer corps of the respective army. The debate surrounding the study of the initial 1645 list of regimental officers for the New Model Army and the implications this has regarding the radical nature (in political, philosophical, and military terms) of the army, has lasted for over forty years.⁶ John Barratt's work on the wartime experiences of Royalist soldiers considers only the general officers rather than the regimental, taking us even further away from the rank and file.⁷ This officer-centred focus is understandable as sources detailing the activities and history of the officers are more likely to have survived the passage of time either in the form of published memoirs for a popular contemporary audience or in letters surviving in family archives.⁸ Furthermore, even contemporaries only intermittently tracked information on the lower ranks. Casualty lists after a battle would detail officer casualties, as well as numbers of

---

3   Malcolm, *Caesar's Due,* pp.1-6, 54-91,124-149, and also Malcolm, 'A King in Search of Soldiers', pp.251-273.
4   Stoyle, *Soldiers & Strangers: An Ethnic History of the English Civil War.*
5   Andrew Hopper, *Turncoats and Renegadoes: Changing Sides During the English Civil Wars* (Oxford: Oxford University Press, 2014).
6   See Mark Kishlansky, 'The case of the army truly stated: the creation of the New Model Army', *Past and Present,* vol. 81 (1978), pp.64-69; Robert Temple, 'The Original Officer List of the New Model Army', *Bulletin of the Institute of Historical Research,* vol. 59 (1986), pp.50-77; Gentles, *The New Model Army in England, Ireland and Scotland,* pp.16-21 and Ian Gentles, 'The Choosing of Officers for the New Model Army', *Historical Research,* vol. 67 (1994), pp.264-285; Malcolm Wanklyn, 'Choosing Officers for the New Model Army, February to April 1645', *Journal of the Society for Army Historical Research,* vol. 92 (2014), pp.109-125.
7   John Barratt, *Cavalier Generals: King Charles I & His Commanders in the English Civil War, 1642-46* (Barnsley: Pen & Sword Military, 2004).
8   See for example: Turner, *Pallas Armata* and Hopton, *Bellum Civile.* One of the few examples of contemporary soldier's letters see Steve Murdoch, Alexia Grosjean, and Siobhan Talbott 'Drummer Major James Spens: Letters from a Common Soldier Abroad, 1617-1632', *Northern Studies,* vol. 47 (2015), pp.76-101.

enemy cannon and colours captured or lost but offer little detail in relation to the rank and file. Where the casualties amongst the lower ranks were noted these tended to be general estimates. The official Royalist report following the Battle of Edgehill in 1642 serves as an example; it is very precise on the number of colours taken but somewhat vague on the casualties:

> The Rebels in this Battell lost above 70 colours of Cornets and Ensigns; we 16 Ensigns, but not one Cornet; but our Horse relieved not only the Standard, but divers of our Ensigns. For the slain on both sides, the Number is uncertain; yet it is most certain that we killed five for one. It is true, that their Chief Officers having fleeter horses than ours, not so many of their Foot, as ours, were slain and taken Prisoners, to our knowledge as yet; but we lost no Officer of Horse excepting the Lord Aubigny.[9]

Post-battle numbers were perhaps understandably vague as the initial tally could be inaccurate due to wounded men later dying or simply due to absenteeism. Ian Atherton's work on battlefield casualties shows that rank-and-file soldiers killed in battle were buried swiftly, usually on or near the battlefield, and often in convenient mass graves with little effort to officially record their numbers or identity.[10] Where the numbers of rank-and-file troops are specified in detail it is almost always in relation to muster roles and pay warrants where precise figures are necessary for accounting purposes.

Recruitment is often mentioned in other, more general works surrounding the Civil Wars, but these are brief sections within a wider chapter that do not give specific detail beyond its contextual application for the work at hand, such as John Wroughton's study on the impacts of the English Civil War on local civilians.[11] The only studies which heavily focus on recruitment are those works dedicated to a particular army itself, such as the New Model Army or the King's Oxford army. Such works generally provide a number of pages, sometimes a short chapter, on the recruitment for the army under discussion but any comparisons with other armies lie beyond the scope of the book.[12] Charles Firth's influential work on

---

9 *A Relation of the Battel fought between Keynton and Edgehill, by His Majesty's Army and That of the Rebels; Printed at His Majesty's Command at Oxford by Leonard Lichfield, Printer to the University, 1642* (Oxford: 1642); Peter Young, *Edgehill 1642* (Witney, Windrush Press, 1997 reprint), p.253.
10 Ian Atherton, 'Battlefield, Burials and the English Civil Wars' in David Appleby, and Andrew Hopper (eds), *Battle-Scarred: Mortality, Medical Care and Military Welfare in the British Civil Wars* (Manchester: Manchester University Press, 2018), pp.23–39.
11 Wroughton, *An Unhappy Civil War*.
12 A selection of works which include more than a brief section on recruitment would be, Roberts, *Cromwell's War Machine: The New Model Army, 1645–1660* and Gentles, *The New*

the New Model Army is focused on the development of the administration and structure of that army, particularly in contrast with previous Parliamentarian forces and his section on recruitment focuses solely on impressment quotas and impressing former Royalists, arguing that this provided a better quality of soldier than the earlier volunteers to the Earl of Essex's army.[13] Peter Young and Wilfred Emberton's work on the King's Oxford army is an attempt to understand the experiences of Royalist soldiers in the army and dwells only very briefly on why men joined at its formation rather than how they were recruited.[14] Hutton's work on the Royalist war effort focuses on the impact of the wartime administration on local support and considers the success of recruitment (and its financing) as a means to measure this.[15]

Studies of Continental warfare in this period have made rather more of recruitment, showing its impact and importance on both military and civilian policy in the seventeenth century. David Parrott's work outlines the role in recruitment and regimental provision provided by military contractors in the European wars of the sixteenth and seventeenth centuries. Parrott uses this analysis to challenge historiographical assumptions on mercenary usage, state formation, and the military capabilities of European countries.[16] Geoffrey Parker's seminal work on Spain's Army of Flanders illuminates how Spain recruited soldiers for its large field armies for almost 100 years – revealing the achievements of the Spanish crown's long-distance diplomatic and organisational capabilities in the process, as well as the Army of Flanders' dependence on civilian trade and provision networks.[17] These European examples show how a close understanding of the methods of supplying manpower can be used to study topics beyond the formation and reinforcement of armies.

Given the importance of maintaining the units of an army, recruitment was not only about the raising of recruits at the wars' outset but also the sustained reinforcement of fresh recruits. Parker stated that 'Few governments in early

---

Model Army in England, Ireland and Scotland. The surviving records of the New Model Army's formation and subsequent campaigns in comparison to other forces of the period perhaps explain why the best examples are on that force. Even Edward Furgol's research of the Covenanting armies is more␣␣an excellent history and reference guide to the individual activities of Scottish regiments during the war rather than detailing recruitment, see Furgol, *A Regimental History of the Covenanting Armies.*

13   Firth, *Cromwell's Army*, pp.36–40.
14   Young and Emberton, *The Cavalier Army*, pp.22–23.
15   Hutton, *The Royalist War Effort 1642–1646.*
16   David Parrott, *The Business of War. Military Enterprise and Military Revolution in Early Modern Europe* (Cambridge: Cambridge University Press, 2012) and Parrot, *Richelieu's Army.*
17   Parker, *The Army of Flanders and the Spanish Road.*

modern Europe seem to have experienced much difficulty in raising an army', however maintaining it was another matter entirely.[18] James Scott Wheeler suggests that the English army campaigning across Ireland during the 1590s required a staggering 2,000 fresh recruits every month in order to sustain its 17,300 strong establishment.[19] As such the below will focus on how men were recruited and dispatched to their duties, how these recruiting systems developed over the course of the conflicts, and a comparison across the combatants. Through the course of this study, it will be shown that the instruments which raised the most men for the wars were not solely militaristic, instead relying on civilian engagement and contribution for the provision of manpower.

During the British Civil Wars, it was widely accepted that the ideal composition of an infantry regiment was 'ten Companies in a Regiment, consisting of a 1,000 or 1,200 men'.[20] The planned establishment of the Covenanter regiments sent to Ulster in 1642 was of 1,000 men, while the initial planned establishment of the infantry regiments of the Earl of Essex's army was 1,200 men.[21] This number did not include commissioned officers: every company would usually include a captain, a lieutenant, and an ensign, and every regiment would have a colonel, a lieutenant colonel, a sergeant-major (who were also the captains of their companies) and others including chaplain, quartermaster, et cetera. Additionally, there were the non-commissioned officers of two sergeants, three corporals, and two drummers in every company. In regiments of 1,200 men the three most senior companies, those belonging to the colonel, the lieutenant-colonel, and the sergeant-major, were larger than the rest at 200, 160, and 140 ordinary soldiers respectively with the other seven companies at 100 men each.[22] In an infantry regiment of 1,200 rank and file, there would also have been around 40 commissioned officers, and 70 non-commissioned officers.

Amongst the cavalry it was somewhat less clear, as the horse was not always organised into regiments and instead operated as independent troops. The use of cavalry regiments was a relatively recent development of the period, as

---

18   Parker, *The Military Revolution*, p.46, also see pp.53–8 on how difficult it was to maintain armies.
19   James Scott Wheeler, 'The Logistics of Conquest', in Pádraig Lenihan (ed.), *Conquest and Resistance: War in Seventeenth-Century Ireland* (Leiden: Brill, 2001), p.181.
20   David Leslie, *Generall Lessley's Direction and Order for the Exercising of Horse and Foot: Being a Most Exact, Compendeous, and Necessary Direction...* (London, 1642), p.7.
21   Stevenson, *Scottish Covenanters & Irish Confederates*, Appendix Two, 'The Establishment and Pay of the Scottish Army in Ireland, 1642', pp.319–324; Edward Peacock (ed.), *The Army Lists of the Roundheads and Cavaliers...* (London: J.C. Hotten, 1863), p.44; Roberts, *Cromwell's War Machine: The New Model Army, 1645–1660*, p.117.
22   Peacock, *The Army lists of the Roundheads and Cavaliers*, pp.19–44; Roberts, *Cromwell's War Machine: The New Model Army, 1645–1660*, p.128.

Sir James Turner, veteran of fighting in Europe and in the British Civil Wars, claimed 'there were no Regiments of Horse (properly so called) only Troops or Companies' until the middle of the seventeenth century, with Turner himself believing the development occurred during the Thirty Years' War which 'with other changes introduced Regiments of Horse'.[23] When they were formed as regiments these varied between three and six troops. The troop was established at 60 cavalry troopers, not including officers, for the forces to be sent to Ireland in 1641, and this seems to be the usual establishment strength for both Royalists and Parliamentarians during the early years of the Civil Wars as well.[24] What is clear is that the overwhelming majority of the men who served in the armies were private soldiers, and thus the below primarily concentrates on the supply of rank-and-file recruits, as these were the preponderance of necessary enlistments and replacements for a unit to remain in the field. However, the individual soldier's experience of recruitment, and their personal motivations or sentiments regarding their enlistment is not the subject of this study which, instead, is concerned with manpower as a facet of supply, in other words in terms of raw numbers of men. While the concept of individual motivations and experiences are interesting, their study lies beyond the scope of this investigation although the below might serve as a contextual basis for such research. Some of the methods of recruitment were used throughout the British Civil Wars, with others only particular examples, and no system of recruitment was perfect – while impressment was probably the most prevalent form of recruitment, it always relied on the civilian local government to function and was often used in tandem with other methods.

Operational Necessity

All units, not just those actively involved in fighting, needed numerous and sustained replacements throughout the conflicts to not only replenish battlefield casualties but to maintain operational capabilities. Historians estimate that deaths as a direct result of battle, either in combat or by later succumbing to wounds received on the battlefield, accounted for at most one in four of all deaths suffered by early modern soldiers, with some estimates as low as one in ten.[25] Failures or problems in the supply of food or other essentials such as sufficient clothing contributed to any death toll. Men often died from (or were in a subsequently

---

23   Turner, *Pallas Armata*, p.232.
24   Peacock, *The Army lists of the Roundheads and Cavaliers*, pp.19–54; Roberts, *Cromwell's War Machine: The New Model Army, 1645–1660*, p.117.
25   Parker, *The Military Revolution*, pp.55–57; Charles Carlton, *This Seat of Mars: War and the British Isles, 1485–1746* (London: Yale University Press, 2011), p.146.

weakened state and thus more susceptible to) disease, exposure to the elements, malnutrition (all exacerbated by poor shelter and sanitation), tiring marches, large numbers of men gathered in close proximity, and often intermittent provisioning of various supplies.[26] Other debilitating, but not mortal, conditions were another reason soldiers were unable to serve when needed. Even if a soldier survived an accidental injury or disease, or recovered from his wounds taken in battle, the likelihood is that they would be left weakened by the experience and therefore would be of limited use in military service, at least temporarily.

A serving soldier of this period, and later periods, was more likely to die due to accident or disease during wartime than he was to die in combat. The requirements to get such invalids healed, healthy, or at least discharged from service was a major contributing factor to the growing spread of medical care that took place on all sides during the English Civil Wars.[27] It was not simply moral or altruistic motives on the part of the commander but the desire to get trained and even veteran troops back into their companies wherever possible. The need to relieve the military of the necessity to pay wages for those who were no longer of use as soldiers, in the case of the incurable or permanently disabled, also played a part. As surviving petitions of wounded soldiers show, these attempts were at least partially successful as some soldiers continued to serve despite being wounded more than once, whereas others had to leave military service altogether due to no longer being suitable for the rigours of soldiering.[28] Wilde Robinson of Staffordshire received 'many and sundry wounds' when he served as a soldier for Parliament, 'both in England and Scotland'.[29] The Royalist soldier Martin Prince was 'wounded at Edgehill in his head and was wounded at the storming of Bristol in his shoulder; and was wounded again at Alesforth … in his knee of which he was ever since Lame.'[30] Both of these men suffered wounds but recovered sufficiently to continue serving as soldiers until a later wounding forced their discharge. Such men would have

26 See Pádraig Lenihan, *Fluxes, Fevers, and Fighting Men: War and Disease in Ancien Régime Europe, 1648–1789* (Warwick: Helion, 2019).
27 See Eric von Arni, *Justice to the Maimed Soldier: Nursing, Medical Care and Welfare for Sick and Wounded Soldiers and their Families during the English Civil Wars and Interregnum, 1642–1660* (Aldershot: Ashgate, 2001).
28 Extensive work is currently being undertaken by scholars from multiple UK universities to transcribe and study the petitions of wounded soldiers from across the British Isles in the Civil War Petitions Project. See www.civilwarpetitions.ac.uk.
29 'The petition of Wilde Robinson of Draycott in the Clay, Staffordshire, 14 July 1657', Civil War Petitions, <https://www.civilwarpetitions.ac.uk/petition/the-petition-of-thomas-heathcott-of-hope-derbyshire-16-july-1689/≥ Accessed 13 July 2021.
30 'The second certificate for Martin Prince of Barwick in Elmet, West Riding of Yorkshire, January 1670', Civil War Petitions, <https://www.civilwarpetitions.ac.uk/certificate/the-second-certificate-of-martin-prince-of-barwick-in-elmet-west-riding-of-yorkshire-january-1670/≥ Accessed 13 July 2021.

been lucky as despite treatment even a light wound would have run the risk of infection and subsequent complications, possibly leading to death or discharge.[31] Contemporaries recognised the near impossibility of an officer maintaining their unit's numbers at anything near establishment strength for very long and there was widespread acceptance that companies and regiments would inevitably campaign at less than full establishment strength. Gervase Markham's advice to would-be officers reading his *Souldiers Grammar* – published in 1615 as a cross between a treatise on practical warfare and a drill manual (republished in 1626 and again in 1639) – was to bear in mind that:

> the warre is a knowne enemy, and who knowes not that sicknesse, mortality, slaughter, ill diet and lodging, hunger, cold and surfeites doe so attend upon Armies, that by them companies are exceedingly weakned and made lesse, so that he which mustereth one hundred men if he bring three score and ten able men into the field to fight, is oft held for a stronge company.[32]

Events during the British Civil Wars would further support Markham's view. An extreme example can be found amongst the Earl of Essex's Parliamentarian army. After capturing Reading from the Royalists in April 1643, disease swept through his regiments causing illness, death, and desertion which resulted in a huge drop in the army's strength. Essex himself reported to the House of Lords in July of that year that only half his infantry were fit for service: 'The Number of Foot Three Thousand marching Men, at least Three Thousand sick, occasioned by the Want of Pay, ill Cloathing, and all other Miseries which attend an unpaid, sickly Army.'[33] Surviving muster rolls appear to bear out Essex's claim, for example Sir James Holborne's infantry regiment had 660 men in February 1643, 473 in May, and only 290 in August out of an establishment (on paper) of 800 men.[34]

31　Stephen Rutherford, 'A New Kind of Surgery for a New Kind of War: Gunshot Wounds and Their Treatment in the British Civil Wars' in Appleby and Hopper (eds), *Battle-Scarred: Mortality, Medical Care and Military Welfare in the British Civil Wars* (Manchester: Manchester University Press, 2018), pp.67–68.
32　Gervase Markham, *The Second Part of the Soldiers Grammar: Or a Schoole for Young Soldiers … For the Training, and Exercising of the Trayned Band…* (London, 1627), pp.47–48.
33　*LJ*, VI, p.160, 31 July 1643, State of the Army, from the Lord General.
34　TNA SP 28/143, Part I, Captain Francis Vernon's account book; Scott and Turton, *Hey For Old Robin!*, p.198; Davies, G., 'The Parliamentary Army under the Earl of Essex, 1642–5', *The English Historical Review*, Vol. 49, No. 193 (January 1934), p.40. This establishment strength of 800 men, rather than the more usual 1,000 or 1,200, will be made clear later in the chapter.

Beyond death or illness, another challenge facing both military commanders and civilian administrators in manning the armies of the British Civil Wars was desertion. Most armies in the conflict suffered from desertion to a greater or lesser degree, but there were some instances notable for a significant volume of this. During the preparations for the Naseby campaign the New Model Army suffered a desertion rate amongst its recruits of one man in two.[35] In this case, the recruits' desertions appear to have been simply attempts to avoid military service. However, at other times, men would desert because of poor treatment, with pay arrears being a leading reason. Work by Ann Hughes on the forces in Warwickshire suggests that units that were in regular receipt of sufficient pay suffered far less from desertion than less regularly paid units.[36] There are also contemporary accounts of soldiers deserting from one regiment to enlist with another on the same side for better pay or conditions – the Earl of Essex lost many of his soldiers in this manner during the formation of Sir William Waller's army in early 1643 with 'the present Regiments much lessened, listing themselves elsewhere for the new Army, expecting better Pay and Cloathing, and, upon their going hence, are entertained and protected.'[37] This appears to have been an ongoing problem as in November 1644 Colonel Edward Massey, commander of Parliament's forces at Gloucester, complained his garrison was lacking sufficient supplies and funds and that subsequently:

> All my best men run away for lack of clothing and other requisites to protect them against the cold, and take service in other parts and Associations where they may have a better and surer entertainment. For it seems there is such a liberty given [to troopers] that all comers are welcomed by every Association without enquiry so that they be well mounted or appointed.[38]

Similar behaviour has dogged volunteer enlistment and bounty incentives in armies throughout history where men would repeatedly enlist for the bounty, desert, and then attempt to enlist in another unit to gain another bounty.[39] However, this form of desertion to find better service in allied forces is treated differently to defecting to enlist in the opposing forces, which was a significant

---

35 Gentles, *The New Model Army in England, Ireland and Scotland*, p.33.
36 Hughes, *Politics, Society and Civil War in Warwickshire*, pp.199–201.
37 *LJ*, VI, p.160, 31 July 1643, State of the Army, from the Lord General.
38 *CSPD 1644*, p.131, 18 Nov., Col. Edw. Massie to the Committee of both Kingdoms..
39 See Philip Haythornthwaite, *British Infantry of the Napoleonic Wars* (London: Arms and Armour Press, 1987), pp.6–8 and David Heidler and Jeanne Heidler, *Encyclopaedia of The American Civil War: A Political, Social, and Military History* (W. W. Norton, 2002), pp.256–258 for bounty enlistments during the Napoleonic and American Civil Wars respectively.

Dévastation d'un monastère (Looting a monastery), from The Miseries and Misfortunes of War, Jacques Callot (Rijksmuseum, Amsterdam)

factor in the English Civil Wars particularly. This form of defection, or turncoat behaviour, is covered below as a facet of recruitment. In addition to active desertion, units of all armies suffered from what is best described as absenteeism. This not only included detached service, where soldiers were seconded to other duties away from the regiment, but also straggling where men became separated from their regiments on the march, or following a battle, became lost and adrift and struggled to re-join their units, or simply wandered away in search of food or entertainment.[40] The problem of straggling was perceived as being significantly detrimental to an army's strength so much so that it was mentioned clearly in the Articles of the various armies of the wars. Alexander Leslie, Lord General of the Covenanter Army, was clear that 'In marching, no man shall stay behind without leave: No man shall straggle from his Troop or Company: No man shall march out of his ranke, and put others out of order, under all highest paine.'[41] For the Parliamentarian army formed in 1642, straggling 'from his Troop or Company, or to March out of his rank' and absenteeism from camp were both punishable by death.[42] The Royalist Articles of 1642 stated that 'No Souldier shall depart from his Captain without licence, though he serve still in the Army, upon pain of death'

40　Donagan, *War in England*, pp.273–274.
41　*Articles and Ordinances of Warre: for the Present Expedition of the Army of the Kingdome of Scotland. By the Committee of Estates, and His Excellence, the Lord Generall of the Army* (London: 1644), pp.7–8.
42　*Laws and Ordinances of Warre, Established for the Better Conduct Of The Army, By His Excellency the Earl of Essex, Lord Generall Of the Forces Raised by the Authority of the Parliament, For the Defence of King and Kingdom.* (London: 1643)

and 'No man shall depart a Mile out of the Army, or Camp, without Licence, upon pain of death.'[43] Gathering in these wandering and errant soldiers was amongst the many responsibilities of the regimental and army Provost Marshals.[44] Provost Marshals were officers responsible for maintaining discipline in their regiment and enforcing the army's Articles of War, there was usually one per regiment and a senior one in an army to coordinate them.[45] In November 1644, 'two Welchmen' were hanged by the Royalists 'for running away'.[46] In practice, despite the above example, broad implementation of such punishments for deserters and stragglers was uncommon. Stragglers often found their way back to their unit, either of their own volition as they caught up with the units or by being collected by the Provost Marshal's men. This straggling was such a common occurrence that regimental and company officers, perhaps seeking to not risk turning straggling into full on deserters, frequently dealt with the misconduct 'in house' rather than seeking to apply the prescribed punishment. Captain Kightley, for instance, redistributed stragglers' wages for the period of their absence 'some of them for two dayes, some three dayes, and some foure dayes, which time they were gone from mee, and give their pay to the rest of the souldiers', thereby also rewarding those men who remained with the unit.[47]

Units which fell too far below strength on campaign would commonly be seconded to garrison duties. When Sir Ralph Hopton was made Governor of Bristol after its capture in 1643, he was left with 'six verie weak Regiments of foot, in all not making above 1200 men' to act as a garrison.[48] On other occasions a regiment which was significantly below strength might be disbanded with the remaining men enlisted into other units, such as the absorption of multiple understrength regiments into the New Model Army (see below). Despite these efforts to maintain effective field units, few regiments in the British Civil Wars remained at establishment strength for long, if it had even reached the initial 1,000 or 1,200 men at its formation. The more pre-eminent a regiment and its commander within the military structure the more likely it was to be closer to full strength

---

43 *Military Orders and Articles Established by His Majesty for the Better Ordering and Government of His Majesties Army Also Two Proclamations, One Against Plundring and Robbing, the Other Against Selling or Buying of Armes and Horse, with Some Other Additions* (Oxford: 1642), articles 11 and 30.
44 R.M. Ball, 'After Edgehill Fight', Historical Research, Vol. 67, No. 162 (1994), p.113.
45 Turner, *Pallas Armata*, p.223.
46 Richard Symonds, (C.E. Long & I. Roy, eds), *Diary of the Marches of the Royal Army* (Cambridge: Cambridge University Press, 1997, first published 1859), p.179.
47 Edward Kightley, *A Full and True Relation of the Great Battle Fought Between the Kings Army, and His Excellency, the Earle of Essex, Upon the 23. of October* (London, 1642), pp.6–7.
48 Hopton, *Bellum Civile*, p.60.

compared to less prestigious units. Peter Young and Wilfred Emberton claim that Prince Rupert's regiment of horse, the personal regiment of the King's nephew, did manage to maintain an almost full complement of men on its regimental strength for almost four years of war.[49] While the success of these senior regiments in securing soldiers may have been connected to the prestige of serving in such units, it is also possible that the more important a unit, the greater the likelihood of it being a priority for pay and supplies and thereby being more attractive to recruits. The huge amount of manpower constantly lost to the attrition of disease, desertion, intermittent battle, skirmish, and other causes needed to be replaced if an army was to remain effective.

Returning Veterans

In the interests of completeness, it is worth considering the role of veterans returning to the British Isles from fighting on the Continent. Historians have previously highlighted the high level of military knowledge and experience that foreign service veterans disseminated across the British Isles during the military developments of the Thirty Years' War. Both Mark Fissel and Charles Carlton argue that allowing their subjects to join the armies of foreign princes was an essential part of Stuart foreign policy, with Scottish and English regiments being raised for service in the (Protestant) armies of Denmark, Sweden, and The Netherlands, as well as Irish regiments for the armies of (Catholic) France and Spain.[50]

There appears to have been widespread acknowledgement of the usefulness of the skills and experience that the veterans possessed. Charles I had attempted to reform the militia in England, commonly referred to as the Trained Bands, during his rule with varying success, with an insistence on sending returning veterans of the Thirty Years' War to instruct and train these county militias. These 'muster masters' were to improve the training of the Trained Bands and introduce them to current methods of warfare.[51] During his preparation for the Bishops' Wars, Charles repeatedly considered the viability of recruiting experienced regiments from overseas service. These included hiring Spanish veterans from the Army of

---

49   Young and Emberton, *The Cavalier Army*, p.25.
50   See Fissel, *English Warfare, 1511–1642*, p.256 and Carlton, *This Seat of Mars*, pp.90–92. For the Scottish experience in foreign armies see: Steve Murdoch (ed.), *Scotland and the Thirty Years' War, 1618–1648* (Leiden: Brill, 2001), particularly the introduction, pp.1–23; Murdoch and Grosjean., *Alexander Leslie and the Scottish Generals of the Thirty Years' War*; Matthew Glozier, *Scottish Soldiers in France in the Reign of the Sun King: Nursery for Men of Honour* (Leiden: Brill, 2004); David Worthington, *Scots in the Habsburg Service, 1618–1648* (Leiden: Brill, 2004).
51   Fissel, *English Warfare, 1511–1642*, p.69; Carlton, *This Seat of Mars*, p.89.

Flanders or hiring experienced Danish regiments from his uncle Christian IV of Denmark. In exchange the King had to supply money, ships to transport them, and fresh levies to replace them. Given that he was struggling to raise levies for his own armies at home at the time, as well as his extremely limited budget, it is no surprise that these plans did not come to fruition.[52]

Many Scottish veterans returned to Scotland in 1638 when the Covenanter leadership requested them. This provided the Covenanters with a large pool of trained and experienced manpower which contributed to the formation of their own forces. Many of these veterans were selected as non-commissioned or commissioned officers and were subsequently dispatched across Scotland as drill masters for fresh recruits. Furthermore, the Covenanter government required that every regiment's lieutenant colonel and major, as well as every company's ensign and two of its sergeants, be drawn from these veterans.[53]

Returned veterans were also likely to have brought back more tangible assets. For example the Swedish Privy Council decommissioned Alexander Leslie as a Swedish Field Marshal at his own request and discussed the possibility of the compensation for his loyal service being in the manner of military supplies of muskets and artillery.[54] Finally, one of the aims of the Cessation of Arms between Royalist and Irish confederate forces in Ireland in 1643, was to allow the release of the veteran English forces fighting in Ireland for service with the Royalist armies in England.[55] Apart from the shipping of veteran regiments over from Ireland in 1643 and 1644 large numbers of rank-and-file soldiers do not appear to have returned from other wars overseas to engage with the British Civil Wars. The returning veterans were largely officers, who made up only a small percentage of the overall manpower in the conflicts. However, as was the case with the Covenanter forces, when available in sufficient numbers to have an impact on training and thus imparting their experience to fresh recruits, these veteran officers provided a pool of knowledge and experience that could benefit their forces, even if the bulk of the manpower was raised by other means.

---

52   For a detailed summary on these diplomatic attempts to recruit foreign forces, see Fissel, *The Bishops' Wars: Charles I's campaigns against Scotland 1638–1640*, ch.4, especially pp.162–173.
53   Furgol, *A Regimental History of the Covenanting Armies*, p.2; Reid., *Crown, Covenant and Cromwell*, p.6.
54   Murdoch and Grosjean., *Alexander Leslie and the Scottish Generals of the Thirty Years' War*, p.95.
55   John Lowe, 'The Campaign of the Irish Royalist Army in Cheshire, November 1643–January 1644', *The Historic Society of Lancashire & Cheshire* Vol. 3 (1959), pp.47–48.

The Militia

The English government had planned to draw on manpower with pre-existing experience from another source during the Bishops' Wars of 1639 and 1640. These were to be recruited from the county militia. Some of the militia, notably the Trained Bands of London and elsewhere, also saw action during the English Civil Wars so a brief outline of the militia system is necessary.[56] The Trained Bands were local militia regiments organised on a county and town basis. By 1638, membership of these militia regiments, both infantry and cavalry, was nominally composed of the wealthy members of local society, 'householders of good condition, or yeomen's sons' below the gentry.[57] The Trained Bands were expected to source their own weapons and armour, so only those with sufficient funds could afford modern equipment and keep it maintained. Furthermore, these elements of society were held to have a vested interest in defending the nation from both foreign invasion, and internal rebellion. However, in many areas the militiamen simply refused to turn up for training, or to pay for their equipment. By 1638, the Tudor Militia statute had been repealed for over 30 years and many in England, particularly amongst those liable for militia service, felt that the militia and the Trained Bands was now a thing of custom rather than law.[58] This strengthened a growing public resistance to attendance, membership, and practice. Subsequently, the quality and numbers of practised, equipped, and willing Bandsmen varied from place to place. For instance, the Somerset forces were so unprepared and poorly trained they were effectively nonexistent.[59] In comparison, London's Trained Bands, Lancashire's, and the Yarmouth Artillery Company, were all well-funded, suitably trained, and considered quite formidable by observers familiar with modern Continental practices.[60]

In many areas gentlemen were 'sponsors' rather than active Bandsmen, paying to equip one or more poorer men, rather than having to serve themselves. A 'substitution clause' often meant that when the militia was activated a Bandsman, or their sponsor, could pay for a substitute to take his place. During the Bishops' Wars, particularly in 1640, this substitution clause was made widely available

---

56 For a far more detailed study and assessment of the Trained Bands during the first half of the seventeenth century see Peter Leadbetter, *The Perfect Militia: The Stuart Trained Bands of England and Wales 1603–1642* (Warwick: Helion, 2021)
57 A. Clark, 'The Essex Territorial Force, 1625–1638', *Essex Review*, vol. 18, no.70 (1909), p.68.
58 Carlton, *This Seat of Mars*, p.89.
59 Thomas Barnes, *Somerset, 1625–1642: A County's Government During the 'Personal Rule'* (Oxford: Oxford University Press, 1961), p.264.
60 D. P. Carter, 'The Exact Militia in Lancashire, 1625–1649', *Northern History*, Vol. 11 (1976), pp.87–106; Carlton, *This Seat of Mars*, p.90.

to men selected for the press. However, few of those selected for the press had sufficient money either to bribe the constable or to sponsor another recruit and they were unlikely to possess the necessary influence to persuade the constable to select someone else in their place – unlike the wealthier Bandsmen. The result in the Bishops' Wars was that many of the supposed Bandsmen who served in the King's forces were untrained and inexperienced substitutes who lacked the training and experience expected or hoped for by their commanders.

Charles I appointed officers, led by Sir Jacob Astley, in the summer of 1638 to undertake a review of the Trained Bands in most of the Midlands and the Northern Counties.[61] One of the principal results of this review was to order an increase in membership of the militia by a third. Anyone suitable who claimed they could not serve due to other responsibilities was to lose exemptions from county rates and military obligation.[62] In short, unless they signed up to the militia, they would be subject to more tax, and risk being subject to service in the army. While this meant that the numbers of Trained Band men rose, many of these were 'sponsored' men as wealthy members of society, unable or unsuitable for active militia service, contributed in this way and so avoided the risk of increased taxation. Sponsoring men was not simply a way to avoid active militia service on the part of the wealthy. In many cases a wealthy individual would be assured of his ability to avoid service. The parish officers felt the need for him to pay his rates exceeded the need for his personal military service, as otherwise they would have to pay more themselves to make up for his absence from the tax contribution. Many of the 'sponsored' men were skilled craftsmen or artisans whom the local economy needed.[63] Often these men would be employers as well as employees. Mark Fissell argued that by sponsoring these men into the militia, their business partners or local grandees ensured that these economic contributors were kept safe from the press.[64] This also increased the use of substitutes when the activation of the militia was called out and sponsors sought substitutes in turn for the men they had previously sponsored, further exacerbating the replacement of trained men with inexperienced ones.

During the First Bishops' War, where the northern Trained Bands were kept intact, the militia from the middle of England was used as a pool of men for the

---

61 TNA SP 16/404/88, Letters from King Charles to Sir Jacob Astley, 18 December 1638; CSPD 1638–1639, Nov. 28, Thomas Smith to Sir John Pennington, pp.130–131. For Sir Jacob Astley being made Sergeant Major General; CSPD 1639–1639, Dec. 12, Article 72 p.171 and Dec. 18, the King to Sir [Jacob] Astley, Sergeant-Major General of the Field, p.176 for the lists of Trained Bands Astley was to inspect.
62 Fissel, *The Bishops' Wars: Charles I's campaigns against Scotland 1638–1640*, p.199.
63 Stephen Stearns, 'Conscription and English Society', *Journal of British Studies*, vol. 11, no.2 (May 1972), p.10.
64 Fissel, *The Bishops' Wars: Charles I's campaigns against Scotland 1638–1640*, p.201.

field regiments. The plan was that these regiments were to be formed around a small nucleus of men drawn from militia units and supplemented by the press, with the militiamen providing the lower level officers.[65] This would have provided a trained and experienced cadre of soldiers in every regiment. The regiments with Marquess of Hamilton's expeditionary force were manned by both activated militiamen and impressed regiments raised in Cambridgeshire, Suffolk, Essex and Kent.[66] However, with the substitution clause, in reality most of the 'Bandsmen' who were sent to the rendezvous were substitutes and 'untrained' men, and not the experienced militiamen expected by the government. While nominally supposed to be composed of 1,700 Trained Band men and their equipment, Lord Poulett's regiment raised in the West Country appears to have been composed almost entirely of substitutes with loaned weaponry.[67] Through keeping the northern Trained Bands intact, as well as the reality of parish and county officials able to substitute actual militiamen for untrained substitutes, Charles' activation of the militia was met with little real resistance. Reliance on these local officials as instruments of recruitment continued throughout the wars. However, the attempted use of the militia changed in the preparations for Charles' campaigns of 1640.

In March that year it was announced that members of the Trained Bands themselves were now subject to impressment through use of Commissions of Array, a medieval instrument that subjected the Trained Bands to being selected and forced as recruits into the field regiments. In addition, the King's Council specifically ordered that the best of the militia be selected in the pressing of men.[68] The approach taken by the Council now meant that a man was *more* likely to be selected for service in the Army if he was a militiaman, and one deemed well equipped and well trained. This was an attempt to assemble a much more efficient and far better equipped army than in 1639. The Privy Council's aim was to provide about half of the planned 20,000 infantry from the militia, with the rest being drawn from the press. Understandably the level of resistance was high from the Trained Bands. Quite apart from the political contexts of 1640, these men felt they were being punished for having already performed their duty, as they saw it, to the King and their locality by joining the militia and paying for their own equipment. When offered press money to legally complete their enlistment many militiamen simply refused to take it.[69] The press had long been associated with the meaner elements of society and to compare the Trained Bands to the 'hard bargains'

---

65   NRS GD 406/1/847, Letter from Hamilton to Arundel, 26 May 1639.
66   TNA SP 16/419, Spring 1639 Indentures.
67   Fissel, *The Bishops' Wars: Charles I's campaigns against Scotland 1638–1640*, p.201, see fn.125.
68   Fissel, *The Bishops' Wars: Charles I's campaigns against Scotland 1638–1640*, p.209.
69   TNA SP 16/451/5, Letter from Deputy Lieutenants of Suffolk, 20 April 1640.

normally caught up in the press was deemed by many Bandsmen to be insulting. Extensive resistance also came from local authorities who felt the removal of the militiamen led to unwarranted risks – who would defend the county against invasion or rebellion if the Trained Bands had been weakened by portions being sent into the field regiments?[70] It was also argued that the economy too would also suffer as the Bandsmen composed significant proportions of the most productive elements of their local economies. In a petition by Trained Bands of Hertfordshire explaining why they should not be pressed as soldiers it was claimed that 'the principal trade of the market towns and the chiefest husbandry and tillage in the country pass through our hands, and are directed by us.'[71] They stated they would be more than pleased to contribute to the wars fiscally and both directly and indirectly referred to their right of substitution.[72] This was not always the case as examples do exist of militiamen willing to take the press money and serve in the army such as happened in eastern Northamptonshire.[73] Nonetheless, faced with such resistance slowing the mobilisation of the army, Charles allowed extensive use of the substitution clause, in effect giving such action Royal approval. Few local government officers or Bandsmen failed to take advantage of this opportunity in 1640. These practices ensured that the majority of infantry heading northwards were unskilled, undrilled men, who were understandably resentful.

Impressment

The Stuart Kingdoms made extensive use of impressment in the decades preceding the outbreak of civil war in the British Isles. Regiments raised for service overseas, commanded either by foreign officers or home-grown adventurers, would often have the majority of their ranks filled by impressment, or more simply the press. Stephen Stearns argues that forces raised in the 1620s for Royal service against Spain and France were manned exclusively by the press.[74] The English methods of impressment for the Bishops' Wars (and in later conflicts as we shall see) were very similar to those used during the raising of those regiments for foreign service in the 1620s. On deciding the size of the force to be raised, the Privy Council of England wrote to the Lord Lieutenants of the counties with orders to raise a certain number of men. Despite hoping for numbers of volunteers these never came in large numbers, and the orders included instructions that 'if the said number cannot

---

70   Fissel, *The Bishops' Wars: Charles I's campaigns against Scotland 1638–1640*, pp.203–204.
71   *CSPD 1640–1641*, pp95–97, [April], Petition of the soldiers of the train bands.
72   *CSPD 1640–1641*, pp.95–97, [April], Petition of the soldiers of the train bands.
73   TNA SP 16/454/44.
74   Stearns, 'Conscription and English Society in the 1620s', p.2.

be had then to press the ablest men'.⁷⁵ The Lord Lieutenant would subsequently order his Deputy Lieutenants, who would then allocate numbers of recruits to be raised in the County's administrative divisions: hundreds, wapentakes, lathes, et cetera. The high constables of these areas would then inform the constables of each subordinate parish or subdivision how many men were to be raised within their respective area. It is worth noting here that at this point the process appears to be completely independent of Parliament with instructions from the Privy Council instead being implemented by the County Lord Lieutenants and their subordinates.

The numbers of men allocated to each parish were typically, and logically, based on its size and its population.⁷⁶ The parish constables would then choose who was to be pressed and send them to the high constables, who would in turn send the selected individuals chosen from his hundred on to a rendezvous decided by the Deputy Lieutenants.⁷⁷ The parish constables would have been selected from amongst the parishes' wealthier and respected residents, either elected by their peers of a similar status within the parish, or selected based on a rota system drawn from the same social group. On a rotating basis, this section of parish society would fulfil the role of parish constables, churchwardens, overseers of the poor, and other respected offices within the parish. It was from this pool of wealthy and prominent individuals that much of the militia would also be drawn. It is therefore unlikely that these men would choose to send friends, family members, their own servants or employees, or people on whom the parish relied – the employed and the able-bodied – unless they had no one else to choose from. Indeed, a call for the press was seen as an opportunity to rid the parish of those undesirables who, it was felt, the local society could do without. The use of the press in this way by the local authorities was well established by this time. During the Tudor period this was officially sanctioned as Elizabeth I's regime saw the impressment of 'idle persons and masterless men' into the army for foreign service as an opportunity to improve 'domestic peace'.⁷⁸

Under the Stuarts' rule the orders for the counties, as outlined by the Privy Council, tended to have stipulated that only 'fit and able men' should be selected, being particularly concerned that men deemed 'unnecessary', unemployed, or

---

75   CSPD 1638–1639, p.503, Feb. 25, Further resolutions of the Council of War.
76   Victor Stater, *Noble Government: The Stuart Lord Lieutenancy and the Transformation of English Politics* (Athens, Ga: University of Georgia Press, 1994), p.40.
77   Fissel, *English Warfare, 1511–1642*, pp.87, 105–107; Spring, *The First British Army, 1624–1628*, p.32.
78   HMC, *Calendar of the manuscripts of the Most Hon. The Marquess of Salisbury, KG., etc, preserved at Hatfield House*, XV (London: H.M. Stationery Office, 1930), p.60; Charles Cruickshank, *Elizabeth's Army* (Oxford: Oxford University Press, 1966), p.28.

wastrel should not be sent.[79] This was certainly not a charitable act on the part of the government, rather a concern in making sure that they were getting quality recruits instead of the poorly fed, the dispossessed, or the disabled. Despite this, the constables continued with the practice of seeing the selection of men sent to military service as a way of ridding the parish of the burdensome or of troublemakers. From their perspective, not only would this not damage their local economy or society, but by removing those currently unemployed, or likely to be unemployed, it meant less pressure on the parish poor relief. The parish constables could make the defence that due to the exemptions to impressment, usually based on a minimum income or wealth, or being a member of the local militia (itself having minimum entry requirements based on property and wealth), it made sense to press the poor and the unemployed first and then work their way up the economic scale. During the reign of Charles I's father, James, the pressed men of English parishes periodically sent to replenish the garrisons in Ireland were often filled with recruits whom their officers felt were physically unsuitable for military service.[80] Prisoners 'condemned of felonies' would be used to make up the numbers of recruits with those who were pressed running the risks of a soldier instead of the certainty of the gallows.[81] In 1629 when raising a regiment for service with the King of Sweden, the goals of Newgate and Bridewell supplied prisoners 'to the end they might be employed in the service of the King of Sweden.'[82] In this way it was not unusual for officers to find many of their 'recruits' were too old, or too physically, or mentally disabled to be suitable.

Unsurprisingly, this system of selection for impressment by local authorities was rife with corruption.[83] Not only did parish constables use it to get rid of men they found undesirable, but officials took the opportunity to make money using the leverage of selection when those selected could pay for a substitute in their place.[84] Some unscrupulous parish constables would use the threat of selection for the press to extort money or favours from members of their parish. There are examples of men simply being 'foreign' to the area, as local parish constables rounded up any man that had no local ties, and therefore could fit the description of 'vagrant', to fill up the numbers. Sergeant-Major Leigh, tasked with surveying recruits at

---

79 TNA SP 16/72/48, Secretary Coke to Secretary Conway, 31 July 1627.
80 Malcolm Wanklyn, *The Army of Occupation in Ireland 1603–42: Defending the Protestant Hegemony* (Warwick: Helion, 2022), p.36.
81 *CSPD 1628–1629*, p.568, June 5, Warrant to Sir William Acton and Rowland Backhouse, Sheriffs of London and Middlesex,.
82 *CSPD 1628–1629*, p.568, June 5, Warrant to Sir William Acton and Rowland Backhouse, Sheriffs of London and Middlesex.
83 Fissel, *English Warfare, 1511–1642*, p.109.
84 Fissel, *English Warfare, 1511–1642*, pp.247–249.

Pillage et incendie d'un village (Looting and burning a village), from The Miseries and Misfortunes of War, Jacques Callot (Rijksmuseum, Amsterdam)

Plymouth in 1625, found that they included 4 'purblind' men, a minister, 1 man described as a 'frantic' (a contemporary term for insane or even violently mad), 26 who were over 60, 2 who were lame, 4 foreigners, a further 24 men he describes simply as 'sick', and hundreds he describes only as 'defective', with at least another 200 men having deserted.[85] In fact, so extensive was the poor quality of recruits selected during the 1620s that in 1627, during recruitment for the war with France, the government began the practice of sending military officers to collect the recruits to ensure that they were suitable.[86] As a result, parish constables had to choose more carefully since their selection was going to be reviewed, in theory, by an officer whose own life might depend on the quality of the recruits selected, as well as the pressure from his senior officers for his need to raise a full company for service. This was again implemented when impressment was used in England for both of the Bishops' Wars when officers were sent to the county rendezvous 'to see that able men be pressed'.[87]

Officers would sometimes conduct large numbers of recruits from the county to the army. For example, Captain Gifford was the officer who 'had the command

---

85 TNA SP 16/4/160, Survey by Sergeant-Major Leigh.
86 J. V. Lyle, (ed.), *Acts of the Privy Council of England, 1627,* vol. 42, pp.455–456, (London: HMSO, 1938), A Minute of letters to the Lords Lieutenants of several counties, 31 July 162; Lyle, *Acts of the Privy Council of England, 1627,* vol. 42, pp.480–481, A Minute of letters to the Lords Lieutenants of several counties, 10 August 1627.
87 *CSPD 1638–1639*, p.503, Feb. 25, Further resolutions of the Council of War.

of one and conduct of all three' of the companies of pressed men from county Durham in April 1640.[88] The involvement of company officers appears to have raised the physical quality of the recruit for the Bishops' Wars.

Even so, a brutal form of logic was applied to the selection process as younger bachelors, seasonal labourers, and the unemployed – 'idle and young fellows who most feared or were fittest for service' – would be selected first.[89] Such men would be unlikely to leave dependents, either wives or children, who might then be forced out of necessity to claim assistance or relief from the parish in the absence of their main breadwinner. However, avoiding conscription was not easy even for men with employment or families if the numbers of recruits needed was high. If someone was willing to argue the case for exemption someone else would still be required to fill their place. Even so, those selected this way were far more likely to be from the lower rungs of the economic spectrum.[90] The term 'labourer' was used as a catchall for those individuals who relied on seasonal or part-time work in the fields and industries. These men, not considered essential to the economy and often unemployed out of season, can be found in surviving papers as one of the largest pools of potential recruits at the commencement of the Civil Wars. An indenture from Northamptonshire for 1638 contains the names of almost 920 pressed men, of whom 649 were labourers, servants, or poor craftsmen.[91] In the spring of 1640, the parish officers in London were advised to press able-bodied men from the taverns and public houses.[92] In the small parish of Cratfield in Suffolk, for the period 1640–1660, of the 13 men pressed for service only two owned or rented property.[93]

The example of Northamptonshire also shows how little time was allowed, since the high constables and petty constables were only informed at the very end of March that they needed to provide their allocated number of men to the deputies on 4 April. This experience of impressment amongst the localities, and the knowledge of whom the authorities preferred to press, had a telling effect on English efforts to recruit soldiers for the Bishops' Wars. On 15 March 1639, the Privy Council sent letters out to the Lord Lieutenants requiring the impressment of men for the Army with orders that those pressed 'were to be at Selby by the 1st of

---

88   *CSPD 1640–1641*, p.75, April 28, Sir Michael Ernle, Lieutenant Governor of Berwick.
89   *CSPD 1639*, p.23, April 6, Dr. Robert Sibthorpe to Richard Kilvert.
90   TNA SP 14/178, Indentures for the delivery of recruits levied for Mansfeld's Army, 1624; TNA SP 14/179, Indentures for the delivery of recruits levied for Mansfeld's Army, 1624.
91   TNA SP17E, Enrolment list for East Division, Northamptonshire, 1638; Fissel, *The Bishops' Wars: Charles I's campaigns against Scotland 1638–1640*, p.224.
92   TNA SP 16/448/70, Order to the Aldermen of London, 1640.
93   Lynn Bothelho (ed.) *Churchwardens Accounts of Cratfield* (Suffolk Records Society, vol. 42, 1999), p.20.

April, but not to fail to be there by the 15th of that month.'[94] The selection of men was made more difficult as soon as news of the imminent press was known, because those men most likely to be selected – the unemployed and the unattached – fled into the countryside. One petty constable received the letter informing him of the press 'at third hand and open, so that all the idle and young fellows which most feared or were fittest for the service had notice beforehand to convey themselves out of the way'.[95] Those most likely to be pressed, those with poor employment and few responsibilities, were usually also those individuals most able to make themselves absent. Thus, many parish officers were faced with a much-reduced pool of potential candidates, many of whom would be able to make valid excuses for relief from service if selected. Despite all these problems, which the nature of the evidence does dwell upon, the system could work surprisingly effectively. As Victor Stater argues, the ability of local constables to provide the numbers of men required for the First Bishops' War was impressive, with as many as 20,000 men raised for service and possibly as many as half of these drawn from impressment. Much of their success is overlooked due to the problems amongst the recruits to the Second Bishops' War.[96] But this success had its own repercussions for the rest of the Civil Wars. The results of the press for the First Bishops' War, as difficult as it was for the local constables, meant that many men the parish society saw as 'suitable' for the press had been selected and marched northwards. How many of the men pressed for service survived the campaign we do not know, although there were reports of smallpox in the army's camp in the beginning of June.[97]

With the assemblage of newly pressed men delivered to the assigned rendezvous, the pressed men would then be given 'press money' which signified a man's enlistment. In the 1620s this sum was around four pence per man, but in the Bishops' Wars was a little higher, with some men getting six pence.[98] With the assemblage at the rendezvous, their names on the paper, and the press money in their hands, the men would be considered legally bound to service. In previous decades if a conductor was not available to transport them to their assigned regiment the recruits might be sent home with orders to make themselves ready upon short notice. The inherent risk here was of men not willing to turn up again at the later date once the county had sent them home. During the impressment of troops for the First Bishops' War, the Privy Council gave the constables as short a

94 CSPD 1638–1639, p.574, March 18, Article 130.
95 TNA SP 16/409/2; TNA SP 16/421/44.
96 Victor Stater, 'The Lord Lieutenancy on the Eve of the Civil Wars: The Impressment of George Plowright', *The Historical Journal*, vol. 29, no.2 (June 1986), pp.281 & 292.
97 CSPD 1639, pp.277–278, June 4, Sir Henry Mildmay to Secretary Windebank.
98 Spring, *The First British Army, 1624–1628*, pp.35–36; CSPD 1640, p.226, Undated, Article 18 Memorandum that Edward Sanders.

time as possible between impressing the men and the rendezvous in an attempt to limit the opportunity to desert. In 1639, and again in 1640, company officers from the conscripts' assigned regiment were ordered to collect the men directly from the parish rendezvous and take them on to the general rendezvous of the army.[99] In 1640, regimental officers were 'sent by the Lord-General into the counties to assist in the levying, exercising, [and] conducting' of the pressed recruits.[100] This was to ensure that there would be no gap between the men reaching the rendezvous and then being sent on to serve in the army, again with the intent of limiting opportunities for the recruits to abscond and to ensure that the recruits were of sufficient quality.[101] This was believed to ensure that 'a captain beine at the choice of his own men would prevent [corruption] and look into [selection] better' but in practice it also drastically slowed the rate of recruitment.[102] Officers could not be sent to 'recruit' without first being given sufficient money to support their new soldiers, both as press money and as 'coat and conduct' money to feed the men on the march and to ensure they were suitably clothed for the days of marching.[103] With comparatively few officers per company against the number of men required, and the distance separating the individual parishes, only so many locations could be visited in a short time by these officers. This practice of officers reviewing and conducting men, rather than just collecting the recruits from multiple parishes at a county rendezvous, further slowed the pace of impressment.

Desperate parish constables having already struggled, albeit largely successfully, to recruit sufficient men in time only a year previously were under even greater pressures to provide pressed men for the Second Bishops' War. In fact, failure to provide enough men would sometimes be met with the threat of their own impressment to make up the numbers.[104] The Deputy Lieutenants of Northamptonshire had 'pressed divers other constables for such like miscarriages or neglects'.[105] However, the impressed constables could hope to escape the press if they were 'to return that night to provide fitter men against the next morning.' These ever more desperate parish constables would have been even less willing to accept excuses or to make exceptions compared to the First Bishops' War.[106] The Deputy Lieutenants of Hampshire explained their lack of success in pressing

---

99 *CSPD 1638–1639*, p.503, Feb. 25, Further resolutions of the Council of War.
100 *CSPD 1640*, pp.559–560,Mar. 19, Notes by Nicholas of the proceedings this day at the Council of War.
101 Lyle, *Acts of the Privy Council of England, 1627*, vol. 42, pp.455–456; Stearns, 'Conscription and English Society in the 1620s', pp.3, 17.
102 TNA SP 16/4/162, Memorandum to Mr. Murray of the Council Staff.
103 Stearns, 'Conscription and English Society in the 1620s', pp.13–16.
104 Stater, 'The Lord Lieutenancy on the Eve of the Civil Wars', p.285.
105 TNA SP 16/421/44, Letter from Deputy Lieutenants of Northamptonshire.
106 Fissel, *The Bishops' Wars: Charles I's campaigns against Scotland 1638–1640*, pp.243–244.

enough men for 'reason that many are run away' and many of those that had been pressed 'were so unfit and insufficient that we had just cause to refuse them.'[107]

The addition of increased substitution further exacerbated the problem of availability of recruits. As outlined above, both in 1639 and again in 1640, elements of an infantry regiment were to be drawn from the Trained Bands and in doing so would provide a significant proportion of 'trayned men', with the best equipment they owned, for every unit. This would, in theory, provide a proportion of regimental manpower, perhaps most of the non-commissioned officers, and a proportion of the necessary equipment. However, the substitution clause allowed a militiaman to be replaced with another man from the parish for both a fee and the equipping of the replacement. If they could not get the militiaman, then they could still get an equipped soldier. Fissel argues that this substitution clause was so widely used that most of the 'militia' recruited in both 1639 and 1640 were substitutes.[108] These substitutions were drawn from the same pool of manpower as those men who would also be liable for the press, in effect forcing the constables to widen the selection even further in order to find the numbers of men they needed to impress. With the substitution clause increasing the number of men required, the sense of the wealthy buying their freedom through substitution, the absence of many potential recruits fleeing the press, and the constables pressing men who would normally never expect to be forced into the army in order for the constable himself to avoid fines or impressment it is no wonder that the pressed infantry of 1640 did 'daily commit many notorious and foul outrages and misdemeanours both against their commanders and others our subjects, and that it is impossible to keep them under the command of their officers.'[109]

Despite the inherent problems with the system of impressment outlined by the examples of 1639 and 1640, the use of the parish and local government officials in the impressment of men continued to be used during the British Civil Wars, at least in England. The use of the press, for all its inefficiencies, was likely seen as a more reliable manner of gathering the necessary manpower for the hazards of military service than others. The use of the press in this manner can probably be summed up as the worst system, apart from all the rest, particularly when there was low enthusiasm for serving in the army. Desertion and poor behaviour among the pressed men were nothing new to the authorities, although the problem grew

---

107 BL Add Ms 26781, f.73, Sir Edward Dering's Lieutenancy Book, 1630–1640.
108 Fissel, *The Bishops' Wars: Charles I's Campaigns Against Scotland 1638–1640*, p.225.
109 *CSPD 1640*, p.477, July 15, the King to Sir Jacob Astley; *CSPD 1640–1641*, p.258 June 1, John Nicholas to his son Edward Nicholas, regarding Wiltshire conscripts stealing and rioting; *CSPD 1640–1641*, p.476, July 14, Lieutenant Colonel Gibson to [Edward Viscount Conway] for the murder of an officer; *CSPD 1640–1641*, pp.477–478, July 15, for rioting troops in Staffordshire.

as the wars progressed. Even in 1645, when large numbers of pressed men were successfully absconding from their enforced enlistment, it was probably still seen as the most effective tool available for producing large numbers of men for a service that few men entered willingly, particularly after several years of war. Its price per man also had much to commend it as a volunteer might need several shillings to be enticed to enlist whereas the pressed man cost pennies, and that was mostly paid for by the local authorities.

It was not just England and Wales who provided impressed soldiers for service in the Bishops' Wars as it appears to have been used in Ireland as well. By 1638, the King's Lord Deputy in Ireland, Sir Thomas Wentworth, was strongly in favour of the idea of using Irish troops to put down what he considered a Scottish rebellion.[110] However, for the First Bishops' War Charles contemplated using troops from Wentworth's Irish establishment, that is English regiments that were garrisoning Ireland, as a force to invade Scotland. Instead, Wentworth began raising new regiments in 1639, amongst them a troop of cavalry commanded by the young Earl of Ormond and several regiments of infantry from native Irishmen.[111] Wentworth deputised the organisation and mobilising of this Irish army to his kinsman Christopher Wandesford, and it seems that the bulk of the men were recruited via impressment. The full picture is not entirely clear as there are extremely limited surviving sources for this army. Certainly, many of the rank and file were Catholic as many of them would later join the rebellion in Ireland in 1641. However, it is likely that the majority of their officers were Protestants, as their regimental officers and non-commissioned ranks were selected from Ireland's much smaller peacetime garrison army.[112]

Drawing experienced troops from the small Protestant establishment army would have provided a nucleus of trained men and ensured that trained (Protestant) soldiers had relatively senior positions in any new regiment. According to Wanklyn, no less than 80 percent of the regimental colonels of the 'New' Irish army had been seasoned company commanders from the 'Old' army. However, Wanklyn also shows that not only were a number of junior officers Catholic, but the rank and file were also almost entirely Catholic.[113] It seems that the initial recruits were not of the highest quality, perhaps to be expected from a parish-based press if the English experience of pressed recruits was anything to go by. The Irish Government appears to have assigned the recruitment of regiments to specific provinces of

110 Fissel, *English Warfare, 1511–1642*, p.243.
111 Stevenson, *Scottish Covenanters & Irish Confederates* pp.230–34.
112 P. H. Hardacre, 'Patronage and Purchase in the Irish Standing Army Under Thomas Wentworth, Earl of Strafford, 1632–1640 (Continued)', *Journal for the Society of Army Historical Research*, vol. 67, no.270 (Summer 1989), p.103.
113 Wanklyn, *The Army of Occupation in Ireland 1603–42*, p.151

Ireland, drawing least heavily from Ulster and its Scottish-descended population.[114] It is possible they preferred to rely more on Catholic Irishmen than Protestant Scots-Irish in an army whose primary purpose was the suppression of Scottish Covenanters. After constant drill and training however, these Irish regiments were later to be considered quite proficient with one of their commanders, William St Leger, boasting of the discipline and proficiency of his soldiers, claiming 'Thes are not the men that were at Dublinne or Clonnell. For those were poore stinking Rascally sneaks. Thes are brave gallant fellows shuch as a man would chose if a Crowne lay at stoke. There Cloaths are better, there Persons better and there Mettell is better.'[115] Given the context, it is probable Dublin and Clonnell were the rendezvous for the men on initially being pressed and St Leger is comparing their current state to their initial one. Sources for the period are limited and it is unclear upon what methods the province impressment system in Ireland was based. Irish rebels in 1642 attempted to raise men for military service based on a number of men apportioned per 'ploughland' which seems to have been a subdivision of a parish.[116] Given the English method of conscripting by apportioning numbers of conscripts to be raised at the parish level, this may indicate that this was how recruits had been raised for Wentworth's forces at a local administrative level, and the rebel leaders in the initial stages of the conflict were attempting to duplicate Wentworth's achievement. However, this is simply conjecture.

The English Parliament attempted to institute impressment in February 1642 to raise an army to counter the rebellion which had broken out in Ireland in October of 1641. Regiments of infantry had been raised in the interim, but the desired volunteers had not surfaced in sufficient numbers to fill all the planned regiments being raised. What is interesting is that the final wording of the Act 'for the better raising and levying of soldiers' outlined that 'by the Laws of this Realm none of his Majesties subjects ought to be imprested or compelled to go out of his county to serve as a souldier in the Wars except in case of necessitie of the sudden coming in of strange enimies into the Kingdome or except they be otherwise bound by the tenure of theire lands or possessions.' The Act went on to outline how only:

> by authority of this p[re]sent Parliament that the Justices of the Peace of every County and Riding within this Realm ... may att any time or times ... within theire severall limits and jurisdictions raise levie and impresse so many men to Souldiers Gunners and Chirurgions as shall be appointed by order of the Kings Majestie his heires or successors and both Houses of

---

114 Wanklyn, *The Army of Occupation in Ireland 1603–42*, p.150
115 Bodleian Carte Ms 1, ff.214r–215v, William St Leger to Ormonde, 21 July 1640.
116 Lenihan, *Confederate Catholics at War*, pp.37–38.

Vol sur les grandes routes (Highway robbery), from The Miseries and Misfortunes of War, Jacques Callot (Rijksmuseum, Amsterdam)

Parliament for the said services and to command all and every the high Constables other Constables and inferiour Officers of and within every such County Riding City or Towne Corporate or the liberties thereof respectively by warrant under the hands & Seales of such Justices of the Peace.[117]

It is worth emphasising here that the impressment of the armies for the Bishops' Wars had been completed without funding from Parliament, but by Charles and his Council through the office of County Lord Lieutenants, their deputies and then the High Constables and Constables of the parishes. Here with the wording of this later Act, Parliament was attempting to bypass the Lord Lieutenant and instead mobilise the Justices of the Peace as the senior local authorities, under Parliament's control, to impress soldiers. Although the Militia Ordinance of March 1642 was viewed by contemporaries as the breaking point of Charles and Parliament when the latter attempted to take control of the militia, the earlier Act of February appears in its wording to have attempted to remove from Charles the right, or perhaps the institutional ability, to raise an army.[118] It outlined that the

---

117 'Charles I, 1640: 'An Act for the Better Raising and Leavying of Souldiers for the Present Defence of the Kingdoms of England and Ireland', in John Raithby, (ed.) *Statutes of the Realm: Volume 5, 1628–80* (London: Great Britain Record Commission, 1819), pp.138–139.
118 Clarendon, *The History of the Rebellion and Civil Wars in England*, I, p.570; John Rushworth (ed.), *Historical Collections of Private Passages of State: Vol. 4, 1640–42*

pressing of men for service was illegal; that this current need to press soldiers was only done with the authority of both the King and both Houses of Parliament; and it also bypassed those in influence perceived as being supportive of the King, the Lord Lieutenants of the counties, from any role in impressing the army. Compare this to the methods of raising men by impressment in the Bishops' Wars, and in the decades preceding that. As a reminder, the King's Privy Council informed the Lord Lieutenants, who then ordered their own Deputy Lieutenants, and these in turn operated through the High and Parish Constables. Parliament was not involved in the traditional manner of raising forces by impressment in England. That Parliament feared the Lord Lieutenants of the counties would be inclined to support the King's acts cannot be in any doubt as the later Militia Ordinance sought to replace as many of the Lord Lieutenants as possible.[119] In practice the impressment of men under this Act, if accepted, would have operated in much the same way at its lowest level of implementation, that is at the county subdivision and parish level, as had the impressments of 1639–1640. Although those commanding the impressment had changed, the activity of impressment itself still fell on the local government representatives, the parish constables.

Impressment, a clear and recognised method of raising large armies by 1642, was not initially implemented at the outbreak of the British Civil Wars although it would be, by both sides, within a year. Why impressment was not used initially is unclear, although it was perhaps seen as politically dangerous by both factions. The split in authority between the King and Parliament, as well as the subsequent divisions of loyalties that spread over the course of 1642–1643 likely prevented its effective implementation as neither the King nor the Parliamentary opposition could count on complete control of the counties. As both sides were attempting to gather wider national support the use of impressment would have not only required the active participation of local elites, and of a civil local government structure that was becoming divided in their loyalties, but the dislike of impressment generally meant that it was not a device which would have earned local support amongst the wider population for whoever employed it. The first to use such methods would possibly lose the very local support they were so desperate to consolidate. Parliament's publications were quick to use rumours of impressment in April 1643 by Royalist regional officers such as Lord Capel who, it was alleged, 'presseth and enforceth men to serve him because few or none there offer themselves as volunteers for his service' while Prince Rupert, it was claimed, 'gathereth up all

---

(London, 1721), 'Historical Collections: The Militia Controverted', pp.516–552. Lois Schwoerer, '"The Fittest Subject for a King's Quarrel": An Essay on the Militia Controversy, 1641–1642', *Journal of British studies*, vol. 11, no.1 (November 1971), pp.45–76.
119 *LJ*, IV, p.625, 5 March 1642, Ordinance of Parliament for the Safety and Defence of the Kingdom.

sortes of men, by menaes and threates'. This was perhaps an attempt to undermine support for the King by highlighting his use of the hated impressment.[120]

Following the breach between Charles and Parliament in England they must both have recognised the damage to their political support which might occur from relying on a press to raise men, even as they each began raising volunteer regiments in the summer of 1642. The split between King and Parliament may also have made the practical implementation of a press at the local government level doubtful at a time when both factions were still vying for local support in those first months. However, as both support and control of local regions coalesced in the first year of the English Civil War, both King and Parliament, driven by the necessity to raise new regiments and to reinforce existing ones, began using impressment. Parliament passed an Ordinance on 10 August 1643 which empowered Deputy Lieutenants of the counties to conscript men in their respective areas. These men and the County Committees of Parliament were 'authorised from time to time, untill other Order be taken by both Houses of Parliament, to raise, leavy, and Imprest such number of Souldiers, Gunners, and Chirurgions, for the defence of the King, Parliament, and Kingdome'.[121] This impressment system was still to be implemented through the parish constables as it always had been, however this time it was under the authority and direction of the Parliamentarian County Committees and the Deputy Lieutenants who by this point were Parliamentarians, rather than through the Lord Lieutenants as Charles had ordered in 1639 and 1640. The new Ordinance of August 1643 commanded:

> all Constables, and other Officers, to be aiding and assisting to them in the said service of Impresting; All which persons so to be Imprested, and every of them, shall have such Imprest Mony, Coat and Conduct Mony, Wages and Entertainment, and other necessary charges and allowances, as shall be fit and convenient, according to the discretion of the Committees and Deputy Lieutenants, or any two or more of them respectively.[122]

Six days later, another Ordinance called for 20,000 men to be pressed for service.[123] The Ordinance of 10 August 1643 granted this right to impress soldiers to both

---

120 *Certaine Informations from Severall Parts of the Kingdome*, Issue 13, April 10 (London: 1643), pp.101–102.
121 *LJ*, VI, pp.174–177, 10 August 1643, Ordinance for pressing Soldiers, &c.
122 *LJ*, VI, pp.174–177, 10 August 1643, Ordinance for pressing Soldiers, &c.
123 *LJ*, VI, p.183, Ordinance for the speedy raising 20,000 Soldiers, in the Six associated Counties of Norfolk and Suffolk, &c.

the Militia Committee of London and to the 'Committees of Parliament in every county'.[124]

By the summer of 1643, Parliament felt secure enough in its own authority to compel a press without recourse to the King as it had in 1642 for Ireland. By August 1643, within the counties and areas under their control, with the corresponding Deputy Lieutenants of their own choosing installed alongside established county committees of their own, there would have been no conflict of authority as there was in early 1642 to challenge or oppose the implementation of a press from Parliament. The existence, by the summer of 1643, of multiple military garrisons and forces within those areas would have also lent further strength to their authority. Parliament may have felt that impressment was absolutely necessary and unavoidable at this point in the war. The loss of manpower Essex's army had suffered following the disease-ridden siege of Reading in April was certainly a factor in needing more recruits. The necessity to rebuild the Southern Association army under Sir William Waller after a slew of Royalist victories in the West over the course of 1643 further drove the need for fresh manpower. The Parliamentarian defeat at the Battle of Roundway Down on 13 July and Prince Rupert's capture of Bristol on 26 July meant that by early August Parliament was desperate to rebuild its armies in the face of an apparent Royalist surge.[125] Yet, apart from who was issuing the authority to the counties, the impressment would still have to be undertaken by the parish constables as it always had been. They would again be responsible for selecting the men who were pressed, finding the money to feed and clothe them, and for paying the conductors to escort the new conscripts to the assigned rendezvous. Constables were still met with threats and punishments if they failed to meet their allotted number of impressments, including the fining of the constables for every man under their assigned total they presented. According to Clive Holmes parish constables in Parliament's Eastern Association could be fined between £2 and £3 for every man they were short, and sometimes more.[126] Resentment towards recruitment and the subsequent desertion amongst the pressed men appears to have been an increasing problem for Parliament, perhaps over and above what it had been in 1639 and 1640, where the pressed men tended to desert *en route* to the rendezvous. At times the military had to be involved such as when pressed men rioted in Cambridge in the autumn of 1643, and a troop of Parliamentarian cavalry was needed to help subdue them, together with the local

---

124 *LJ*, VI, pp.174–177, 10 August 1643, Ordinance for pressing Soldiers, &c.
125 Lipscombe, *The English Civil War: An Atlas and Concise History*, pp.114–122.
126 Holmes states that fines might go as high as £10 in for a 'recalcitrant constable'. Holmes, *The Eastern Association in the English Civil War*, endnote 23, p.280.

townsmen. After 'having killed some, and wounded others' of the pressed men, the survivors were marched off to join the army.[127]

The introduction of impressment in Royalist areas also began in 1643 but on a more intermittent basis than in Parliament's, perhaps accounting for the rumours that the Parliamentarian press made use of, as seen above. Throughout the course of 1643, beginning in May, the King had issued individual colonels with the right to impress men to fill their regiments.[128] When this form of impressment was used, the regimental officers would show this right and authority to the local county officials, again presumably the Deputy Lieutenants or higher Constables. The Deputy Lieutenants at least, and possibly the Constables, would not have been able to keep their authority in Royalist controlled areas if they retained overt Parliamentarian sympathies. Again, the men would be recruited through the parish constables following the instructions and allocations of the Deputy Lieutenants, with the recruits being dispatched to the rendezvous chosen by the regiment. However, it was not until the spring of 1644, with the establishment of the Royalist Parliament at Oxford, that a more widespread system of impressment was rolled out by the Royalists with the creation of the new 'investment committees' in every Royalist controlled county to take charge of the impressment.[129] On 11 March 1644, the Royalist Parliament voted that 6,000 men needed to be impressed immediately to fill up the depleted ranks of the army in Oxford.[130] In April 1644 the constables of the Hundred of Potterne and Cannings in Wiltshire received a Royalist order for the impressment of 21 'able men' which detailed the type of men to be impressed for service as 'common soldiers':

> *First.* The persons you are to impress for this service, you shall make choice of such as are of able bodies.
> *Secondly.* Such as are for their quality fit to be common soldiers.
> *Thirdly.* Such as are fit for their age.
> *Fourthly.* Such as are single men rather than married men.
> *Fifthly.* Such as are being single men, are not housekeepers.
> *Sixthly.* Such as not being housekeepers, are out of service rather than such as are in service.
> *Seventhly.* Such as are mechanics, tradesmen, or others, rather than husbandmen; but not mariners.

---

127   *The Parliament Scout Communicating his Intelligence to the Kingdome*, 16 (October 6, 1643).
128   Hutton, *The Royalist War Effort 1642–1646*, p.95.
129   Hutton, *The Royalist War Effort 1642–1646*, p.95.
130   Hutton, *The Royalist War Effort 1642–1646*, p.93.

Eighthly. Next you shall take care that they be conveniently apparelled either of their own or by the assistance of the parish where they are impressed.[131]

This list of requirements, demanding where possible single, unattached men, preferably unemployed fits the type of recruit the parish could most afford to lose. What is interesting is the preference to not press husbandmen, suggesting the army preferred to leave the food production of farms and other land alone. However, they were still relying on the parish to do the selection, within set limits, and to clothe and transport the men to the rendezvous. In effect, the army was relying still on the influential local civil elites to operate in conjunction with, and give orders to, the local civilian county and parish officials regarding the impressment of soldiers. A common thread throughout this study is how the military was dependent, even reliant, on the civilian population in order to supply their military forces, in this case for local officials and structures to provide the army with the necessary manpower. It is also worth noting that this administration via constables was also the system used throughout the war for raising taxation. The parish constable was key to providing the sinews of war.[132]

That it took Parliament over a year and the Royalists nearly two years before widespread implementation of systems of impressment, which were in any case based on the long-established structures, is more a reflection of their need to consolidate and establish their own authority in the areas they controlled rather than the building of completely new impressment structures. This is a similar pattern to the implementation of taxation where Parliament would apply a new method of financing the war, such as the excise, which would be followed a few months later by the Royalists implementing similar taxes in the areas under their control.[133] Although this is outside the focus of this study, the lag between Parliamentarian and Royalist implementation could be worthy of investigation. Perhaps it reflects different methods or degrees of centralisation of administrative authority between the two, or even of perceived popular support or different concerns over possible resistance.

While the implementation of conscription was intended to bring the existing regiments up to strength it does not seem to have been able to match attrition rates.

---

131 James Waylen, *A History Military and Municipal of the Town (Otherwise Called the City) of Marlborough and more Generally of the Entire Hundred of Selkley* (London: John Russel Smith, 1854), pp.205–206.
132 Joan Kent, 'The English Village Constable, 1580–1642: The Nature and Dilemmas of the Office', *Journal of British Studies*, vol. 20, no.2 (Spring, 1981), pp.26–49.
133 John Morrill, *The Revolt of the Provinces: Conservatives and Radicals in the English Civil War, 1630–1650* (London: Longman, 1980), pp.81–84.

Desertion appears to be the largest cause, particularly when facing poor conditions during a campaign. Shortly after the Royalist army had withdrawn following the Second Battle of Newbury in October 1644, Parliamentarian officers counselled against a pursuit of the retreating Royalist forces claiming 'such a march would reduce [the army] to nothing, many of the soldiers already deserting by reason of the coldness of the weather and want of provisions.'[134]

By 1645, despite numerous rounds of impressment across all of the associated counties, the three main field armies of Parliament were desperately understrength. The New Model Army was assembled in the spring of 1645 by amalgamating many of the regiments of the three main Parliamentarian field armies of the Earl of Essex and of the Eastern and the Southern Associations. In total Essex's eight remaining infantry regiments contributed 3,048 foot and surviving muster rolls for the winter of 1644–1645 show that Essex's personal regiment had a strength of 643 men.[135] This means that the rest of the infantry regiments of Essex's forces were operating at less than half of their establishment strength of 800. The Eastern Association forces, according to surviving musters, were operating far below even that with Crawford's regiment of foot at 267 men and Pickering's at 243.[136] Even with the 3,048 men from Essex's infantry, 3,578 from Manchester's and a further 600 men from Waller's forces, an additional 7,174 were needed to bring the planned 12 infantry regiments of the Army up to their full establishment strength of 1,200 men each (14,400 men total establishment strength).[137] The balance of the necessary manpower was supplied by further impressment from across Parliament's controlled counties with the pressed men arriving to the rendezvous at Windsor in April 1644, via Staines-on-Thames.[138] By this point in the war the use of impressment appears to have been meeting strong local resistance with recently pressed men deserting and their county of origin making little effort to find and return them. Sir Thomas Fairfax wrote in late June 1645 that:

> The Difficulty of raising Recruits in the associated Counties, which are so populous, and their suffering Men that run from the Army to return and continue unquestioned among them, and unsent up to the Army, as

---

134 *CSPD 1644–1644*, pp.82–83, October 30, Sir A. Johnstone and John Crew, MP to the Committee of both Kingdoms.
135 HMC, *Thirteenth Report, Appendix, The Manuscripts of his Grace the Duke of Portland, Preserved at Welbeck* Abbey, I (London: H.M. Stationery Office, 1891), p.215.
136 Holmes, *The Eastern Association*, Appendix 8, p.238.
137 HMC, *Thirteenth Report, Appendix, The Manuscripts of his Grace the Duke of Portland*, I. p.215; Godfrey Davies, 'The Formation of the New Model Army', *The English Historical Review* vol. 56, no.221 (Jan 1941), pp.103–105; According to Firth, *Cromwell's Army*, pp.35–36 a total of 8,500 were eventually pressed for the creation of the New Model Army.
138 Davies, 'The Formation of the New Model Army', pp.104–105.

this seems strange, so the latter (if no Course be taken to redress it) will certainly be such Encouragement to those in the Army to quit it, that it will be impossible for me to keep it up, though I should be recruited every Day.[139]

Ian Gentles has previously stated that Parliament found 'conscripting infantry in 1645–6 was like ladling water into a leaky bucket', which is very similar to Parrott's analogy of water from an intermittent tap attempting to fill a bath without a plug.[140] The sense of a draining and repetitive task unable to be fully completed is shared by both analogies. This certainly appears borne out by the surviving evidence. Parliament attempted to prevent the desertion of these men 'who have been lately levied and imprested for Soldiers' who 'daily run away and depart from their Colours' by delegating the authority to administer the death penalty to any such deserters for six months in June 1645.[141] Even after the dramatic victory of the New Model Army at the Battle of Naseby on 14 June 1645, men from the victorious army deserted in their thousands.[142] From July 1645 Parliament was sending representatives to the county committees to ensure that deserters would be punished and fresh conscripts raised.[143] Colonel John Venn, in charge of the military rendezvous at Northampton and responsible for dispatching freshly raised conscripts to their assignments, stated that the Committee of Lincolnshire had 'quartered [the conscripts] in the Country, where almost Half ran away.'[144] The expansion of Parliamentary authority during the campaigns of 1645 and 1646 into areas which had formerly been either contested or were under Royalist control led to a new kind of pressed man being selected by the local constables – former Royalist soldiers. Venn continued, 'The Reason is, most Countries press the Scum of all their Inhabitants, the King's Soldiers, Men taken out of Prison, Tinkers, Pedlars, and Vagrants that have no Dwelling, and such of whom no Account can be given.'[145]

---

139 *LJ*, VII, pp.462–465, 28 June 1645, Letter from Sir T. Fairfax, for Directions how to act; for his Army to be recruited with Men and Horses; and for some Means to be taken to prevent his Soldiers from deserting.
140 Gentles, *The New Model Army in England, Ireland and Scotland*, p.33.
141 *LJ*, VII, p.461, 27 June 1645, Ordinance to Prevent Desertion from Sir T. Fairfax's Army, by Execution of Martial Law on Delinquents.
142 Gentles, *The New Model Army in England, Ireland and Scotland*, p.34.
143 *CJ*, IV, 1 July 1645, pp.191–193 1 July 1645.
144 *LJ*, VIII, p.268, 11 April 1646, Letter from Colonel Venn, that he had sent Recruits to Colonel.
145 *LJ*, VIII, p.268, 11 April 1646, Letter from Colonel Venn, that he had sent Recruits to Colonel.

La revanche des paysans (The peasants fight back), from The Miseries and Misfortunes of War, Jacques Callot (Rijksmuseum, Amsterdam)

The period of impressment from 1643 to 1646 appears to have been one of growing military involvement in the delivery of pressed men. Constables initially escorted, or at least accompanied, their pressed charges to the county rendezvous in order to have their selections approved by the authorities, being threatened with punishment if they did not meet approval. In response to the first round of impressment for Parliament in September 1643, it was the parish constables who had to watch over the pressed recruits 'in the nature of so many gaolers'.[146] Elements of the armies rather than the local militia were used to escort the reluctant conscripts on to their military destination. During April 1645 'soldiers lately pressed in Kent' for the New Model Army mutinied. Cavalry and local militia units brought them back under control and marched the recalcitrant conscripts north where they were dispersed into the various New Model regiments.[147] The situation had not improved a year later when in April 1646, Colonel Venn marched reluctant pressed recruits with 'Two Troops of Horse to convey them' sending the pressed men marching unarmed and dispatching their 'Arms after them' to prevent any armed mutiny.[148] In its struggle to find enough recruits in the face

---

146 Morant Manuscripts, 47, f.59, quoted in Holmes, *The Eastern Association*, p.167.
147 *CSPD 1644*, p.411, April 15, The same to Col. Ludlow; p.426, April 20, the same to the same; pp.436–437, April 26, Proceedings at the Committee of both Kingdoms.
148 *LJ*, VIII, p.268, 11 April 1646 Letter from Colonel Venn, that he had sent Recruits to Colonel.

of such problems Parliament had to continually extend the use of impressment throughout 1645 and into 1646 in desperate attempts to supply the New Model Army with the manpower it needed to remain operational, including the granting Fairfax the right to 'imprest Men upon Occasions as he marches'.[149]

The method of impressing them remained the same with the burden falling on the county and parish authorities. The extensive use of conscription at all levels of the war required strong local civilian engagement in order to both function and remain effective, as even if military officers became more involved in attempting to limit desertion the growing resistance to impressment from 1644 onwards amongst the civilian authorities prevented the return of conscripts who had managed to abscond home. As with a civilian transport infrastructure that ultimately was beyond the complete control of the military, so was it impossible for recruitment to function without a willing, or at least pliable, civilian administration.

Not all pressed men were looked down upon and, in some cases, they may have even been considered to have been of better quality than volunteers. Of the 5,000 recruits sent to Ireland from England in May and June of 1651, the pressed men were 'choicer men' than the volunteers, the latter 'were so full of children ... who are fitter for school than manlike exercises'.[150] If true this seems a remarkable change from the experiences of the press from the 1620s and the problems recruiting the New Model Army in 1645–1646. Perhaps this view was more a reflection on the quality of the volunteers amongst the reinforcements than a true endorsement of the pressed men. However, if we look at the experience of recruitment in Scotland during the British Civil Wars, we will see that the process of recruitment by selection was not always one which provided poor quality recruits.

Scottish Enrolment

While Scotland had raised military forces prior to 1638 these had been based on writs for limited numbers of men and composed under the orders of the Scottish Privy Council who in turn drew their own authority as being representatives of the King, himself resident in London. Edward Furgol estimated that 25,000 Scots served in the Swedish and Danish armies alone between 1626 and 1632 which would be about ten percent of all adult males in Scotland at the time.[151] Steve Murdoch and Alexia Grosjean concluded that as many as 50,000 Scots served with

---

149 *LJ*, VII, p.457, 26 June 1645 and to continue Sir T. Fairfax's Ordinance for pressing Men; *CJ*, IV, p.383, 23 December 1645; p.418, 26 January 1646.
150 Firth, *The Memoirs of Edmund Ludlow*, I, p.278.
151 Edward Furgol, 'Scotland Turned Sweden: The Scottish Covenanters and the Military Revolution, 1638–1651,' in John Morrill (ed.), *The Scottish National Covenant in its British Context* (Edinburgh: Edinburgh University Press, 1990), pp.140–142.

anti-Hapsburg forces during the Thirty Years' War.[152] Many of these men were recruited via impressment as the Privy Council of Scotland was often forced to use methods similar to the Privy Council in England to recruit sufficient soldiers for regiments sent on overseas service. When discussing recruits for such service, the Scottish Privy Council stipulated that 'all Egyptians [gypsies], strong and sturdy beggars and vagabonds, ydle and masterless men … should be apprehended.'[153] A month later, the same Privy Council ordered each parish to provide lists of all the 'masterless men' in their area as possible recruits.[154] The key element of impressment in Scotland in the early seventeenth century was that it required permission from Scotland's Privy Council, the King's representative body when James, and later Charles, were resident in England.

In raising forces to resist the imposition of Anglicanism following the upheavals of 1637, the Covenanter government had to take a new approach. By taking arms against their King the Covenanters no longer had access to the Privy Council's authority, through its Royal proxy, to call a press. To raise a national army to defend Scotland, in defiance of the King, a new authority and a new system of recruitment was needed.[155] The basis of this new authority to levy and raise men was formed upon the National Covenant, as expressed by the Tables, which was for all intents and purposes the Covenanter government. The new recruitment system that emerged was different to both the previous Scottish and the contemporary English approach to impressment. It was so different that to use the same term of impressment for both is misleading, regardless of accuracy. Unlike England, Scotland had no countrywide militia upon which to base any recruitment or to suborn into a new system of recruitment. Instead, a system of selection and organisation of recruits had to be built largely from scratch and making best use of what other social authority was available and willing; its reliance upon local officials and clergy, rather than opting for a new, more military-focused infrastructure, illustrates most clearly the tendency for British Civil War supply systems to first and foremost be civilian systems.

This social authority appears to have been readily available as, through the nationwide signing of the National Covenant, almost all adult males across most of Scotland had agreed to defend the true religion 'according to our vocation and

---

152 Murdoch and Grosjean., *Alexander Leslie and the Scottish Generals of the Thirty Years' War*, p.39.
153 David Masson (ed.), *Register of the Privy Council of Scotland, 2nd Series, Volume 1: 1625–1627* (Edinburgh: H.M. General Register House, 1899), pp.565–566.
154 Masson, *Register of the Privy Council of Scotland*, I, pp.603–605.
155 Furgol, *A Regimental History of the Covenanting Armies*, pp.3–6.

power all the days of our lives.'¹⁵⁶ The Tables established committees of war at the shire level, and incorporating the towns and burghs within these committees. The committees were responsible for the implementation of orders coming from the Tables, and later the Covenanter controlled Scottish Parliament and Privy Council. According to Edward Furgol, the local committees made best use of existing local officials in order to register, or enrol, recruits.¹⁵⁷ Local government officials and local church representatives worked together to compile these lists and the traditional councils in the towns along with the clergy in rural parishes were each responsible for listing eligible recruits within their areas of responsibility. In both urban and rural locations the influence of the local church in encouraging the selected recruit(s) to serve when called for was invaluable, especially when they could make use of the National Covenant as a motivator. This is a completely different system to earlier impressment in Scotland and the contemporary methods used in England. All those eligible to serve were listed, with the Committee choosing those best suited and, at least in theory, these were not the ones the parish could most afford to lose. The Scottish Covenanters had only two very simple distinctions for parish recruits – sufficiently able bodied so as to be suitable for military service, or not. There appears to be less evidence of the widespread exemption through wealth as there was in England. The local shire committees were determined that only those suitable and able were selected.¹⁵⁸ A parish minister in Dundee was criticised when he compiled his list solely from the communion roll, due to fears of the suitability of those enrolled, as he would have included all age-appropriate men but not necessarily those physically able or suitable.¹⁵⁹ Furgol believes that the division in local and national church support for the Engagement in 1648 was a major element as to why that army raised in Scotland failed to meet anything like its required numbers of recruits.¹⁶⁰ The engagement of local elites in the system created by the Covenanters in 1638 ensured their support particularly as they were encouraged to provide many of the officers for those regiments. Sending your son off to war as an officer may well have encouraged a deeper investment in looking for suitable rank-and-file soldiers to go with him.

156 'National Covenant, solemn agreement inaugurated by Scottish churchmen on Feb. 28, 1638, in the Greyfriars' churchyard, Edinburgh (1638)', Reformation History, <http://reformationhistory.org/nationalcovenant.html≥ Accessed 12 March 2020.
157 Furgol, *A Regimental History of the Covenanting Armies,* p.3; Laura Stewart, 'Military Power and the Scottish Burghs, 1625–1651', *Journal of Early Modern History,* Vol. 15 (2011), p.71.
158 Fissel, *The Bishops' Wars: Charles I's campaigns against Scotland 1638-1640,* p 245.
159 Stewart, 'Military Power and the Scottish Burghs', pp.74–75.
160 Edward Furgol, 'The Religious Aspects of the Scottish Covenanting Armies, 1639–1651', DPhil Thesis (University of Oxford, 1983), pp.40–41.

Potential Covenanter rank-and-file recruits underwent training even before a proportion of them were called up. In this way they ensured that their regiments contained a cadre of experienced officers to train and organise the other officers, and to train the recruits raised locally who had already undergone at least basic training upon selection. This system of compulsory enlistment and training prior to actual recruitment proved so successful that it would be adhered to by various Scottish Governments until 1651.[161] It meant that when the Tables' Committee for War called for numbers of men from parishes they would already have been at least partially drilled. The military tactics and equipment that evolved in the seventeenth century were not only expensive in terms of weaponry but also required extensive levels of drill and large numbers of men.[162] The leaders on both sides during 1638–1640 attempted to use or adapt recruitment methods that would mitigate these problems as much as possible, with the Scottish attempts, for all the reasons outlined above, being more successful.

There were, nonetheless, still heavy elements of impressment and coercion within the Scottish system as enrolled men were selected for service by local authorities rather than this being entirely voluntary. However, those who served still had to be encouraged or cajoled to actively enlist, rather than simply being ordered to, and some were even rewarded for their service. For instance, recruits from the burgh of Kirkcudbright 'were admitted free burgesses of the town, as a reward for their services.'[163]

With the local church, the local elites, and the parish authorities in Scotland invested in, and actively participating in, the system of recruitment, a potential soldier had few ways of appealing or avoiding service. Even if he considered deserting, he would have known that the entirety of the local parish authorities were actively arraigned against him. The Scottish parish recruits themselves, even if they wished to, had less means of resisting coercion based as it was on perceived duty and responsibility, and in defence of their Kirk and country. Scotland's methods ensured that those chosen to serve as soldiers had a unified societal coercion encouraging them to accept their assigned duties and backed by the National Covenant. If this is the case, that Scottish enrolment was more successful than English impressment because of popular support amongst the recruits, it could reflect wider public opinion into the perceived worthiness of

---

161 Furgol, *A Regimental History of the Covenanting Armies*, p.3.
162 The development of tactics and the increasing costs of military operations and training throughout the early modern period more broadly across western Europe is neatly summarised in Parker, *The Military Revolution*. For an English perspective see Fissel's *English Warfare, 1511–1642*.
163 J. Nicholson (ed.), *Minute Book of the War Committee of the Covenanters in the Stewartry of Kirkcudbright, 1640 and 1641* (Kirkcudbright, J. Nicholson, 1855), p.235.

the war effort. The local authorities in Scotland appear more actively engaged in the recruitment process than those in England, where local authorities appeared more reluctant. Perhaps the difference was that the wars were seen as being in the 'national' defence by Scottish recruits whereas perhaps Englishmen felt that the wars with Scotland, and even civil war in England, were not something many of them supported.

Noble Summons

For the First Bishops' War in 1639, King Charles could not rely on parish impressment to recruit his cavalry. Cavalrymen of the period were more expensive to raise and equip than infantry, each trooper requiring armour, a sword, pistols, a carbine, various other items of equipment, as well as his mount, saddle, bridle, and other furniture for the horse. The weaponry itself was more expensive, with cavalrymen requiring rarer and more expensive flintlock or wheel-lock mechanism firearms instead of the infantry's commonplace matchlock.[164] Impressment fell more heavily on the poorest in society, many of whom even had to be clothed at a cost to the parish before joining their regiment. Charles needed a different method to recruit his cavalry in 1639 and he opted to rely on the traditional military obligations of the nobility in times of war, specifically focusing on those with estates or titles near the Scottish border, likely by emphasising their part in their traditional role to defend the border against invasion from the north. To that end Charles sought legal advice on the crown's right to call on the English nobility to provide him with military support, receiving the response that the King could 'command all holding offices or lands in the posts adjoining Scotland to repair well arrayed and to stay there during your pleasure'.[165]

At the end of January 1639, the King sent letters to the nobility who held land or title in Northern England calling on them to 'attend our Royal person and standard at York, by the 1st of April next, with equipage and horses, as your birth, your honour, and your interest in the public safety oblige you unto, and as we have reason to expect.'[166] According to a letter from the Lord Chief Justices and Judges sent to the King, those nobles who held estates in Cumberland, Northumberland, Durham, and Westmoreland had not been relieved of their duties to 'perform upon the borders for the defence of this kingdom of England' even with the union of the

---

164 Edwards, *Dealing in Death*, pp.6–7.
165 HMC, *Twelfth Report, Appendix Part II, The Manuscripts of the Earl Cowper, K.G. Preserved at Melbourne Hall, Derbyshire*, II (London: HMSO, 1888), p.187.
166 CSPD 1638–1639, pp.366–367, Jan 26, the King to William Lord Grey of Wark; for entries for other copies of similar letters to other nobles see CSPD 1638–1639, p.367, Jan 26.

crowns of Scotland and England.[167] Use of the knightly instrument of summons would mean the initial recruitment and equipment costs, as well as conveyance to York, would be at the expense of the nobility rather than of the King himself. Once the cavalry reached York they would become part of a Royal Army with their wages from thereon being paid by the army rather than the nobles. However, the problems attending on such mobilisation were many, even with the legal advice Charles had been given. Although he had sent out his summons in early January, many of the nobility, particularly those residing in the West and the North of England, furthest from London, did not receive that initial summons until early February. Simply because they held lands in the English Counties adjoining Scotland did not mean they lived there themselves. This meant that for many of these nobles they had less than two months to raise and equip their cavalry troopers.

How many men each noble was to provide was left vague, with the summons only stating as many as 'your birth, your honour, and your interest in the public safety oblige you unto, and as we have reason to expect.'[168] Many of the nobility summoned were either elderly (such as the Earl of Middlesex), under age (as was the case with the 12 year old Lord Herbert), or not even in the country as in the case of the Earl of Leicester and the Earl of Oxford. Leicester was in fact in Paris at that time serving as Charles' ambassador and claimed, 'I am in a great strait between the inobservance of the King's commandment and the abandoning of his affairs which now are in my hands only'.[169] Those nobles who did make strenuous efforts to provide cavalry for the army still appear to have struggled in doing so. Many of the weapons and equipment in England had already been secured for use by the Royal Army and attempts by nobles and their agents to purchase equipment in London were met with frustration. William Montagu, attempting to secure the necessary equipment for his family's cavalry contribution, complained that 'The King commands armour and pistols, and sets all the armourers and pistolers a-work for himself.'[170] Charles's need for campaign funds in the early spring further disrupted the summons for cavalry by informing the nobility that ready cash would be acceptable in lieu of military service. The Earl of Bridgewater, in the process of raising a small force of cavalry, wrote to the Secretary of State in

---

167 *CSPD 1639*, p.100, April, The Lords Chief Justice and Judges to the King.
168 *CSPD 1638–1639*, pp.366–367, Jan. 26, the King to William Lord Grey of Wark.
169 For the avoidance of nobles to the service see: SP 16/413/106 Letter from Earl of Middlesex to Secretary Coke, 28 February 1639; SP 16/412/115, Letter from Lord Herbert to Secretary Coke, 13 February 1639; *Twelfth Report, Appendix Part II*, II, p.213, 'Leicester to Coke 25/15 February 1639'.
170 HMC, *Manuscripts of the Duke of Buccleuch and Queensberry, preserved at Montagu House*, I (London: HMSO, 1899), p.282, 'William Mountagu to Lord Mountagu, 14 March, 1639'.

response that 'the King is pleased to spare my horse, and expecteth to receive from me £1,000. Mr Secretary, I cannot expend and disburse my moneys and have them ready lying to me.'[171]

Delayed summons, a short timeframe, lack of available equipment, and confusion over sending troops or money all help to explain why only 800 horsemen appeared at York in answer to the King's summons. However small this contingent might sound, Fissel highlights that the costs to the King's Exchequer to raise the equivalent of more than a dozen troops of cavalry had been minimal at around £12 per trooper.[172] Before the wars, an above average horse may have cost between six and eight pounds by itself, so with saddle and other equipment, and initial wages for the trooper, not to mention arms and armour during a period of peak demand this was likely a seen as a bargain.[173] It could be called a qualified success, as the Army succeeded in gaining cavalry even if perhaps not in the numbers that Charles had hoped for. This limited success seems to have encouraged the King to issue a more wide-ranging summons for service in the Second Bishops' War. The 1640 summons appear to have been sent to not just those holding land and titles in the North of England but to others as well. The summons, sent out on 20 August 1640, were for 'all such as hold of his Majesty by grand Sergeantry, Escuage, or Knights-Service' to 'be ready furnish'd with Horse and Arms for performance of their said Services.'[174] Again, we cannot be sure why there was a delay in sending out the summons, however, there were no cavalry raised in this manner able to join the Army before the decisive Covenanter victory at the Battle at Newburn on 28 August. There was simply insufficient time for such recruits to have made it to the army in the eight days between when the summons were issued, let alone received, and when the battle took place. After this, attempts to raise cavalry by noble summons were not repeated.

'By Beat of Drum'

Recruitment for the Bishops' Wars was not supplied by volunteers in England, focused as it was on impressment, militia, and substitution. Furthermore, the enrolment system in Scotland ran along different concepts of responsibility to

---

171 HMC, *Twelfth Report, Appendix Part II*, II, p.216, 'Bridgewater to Coke, 14 March 1639'.
172 Fissel, *The Bishops' Wars: Charles I's campaigns against Scotland 1638–1640*, p.160.
173 Peter Edwards, 'The Supply of Horses to the Parliamentarian and Royalist Armies in the English Civil War', *Historical Research*, vol. 68. no.165 (February 1995), pp.121–140.
174 'On the twentieth of August the King published a Proclamation to summon all such as hold of his Majesty by grand Sergeantry, Escuage, or Knights-Service, to do their services against the Scots, according to their tenures' in John Rushworth (ed.), *Historical Collections of Private Passages of State: Vol. 3, 1639–40* (London, 1721), pp.1227–1228.

serve. The first time that large numbers of rank-and-file volunteers were recruited for the British Civil Wars, was in response to the rebellion in Ireland in the autumn of 1641.

The English Parliament was made aware of the Irish rebellion on 1 November 1641 and the Commons resolved that 'a Drum shall be forthwith beaten, for the Calling in of Volunteers to this Service for Ireland.'[175] That same day they also directed that a bill be drawn up 'for the Pressing of Men for this particular Service for Ireland'.[176] It appears that the English Parliament was doubtful of securing enough volunteers and wanted to implement a press to ensure they sourced sufficient recruits. Parliament's choice of trying to institute a press alongside calling for volunteers may have been due to the recognition that most Englishmen had absolutely no desire to fight in Ireland. Although Parliament had initially called for volunteers for the raising of 6,000 infantry and 2,000 cavalry to counter the Irish rebellion this target for recruitment was further increased by an additional 10,000 infantry. However, Parliament's attempts to institute a press on the same day as calling for volunteers might also have been part of a dual approach to recruitment in order to raise an army more swiftly and not solely due to doubts of sufficient numbers of willing volunteers.[177] In fact, it appears that the initial volunteer recruitment appears to have been very positive. For example, the recruitment to Sir Simon Harcourt's regiment in Cheshire began in mid-November and he landed in Dublin at the end of December with his regiment being reported as being 'compleat' with an additional 'Four or Five hundred more chearful Voluntiers' accompanying him, over-and-above his full complement.[178]

This initial success appears to have led Parliament to issue further commissions for volunteer regiments. An additional six infantry regiments including 'Two Regiments of One thousand Foot in a Regiment, be forthwith raised of Voluntiers out of the Western Counties.'[179] The raising of Harcourt's regiment may have benefitted in its recruitment numbers from displaced Protestant Irish refugees who had fled across the Irish Sea to Chester, Cheshire's main port and an important connection between England and Ireland for many years, with local recruitment further stimulated by its proximity to the rebellion. The assistance of the local MPs, notably Sir William Brereton, also likely aided in the finding of

---

175   *CJ*, II, pp.304–305, 3 November 1641, Volunteers for Ireland..
176   *CJ*, II, pp.304–305, 3 November 1641, Pressing Soldiers for Ireland.
177   *CJ*, II, p.304; *LJ*, IV, p.421, Votes of the Commons, concerning Ireland; *CSPD 1641, p.164*, Nov. 11, Capt. Robert Fox to the same.
178   *CJ*, II, p.351, Irish Affairs, Forces for Ireland.
179   *CJ*, II, p.351, 21 December 1641, Irish Affairs; p.359, 28 December 1641, Irish Affairs; CSPV *1640–1642*, p.285.

local volunteers.[180] By January 1642 Parliament was still trying to establish a press reportedly sparing 'no efforts in this city to forward the levy of 10,000 English for [Ireland's] defence' but apparently without much success.[181] Their determination to secure this impressment is curious as there were still numbers of volunteers coming in, although perhaps not in the numbers or at the rate deemed necessary, or hoped for. For example, the Earl of Leicester's regiment of 1,500 men was granted commissions on 11 December 1641 and within 10 days had its recruiting funds voted for and issued. This allowed the new regimental officers to be able to begin recruiting on receipt of the money before Christmas. By 8 January 1642, less than three weeks later, the companies of the regiment were being filled.[182] These were not the only troops raised, as 300 cavalry were mustered at the beginning of January, and a further 300 cavalry and 300 dragoons would be mustered by the middle of March 1642.[183] The cavalry was a volunteer arm and the troopers needed sufficient property and money to be able to provide their own mount and much of their equipment. However, the increasing tensions between the King and Parliament appear to have impacted the ability to raise further regiments. Charles's insistence on wanting officers from his former English army of 1640 to hold commissions in the next wave of regiments that Parliament had planned was one of these sticking points, as was Parliament's attempts to take all non-rebel forces in Ireland into Parliamentary pay, thereby in theory making them answerable to Parliament rather than the King.[184]

The associated increase in costs necessary to pay for Irish troops appears to have affected the money available for English volunteer recruiting. An enlistment bounty was one of the key enticements for volunteers to enlist, and the professional officers being assigned to the new regiments may have lacked the personal credit and wealth to extend these bounties, instead relying on funds issued by Parliament such as the funds voted for both Harcourt's and the Earl of Leinster's regiments in the first few weeks. Bounties were different from press money, and not just in

---

180 *LJ*, IV, p.437, Propositions concerning the Irish Affairs agreed to; *CJ*, II, p.313, Raising Soldiers for Ireland; *CJ*, II, pp.351–352, Forces for Ireland; *CJ*, II, pp.361–362, Forces for Ireland; Robert Armstrong, 'The Long Parliament Goes to War: The Irish Campaigns, 1641-3', *Historical Research*, vol. 80, no.207 (February 2007), p.8.
181 *CSPV 1640–1642*, p.273, Jan 10, Gio. Giustinia, Venetian Ambassador in England, to the Doge and Senate.
182 *CJ*, II, pp.346–347, Forces for Ireland; *CSPD 1641–1643*, p.203, Dec 16, Captain Guy Molesworth; TNA SP 28/1B, ff.424 & 432, Leicester's warrants, 1641–2; TNA SP 17/H/7, f.19, Documents relating to the military in Ireland.
183 TNA SP 17/H/7, f.23, Documents relating to the military in Ireland.
184 For the King's choice of officers being placed on half-pay see SP 28/1B, pt. I, ff.406, 408, 410, 412, 414, 416. For Parliament taking forces into their pay see *CJ*, II, pp.359–361, 365, 380.

the amount, which was usually substantially higher. Pressed men could receive something as low as four pence to signify their enlistment, whereas a volunteer was enticed with amounts of a shilling or more. However, regular pay of these English recruits while in England appears to have been contested, with the House of Lords arguing in November of 1641 that they 'should receive no pay till they were ready to march against the enemy' which the House of Commons apparently agreed to.[185] This decision may have been one of the reasons why recruitment of volunteers in England was slow, with what was meant as a cost-saving exercise for Parliament and an incentive to hurry regimental officers over to Ireland, in fact negatively impacting recruitment. The growing expense could also have been another reason Parliament was advocating for a press, so that initial costs of recruitment would be borne by the local parishes and counties rather than by Parliament. Another reason might have been the belief that men might be recruited faster through impressment. Volunteers required willing men to be found, or at least men to be persuaded, as well as cash on hand for enlistment bounties, whereas with impressment all of the initial time, expense, and effort was borne by parish officials. Parliament's responses to ongoing developments in Ireland also negatively impacted the gathering of recruits for the new regiments. For example, the deployment of Sir Charles Vavasour's regiment of foot, then mustering in Devon and Cornwall, to Munster was delayed when, in January 1642, Parliament stripped Vavasour of 200 of his recent recruits to 'be forthwith sent over to Duncannon Castle in the province of Leinster and money for them' with Vavasour being ordered to find a further 200 men to replace them, which delayed his regiment's deployment even further.[186] In April 1642, Parliament decided to try to raise another 10,000 soldiers from the English counties under a new 'Colonel-Generall' serving under the Lord Deputy of Ireland. 5,000 of whom were be to dispatched into Munster, principally funded by the separate Adventurers' Act of the previous month.[187] However, these efforts were blocked by a Royal refusal to grant the power to levy troops – even at this late stage there was clearly a limit to Parliament's own authority to raise troops without working with the King's authority.[188] The other regiments of infantry confirmed in December 1641 began mustering again in April after new funds had become available. These regiments

---

185 *LJ*, IV, p.437, Propositions concerning the Irish Affairs agreed.
186 *CJ*, II, p.365, Irish Affairs and p.394, Levies for Ireland; Wilson Coates, Anne Young, and Vernon Snow (eds) *The Private Journals of the Long Parliament: 3 January to 5 March 1642* (New Haven: Yale University Press, 1992), Moore, 17 January 1641/2, pp.99–100.
187 CSPI 1633–47, 18 April, Propositions of the Lord and other Commissioners for Irish Affairs, p.361.
188 LJ, V, 25 April 1643, Committee to prepare a Commission, for pressing Men to make up the Deficiency in the Number, pp.15–16.

Spanish garrison leaving Maastricht in 1632. Jan van de Velde (II), after Jan Martszen the Younger, 1632 (Rijksmuseum).

were raised from across England, with companies of Sir Fulk Hunk's regiment having been recruited in Yorkshire and the inhabitants there requiring repayment for the costs of quartering the regiment as it mustered.[189] The four month delay in recruiting these regiments until money from the new Adventurers' Fund became available, suggests a lack of money was hampering the volunteer enlistment, again reinforcing the theory that Parliament's desire for a press in 1642 was at least partly driven by a need to recruit men but with a need to defray the initial costs of recruiting onto the counties.

189 CJ, II, 18 April 1642, Col. Huncks, &c, p.533; CJ, II, 16 May 1642, Huncks' Arrears, p.573.

Recruitment of units within Ireland itself continued, with regiments being raised from among the Protestant refugees who had fled to Dublin and other holdouts.[190] As the situation in Ireland became clearer, the English Parliament was able to clarify some of its earlier orders. Half of Sir William St Leger's infantry regiment was initially to be raised in England, but instead the regiment was formed entirely in Ireland by merging into it several independent companies of local troops raised by Munster Protestants and by recruiting heavily amongst local refugees.[191] How these local militia companies were initially organised before being taken into English pay is unclear, as the sources in Ireland which might enlighten us have not survived, although it appears that part of the process of being taken into the English Parliament's pay served to consolidate them into more official regiments.[192] By 17 July 1642 volunteer units in Ireland, including those raised locally, totalled 11,700 men in Ulster, 16,500 men in Leinster, 2,140 men in Connaught, and 4,460 men in Munster – a grand total of 34,800, of whom at least 10,000 had been recruited across England and Wales. Robert Armstrong claimed that the exact moment when Parliament stopped actively recruiting for Ireland and prioritised their concerns with the King can be pinpointed to 30 July 1642 when it resolved to use £100,000 from Adventurer funds for the suppressing of the Irish rebellion towards the cost of raising of an army under the Earl of Essex for service in England.[193]

Cavalry units were raised somewhat differently to the infantry, being drawn from a wealthier class of men who could afford their own mount and equipment. Parliament had decided that a regiment of horse for Ireland was to be composed of five troops each of 100 troopers, though this later appears to have been reduced to 60 troopers.[194] Details on the earlier raising of the cavalry are unclear. It appears that there was a plentiful supply of volunteers to serve as cavalry in Ireland as, despite having sent several hundred cavalrymen across both as formed regiments of horse and as independent troops, there were still an excess of volunteers ready to serve even after these units were formed and dispatched. This plentiful supply of volunteers is curious as typically service in Ireland was seen as unpleasant and hazardous, and this continued into the British Civil Wars, with English recruits

---

190 According to Armstrong, these local units functioned more as militia for the towns and refugees around which they had gathered rather than as part of a marching army. Armstrong believes a model for their behaviour is the Netherland's militia units' details to be found in Parker, *The Army of Flanders and the Spanish Road*, pp.47–48; See Armstrong, 'The Long Parliament Goes to War', p.86, fn.78.
191 HMC, *Calendar of the Manuscripts of the Marquess of Ormonde, K. P., Preserved at Kilkenny Castle*, I (London, 1895), p.125.
192 Ian Ryder, *An English Army for Ireland* (Newthorpe: Partizan Press, 1987), pp.7–17.
193 Armstrong, 'The Long Parliament goes to war', p.89.
194 Ryder, *An English Army for Ireland*, p.7.

often showing a strong dislike at the prospect. In January 1642, when news of the Irish rebellion was still fresh 'the aversion of the people to go [to Ireland]' was apparently slowing recruitment.[195] In May 1649 troop transports for Ireland were delayed embarking soldiers due to the 'distemper' in those regiments 'designed for that service'.[196] Scottish soldiers also appear to have been reluctant to serve in Ireland. In March 1642, Scottish veterans from the Second Bishops' War had to be encouraged with bounties of 'seven dollars' for 'everie souldiour who served in the last expedition to Newcastle and is now content to goe in this armie to Ireland.'[197] The conditions in Ireland were clearly not to the soldiers liking as after landing in April 1642, by June substantial enough numbers of them were deserting from 'the armie, leav[ing] thair cullors and, without anie warran[t], come home to [Scotland]' that a proclamation ordering the death penalty for such soldiers had to be issued to the army in Ulster, and to the authorities on Scotland's western coast.[198] However, in England the steady stream of men coming forward as cavalry volunteers might have been a popular response to the Catholic uprising. Many Protestants in 1641 and 1642 viewed the rebellion as a religious struggle and were outraged by overblown reports of massacres, rapes, and forced conversion.[199] Perhaps this partially explains the enthusiasm amongst some Englishmen for Irish service, at least in the initial response to the rebellion. Nonetheless, this stream of cavalry recruits required organising.

In June 1642, in preparation for raising further cavalry for Ireland it had been advertised that men who were able to 'find and maintain' themselves a horse and sufficient cavalry equipment who wished to volunteer needed to register their address at the Guildhall in London.[200] As soon as the list reached 60 names those would be enrolled in a troop and a Committee from the House of Lords would assign officers to their command and begin their training.[201] On 30 July the English Parliament ordered that cavalry forces raised to fight in Ireland, but still awaiting transport, were to 'attend the Lord General, for his Commands, to serve here in this Kingdom, for the Defence of the King and Parliament.'[202] As a result,

---

195 *CSPV 1640–1642*, p.273, Jan 10, Gio. Giustinia, Venetian Ambassador in England, to the Doge and Senate.
196 *CSPD 1649–1650*, p.149, May 19, Council of State to Capt. Geo. Bishop [of Bristol].
197 Peter Brown, (ed.), *Register of the Privy Council of Scotland, 2nd Series, Vol. 7, 1638–1643* (Edinburgh: HM General Register House, 1906), p.228.
198 Brown, *Register of the Privy Council of Scotland, 1638–1643*, pp.220–221.
199 Jane Ohlmeyer, 'The Wars of Religion, 1603–1660' in Thomas Bartlett and Keith Jeffrey (eds), *A Military History of Ireland* (Cambridge: Cambridge University Press, 1997), p.180.
200 *LJ*, V, p.122, 9 June 1642.
201 *LJ*, V, p.142, 17 June 1642 Message from the House of Commons with a Resolution for putting in Execution the Propositions for raising Horse.
202 *CJ*, II, p.698, 30 July 1642, Forces intended for Munster.

some of the men who had volunteered to fight against the Irish rebels would find themselves riding in Parliament's army against their King; not all soldiers who were redirected into Parliament's service in such a way were happy to do so.

The Civil War began in earnest in the late summer and autumn of 1642, when both King Charles and Parliament actively, and openly, began to recruit regiments of volunteers. The King issued Commissions of Array and Parliament passed the Militia Ordinance but neither had much practical application in the raising of troops. Instead, both sides issued their leading supporters with military commissions to raise regiments. The Parliamentary commission given to the Earl of Essex to be Captain General of the Army gave him the authority to 'raise and levy Forces, as well Men at Arms, as other Horsemen and Footmen of all kinds' and 'to also to appoint a Lieutenant-General of the Troops of Horse and all such Commanders and Officers as shall be necessary and requisite for the Government and Command of the said Army'.[203] Under Essex's authority, commissions as colonel were issued to individuals who then began the process of recruiting to their new infantry regiments. These colonels in turn appointed company commanders who were then issued with levy money to cover the cost of enlisting soldiers including an enlistment bounty and equipment costs. In Parliament's case this was set at 10 shillings per man.[204]

The Royalist infantry was raised in a similar manner, as was their cavalry, although the new colonels were often expected to fund their own bounty, whereas the Parliamentarian initial signing funds were channelled through Parliament's committees regardless of their source. Royalist commissions stated that recruits needed to be volunteers, and the large associated financial costs of raising a regiment explains why so many of the early war colonels came from wealthy backgrounds.[205] Taking the example of Lord Paget's regiment of foot; in August 1642, Lord Paget was granted a colonelcy from the King and set about recruiting his regiment.[206] Although Paget was responsible for funding the regiment, he assigned a veteran soldier as his lieutenant colonel. The captaincies of the regiment's companies were largely assigned to the sons of gentry families from across Staffordshire and the surrounding counties.[207] Lieutenants were sent out

---

203 For the Earl of Essex's Commission of 16 July 1642, see Firth and Rait, *Acts and Ordinances of the Interregnum, 1642–1660*, I, pp.14–16.
204 TNA SP 28/1A, ff.29 & 64.
205 Barratt, *Cavaliers: The Royalist Army at War*, pp.9–10.
206 HMC, *Fifth report of the Royal Commission on historical manuscripts, Part I Report and Appendix*, p.141; Aaron Graham, 'The Earl of Essex and Parliament's Army at the Battle of Edgehill: A Reassessment', *War in History*, Vol. 17, No. 3 (2010), p.278.
207 HMC, *Thirteenth Report, Appendix, The Manuscripts of his Grace the Duke of Portland*, I (London: HMSO, 1891) p.63.

across Staffordshire to 'raise volunteers' by 'beat up of drum'.[208] These recruiting officers of Paget's carried personal letters of introduction from Paget to local elites, both to inform them that he had ordered 'this gentleman one of my officers to beat up my drummes in your parts' and to request their assistance.[209] Hutton says that Paget's regiment was fully recruited in this manner within one month which suggests a success of volunteer enlistments not unlike Harcourt's regiment for Ireland the previous year.[210] A record of Royalist recruitment survives for the town of Myddle in Shropshire during the winter of 1642–1643. Warrants were issued by a local Commissioner of Array for all the men of Pimhill Hundred 'housholders with theire sons, and servants, and sojourners, and others' between the age of sixteen and sixty to appear at a local landmark on a particular day. There an officer read out 'a proclamation, that if any person would serve the King, as a soldier in the wars, hee should have 14 groats a weeke [over four shillings, a groat is a 4d piece] for his pay'.[211] Officers could also make use of their pre-existing social networks to gather recruits, for instance landlords encouraging tenants, the wealthy their servants, and men who had served in the local militia approaching their former comrades. The Royalist officer at Pimhill for example, was a close associate of Sir Paul Harris, a local Royalist Commissioner.[212]

The degree of freedom in the recruits under such circumstances is not wholly clear, but they do appear distinctly different from the allocated, and altogether unwilling, impressed recruits who would come to make up much of the armies as the wars progressed. The men were promised a signing bounty as a major part of their enlistment, making it a symbolic and contractual obligation. It had long been a practice to issue recruits with money on their recruitment and the handing over of this money appears to have been seen as legally binding the recruit to service as in the case of the pressed men seen earlier.[213] In 1643, Sir Samuel Luke, commander of the Earl of Essex's scouts, recorded Royalists recruiting by 'beate upp drumes dayly in seuerall townes' and offering two shillings bounty on enlistment.[214] The

---

208 HMC, *Thirteenth Report, Appendix, The Manuscripts of his Grace the Duke of Portland*, I, p.63.
209 HMC, *Fifth report of the Royal Commission on historical manuscripts, Part I Report and Appendix*, p.141.
210 Hutton, *The Royalist War Effort 1642–1646*, p.23.
211 Richard Gough, *Antiquities & Memoirs of the Parish of Myddle County of Salop* (Shrewsbury: Adnitt & Naunton, 1875), p.67.
212 Gough, *Antiquities & Memoirs of the Parish of Myddle County of Salop*, p.67.
213 During 1640, the refusal of selected militiamen to take the 'press money' was how they proclaimed their refusal to serve in the army. See TNA SP16/451/5, Letter from Deputy Lieutenants of Suffolk, 20 April 1640.
214 Sir Samuel Luke, *Journal of Sir Samuel Luke: Scoutmaster to the Earl of Essex 1642–1644*, (ed.) I.G. Philip (Oxfordshire Record Society, 1950–1953), p.38.

dramatic increase in recruitment bounties in 1643, following the initial recruiting wave of 1642, compared to the pressed enlistment payment of as little as four pence argues for an increasing bounty offer in an attempt to encourage recruits. The first wave of Royalist recruits in 1642 from the parish of Myddle who 'went for soldiers, when the King was att Shrewsbury' appear drawn from the lower ends of the economic spectrum of the parish. These included Richard Chaloner, an illegitimate son who was 'partly maintained by the parish', an unnamed itinerant tailor described as an 'idle fellow' with 'noe habitation', as well as two men described only as sons of a previous, or 'sometime', innkeeper.[215] Such recruits as these –the unemployed, the homeless, those on parish relief, and the unattached–would have been, in the eyes of parish authorities, the most likely to have faced impressment in other circumstances. It is interesting to consider that when impressment would be reintroduced later in the wars, many who would have been obvious candidates for potential conscripts had, it appears, already marched off to war of their own volition at the outbreak of the war in England. These promises of money and glory do appear to have initially appealed to many young and unattached recruits on both sides. In September 1642, the Venetian ambassador in London wrote that Parliament's new recruits were 'for the most part of tender age, entirely without discipline and unaccustomed to hardship or the handling of weapons', while in October 'many young boyes' were reported to be joining the King's army.[216]

Such was the need for more recruits that Parliament passed an Ordinance in November 1642 guaranteeing legal and financial protections for any apprentice that enlisted including 'their Sureties and such as stand engaged for them shall be secured' and that 'the Masters of such Apprentices shall be commanded and required to receive them again into their Service, without imposing upon them any Punishment, Loss, or Prejudice, for their absence.'[217]

Despite such efforts, the numbers of recruits were far below what had been hoped or planned for, with Parliament having difficulty finding enough willing recruits to complete their regiments of infantry, both those still mustering in the city and those with Essex's army. The struggle to find enough recruits explains their attempts to encourage further recruitment amongst London's apprentices by means of the November Ordinance. The initial plan was that the regiments were

---

215 Gough, *Antiquities & Memoirs of the Parish of Myddle County of Salop*, pp.16–17.
216 CSPV 1642–43, Aug 15, Giovanni Giustinian, Venetian Ambassador in England, to the Doge and Senate. pp.122–123; Donagan, *War in England, 1642-1649*, p.220; *A Continuation of the late proceedings of His Majesty's Army at Shrewsbury, Bridge-North and Manchester* (1642), p.6.
217 For Parliament's Ordinance of 1 November 1642 see *LJ*, V, pp.424–429, 'Order Concerning Apprentices that list Themselves for Soldiers'; Firth and Rait, *Acts and Ordinances of the Interregnum, 1642-1660*, I, p.37.

to be composed of 1,200 men which, as already established, was widely accepted in the period to have been the ideal strength for an infantry regiment.[218] However, despite recruiting having started in earnest at the beginning of July 1642, by the end of August colonels were receiving only enough money for around 800 men each. The three regiments commanded by Lord Robartes, the Viscount Saye and Sele, and the Earl of Stamford all received only £400 money for enlistments, enough for only 800 men at the 10s. per man outlined by Parliament for the bounty and equipage of each soldier.[219] The Parliamentary Ordinance of 23 September does suggest it was a lack of willing recruits and not a shortage of ready money:

> And such Regiments or Troops as shall fail herein, or shall not consist of such Number as is before specified, that is to say, a Regiment of Foot of Four Hundred, and a Troop of Horse of Forty, shall be cashiered, and also liable to such further Punishment as, upon Examination of the Cause of their Failing and Neglect, shall be found that they have deserved; and the Common Soldiers of such Regiment, or Troop, so cashiered, shall be disposed of, for the filling up and recruiting of others.[220]

Therefore, Parliament was already struggling to fill its regiments with recruits before it started to court the apprentices. The responsibility of recruiting the companies appears to have fallen on the individual company captains and the regimental colonel. Those company captains who had their own companies up to strength, despite their regiment being due to be disbanded, were not themselves threatened with cashiering:

> Yet, in regard the Captains of some Regiments, which have not the Number of Four Hundred, may have been careful to raise and compleat their own Companies, and that there is no Reason they should suffer for the Default of others, either the Colonel or other Captains that have not been so careful: It is thought fit, That such Captain of any Regiment now to be cashiered as shall have his Company compleat, and shall be continued in his Entertainment, together with his Company, and shall march unto

---

218 Lord Robartes' regiment was initially intended to be 1,200 strong see their initial pay warrant of 20 August 1642: TNA SP 28/1A, f.123; For the widespread acceptance that this remained the standard see Firth, *Cromwell's Army*, pp.22–23; Samuel Gardner, *History of the Great Civil War, Volume One 1642–1644* (London, 1987), p.42; Young, *Edgehill 1642* pp.96–99.
219 A new pay warrant for Lord Robartes issued on 30 August expects only 800 men, at £400 see TNA SP 28/261, f.42. For Stamford's and Saye and Sele's receiving only £400 (the same as Robartes' regiment of 800 men) see TNA SP 28/1A, ff.29, 64.
220 *LJ*, V, p.371, 23 September 1642, Order to send the Soldiers to the Rendezvous.

the Place where the Lord General shall be, to be disposed of by him in any other Regiment, or otherwise employed as his Lordship shall think fit.[221]

These methods of disbanding critically understrength regiments, transferring recruits, encouraging legal protections for enlistment, and merging full strength companies into less critically understrength regiments, appear to have been used to bring the overall size of the Parliamentarian regiments to around 800 men by the end of October. This suggests that the 400 minimum outlined in September was eventually deemed far too small to be effective and further consolidation and recruitment must have followed. With surviving pay warrants being incomplete basing our assumptions solely on them is inconclusive. However, it is still possible to establish that Parliamentarian regiments in Essex's army were composed of at least 800 men. This can be confirmed by comparing the surviving pay warrants we do have against the surviving records of supplies sent to those regiments. John Hampden's regiment of foot mustered for pay on 17 October 1642 with a strength of 963 men, and also received 1,000 sets of clothes a week later on 24 October.[222] Likewise Colonel Thomas Grantham's regiment received 800 sets of clothing and footwear weeks after receiving food supplies for the same number.[223]

Despite the period of consolidation of understrength regiments, cashiering of unsuccessful recruiters, transfers, and intensified recruitment attempts where necessary, the Parliamentarian regiments marched to war at around 80 percent of their initial planned strength, even before the vagaries of campaigning took their toll.[224] Taken together this hardly suggests overwhelming success in 'beating the drum'. Unfortunately no records in such detail survive for the early Royalist forces, however both the Royalists and Parliament continued to recruit in this way as they marched across England before finally meeting at the Battle of Edgehill on Sunday, 23 October 1642.[225]

According to Chris Scott and Alan Turton, much of the manoeuvring of both the King's and Essex's armies across the Midlands in the autumn of 1642 were attempts to find more recruits for themselves while also attempting to deny potential recruiting areas to the opposing side.[226] Aaron Graham's article

---

221 *LJ*, V, p.371, 23 September 1642, Order to send the Soldiers to the Rendezvous.
222 TNA SP 28/261, f.307.
223 TNA SP 28/2A, f.88; TNA SP 28/261, f.185.
224 Hampden's regiment of 963 men on an establishment of 1,200 is 80 percent, and Grantham's at 1,000 is 83 percent of the planned 1,200 men.
225 Malcolm, 'A King in Search of Soldiers', pp.251–73; Malcolm Wanklyn and Peter Young, 'A King in Search of Soldiers: Charles I in 1642. A Rejoinder', *Historical Journal*, Vol. 24 (1981), pp.147–154; Hutton, *The Royalist War Effort 1642–1646*, pp.22–23 & 28.
226 Scott and Turton, *Hey For Old Robin!*, pp.34–35.

reassessing the Earl of Essex's army at Edgehill states that by the time the battle was fought in late October Parliament had accepted the strength of most regiments to be at 800 rather than the initially planned 1,200.[227] This method of recruiting was at least sufficient to keep the Parliamentarian regiments at around the same strength level as when they had departed London, despite desertion and death caused by low pay and poor conditions on campaign. The letters of Nehemiah Wharton, a Parliamentarian sergeant in Denzil Holles's Regiment of Foot, gave some indication of the conditions under which Essex's troops struggled in the autumn of 1642, including marches 'without any sustenance, insomuch that many of our soldiers drank stinking water'.[228] Conditions remained poor a month later as 'by reason of the rain and snow, and extremity of cold, one of our soldiers died by the way, and it is wonderful we did not all perish.'[229]

The Royalists were able to recruit a field army in less than three months. Historians differ on the exact figures but agree that the King's army at Edgehill was a comparable size to Essex's at around 12,500 infantry and cavalry for the Royalists and around 13,500 for Parliament.[230] This Royalist force was in addition to leaving garrisons and having regiments still mustering in the west, without the advantage of London's large population centre and without making use of troops which had already been raised for Ireland which had been redirected into Essex's army. Similar to Parliament, the Royalists seem to have not used impressment to initially fill their regiments, relying likewise by 'beat of drum'. The lack of Royalist paperwork surviving for the period is frustrating given that the Royalists' ability to field a comparably sized army to Parliament, with other Royalist forces still being raised elsewhere in England, suggests at least a similar measure of success in the method of recruitment that Parliament enjoyed. However, without the surviving evidence of either regimental pay lists or equipment receipts for the Royalists it is impossible to be sure.

It is quite possible that the initial regiments on both sides during the first wave of recruitment could have been left with quite a strong regional identity, at least amongst the rank and file. In the case of Parliament, the Lord General's regiment initially recruited heavily in Essex, Hampden's and Ballard's were both heavily recruited in Buckinghamshire, and both Lord Brooke and Denzil Holles largely

---

227 Graham, 'The Earl of Essex and Parliament's Army at the Battle of Edgehill: A Reassessment', pp.278–279.
228 *CSPD 1641-1643*, p.384, Sept 3 [1642], Nehemiah Wharton to George Willingham.
229 *CSPD 1641-1643*, p.398, Oct. 7 [1642], Nehemiah Wharton to George Willingham.
230 I have taken an average of the estimates from a selection of the following historians, for their particular estimates of the strength of both sides see: Young, *Edgehill 1642*, pp.78–102; Scott, Turton, von Arni, *Edgehill, The Battle Reinterpreted*, pp.53–72; Lipscombe, *The English Civil War: An Atlas and Concise History*, Appendix 1, pp.330–331.

A scene from Spanish military camp, siege of Breda 1624-1625. Jacques Callot, 1628 (Rijksmuseum)

recruited their regiments in London.[231] For the Royalists, the colonel would often focus his initial recruitment in areas where he held influence, possible being able to find officers and men from amongst his family and extended client and social networks. The Royalist Earl of Derby played a large part in recruiting an estimated 3,000 soldiers for King Charles's service in Cheshire where Derby had extensive estates.[232] Lord William Paget's Royalist regiment was almost entirely recruited from Staffordshire where Paget held land and estates.[233] It is probably no coincidence that at least some of the Parliamentarian colonels had connections in the areas that their regiments were recruiting from as well. For instance John Hampden held estates in Buckinghamshire while Lord Brooke had a house in London and extensive contacts within the City of London.[234] The Earl of Manchester attempted to maintain this local character in his own Parliamentarian Army of the Eastern Association stating 'Those countyes out of which the regimentes were at first raised I had appointed to supply the defectes of such regimented as were by them raised,

---

231 Davies, 'The Parliamentary Army under the Earl of Essex', p.33.
232 Barratt, *Cavaliers: The Royalist Army*, pp.9–10.
233 HMC, *Fifth report of the Royal Commission on Historical Manuscripts, Part I Report and Appendix*, p.14; Goodwin, G., and Sutton, J., 'Paget, William, sixth Baron Paget (1609–1678), politician' *Oxford Dictionary of National Biography* (online ed.) <https://doi.org/10.1093/ref:odnb/21123>.
234 C. Russell, 'Hampden, John' in *Oxford Dictionary of National Biography* (online edition). <https://doi.org/10.1093/ref:odnb/12169>; A. Hughes, 'Greville, Robert, second Baron Brooke of Beauchamps Court' in *Oxford Dictionary of National Biography* (online edition) <https://doi.org/10.1093/ref:odnb/11518>.

and I found this way to give the best satisfaction to the counties, and made the soldiers more united among themselves.'[235] This local nature of the initial stage of recruitment could, at first glance, substantiate Clarendon's claim that the Royalist army was raised by grandees and landowners recruiting their tenants into military service.[236] While not entirely accurate, it is clear that the local nature of the initial wave of recruitment, and the social standing of the initial wave of colonels on both sides, probably lends credence to Clarendon's claim.

However, the situation was not as simple as that since even a magnate's influence, wealth, and local importance of their estates could not guarantee allegiance where it ran contrary to local sentiment. Both the Marquess of Hertford and the Earl of Bath, for example, failed to implement the Commission of Array in Marlborough and South Moston despite holding influence through their estates and properties in the area.[237] Local populations in Warwickshire, North Devon and Yorkshire's West Riding remained strongly supportive of Parliament despite the majority of the local gentry in those areas supporting the Royalist cause.[238] It is likely that the Royalist magnates, where successful, benefited from the same advantages locally raised forces had in gathering men to recruit, such as making use of local knowledge, swaying local interests, and making full use of their social networks, but perhaps on a larger scale given their larger wealth and influence.

How long this regional identity lasted is unclear. In some areas, such as amongst the Royalist Cornish troops, it was retained for quite some time. Five infantry regiments were raised in Cornwall in October 1642, in July 1643 these were each still about 600 men strong. Mark Stoyle has shown that despite losing hundreds of men and three out of the five original colonels by August 1643, they were still identifiably Cornish and appear to have been reinforced with local recruits as they campaigned through Cornwall and the southwest well into 1644.[239] However, this identifiable 'Cornish Army' was perhaps an anomaly, largely campaigning around their original area of formation where 'local' recruits would have been

---

235 'Earl of Manchester to the Committee of Both Kingdomes Sitting at Derby House, 14th August, 1644', printed in D. Masson (ed.), *The Quarrel Between the Earl of Manchester and Oliver Cromwell: An Episode of the English Civil War* (Camden Society, New Series, Vol. 12, 1875), p.13.
236 Malcolm, 'A King in Search of Soldiers', provides a Parliamentarian view on the recruitment of Royalist infantry, perhaps not deliberately, but heavily flavoured by her choice of sources, see also Wanklyn and Young, 'A King in Search of Soldiers: Charles I in 1642. A Rejoinder', especially pp.147–149.
237 Underdown, *Somerset in the Civil War and Interregnum*, p.31; Stoyle, *Loyalty and Locality: Popular Allegiance in Devon*, p.143.
238 Ann Hughes, *The Causes of the English Civil War* (London: Palgrave, 1998), p.140.
239 Mark Stoyle, 'The Old Cornish Regiment, 1643–44', *Cornish Studies*, vol. 16 (2008), pp.31–36.

available. For many other regiments, recruits would have come from a much wider geographical area as drafts of pressed men and recruits were taken in on campaigning, particularly the recruitment of prisoners, as we shall see. This would have meant that any regional identity would have been very tentative for regiments in the field armies.

After the Edgehill campaign ended in stalemate in November 1642, the hopes for a quick campaign and swift victory was replaced with the need to raise further regiments. It appears that the success of the initial wave of volunteers in the late summer and autumn of 1642 convinced the Royalists that there were more potential recruits available. Additional colonels were granted commissions and dispatched from Oxford to areas now under Royalist control, and to the recruiting grounds of the previous year. However, these new colonels were often veteran soldiers selected for their military experience rather than men of power and influence in the areas they were sent to recruit in. For example, in the early spring Colonel Sir Michael Wodehouse, a professional soldier, was to recruit a regiment in North Wales and was dispatched from Oxford accompanying Lord Arthur Capel, the newly appointed Lieutenant-General of North Wales, Cheshire, Shropshire and Worcestershire.[240] Capel himself was expected to recruit men for local forces in the area under his command and taken together this suggests a Royalist belief that enough potential recruits existed for not only more infantry regiments for the King's main field army but also for local regiments as well. How successful Sir Michael was in his recruitment is not altogether clear as in September of 1643 he rejoined the King's army with the 700 men of his 'Prince of Wales regement'.[241] Given his parallel role as Capel's 'Serjeant Major generall of the foote' over the preceding spring and summer, this speaks to either a successful recruitment drive and hard campaigning with no subsequent opportunity to refill the losses, or of a particularly difficult recruitment drive lasting months with only limited success.[242] Alternatively, it could have easily been a combination of both, as losses to regiments outside of battle had multiple causes as outlined above – a regiment on campaign might not have had the recruiting opportunities to fully replace the wastage of manpower it was suffering due to battle, straggling, disease, or desertion.

---

240 W. Phillips (ed.), 'The Ottley Papers relating to the Civil War', II, *Transactions of the Shropshire Archaeological and Natural History Society*, 2nd Series, Vol. 7 (1895), pp.300–301.
241 William Day (ed.), *The Pythouse Papers: Correspondence Concerning the Civil War, the Popish Plot, and a Contested Election in 1680. Transcribed from Mss. in the Possession of V. F. Benett-Stanford* (London: Bickers, 1879), p.17.
242 Phillips, 'The Ottley Papers', II, pp.300–301.

At the initial outbreak of war, smaller forces were raised by supporters for service in their respective localities. Sometimes these forces were initially well armed and equipped companies, often paid and outfitted either wholly or partly by local gentry. These would usually develop in areas where no regiment was being mustered nearby that would otherwise form the centre of recruitment efforts. These local musters would be performed in much the same way as the more official regiments, with commanders and sponsors of the forces recruiting in their locality and making use of local loyalty and enthusiasm. John Ashe in Somerset, for example, raised and armed 'a troop of horse, a company of foot, and a company of dragoons for ye service of ye west country' all of this purportedly costing him more than £3,000.[243] As the recruitment of new regiments continued into 1643, these local companies would often find themselves folded into the strength of an officially commissioned regiment. Such was the case of cavalry troopers raised by various clergymen in Somerset, when in August 1643 King Charles ordered that these cavalry troops report to a new cavalry regiment then being recruited in Somerset.[244] Even as late as 1645, a reported 3,000 strong force from the locality joined Sir Thomas Fairfax's siege lines before Bristol when the New Model Army invested the town.[245] Unfortunately there is little detail as to the type of forces these were, except that the officers of the New Model Army felt their capabilities were suspect.[246] This might suggest local populist forces of 'clubmen' as compared to well armed and equipped troops.

Overall, the recruitment through 'beat of drum' seems to have been heavily dependent on a combination of enthusiasm and ready money for enlistment bounties. The recruitment of men for Ireland, and later for both Royalist and Parliamentarian forces, appears to have slowed as enthusiasm and ready bounty money waned and recruits needed to be found by other means. As discussed, other forms of recruitment, such as impressment, required the active participation and involvement of local society elites from local nobles and gentry through to parish constables and, in a similar manner, so too did recruitment by 'beat of drum'.

---

243 Wroughton, *An Unhappy Civil War*, p.40.
244 George Harrison, 'Royalist Organisation in Wiltshire, 1642–1646', PhD Thesis (Royal Holloway, University of London, 1963), pp.192, 277.
245 Joshua Sprigg, *Anglia Rediviva Englands Recovery Being the History of the Motions, Actions, and Successes of the Army Under the Immediate Conduct of His Excellency Sr. Thomas Fairfax* (London: 1647), pp.110–111.
246 Sprigg, *Anglia Rediviva*, p.111.

Changing Sides

The concept of a defector or a turncoat is more nuanced than you might expect. The study of conflicting allegiances, and which ones determined someone's personal loyalty, runs through much of the modern historiography of the British Civil Wars. Local studies which attempt to ascertain why particular regions and principles chose either the King or Parliament have made it clear that allegiance was neither binary nor straightforward in deciding which side men might fight for.[247] The motivations of the rank and file are difficult to establish, but both Carlton and Gentles have assumed, probably correctly, that the pressed infantry were not particularly motivated by either religion or politics.[248] However, my concern here is to consider defection as a facet of recruitment and its impact on operational capabilities.

In the initial stages of the Irish rebellion, many of the 'troops' fielded by the rebels were armed insurgents from the local population. However, as the rebellion took hold the insurgency armies were bolstered by other sources of soldiers. A large pool of trained recruits for the rebellion were the disbanded soldiers of the Earl of Strafford's Irish Army, or the 'New Army', raised to fight against the Covenanter forces in 1640. This stood differently to the Anglo-Irish army of occupation, or the 'Old Army', established since 1603. Despite the New Army's disbandment beginning in May 1641 these soldiers had not actually gone home. Instead most of the remaining 8,000 infantry had been recruited into new regiments destined for foreign service, the King giving 'licence for the departure of these men, so that Ireland will be quite relieved of them.'[249] Curiously the embarkation of these troops appears to have been deliberately delayed, with historians debating if their delay was part of a conspiracy amongst the Irish nobility or even one including King Charles himself.[250] The Irish Parliament blocked their departure in early August,

---

247 A brief selection of the most influential of the studies on the topic of regional allegiance would include Everitt, *The Community of Kent and the Great Rebellion*; Underdown, *Somerset in the Civil War and Interregnum*; Morrill, *Cheshire 1630–1660: County Government and Society*; Anthony Fletcher, *A County Community in Peace and War: Sussex, 1600–1660* (London: Longman, 1975); Ann Hughes, *Politics, Society and Civil War in Warwickshire*; Stoyle, *Loyalty and Locality: Popular Allegiance in Devon*.
248 Charles Carlton, *Going to the Wars: The Experience of the British Civil Wars, 1638–1651* (London: Routledge, 1992), pp.255 & 264; Gentles, *The New Model Army in England, Ireland and Scotland*, p.33.
249 *CSPI 1633–1647*, p.281, 7 May, Copy of Resolutions taken for disbanding the New Irish Army of 8,000 men.
250 See for example Michael Perceval-Maxwell, 'The "Antrim plot" of 1641 – A Myth? A Response' *The Historical Journal*, vol. 37, no. 2 (1994), pp.421–430 and Jane Ohlmeyer, 'The Antrim Plot of 1641: A Rejoinder' *The Historical Journal*, vol. 37, no. 2 (1994), pp.431–437.

but it was the English Parliament that subsequently blocked these regiments from going overseas in September 1641.[251] In October of that year many of these men subsequently joined the rebellion. Later in 1641, a Patrick Dowd testified that he encountered 'a Company of a hundred men' from the regiment of 'the Lord Taff' which had joined the rebellion.[252] Viscount Theobold Taaffe was one of the new colonels of one of the foreign service regiments raised from the men of the disbanded New Irish army.[253] At least four of the colonels in total joined in the rebellion so it is possible as many as 7,000 of the former New Irish army, of whose training St Leger had thought so highly in 1640, joined the insurgents in 1641.[254] Trained soldiers might well have come from another source as well – the Old Irish army which by 1638 amounted to at least 2,000 men in 40 companies of infantry.[255]

An investigation in the winter of 1641 into the religious make up of the Old Army, following the outbreak of rebellion, revealed numbers of both Irish Catholics and suspected false Protestants in it. These had likely been recruited to maintain muster strength within the army in the previous years of peace as no new drafts of replacements had come from England for over 15 years. It is also possible that some were more recent recruits enlisted into the Old Army garrison companies since the outbreak of the rebellion in the preceding months.[256] Freshly recruited Irish Catholic soldiers in government service deserted in large numbers when government troops fought the insurgents during the early stages of the rebellion. In November 1641, county Wicklow government forces composed of 'raw levies' which were 'mostly Irish' deserted to the rebels in such numbers that 'In some cases not above six or seven out of a company of forty remained on our side.'[257] Catholic government soldiers taken by the insurgents during a rout or taken prisoner in battle appear to sometimes have been spared by neighbours and acquaintances amongst the rebels and were subsequently recruited into the rebel forces that way.[258]

---

251 *CSPI 1633–1647*, p.350, 8 Aug, Petition of Theobald Taaffe, James Dillon, John Barry… etc.
252 1641 Depositions, Trinity College Dublin, 'Examination of Patrick Dowd, 25/11/1652', Ms 831, ff.079r–080v, <https://1641.tcd.ie/index.php/deposition/?depID=831079r079> Accessed 16 September 2020.
253 *CSPI 1633–1647*, p.281, 7 May Copy of Resolutions taken for disbanding the New Irish Army of 8,000 men.
254 Lenihan, *Confederate Catholics at War*, p.45.
255 Wanklyn, *The Army of Occupation in Ireland 1603–42*, pp.36, 111, 114–115.
256 Wanklyn, *The Army of Occupation in Ireland 1603–42*, pp.200–203.
257 *CSPI 1633–1647*, p.350, 25 Nov. Extract of the Lords Justices and Council to the Lord Lieutenant of Ireland.
258 1641 Depositions, Trinity College Dublin, 'Examination of James McConnell, 12/3/1653', MS 838, ff.075v–076r, <https://1641.tcd.ie/index.php/deposition/?depID=838075v139> Accessed 22 September 2020; 'Examination of James Carroll, 2/1/1642', MS 816,

In 1643 the Cessation of Arms, and the subsequent conflicts between co-religionist forces, meant that desertions to an enemy could be a viable option for both Protestant and Catholic soldiers. Traditional historiography has assumed that mercy was rarely shown to enemy soldiers of differing religion, with both Protestant and Catholic forces having given little mercy to the soldiers of opposing armies for much of the war. Following the Battle of Dungan's Hill in 1647, it is possible that 3,000 Irish soldiers were killed while attempting to flee or surrender.[259] However, there is evidence that known Catholic Irishmen, even those identifiable as former rebels, were recruited into the New Model Army as that army's campaign for the reconquest of Ireland progressed. Some of this recruitment may not have been willing as Cromwell forced 'fourescore and fifteen' Irish prisoners from Wexford 'taken to be Pioneers', labourers, with the army.[260] Following the surrender under terms of the Catholic garrison of Carlow, the Royalist commander in Ireland claimed many of the garrison went on to 'serve the rebels'.[261] It is also possible that the New Model Army recruited directly from Ireland rather than merely enlisting prisoners. Writing in 1680, Edmund Borlase claimed that 'the Irish (in all Quarters of which the Enemy were possessed) not only submitted and compounded, but very many of them enter'd into their Service, and marched with them in their Armies.'[262] Catholic veterans were likely still serving within the ranks of the Commonwealth forces in 1652 when Commissioners for the Transplanting of Catholics into Connacht wanted to know what to do with those 'Papists that first served in the rebel army, but then took service under the Commonwealth, if still on muster.'[263]

In England, as the Civil War continued and the need for recruits on both sides became more urgent, both Parliament and the Royalists attempted to recruit men of the opposing armies and tempt them into defecting. This was often by making use of proclamations which offered clemency and forgiveness to soldiers currently in arms against them. On 19 April 1645, the King argued that the removal of the clause protecting the King's person from General Fairfax's commission indicated that Parliament now aimed at destroying the very monarchy itself, thus amnesty was offered to Parliamentarian soldiers who would join the Royalist cause. This

---

ff.037r–038v, <https://1641.tcd.ie/index.php/deposition/?depID=816037r019≥ Accessed 20 September 2020.
259 Hopper, *Turncoats & Renegadoes*, p.87, fn.66.
260 *A Perfect and Particular Relation of the Several Marches and Proceedings of the Armies of Ireland...* (London: 1649), p.8.
261 Bodleian Carte Ms.26 f. 263, 3 August 1650, Ormond to Clanricarde.
262 Edmund Borlas, *The History of the Execrable Irish Rebellion Trac'd from Many Preceding Acts to the Grand Eruption the 23 of October, 1641...* (London: 1680), p.281.
263 Quoted in John Prendergast, *The Cromwellian Settlement of Ireland* (New York: P. M. Haverty, 1868), pp.96–98.

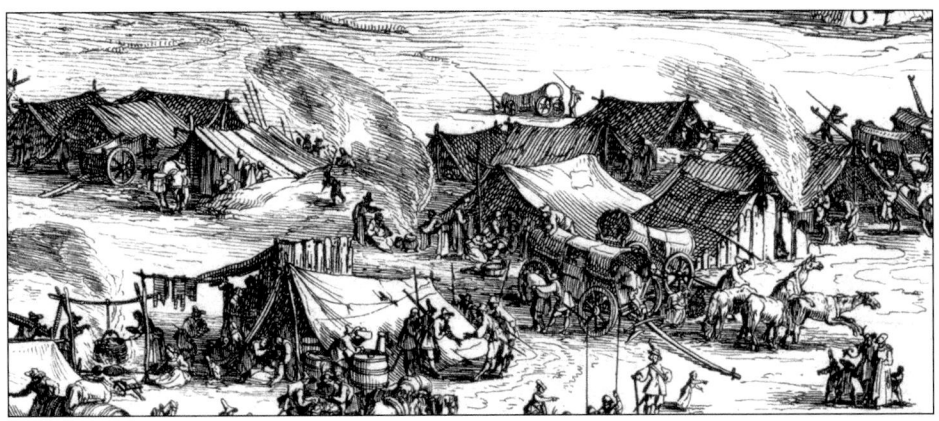

Another scene from Spanish military camp, siege of Breda 1624-1625. Jacques Callot, 1628 (Rijksmuseum)

proclamation extended a pardon to any such soldiers providing they submitted by 31 May.[264] Charles Carlton has interpreted these proclamations to suggest the Royalists were suffering recruitment issues whereas Andrew Hopper argues that they may suggest the Royalists perceived widespread discontent amongst Parliamentarian soldiers.[265]

Cavalry troopers in particular, being more mobile and with the individual regiments and troops often being more dispersed both when on campaign and in quarters, were more likely to have an opportunity to defect to the enemy than the average infantryman.[266] At Edgehill, Sir Faithful Fortescue and his troop of Parliamentarian horse turned their coats at the outset of the battle and joined the Royalist cavalry attack. In Fortescue's case, his troop had initially been raised for service in Ireland and was one of the units who were instead redirected into the Earl of Essex's army when this was formed. There were also other instances of cavalry defecting to the enemy, including when Sir Richard Grenville led almost 20 troopers to desert to join the Royalists in March 1644.[267] Apparently, four complete troops of Royalist horse, with their captains, deserted to a Parliamentarian force under Colonel Horton in 1648.[268]

264 James Larkin, (ed.), *Stuart Royal Proclamations. Vol. 2: Royal Proclamations of King Charles I, 1625–1646* (Oxford University Press, 1983), p.1063–1065.
265 Carlton, *Going to the Wars*, p.197; Hopper, *Turncoats & Renegadoes*, p.84.
266 Hopper, *Turncoats & Renegadoes*, p.88.
267 Luke, *Journal of Sir Samuel Luke*, p.261.
268 Bodleian Tanner Ms 57, f.67.

In the case of infantry, the most frequent situation in which large numbers of pikemen or musketeers could change sides was following their surrender, usually after a battle or a siege when their captors offered the prisoners the chance to enlist. For many soldiers, miles from home and without food or money, such a choice was the only safe and practical option. This form of mass defection was crucial to acquiring replacement men, many of whom would have already been trained and may have been veteran soldiers as well. Indeed, this partially enforced recruitment made these soldiers' side-changing slightly less objectionable to their former comrades, at least less so than voluntary and premeditated desertions. Carlton has estimated that a total of over 32,000 Parliamentarians and 83,000 Royalists were taken prisoner across England and Wales in over 600 separate engagements during the English Civil Wars.[269] Such large numbers indicate that there was potential for many soldiers to change sides following their capture.

Mass side-changing began early in the English Civil War; following the surrender of Banbury on 26 October 1642, most of the 600 men in the Earl of Peterborough's Parliamentarian regiment re-enlisted as Royalists. It is interesting to note that again many in this regiment had been men who had initially been raised for service in Ireland rather than for Parliament.[270] Similar to Fortescue's troop, this may well have been a factor in their decision to change sides, having initially enlisted as volunteers to fight Irish rebels and not the King. After Prince Rupert's capture of Cirencester in the following February 1,000 Parliamentarian soldiers were marched to Oxford. Given insufficient food and clothing, and exposed to the winter weather, many agreed to enlist with the Royalists rather than perform hard labour on the Oxford defences under similar conditions as experienced during the march. Many who refused this initial offer changed their minds in subsequent weeks.[271] Parliament also attempted to recruit the 1,500 Welsh prisoners they captured on 25 March 1643 and several of these soldiers later served in Parliament's garrison of Gloucester.[272] When the Royalists captured Bristol in late July 1643, as many as 1,000 men of the former garrison enlisted with the Royalists. Surviving sources from both sides contradict each other on what induced these men to do so with their former commander, Nathaniel Fiennes, claiming his men only agreed to enlist with the Royalists after 'pillaging our Souldiers as well Officers as others and by threats and inticements drawing off our

---

269 Carlton, *Going to the Wars*, pp.203–204.
270 *A Relation of the Battel Fought Between Keynton and Edgehill, by His Majesty's Army and That of the Rebels*.
271 Luke, *Journal of Sir Samuel Luke*, pp.10 and 13.
272 Wroughton, *An Unhappy Civil War*, p.54.

Souldiers to serve them.'²⁷³ This is perhaps corroborated by Samuel Luke's claim that the Royalists 'compelled them to take upp armes for the King and wounded and beate them that would not.'²⁷⁴ Whereas the Royalists claimed the opposite, that 'at least 1000 of the garrison soldiers very willingly' chose to turn their coats, and Fiennes's own officers testified that these defections were so numerous because Fiennes had so badly mishandled both the siege and the surrender of the city.²⁷⁵

Initially their new comrades and officers could be suspicious of such recruits, doubting that their loyalties had truly or completely changed – possibly as a reflection of the nature of their recruitment (if it was different to their own). A company of veteran volunteers, even one with several pressed men in their ranks, might be wary of serving alongside those who had until recently been their enemies. The first 'batch' of Parliamentarian-turned-Royalist soldiers from Cirencester was dispersed amongst Reading's garrison companies by Rupert in exchange for soldiers out of the garrison. The Governor of Reading was distinctly unenthusiastic about his new soldiers, writing to the King that 'hee needed not to have sent him more enymies for hee had enowe [enough] already'.²⁷⁶ What is also clear, however, is that such men could rapidly gain acceptance amongst their new comrades if they showed themselves willing to fight well.²⁷⁷ How compulsory, or not, these defections were in each case remains uncertain, although the experience of recently surrendered troops were undoubtedly terrifying for the men. The Earl of Essex's infantry which surrendered at Lostwithiel in 1644 was subjected to extensive harassment and violence as they marched past the Royalist ranks, with threats called at them about what might befall them if they did not enlist with the victorious Royalists.²⁷⁸ It is not surprising then that captured soldiers claimed to have been unwillingly recruited in an attempt to gain better treatment and perhaps gain the offer of enlistment by their captors. Following the successful defence of Hull by Parliamentarian forces in October 1643, amongst the 140 Royalist soldiers captured through the course of the siege some claimed that they were 'array'd [i.e. pressed] men' and were subsequently allowed to enlist with the garrison.²⁷⁹

---

273 Nathaniel Fiennes, *A Relation Made in the House of Commons by Col. Nathaniel Fiennes Concerning the Surrender of the City and Castle of Bristoll, August 5. 1643...* (London: 1643), p.11.
274 Luke, *Journal of Sir Samuel Luke*, p.130.
275 Samuel Seyer, *Memoirs Historical and Topographical of Bristol and its Neighbourhood, from the Earliest Period Down to the Present Time* (Bristol: J. M. Gutch, 1823), II, pp.411–413; Lynch, *For King & Parliament: Bristol in the Civil Wars*, p.105.
276 Luke, *Journal of Sir Samuel Luke*, p.13.
277 Hopper, *Turncoats & Renegadoes*, p.86.
278 Hopper, *Turncoats & Renegadoes*, p.86.
279 *Hulls Managing of the Kingdoms Cause: Or A brief Historicall Relation Of The Severall Plots and Attempts Against Kingston upon Hull...* (London, 1644), p.24.

Men might also attempt to desert if they perceived that the circumstances had changed to allow it. Following the Cessation of Arms in Ireland in September 1643, English troops who had been fighting the Irish Confederate forces were recalled to England to serve the King. On several occasions these veterans took the opportunity to defect to Parliamentarian forces. Following the Royalist defeat at Nantwich on 25 January 1644, perhaps 1,500 of 'the Com'on sorte' were captured by Parliamentarian forces and afterwards 'many of theim took up Armes'.[280] It seems that amongst these turncoats was an almost complete company of 'firelocks' who went on to serve extensively with Parliamentarian forces under Sir William Brereton. Brereton appears to have mounted them, subsequently describing them as 'choice dragoons – firelocks which were soldiers in Ireland largely mounted.'[281] Lord Byron, commanding the Royalist forces in Cheshire, where many of these troops fought and subsequently turned their coats, felt they were all infected with disloyalty 'Poisoned by the ill-affected people here'.[282] He recommended that only native Irish troops be brought over claiming 'I would wish they were rather Irish than English; for the English we have already are very mutinous.'[283] Byron seemed to believe that the Irish would fight harder and not defect as the Catholic Irish soldiers believed that they would receive no quarter from Parliamentarian forces. Parliamentarian officers took advantage of this low morale amongst the English veterans in England by encouraging desertions with promises of settlement of back pay for any officer that brought his men over to join Parliamentarian forces.[284]

As the First Civil War drew to a close, particularly following their victories during the Naseby campaign in 1645, the New Model Army took many defeated former Royalist troops into Parliamentarian service. Of the 2,000 released prisoners taken at the Battle of Langport in July 1645, 800 of them enlisted in the New Model Army. At the surrender of the castle and town of Bridgwater later that month another 500 Royalist prisoners from the surrendered garrison joined the New Model.[285] Royalist veterans found their way into Parliamentarian service in less direct manner as well. As mentioned earlier, many former Royalist soldiers attempting to return home had the misfortune to be selected for the press, either

---

280 Thomas Malbon (J. Hall ed.), *Memorials of the Civil War in Cheshire and the Adjacent Counties*, (Record Society of Lancashire and Cheshire, 1889), pp.114–115.
281 Robert Dore (ed.) *The Letter Books of Sir William Brereton. vol. 1* (Gloucester: Lancashire and Cheshire Record Society, Vol. 123, 1984), p.610., also listed under Captain Holt's firelocks in a list of Cheshire forces, p.325.
282 Lowe, 'The Campaign of the Irish Royalist Army in Cheshire, November 1643–January 1644', pp.70–73.
283 Carte, *A Collection of Original Letters and Papers*, I, p.39.
284 Lowe, 'The Campaign of the Irish Royalist Army in Cheshire, November 1643–January 1644', pp.53–55.
285 BL Add. MS 18979, f.204.

as strangers passing through a parish or from being selected for impressment after they had returned home. In Yorkshire during 1646 it appears Scottish regiments were also recruiting locally and to such an extent that worried commanders called for an investigation into the number of former Royalists serving in the army. At least one Scottish cavalry regiment had to be disbanded as a consequence of this investigation, due to the number of former Royalists serving as troopers within the ranks.[286]

The recruitment of former enemies into the ranks had a further advantage beyond simply re-filling the ranks of their regiments which had been thinned from disease, battle, or desertion. It also prevented these veteran troops from being re-enlisted amongst the dwindling ranks of their enemy, for whom large numbers of such experienced troops were often irreplaceable. Furthermore, as knowledge of Royalist military defeats and defections to Parliament became more widespread this in turn would have encouraged further defections. According to Gentles, the recruitment of former Royalists to the New Model Army was so widely known that it was often used to declaim against the army by those factions within Parliament who were either opposed to the costs of the army itself, or to particular government policies around it.[287] However, the New Model Army's commander, Sir Thomas Fairfax, had very few concerns about these recruits himself and seems to have preferred gaining veteran and motivated troops in this manner compared to relying on the recruits drawn from the increasingly inefficient press system, upon which his army was at least nominally supposed to rely. Given the problems he had relying on the press discussed above, this is perhaps understandable. Fairfax claimed that 'The best common soldiers he had' were former Royalist troops whose previous commanders 'had made them good soldiers'.[288] However, by July 1647 the recruitment of former Royalists had become so politically contentious amongst the civilian authorities within Parliament that Fairfax had to order that all former Royalists recruited in that year 'since the Muster preceding the last Muster' were to be discharged ordering his officers to 'expunge the Names of all such Cavaliers out of the Muster Rolls as they shall have put out of their Troops or Companies.'[289]

---

286 LJ, VIII, 2 June, English Commissioners Paper to the Scots Committee, for Removal of all Englishmen that have served the Enemy, and not conformed to the Ordinances of Parliament, out of the Scots Army, pp.348–349; LJ, VIII, p.366, 8 June, Order of the Scots Committee, for discharging those from their Army against whom there is just Cause of Complaint.
287 Gentles, *The New Model Army in England, Ireland and Scotland*, p.153.
288 Philip Warwick, *Memoires of the Reign of King Charles I* (London, 1702), p.305.
289 John Rushworth (ed.), *Historical Collections of Private Passages of State: Vol. 6, 1645–47* (London, 1722), see 'The Order of the General for expunging Cavaliers out of the Muster Rolls 21st July 1647', p.639; Firth, *Cromwell's Army*, p.37.

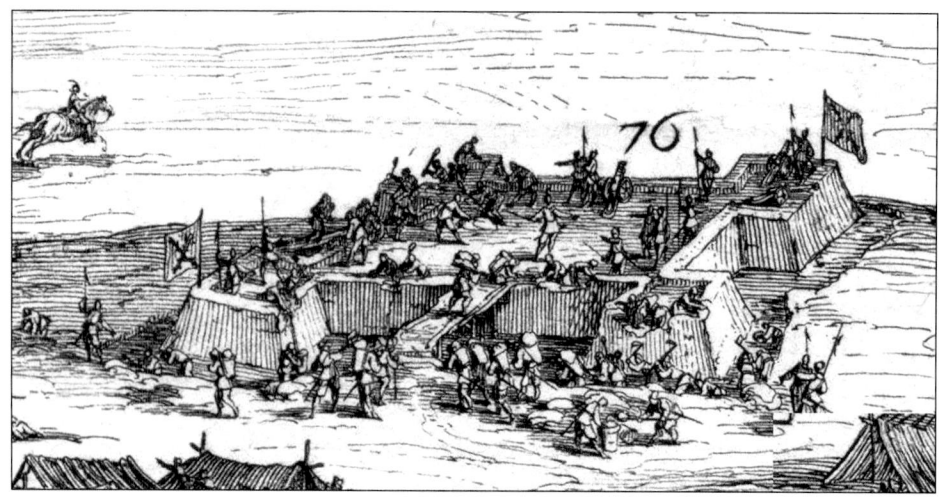

Spanish field fortifications during the siege of Breda 1624-1625. Jacques Callot, 1628 (Rijksmuseum)

Not all former Royalists who enlisted with Parliament had found their way into the New Model Army. Large numbers of former Royalist soldiers were sent to Ireland for service with Protestant forces there rather than being incorporated into the New Model. This was seen as not only a way of getting Royalist veterans away from England, where they might otherwise find their way back into Royalist service, but as a useful tool for reinforcing the Protestant forces in Ireland with experienced soldiers who had little recourse to oppose their deployment to an unpopular posting. There were concerns that sending former Royalists to serve as part of Parliamentarian forces in Ireland might lead to their defection back to the Royalist forces still active there. This was further exacerbated by reports of soldiers' claims that 'they have served [the Royalists], and say they will do so again.'[290] In some instances, such as the recruits amongst Colonel Tothill's Parliamentarian regiment, men were required to take an oath of loyalty in an attempt to counter such a possibility.[291]

Deserters of one army could be encountered by the opposing side without the latter seeking to enlist them. On the battlefield, routing enemy soldiers could often simply be relieved of their goods. Captain Edward Kightley, a Parliamentarian troop captain, wrote of his encounter with routing Royalist soldiers at the Battle of Edgehill, 'I tooke away about tenne or twelve horse, swords, and armour, I could

290 Quoted in Hopper, *Turncoats & Renegadoes*, p.94.
291 Hopper, *Turncoats & Renegadoes*, p.94.

have killed 40 of the enemy, I let them passe disarming them, and giving the spoile to my Troopers.'[292] Enemy deserters might be recruited by the receiving forces, but on other occasions might simply be sent on their way with oaths not to take up arms again. Such was the case at Aylesbury in 1646, when a Royalist officer demanded the return of deserters from his own forces who had fled to the Parliamentarian garrison in the town. The Governor of Aylesbury, Thomas Mulstrode, replied that he had already sent the Royalist deserters on to their own homes adding that 'This garrison is not suffered to be a receptacle for your fugitives.'[293]

As already noted, commanders attempted to prevent desertion by the threat of harsh penalties, including death, if a man was caught deserting or straggling.[294] Desertion to the enemy seems to have warranted harsher treatment than simply deserting military service, and certainly harsher than straggling. As Hopper states, such punishments were not always applied in practice, with the circumstances of the man who turned his coat and the wider circumstances surrounding his capture often taken under consideration.[295] The death penalty against defectors was generally applied only when the identity of the turncoat and his previous service was clear and his death would, it was believed, serve as exemplary punishment to his erstwhile comrades. The Earl of Essex captured several of his former soldiers amongst the Reading garrison after it surrendered; these men were tried by court-martial and hanged.[296] Prince Rupert likewise had a dozen Parliamentarian prisoners hanged when it was clear they had previously served in the Royalist army.[297] Thomas Fairfax, very early in the New Model Army's existence and determined to emphasise the importance of discipline, ordered a deserter hanged at Wallop in May 1645. The gallows were very deliberately chosen: the deserter and one other criminal 'were executed upon a Tree, at Wallop, in the way of the Armies march, *in terrorem*' as a clear reminder on the punishment to such behaviour.[298]

Conclusion

The various methods of recruiting during the British Civil Wars were each only partially successful, with problems attending all methods applied to maintain an

---

292 Kightley, *A full and true relation of the great battle fought between the Kings army, and His Excellency, the Earle of Essex, upon the 23. of October* (London, 1642), p.4.
293 Quoted in Donagan, *War in England*, p.302.
294 *Laws and Ordinances of Warre, Established for the Better Conduct Of The Army, By His Excellency the Earl of Essex, Lord Generall...* (London: 1643).
295 Hopper, *Turncoats & Renegadoes*, p.179.
296 Clarendon, *The History of the Rebellion and Civil Wars in England*, IV, p.42.
297 Donagan, *War in England*, p.276.
298 Sprigg, *Anglia Rediviva*, p.15.

army in the field. Even the system so efficiently used in Scotland was unable to keep Scottish regiments operating outside of their home country at full strength, forcing the regimental commanders to recruit local English replacements. The need for local manpower on campaign appears to have even affected the New Model Army in Ireland, where, according to James Scott Wheeler, even though Cromwell 'demonstrated a mastery of the logistical aspects of warfare' the army he commanded still required local recruits, including Catholics, to maintain its strength in the field.[299] Both of these examples challenge the broad historical assumptions we have on the period, with the idea of a 'Godly' army recruiting whatever warm bodies they could get their hands on in order to remain operational, transcending concepts of both religion and ethnicity. These flawed recruitment systems worked best when used in conjunction with one another, as regiments raised by 'beat of drum' would be later reinforced by impressed soldiers, and then by both from recruiting locally and amongst their defeated enemies.

What is clear, and perhaps most important, is that none of these recruitment methods could have worked without the active participation of pre-existing local civilian structures. Again, the pattern which was seen elsewhere above emerges, that the military was extremely reliant on active civilian engagement in order to operate a functioning method of supplying its forces, this time with manpower. Whether it was the local parish constable selecting the men to be pressed, the official assisting in the creation of recruitment lists, or of local elites providing their tacit support in encouraging local volunteers, the military remained heavily dependent on its relationships with local civilians, even as it took some of them off to war. Even recruitment of deserters or the enlistment of prisoners would not have been possible if the soldiers had not first been enlisted with the opposing army through other forms of recruitment. This appears to have been recognised by the military, where the ideal pressed recruit was someone who both the parish could spare, and the army could make use of. However, increasing and persistent demands for more manpower to replace those lost to battle, ill-health, desertion, or other forces, meant that the numbers of men required by press far exceeded the pool of those a parish could do without, or felt that it could. In the case of the English Civil War, this pool may have already been partially drained by the various rounds of impressment in the Bishops' Wars, and further impacted by the volunteer enlistments of men to combat the Irish rebellion, and those at the outbreak of civil war in 1642 having already been enticed to serve by the beating of the drums.

---

299 Wheeler, *Cromwell in Ireland*, p.3.

4

Provisioning

Providing the men of the armies with the requisite food, drink, shelter, and clothing necessary to maintain them in the field will be the focus of this chapter. It may seem strange to not cover weapons or mounts, with the focus on this work being the operational realities of provision. However, the majority of a soldier's time was not spent fighting, and he still needed to be fed, clothed, and sheltered every day. Arms and horses have been covered by other studies as has the provision of more martial supplies, so rather than repeat work by others this chapter will focus on the operational realities of supplying armies in the field instead of how they were equipped.

Supplying an army with the essentials of food, clothing, and shelter was as fundamental to the operational capabilities of that force at any strategic or tactical level as their weaponry. If the army lacked either sufficient clothing or suitable shelter the men could suffer from exposure, illness, and low morale. Without food and drink the army would simply fall apart, and the previously effective force of now starving soldiers would have either deserted or mutinied. Yet this element of supply is one of the least studied and least understood of early modern armies. This gap in knowledge is perhaps understandable as at a basic level the study of how soldiers were supplied with their food, drink, and shelter is challenging due to limited surviving source material. Most of that which has survived tends to originate from civilians detailing the costs and losses of feeding unwelcome soldiers who had been imposed on their household in the system of free quarter. This 'quartering', where soldiers were divided amongst civilian households and fed by the civilians they were billeted with, will be considered in detail later. Here it is worth noting that 'free quarter' simply referred to the fact the soldiers concerned were not reimbursing the civilians immediately for the shelter and sustenance the soldiers received while quartered. Many documents detailing such lack of payment survive in the National Archives as part of the SP28, known as the Commonwealth Exchequer Papers, particularly the surviving accounts of The

Committee for Taking the Accounts of the Kingdom. However, in such a context the soldiers themselves are most often cast as intruders and plunderers, guilty of exploiting and abusing civilians and their property, rather than as recipients of the system of quartering themselves. Even those few works by historians which focus specifically on the quartering of troops on civilians continue to focus more on these negative impacts felt by civilians rather than why, or how, the system of quartering was implemented or its efficiency for the army as a whole and the soldiers specifically.[1]

Despite the importance of provisions to a soldier's physical capabilities, his morale, and his loyalties, there has been little work done on how the armies during the Civil Wars were provisioned. The exceptions to this are the historians whose work details the New Model Army, the records of which tend to be more substantial than other forces. However, even historians of the New Model Army such as Ian Gentles pay provision short thrift – in the two pages he dedicated to the feeding of the New Model Army over a period of eight years, he summarised simply that the army 'fundamentally lived off the countryside where it was located'.[2] Charles Firth, and later Henry Reece, both dedicate parts of their separate studies of the New Model to its use of free quarter as a method of supply. In the case of Firth, he argued that it was the only way the army could remain functioning as a cohesive force and thus focused on how the New Model Army's 'Commissariat', those officers in the army responsible for provisioning the troops, used free quarter to support the soldiers.[3] Reece studied the political and social ramifications of free quartering. This includes the attempts made to remove the New Model Army from its reliance on free quarter as the force transitioned into an army of occupation (in Scotland and Ireland) and permanent standing (in England and Wales) in the years following the Civil Wars.[4] As we shall see, this is partly true but not completely so. It misses opportunities for considering the operational realities that generals of the period had to contend with, and the complexity of interactions between soldiers and civilians which are so often lost to history. As discussed in previous chapters, this dearth of detailed study is not limited to provisions and simply follows the patterns in existing scholarship with a focus away from aspects of supply towards topics considered either more 'exciting' or with a greater weight

---

1   Anne Oestmann, 'Billeting in England During the Reign of Charles I, 1625–1649: The Case of Tickhill/Yorkshire', *Arbeitskreis Militär und Gesellschaft in der Frühen Neuzeit e.V.*, vol. 10, no.1 (2006), pp.74–90.
2   Gentles, *The New Model Army in England, Ireland and Scotland*, pp.45–47.
3   Firth, *Cromwell's Army*, particularly chapter nine.
4   Henry Reece, *The Army in Cromwellian England, 1649–1660* (Oxford University Press, 2013), pp.98–115.

of existing historiography and fuller sources behind them, such as battles or political studies.

This shortfall of research is not repeated in the study of European early modern armies where there has been significant work on military food supply in other conflicts, revealing the importance of studying supply. Geoffrey Parker's *The Army of Flanders and the Spanish Road, 1567–1659* takes a detailed look at how the Army of Flanders fed its soldiers.[5] While Parker does discuss the feeding of the army operating in The Netherlands, his focus is on the supply of food for the *tercios* as they marched along the Spanish Road, the trade route and military highway which linked the Spanish Netherlands with the wider Spanish Empire in Italy and the Mediterranean. Parker concludes that the Spanish authorities were deeply involved in organising markets at regular intervals along the road from whom the marching *tercios* could purchase the victuals that they needed. Parker's study of provisions for the Army of Flanders revealed the complex interconnectivity and successful operation of early modern Spain's diplomatic arrangements, bureaucratic apparatus, and military administration. This method of providing food for the soldiers to pay for themselves out of their wages was a familiar situation across Europe during the early modern period. John Lynn's work on France in the later seventeenth century, with regard to army provisions, studies the French method of establishing regional and local magazines for use by both garrisons and the marching armies. Lynn argues that without the use of this magazine system the French army could not have grown to the huge size it did, numbering 400,000 soldiers at its highest during the early modern period.[6] The common thread of food supply for early modern warfare in Europe was the lack of daily rations issued by the army's governing authority at the authority's own expense. Soldiers were instead expected to buy their food themselves. Even when the authorities supplied food directly out of magazines, the soldiers' pay would be subsequently docked to cover the costs, usually above the value of the food to reflect attendant costs of storage and transportation. This represented the ideal more than the reality as on occasion, soldiers had to make do with only 'two pound of bread' to last them all week.[7]

It may be worthwhile to quickly add a few definitions. Seventeenth century soldiers referred to their food and drink interchangeably as victuals (or vittles), entertainment, proviant, and other less common terms. There is no consistency in the use of these terms across contemporary accounts and sources. Such accounts

---

5 Parker, *The Army of Flanders and the Spanish Road*, Parker's first edition was in 1972.
6 John Lynn, 'Food, Funds, and Fortresses: Resource Mobilization and Positional Warfare in the Campaigns of Louis XIV', in John Lynn, *Feeding Mars*, pp.137–160.
7 Turner, *Pallas Armata*, p.201.

use the term quarter to refer solely to lodgings, or to lodgings which also provided food and drink. In this chapter, and outside of quoted text, I have used the word 'victuals' as a general term for the combined provision of food and drink. Billeting is used for the imposition of soldiers on civilian households for shelter and when discussing billeting soldiers being fed the contemporary term quartering or quarter is used.

The range of sources available for a study concerned with the operational supply of provisions is again limited. As mentioned above, surviving accounts exist in SP28 but these focus almost entirely on the costs associated with Parliament's war effort. There is no single useful source suitable to tackle this question as the ephemeral nature of receipts and promissory notes means that they rarely survive in great numbers. Without such evidence in sufficient quantity, it is impossible to compile datasets of documents for study. Sources detailing the methods of provision and the associated realities are instead drawn from a range including contemporary military publications, letters from military officers, government reports and orders from central authorities, and local parish accounts. Some of the most important of these local records come from the surviving accounts of parish constables. When resources were drawn from their parish for military use, whether food, money, fodder, or other goods, the local constable often entered these into their account books. As such, surviving examples of these accounts can provide insight into the forms and types of resource drawn from localities for military use. However, the surviving accounts are incomplete with very few covering more than a brief period pertaining to their own small geographical area and so they provide limited insight into military provisioning systems without the context of other sources.[8]

Therefore, in order to understand how military provisioning systems of the period were organised a wide range of sources are necessary to link the realities of provisions, food, and clothing of the period, to the planning of the military and governments. Fortunately, there have been extensive studies on how seventeenth century people stored and prepared their food. One of the most useful of these, for the purpose of contextualising soldiers' food, is *The Soldier's Life in the English Civil War* by Stuart Peachey.[9] Based on surviving contemporary journals, recipes, and guides to housekeeping and farming, as well as extensive experimental archaeology, this work provides an insight into the foods available to both contemporary civilians and to soldiers in garrisons and on campaign.

---

8   For an overview on the office of these parish constables see Joan Kent, 'The English Village Constable, 1580–1642: The Nature and Dilemmas of the Office', pp.26–49.
9   Stuart Peachey, *The Soldier's Life in the English Civil War: Organisation, Food, Clothing, Weapons, and Combat* (Bristol: Stuart Press, 2016).

While Peachey's work is heavily focused on England, many of the findings on food storage and preparation would hold true for most of the British Isles, although some regional differences in diet would be expected. It is very possible that much, if not most, of the poor behaviour reported of soldiers was at least partly a result of the circumstances that quartering (free or not) placed upon the soldiers, with quartering itself being a necessary evil used to keep troops in the field.

The Realities of Provisioning

The ideal arrangements for provisioning an army in the field as laid out by contemporary military manuals relied heavily on two officers – the quartermaster and the commissary of victuals. Ideally the role of quartermaster was filled by experienced officers, who, according to Sir James Turner, needed to 'be men of metal, who have learned some Arithmetick, and have some skill of Castrametation [the making or laying out of a military camp]'.[10] Most regiments had only a single quartermaster, although troops of cavalry might have one each according to Henry Hexham's *Principles of the Art Military*.[11] The quartermaster was responsible for dispersing any victuals received 'and divide it proportionably out' across the regiment.[12] He was also responsible for assigning quarters to the different regimental companies, and if necessary 'to go before' the regiment to locate and identify such locations. If the regiment was marching with part of an army, the regimental quartermaster received such locations 'as the General Quarter-master assigns to him, and divide them proportionably to the Regiment.'[13] The victuals and other provisions the quartermaster might receive would likely come from the army's commissary of victuals, who was responsible for locating and dispersing supplies the army gained to the various regiments. During this period the title 'commissary' appears to have indicated an officer subordinated to a particular position. Henry Hexham describes the office of Commissary-General of the Victuals in his work on the Dutch army, while in the New Model Army Henry Ireton was Commissary-General of Horse, a senior general of horse below the Lieutenant-General of Horse, but with no responsibility towards victualling.[14]

---

10   Turner, *Pallas Armata*, p.224.
11   Henry Hexham, *The First Part of the Principles of the Art Military Practiced in the Warres of the United Netherlands* (Delft, The Netherlands, 1642), p.2.
12   Turner, *Pallas Armata*, p.223.
13   Turner, *Pallas Armata*, p.224.
14   Henry Hexham, *The Second Part of the Principles of Art Military, Practised in the Warres of the United Provinces Consisting of the Severall Formes of Battels* (Delft, The Netherlands, 1642), p.3.

Hexham describes the responsibility of the Commissary-General of the Victuals as:

> Wheresoever the Army shall land, march, or lodge, all the victuals found in such places, shall be seized upon by him, and a proportion set out by him for the present use of the Troupes, there quartered, and the rest reserved as part of the generall store and Magazine of victuals, and to that end, he himselfe shall go, or send an under officer, or the clarke to attend the Lord Marshall, or Quarter master generall, when he goes to view and appoint him his quarter.[15]

However, the commissary of victuals in early modern armies, particularly in the British Civil Wars, does not seem to have held extensive responsibility for the hundreds of wagons and teams necessary to supply an army with large amounts of prepared food. The obvious question which follows is 'if not the commissary of victuals, then who?' As far as we can tell it was no one in particular, as there was simply no large pool of organised wagons which followed the army for the sole purpose of carrying provisions. Instead, the commissary of victuals appears to have been more of an administrative role with only a small staff and very few wagons at most. These were responsible for the organisation of gathering and distributing whatever victuals and supplies the army encountered each day, often supplemented instead by locally acquired transport. It was likely that foragers, troops who ranged out from the main marching body to locate nearby supplies, would officially report to these commissary officers. Edward Orpin, Commissary for the Victuals to the New Model Army, had only two deputies and two clerks according to surviving pay warrants, and with no mention of drivers.[16] Furthermore, unless he inherited substantial numbers of wagons and teams from the trains of the armies which merged into the New Model, of which there is no evidence, he does not appear to have had a large number of wagons under his command and the receipts for new wagons for the New Model Army do not suggest any.[17]

Supplying fresh (or even reasonably edible) food to an army in the field during the early modern period, regularly and in sufficient quantities to be useful, was an almost insurmountable problem. This was not simply due to monetary issues or unwillingness on the part of general officers to ensure that their men were properly cared for. The need to properly provision their troops was a constant concern for early modern generals as unfed troops were prone to desertion either

---

15 Hexham, *The Second Part of the Principles of Art Military*, p.3.
16 TNA SP 28/19, f.1, Pay Warrant date 25 April 1645.
17 Mungeam, 'Contracts for the Supply of Equipment', p.114.

permanently or through slipping away to forage for food for themselves rather than starve. Poorly fed men were also more susceptible to disease or straggling through exhaustion. As we saw in the previous chapter on recruitment, hunger, disease, desertion, and straggling were key concerns for military officers of the period. While the science of the human immune system and minimum calorie requirements were not understood to the same degree as it is today, generals of the time were very well aware that underfed men were often sickly and also noted that men on a repetitive diet could swiftly become ill. The Earl of Cork commented that nothing but barrelled biscuit, butter, and salt beef to eat and only water to drink made for 'a rich churchyard and weak garrison'.[18] The challenge for generals during the British Civil Wars was overcoming fundamental issues in supplying food to their forces. As we have seen in earlier chapters, the armies on all sides of the conflicts suffered to varying degrees with difficulties in maintaining and running an effective and reliable transport infrastructure. These limitations on the transportation capabilities of armies impacted the ability to provision soldiers in the field.

With regard to food, the amount (at least on paper) required to feed a soldier in the Civil Wars was 2lbs of bread and 1lb of meat a day, although it was accepted that the latter could be substituted for 1lb of cheese. According to Sir James Turner, 'The Ordinary allowance of a Soldier in the field, is daily two pound of bread, one pound of Flesh, or in lieu of it, one pound of Cheese, one pottle of Wine, or in lieu of it, two pottles of Beer'.[19] General George Monck recorded in January 1657 that the allowance for the New Model Army soldiers in Scotland was for 'each man 2lb of bread and a quarter of a pound of cheese per diem'.[20] Francis Markham, a veteran of several wars and who saw service in Dutch, English, and German armies, noted how daily rations were flexible and 'must be rated according to the plenty of the store and the prizes [prices] by which they are attained'.[21] In June 1644, following concerns that soldiers in the garrison at Oxford were not being fed properly, an order was issued that 'bread and Cheese according to the usuall proporcon [proportion] of one pound in bread and half a pound in Cheese to each man'.[22] The Mayor of Oxford was directed to 'use his utmost endeavuor and diligence in assisting' the military officers assigned to this task.[23] This last example is roughly half the recommended allowances listed above and is likely due to the men being

---

18 Henry Townsend (ed.), *The Life and Letters of the Great Earl of Cork* (New York: E.R. Dutton, 1904), p.434; Ryder, *An English Army for Ireland*, p.26.
19 Turner, *Pallas Armata*, p.201.
20 General Monck's Order Book 15 January, 1656/57 quoted in Firth, *Cromwell's Army*, p.227.
21 Markham, *Five Decades of Epistles of Warre*, p.103.
22 Toynbee, *The Papers of Captain Henry Stevens*, p.25.
23 Toynbee, *The Papers of Captain Henry Stevens*, p.26.

in a garrison which, only days before, had been under siege by Parliamentarian forces for over a week. A longer siege could lead to even greater privation. On 28 April 1646, the Royalist garrison of Lichfield, which had been besieged since March (and would surrender on terms in July), was reported by one deserter to have been on a daily allowance of 'half a pound of bread and half a pound of cheese a day or half a pound of beef'.[24] Their daily allotment of drink was a single pint of beer and several of the soldiers supplemented their allowance with horseflesh from those horses which had died for want of feed.[25] Some of the defenders claimed this was too little with 'six men imprisoned for asking for provision' and at least one man deserting to the besiegers 'by reason of the scarcity of victuals'.[26]

Returning to the challenges of supplying an army with food, a foot regiment of 1,000 men required, theoretically, the best part of a ton of bread (2,000lbs), and half a ton (1,000lbs) of either meat or cheese every day. Even with the large wagons in the South-East of England with their teams of six horses, this daily ration would require a full wagon load for the food alone every two days, leaving aside the drink and the weight and bulk of the sacks and barrels in which the food was transported. If operating in areas where these vehicles were uncommon, where the army would be dependent on packhorse or carts, the daily allowance for such a single full strength regiment would require daily deliveries by at least one, maybe two carts, or perhaps more than a dozen packhorses. The realities of sourcing, supplying, and operating such a huge number of vehicles and beasts at daily dispatch intervals and along uncertain routes, even in secure areas without fear of weather or enemy patrols, and to the precise current location of the particular regiment was extremely difficult.

The emphasis on bread and meat (or cheese) in the daily allowance is because these were the commonplace and readily available foods of the period capable of remaining edible without spoiling for some time (although this did vary). Other food types could travel well over long distances, but these tended to be extensively preserved such as salted meat. Heavily preserved salted meat required considerable preparation time and effort after delivery to be put into a consumable condition. Bread, along with cheese and freshly cooked meat, could be easily transported and needed little in the way of preparation by the soldiers when they received it. Francis Markham noted that 'the victuals which is most easie for carriage, and

---

24 Ian Atherton and Ivor Carr (eds) *The Civil War in Staffordshire in the Spring of 1646: Sir William Brereton's Letter Book, April–May 1646* (Staffordshire Record Society, Collections for a History of Staffordshire, 4th series, vol. 21, 2007), pp.178, 190; Hutton, *The Royalist War Effort 1642–1646*, pp.202–203.
25 Atherton and Carr, *Sir William Brereton's Letter Book, April–May 1646*, p.190.
26 Atherton and Carr, *Sir William Brereton's Letter Book, April–May 1646*, p.190.

the longest lasting, as Bisket, Beefe ready boyld, cheese, or the like.'[27] Biscuit was a hard, dense, and small loaf which could be stored for lengthy periods of time such that it could safely be kept in barrels and stockpiled.[28] Without extensive, reliable, and efficient means of delivering food to troops daily over distance and across a wide and varied theatre of operations, generals were often forced to rely on systems where troops could source their food as close as possible to where they were located.

Another element which would have affected the amounts of food available for soldiers in the area would have been large numbers of supernumeraries accompanying the soldiers on campaign. Most often referred to as camp followers, for any large army in the field, they were the non-military following of an army and certainly added to the number of people needing to be fed. Although the numbers are impossible to ascertain in the context of the British Civil Wars, we know that almost all contemporary armies in Europe had large numbers of non-combatants following an army for familial or business reasons. According to Parker, the Army of Flanders and other European forces acknowledged this practice simply by referring to the numbers of 'mouths' to be fed rather than the number of soldiers.[29] We know that camp followers accompanied at least some of the armies of the British Civil Wars, particularly the Royalist army at Naseby where women accompanying the Royalist army were attacked and mutilated by Parliamentarian cavalry.[30] Unfortunately, numbers of camp followers for particular armies in the Civil Wars cannot be ascertained, particularly as even the numbers of fighting men themselves are often only estimates. If contemporary European experience was any indicator, there could have been a substantial number of these camp followers on campaign. However, no source that I have identified, military or civilian, discusses the necessity of feeding such non-combatants during the Civil Wars, leading us to assume that where they accompanied an army they had to either fend for themselves or share in the soldiers' provisions. Camp followers apparently increased in number following the British Civil Wars when the victorious New Model Army was redirected as an army of occupation, particularly in Scotland. According to Keith Roberts, the more permanent nature of the occupation garrisons in Scotland in the 1650s allowed for the establishment of more European-style semi-permanent communities of soldiers' families, sutlers and other camp followers.[31] Curiously, the numbers of receipts or complaints from

---

27 Markham, *Five Decades of Epistles of Warre*, p.103.
28 Peachey, *The Soldier's Life in the English Civil War*, pp.150–151.
29 Parker, *The Army of Flanders and the Spanish Road*, p.79.
30 Mark Stoyle, 'The Road to Farndon Field: Explaining the Massacre of the Royalist Women at Naseby', *The English Historical Review*, vol. 123, no.503 (2008), pp.895–923.
31 Roberts, *Cromwell's War Machine: The New Model Army, 1645–1660*, pp.271–272.

the English Civil Wars regarding free quarter, or plundering by soldiers, do not mention camp followers as far as I have seen. If this is for the obvious reason that only soldiers were often encountered and not camp followers, then taken with the lack of other evidence, I would suggest that the numbers of camp followers in campaigning armies of the Civil Wars, if they did travel with other armies and forces like the unfortunate women at Naseby, were likely substantially smaller in number, in both absolute and proportional terms, than those accompanying many contemporary European forces.

Perhaps the most important implement in providing for the needs of the soldiers in the British Civil Wars, was the common knapsack. It was seen as one of the most basic items of equipment for a soldier, and even before a soldier was issued with his weaponry or received training he was often issued with a knapsack (or snapsack). It was stipulated by King Charles to the Lord Lieutenants in February 1639 that newly recruited English soldiers 'be provided with knapsacks at the charge of the county.'[32] For the English soldiers recruited in 1640, it seems the Council forgot to order that recruits from Rutland and Leicester were to have them, but the Earl of Huntingdon and his son Ferdinando, the Lord Lieutenants of Rutland and Leicester, 'presumed to do one thing of ourselves which we think you did not command us, which was to furnish them with knapsacks.'[33] Parliamentarian soldiers in September of 1642 seized three donkeys 'which they loaded with their knapsacks'.[34] The importance of issuing soldiers with knapsacks continued throughout the British Civil Wars.

Thomas Barnes was paid to transport '180 blew coates and 180 snapsacks' to St Albans.[35] As Barnes was also conducting '5 souldyers to the Committee' at the same time, these were possibly for an issue to newly pressed men.[36] In 1646, the regiment of Colonel Wetton was issued 'clothes, arms, knapsacks, &c. from the store'.[37] In September 1645, Michaell Raynor was contracted to provide '5000 snapsacks att 9d ye piece' and in December that year Raph Ferbanke was contracted to provide a further '3000 Snapsacks large & of good leather at 8s a dozen'[38] Made from leather or other sturdy materials, they were the method by which a soldier carried his personal effects, and more importantly, any food he had.

32 CSPD 1638–1639, pp.513–514, Feb, the King to the Lords Lieutenants.
33 *CSPD 1640–1641*, p.340, June 24, Henry Earl of Huntingdon and Ferdinando Lord Hastings to the Council.
34 *CSPD 1641–1643*, p.384, Sept. 3 [1642], Nehemiah Wharton to George Willingham.
35 TNA SP 28/231, Thomas Barnes bill re carrying coats [undated].
36 TNA SP 28/231, Thomas Barnes bill re carrying coats [undated].
37 *CSPI 1633–1647*, p.512, 1646. James Cook, the Commissary at Liverpool.
38 Mungeam, 'Contracts for the Supply of Equipment', pp.53–115 ff.9r, 87.

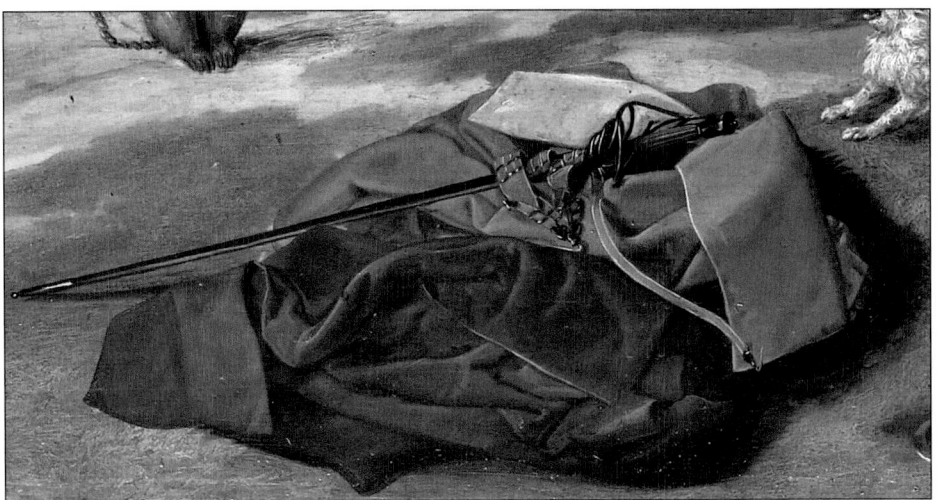

A pile of soldier's equipment including, at right, a snapsack (or knapsack – the tubular item with a shoulder strap). Detail from 'The Fête Champêtre', Dirck Hals c.1627. (Public domain, Rijksmuseum, Amsterdam)

The capacity of these bags were clearly substantial as soldiers aboard Hamilton's fleet in May 1639 had 'no means of victualling but what they carry in their knapsacks, with which they are fitted for 14 days.'[39] For the Parliamentarian forces at the Second Battle of Newbury in October 1644 'most of them had 3 dayes provision prepared by Command in his snapsack.'[40] Lord Inchiquin when planning for his campaign in the summer of 1644 wrote 'unto all the guarisons' nearby to secure supplies in order to 'furnish the souldiers knapsaks for the feild' and thereby managed to secure 'five daies provision'.[41] The knapsack served to act as a reserve for the soldier as early modern military transportation limitations and the vagaries of campaigning could not guarantee a daily supply of provision. In September 1644 the London Brigade of Trained Bands on campaign with the Earl of Essex's forces often 'could get no accommodation either for meat or drink, but what we brought with us in our snapsacks' and throughout the campaign they found themselves with 'no provision but what little every one had in his Snapsack'.[42] For soldiers in

39 *CSPD 1639*, p.210, May 22, Sir John Pennington to Captain George Carteret.
40 John Vicars, *Magnalia Dei Anglicana. Or, Englands Parliamentary Chronicle.* (London: 1646), p.58.
41 Carte, *The Life of James, Duke of Ormond*, VI, p.169.
42 Foster, *A True and Exact Relation of the Marchings of the Two Regiments of the Trained-Bands of the City of London*, pp.9–10

garrison, knapsacks seem to have been unnecessary, and only issued when out on patrol. Soldiers at Gloucester in December of 1645 were 'ordered to furnish themselves with knap-sacks and provisions' before marching out.[43] However useful the knapsack was, filling it was another matter and it appears to have been used as a reserve for when other methods of supply failed.

With regard to drink for soldiers during the wars, little is known. There are no records of canteens being issued for any of the armies of the period which begs the question of how men carried water with them on the march. It is likely that any drink for marching troops was instead carried within their knapsack in bottles. Soldiers on the march appear to have had to make do with whatever sources of water were available until they reached their quarters where they might find something like small beer to drink brewed locally.[44] Soldiers could always be assured of something to drink from civilian towns such as the 'Bread, Beer & Cheese' that Captain Jackson's and Captain Church's men received while in Uttoxeter.[45] The victuals that foragers secured to be sent down to the army included drink, with 'bottles of wine, and barrels of beer' such as those sent from London to the Earl of Essex's forces.[46] However, if there was not enough of this available locally or to carry over into the following day's march soldiers had to make do with what they could find at, or near, the roadside. In the autumn of 1642 Parliamentarian soldiers had to make do with drinking 'stinking water' while they marched.[47] On other days they were able to refresh themselves from 'pleasant springs of water'.[48] The provision of drink appears to have been provided though the same methods as food, and rarely provided separately.

Before discussing the methods of supplying food and clothing for the army, we need to look at the supply of fodder for the animals. There were always large numbers of animals pulling or carrying the supplies that the armies relied upon. Additionally, the armies themselves had huge numbers of horses, not just in the artillery and baggage trains, but also in the regiments and troops of cavalry and dragoons as well. The need to provide these animals with the correct diet was paramount. Cavalry horses trapped in the besieged close at Lichfield in 1646 rapidly succumbed to weakness and starvation, and this was almost certainly

---

43 Vicars, J., *Magnalia Dei Anglicana. Or, Englands Parliamentary Chronicle*, p.330.
44 CSPD 1641–1643, pp.379–380, Aug. 26 [1642], Nehemiah Wharton to George Willingham.
45 David Cooper, 'The English Civil War in Staffordshire: The Experience of Uttoxeter', *Staffordshire Studies*, Vol. 19 (2008), p.74.
46 Firth, *Cromwell's Army*, pp.215–216.
47 CSPD 1641–1643, p.284, Sept. 3, Nehemiah Wharton to George Willingham,.
48 CSPD 1641–1643, p.382, Aug. 30, Nehemiah Wharton to George Willingham.

due to a lack of hay or grass.[49] Horses can survive on such alone but working animals, such as cavalry mounts and draught horses, require a daily portion of cereals and other foods like oats to get the energy needed to perform their roles. According to Gavin Robinson's study of the supply of horses in the Civil War these were not small amounts, however, attempting to estimate how much a horse of the period needed, how much it was fed, and how much this cost is difficult.[50] Unfortunately, we have little surviving evidence of the securing of food supplies for horses. Much of the cereal crops such as barley or oats that a horse could eat so too could men, and it is likely that many records of the amount of such produce secured by the armies were at least partially for the horses' use. Throughout 1643 and 1644 the Nottinghamshire village of Upton was regularly required to provide passing cavalry troops and the garrison of Newark with horse feed which included supplies of oats, peas, and hay.[51] Likewise, throughout 1644 and 1645 the parish of Mavesyn Ridware in Staffordshire sent regular supplies of oats to the nearby garrison at Lichfield where Colonel Bagot's cavalry regiment was based.[52]

It is worth noting that in this period the charge of quartering a cavalry trooper was higher than quartering an infantryman to reflect the extra cost of feeding the former's mount. According to Charles Firth, the standard reimbursement cost of quartering troops was set at six pence a day for infantrymen, and eight pence for a cavalryman.[53] However, according to the constable accounts of the manor of Manchester, while the cost to the community of quartering infantrymen was indeed around six to eight pence each a day, a trooper and his horse cost the parish at least one shilling and six pence a day, sometimes more.[54] These parish constables' accounts match closely with the estimates from the Royalist Council of War who stated that 4,000 cavalry of the King's army quartered in the country around Oxford needed £2,100 a week, or more precisely, one shilling six pence per trooper per day.[55] These cavalry units had to be quartered in locations able to

---

49   Atherton and Carr, *Sir William Brereton's Letter Book, April–May 1646*, p.190.
50   Robinson, 'Horse Supply in the English Civil War, 1642–1646', pp.208–210.
51   Martyn Bennett (ed.), *A Nottinghamshire Village in War and Peace: The Accounts of the Constables of Upton, 1640–1666* (Nottingham: The Thoroton Society of Nottinghamshire, Vol. 39, 1995), pp.12, 14–15.
52   Staffordshire Record Office D3712/4/1, Mavesyn Ridware Parish Book, 1642–1698, ff.20–26; Atherton, 'Royalist Finances in the English Civil War: The Case of Lichfield Garrison, 1643–5', pp.38–39.
53   Firth, *Cromwell's Army*, p.217.
54   John Earwaker (ed.), *The Constables' Accounts of The Manor of Manchester from the Year 1612 to the Year 1647, and from the Year 1743 to the Year 1776*, vol. 2 (Manchester, J.E. Cornish, 1892), pp.83, 91, 102, 104, 141.
55   BL Harley MS. 6852, ff.175–178, Papers of the Secretary of the Royalist Council of War, 17th August 1643.

support their mounts in shelter and food, such as inns and farms, or at least with ready access to fields and feed.[56] The impact of large numbers of horses appears to have been too heavy a burden for smaller communities to support for very long at all. In 1644 the village of Upton struggled to supply the demands of several troops of cavalry with sufficient grazing which, according to the local constable, '[de]stroyed the Medow' due to overuse.[57] A detailed description of the short-term requirements for the Royalist cavalry going into winter quarters in November 1642 survives in an order from King Charles:

> to all the colonels of the horse and dragoons of our army, to quarter and billet their respective regiments in such places as we have assigned, and there to take up such necessary provision of diet, lodging, hay, oats, and straw, as shall be necessary for them. And if there shall not be sufficient for such their supply in their quarters, then they are to send forth their warrants to the several hundreds and parishes adjacent, requiring the inhabitants to bring in all fitting provisions for their daily supply. For all which, as for that taken up in their quarters, they to give their respective tickets, and not to presume, upon pain of our high displeasure, to send for greater quantities than will suffice for their numbers of men and horses, and such as may be proportionable to half of each officer's pay by the day, for all manner of diet, lodging, and horse-meat [horses], and half of every ordinary horseman's pay by day for diet only, their horse-meat being to be daily supplied by the counties adjacent to each quarter. In this manner we will that you proceed and continue until such time as the counties wherein they are quartered shall agree of, and settle some other course for their constant and daily supply.[58]

The Royalist command appeared to accept that, in order feed the horses, the surrounding areas would need to contribute rather than just the areas wherein the troopers themselves were quartered. Furthermore, the ending suggests there was an expectation that the regimental commanders and the local civilian authorities would agree or arrange 'some other course' for the 'constant and daily supply' of the cavalry rather than operate on the terms stipulated by the order long-term, suggesting again a level of compromise between the military and the local civilian populace.

---

56   Robinson, 'Horse Supply in the English Civil War, 1642–1646', pp.212–214.
57   Bennett, *A Nottinghamshire Village in War and Peace*, p.13.
58   Warburton, *Memoirs of Prince Rupert, and the Cavaliers*, II, pp.70–71.

Quartering

Quartering was the method of supplying troops by dispersing them amongst local civilian households who, for a daily rate paid by the soldiers, would provide them with both victuals and shelter. This worked reasonably well in theory but was perpetually undermined in reality by the lack of ready money amongst the soldiers as their pay was almost always in arrears. During the Second Bishops' War, Fissel argues much of the poor behaviour of the English troops could be linked to their lack of pay.[59] In March 1641, Ireland's Lord Justices warned that the garrison forces were 'in arrear almost 18 months' pay' with the 'New' army to go unpaid after that month due to shortage of funds.[60] The Irish Government was concerned that if 'left unpaid during the coming months there will surely be disorder among the troops.'[61] In 1644 the Earl of Newcastle and Prince Rupert had to 'pla[y] the orators' at York as the soldiers of the Earl's army were 'in a raging mutiny in the town for their pay.' As mentioned above, the Royalist forces in Ireland were promised their 'arreares that shall bee due to any of them'.[62] By February of 1647 the soldiers of the New Model Army were owed over £330,000 in arrears ranging, for various regiments, between 18 to 43 weeks.[63] The direct result of this shortage of pay was that the soldiers, imposed on civilians through quartering, would have had no means of reimbursing their enforced hosts for their room and board. Without money, householders had to provide for the soldiers in return for a scribbled paper receipt from an officer which promised future reimbursement. Receipts were promises from a higher authority to pay the householder the sum that the soldier could not, the subsequent payment to be deducted from the quartered soldier's eventual pay. An example of the expected behaviour for soldiers of the New Model Army regarding the issue of such receipts was:

> no Officer or Soldier be quartered at any Place, but by the Quarter-master first shewing his Commission if it be required, and by what Authority he takes up such Quarters, and giving a Ticket of the Names of every Person which he shall quarter, expressing of what Regiment, Troop, or Company, the same Person so quartered is, and the Number of Horses there quartered, and at whose House the same are quartered; together

---

59 Fissel, *The Bishops' Wars: Charles I's campaigns against Scotland 1638–1640*, pp.271–272
60 *CSPI 1633–47*, p.260, 8 March, The Lords Justice and Council to [Secretary Vane].
61 *CSPI 1633–47*, p.260, 8 March, The Lords Justice and Council to [Secretary Vane].
62 Carte, *The Life of James, Duke of Ormond*, V, pp.465–467.
63 Ian Gentles, 'The Arrears of Pay of the Parliamentary Army at the End of the First Civil War', *Bulletin of the Institute of Historical Research*, vol. 48, no.117 (May 1975), pp.52–63; Donagan, *War in England*, pp.239–240, 265.

with the Day of the Month; and that thereunto the same Quarter-master subscribe his Name.[64]

Free quartering was widely and understandably loathed by civilians. Large numbers of surviving sources outline the financial costs to civilians for food and drink, not to mention damages and other loss, due to soldiers.[65] The fury against free quarter was such a common loathing that it found its way into printed polemics against both Parliament, and the army. William Prynne, lawyer, author, theologian, and politician called it 'an expresse high violation of our fundamentall Lawes, Rights, Properties and Liberties.'[66] The application of free quartering was practised long before the Civil Wars and was a further cause of conflict between Charles and the English Parliament. The quartering of troops on civilians in the South of England during the wars with Spain and with France through the 1620s caused extensive resentment, particularly as the soldiers lacked regular pay with which to reimburse their hosts. Clause VI of the *Petition of Right* (1628) contained passages against quartering as 'great companies of soldiers and mariners have been dispersed into divers counties of the realm, and the inhabitants against their wills have been compelled to receive them into their houses ... to the great grievance and vexation of the people.'[67]

Quartering, paid or free, was an ad hoc method of feeding troops. Sir James Turner claimed generals used it when 'forc'd for want of money' but who nevertheless needed to keep their troops operational.[68] However it could and did work, despite grievances, provided that the numbers of men allocated and dispersed amongst the civilians did not exceed the capabilities of the local population to feed them. For small numbers of men, the system appears to have worked well enough. Surviving constable accounts had multiple entries for sick or wounded individual soldiers being sustained on the parishes, presumably left there by passing units, until they were well enough to travel. Constables at Upton paid for the 'lodging & meat & drink' of soldiers 'which did lie sicke' in the village throughout the wars.[69] This was also extended to caring for sick cavalry mounts, for example when the local

---

64 *LJ*, VII,pp.376–379, Article 6, 16 May 1645, Instructions for the Commissioners Appointed to Reside with the Army.
65 Many of these sources (at least for damages caused by Parliamentarian soldiers) stem from the Committee for Taking the Accounts of the Kingdom.
66 William Prynne, *A Publike Declaration and Solemne Protestation of the Free-Men of England and Wales, Against the Illegall, Intollerable, Undoing Grievance of Free-Quarter* (London: 1648).
67 'The Petition of Right', UK Parliament Digital Archive, <https://digitalarchive.parliament.uk/HL/PO/PU/1/1627/3C1n2≥, Accessed 28 September 2021.
68 Turner, *Pallas Armata*, p.201.
69 Bennett, *A Nottinghamshire Village in War and Peace*, p.10.

constables paid for 'hay & a pecke of pease' for 'a trooper his horses which did lye sicke.'[70] Other parishes had similar experiences, such as the manor of Manchester where in October 1644 Thomas Ouldan was indebted ten shillings 'for quartring 2 sicke souldiers of S[i]r Tho[mas] F[air]fax one weeke' with John Taylor, Robart Blomeley, Thomas Scocraft, and other householders likewise due money for caring for several more 'of the same souldiers'.[71] In March 1645 other local householders in Manchester, including Titus March and the widow Kenion, had 'sicke souldiers' quartered with them for up to '9 dayes' and the surviving records outline several other occasions such as these throughout the wars in Manchester alone.[72]

'The Siege of Breda', 1628 (detail): Jacques Callot (1592–1635). Etching published by Israel Silvestr, 120.5 × 140.5cm (complete plate) Note the camp and the cattle being herded either by soldiers or by sutlers. (Collection of Princeton University Art Museum. Bequest of Junius S. Morgan, Class of 1888. Public Domain)

For a larger force, being several regiments or a whole army marching together, quartering was more problematic. Large numbers of men attempting to find victuals and shelter all at the same time, and on short notice, meant that the civilians inevitably lacked the resources to feed them and such numbers of soldiers would have rapidly drained local food supplies.[73] This lack of plentiful

---

70 Bennett, *A Nottinghamshire Village in War and Peace*, p.14.
71 Earwaker, *The Constables' Accounts of the Manor of Manchester*, p.104.
72 Earwaker, *The Constables' Accounts of the Manor of Manchester*, pp.72, 79, 94, 121, 123, 136.
73 Gentles, *The New Model Army in England, Ireland and Scotland*, p.45.

food available and to hand was primarily a result of the contemporary methods of storing and preparing food.

The nature of civilian food storage at that time impacted on how much food, both in variety and volume, was available for soldiers, particularly in rural areas where most of the campaigns took place. This is key to understanding the capability of civilians to support large numbers of men on short notice. Soldiers dispersed into quarters following a day's march would have eaten what food was available. Long-term quartering, such as in a garrison, would have produced a different experience as their hosts would have had to adapt to provide for the greater number of mouths for a longer duration. However, the focus here is mainly on the experience of marching armies quartered with civilians who typically stayed only a short period, perhaps one or two nights, with their enforced hosts. If the civilians did not have enough prepared food available to satisfy the needs of the newly arrived soldiers, the hungry troops took what they needed or demanded the household purchase some for them. This behaviour was a common enough concern that Parliament felt the need to include a provision warning against such acts in the instructions for the New Model Army 'That no Inhabitants whatsoever shall be compelled to furnish any Provision, but what he hath in his House of his own; and that no Officer or Soldier shall compel him to do otherwise, upon Pain of cashiering, or such other Punishment as the Commander in Chief shall think fit.'[74]

An essential element of the soldiers' diet was bread, which formed a large part of the civilian diet as well. However, the amount of fresh bread on hand for civilians was limited. After harvesting, the common cereal crops such as wheat, rye, barley, and oats would typically be stored on the stalk, most often in sheafs. The type and availability of cereal crops also varied by region, with oats, for instance, being more common in upland areas than wheat or barley which were more common to lowland areas. Cereals destined for bread flour would be threshed and prepared for the journey to the local mill, but only as much as would keep in flour form, that the civilians expected to use over a period of weeks rather than months.[75] Flour itself was seen as the most vulnerable stage of the process since it was far more susceptible to damp, insect infestation, rodents, or other risks as compared to unthreshed grains. Thus the amount of flour was kept to the minimum necessary to meet the household's requirements between millings, and little more.[76] This was repeated in military storage practice as the Royalist garrison at Lichfield paid £5

---

74 *LJ*, VII, pp.376–379, Article 7, 16 May 1645, Instructions for the Commissioners appointed to reside with the Army.
75 Peachey, *The Soldier's Life in the English Civil War*, p.132.
76 Peachey, *The Soldier's Life in the English Civil War*, p.151.

7s. 'For threshing'.⁷⁷ Thus it can be seen that civilians planned, well in advance, the meals and ingredients they needed for themselves so as to avoid spoilage and waste.

Baking bread, or even pies, from the flour was again not a quick process. According to Peachey, small bread ovens needed between three and four hours to heat up and a further 12 to 16 hours to cook the bread dough, the dough itself needing perhaps a whole day of preparation before the ovens were even lit.⁷⁸ Armies on campaign in the British Civil Wars do not appear to have been equipped with mobile ovens, and the extensive equipment lists for the New Model Army in 1645 make no mention of either mobile ovens or mobile mills. This is reasonably explicable as the lack of certainty over the availability of flour, coupled with the almost 48 hour period necessary to prepare the dough, assemble the oven, warm the oven, and then bake the bread, would render such items only intermittently useful at best. Any ovens (and their subsequent produce) could be as many as two days' march behind the army by the time those ovens had finished baking the first load of bread. Even for a staple as common and basic as bread, fresh amounts could not be prepared and cooked by civilians to feed soldiers quickly in much less than two days. For soldiers on the march all that they had available to eat in overnight quarters was what the civilians already had to hand. This amount would also depend on how recently the householders had either been to the mill or cooked their planned bread. If it was close to the next planned baking or milling day of the household then the quantity of baked food ready and available could have been quite low, the civilians having already run down their household stores. A soldier might have to make do with gruel or pottage cooked quickly from what cereals were to hand in the household. Oats, which in many areas of England were used primarily as animal feed, may well have been a convenient cereal crop on hand when soldiers arrived.⁷⁹ Peas, like cereal crops, were stored dried in their pods on the vine and ready to be removed and soaked overnight, as needed. Dried peas were seen as part of the ration for troops sent on overseas expeditions in the 1620s.⁸⁰ Dried field beans, used as animal feed in England much like oats, could be ground as flour to mix with cereal flour for cheap, coarse bread.⁸¹

However, commanders of troops marching out on campaign preferred to send their troops out with biscuit rather than the type of loaves of bread civilians would have. While biscuit was long lasting and useful for extensive marching, not all

---

77   Ian Atherton, 'The Accounts of the Royalist Garrison of Lichfield Close, 1643–1645', *Staffordshire Studies*, Vol. 18 (2007), p.72.
78   Peachey, *The Soldier's Life in the English Civil War*, pp.132–133.
79   Peachey, *The Soldier's Life in the English Civil War*, p.133.
80   Spring, *The First British Army, 1624–1628*, p.85.
81   Peachey, *The Soldier's Life in the English Civil War*, p.133.

officers rated it as a sustaining, long-term ration, as above with the Earl of Cork. Yet biscuit continued as a common element of military rations, as it could be stored for long periods of time and it travelled easily. It could 'bee put up into Sacks, & laden in Carts to bee caried away' which is how the Royalists transported '8 thousand weight' of biscuit to the field army from Oxford in October 1644.[82] It was also clearly an important element in a garrison's stores as the same warrant ordered that 'soe much of ye Meale as it now in Magazine may bee baked into Bisket, w[i]th all possible speed' to replenish the stores.[83] This hard, durable biscuit appears to have been a staple of a soldier's diet, at least as an emergency ration. The Earl of Cork's comments suggest relying solely on this 'bisket' was not advisable for a soldier's long-term diet. However, it appears to have been an essential food for the soldiers when nothing else was available. Royalist Cornish troops in 1643 had only 'a drie bisquett apiece' daily for at least '3 or 4 dayes' before the Battle of Stratton, as it was all the army had with them and the local area was 'so poore, that it was not able to supply them.'[84] The soldiers on Hamilton's fleet in 1639 who reportedly had 14 days of victuals in their knapsacks probably had this as their staple.[85] It was certainly hard and durable enough to survive transport by sacks and by cart. Although not a part of the civilian diet, it appears that it was supplied by local bakers with whom the military placed orders, suggesting that it was easily made, likely the case with the Oxford stores. The accounts of Edward Russell, the Royalist military storekeeper at Chester, include multiple payments to local bakers for providing his stores with biscuit.[86]

The experience of soldiers in garrison, as well as for soldiers in extended periods of quarter with the same household, was quite different to that of soldiers marching. The local households would have been able to account for the increased demand of bread and, providing supplies of flour were available, would have been able to bake the necessary bread. Additionally, the static nature of the garrison itself meant supplies could be stored far more easily and in far greater quantities than a marching army could carry without large numbers of transport vehicles. The Royalist garrison at Winchester castle surrendered in 1645 after only a brief siege once the Parliamentarian artillery had made several breaches in the ancient walls of the castle. The captured stores included '38 hogsheads of beef and pork; 15,000 weight of cheese; 800 pound of butter; 140 quarters of wheat and meal; 3 hogsheads of French wine; 10 quarters of salt; 20 Bushel of Oatmeale; 70 Dosen of Candles; 30 Load of Wood; 40 Quarters of Charcoale; 30 Bushels of Seacoale; 14

---

82 Toynbee, *The Papers of Captain Henry Stevens*, p.32.
83 Toynbee, *The Papers of Captain Henry Stevens*, p.32.
84 Hopton, *Bellum Civile*, pp.41–44.
85 *CSPD 1639*, p.210, May 22, Sir John Pennington to Captain George Carteret.
86 TNA SP 28/128/12, Accounts of Edward Russel, Chester.

Sheep; 4 Quarters of Fresh Beef; 7000 Weight of Biskets; 112 hogsheads of strong beer' and the garrison numbered '700 men'.[87]

While this might appear a large supply on paper, if we take the recommend allocation of Sir James Turner, two pounds of bread (in this case biscuit), one pound of cheese, and 2 pottles (4 quarts) of beer a day it can be seen that the stores at Winchester were not actually that substantial. 15,000 weight of cheese, that is 150 hundredweight, which is about 16,800lbs, at one pound per day for every man is enough to last the garrison 24 days. For biscuit at two pounds per day the 7,840lbs (70 hundredweight) would last the men on a full ration less than six days. For the beer, at 288 quarts to a hogshead, with 112 hogsheads, would make enough for just over 11 days' supply for the garrison of 700 men. The term 'strong beer' might indicate it could, or would, have been watered down to have stretched it further, and this is based on an ideal daily ration, not the limited ration the soldiers might expect if placed under close siege. The above calculations also do not include the butter, wine, oatmeal, meat, or the almost 4,000lbs of wheat and meal in the stores. However, the estimates do provide an indication that the garrison stores held a few weeks' worth of food at most. One could surmise then that the garrison's daily usage of victuals came largely from the surrounding town. In general, soldiers in garrison tended to enjoy a higher quality of living than those in the marching armies – at least when the latter was on campaign. Soldiers seconded from garrisons and detached for field service complained about the hard living outside of their garrison. The Royalist Major Elias Whalley when on campaign with soldiers drawn from the Lichfield Garrison in 1643 wrote that he was dubious about how to make 'the Lichfield soldiers fight or keep them from mutiny, they being used to so much plenty and ease at home'.[88]

Cheese was seen as essential part of the diet for marching soldiers, either as a supplement itself or as a replacement for other goods, such as being a primary substitute for meat. In 1643 the Lord Justices of Ireland felt that without cheese 'the soldier cannot well march abroad.'[89] Cheese in the seventeenth century, like butter, was common, easily portable, and able to be stored for extended periods. Unlike preserved meat (see below), cheese was also readily available to eat without extensive preparation.[90] The Earl of Orrery, another veteran writing about his military service after the wars, believed both butter and cheese were 'better liked by the Soldiery' as they were ready to eat at need 'without their [the soldiers] labour to cook it, or to get fire to do it', and had the added advantages of making

---

87 Sprigg, *Anglia Rediviva*, p.132.
88 HMC, *Report on the Manuscripts of the Late Reginald Rawdon Hastings*, II, p.111.
89 HMC, *Calendar of the Manuscripts of the Marquess of Ormonde*, I, pp.62–63.
90 Peachey, *The Soldier's Life in the English Civil War*, p.135.

soldiers less thirsty than preserved meat, and being easy to store and 'long kept in good condition'.[91] If soldiers were also issued meat by weight, as Turner and others suggest, than there may have been little allowance made for fat or bone in the cut and, as Laurence Spring points out, possibly making a pound of cheese preferable to a poor cut of meat.[92] It is perhaps for these reasons that cheese was frequently part of the soldier's ration, particularly if more readily available than preserved meat.

The type of meat given to soldiers for their ration is rarely stipulated, which suggests it was whatever was available, whether in season or preserved. Meat itself was a major part of the English diet at the time, with a large proportion being bacon or fish, often preserved by either salting or drying.[93] However, due to the nature of the preservation treatment, whether salting or drying, such meat would have had to undergo extensive preparation before use. At a minimum it would require cutting and soaking in water overnight and depending on the amount of salt used (if it had been salted) possibly with multiple rounds of boiling and soaking, changing the water each time.[94] Again, planning and forethought was necessary to make this food suitable for human consumption. Like the preparation of bread, when large numbers of soldiers were quartered in a vicinity without several days' notice ahead of their arrival, there would not be enough time for civilians to draw their preserved meat from storage, prepare it, cook it, and serve it to the soldiers. The results of which meant that for the soldiers this might well have meant a hungry night or a day's march following little food. Consequently, hungry soldiers might well have taken more than the household felt they could personally spare.

Soldiers who had experience of lengthy marches would have been familiar with the realities of having to rely on both quartering and foraging for their food. This would have included a lack of certainty of there being sufficient food for soldiers at future stops along the march. Given this lack of confidence in future sources of food, it is not hard to understand the soldiers taking any opportunity to secure whatever food sources they could in the present, against an uncertain future. Unfortunately for the civilians, these food sources would very likely have been drawn from the household they were due to depart from, and in which they had been quartering up to that point. A well-known caricature 'The English Irish Souldier' reveals how soldiers were seen by some in the popular imagination at the time – festooned with loot, almost all of it food related. For example, his cap and plume have been replaced with a looted cooking pot and fowl. His weapon has

91 Roger Boyle, *A Treatise of the Art of War*, (London 1677), pp.49 & 125.
92 Spring, *The First British Army*, p.86
93 Peachey, *The Soldier's Life in the English Civil War*, p.134.
94 Peachey, *The Soldier's Life in the English Civil War*, p.134.

been replaced by a chicken and spit, and his bandolier of ammunition with bottles of beer or butter. The overall impression is of a soldier who would much rather take food as loot than to fight.

Given that this image was published in London in 1642, as a response to the raising of troops to counter the rebellion in Ireland, it is likely not a representation of English soldiers in Ireland as few had been sent by the end of 1642. These regiments of English soldiers did not return to England from Ireland until late in 1643 and rumour of their return did not begin until a few months before that, both long after the publication of the cartoon.[95] However, England did have experience of soldiers more recently from the Bishops' Wars, and this image is more likely representative of how Englishmen saw soldiers in general rather than the English veterans in Ireland in particular. Rather more importantly, the soldier is drawn with obvious replacements for this equipment, suggesting the artist expected their audience to understand what he represented – a stereotype of a soldier. This further suggests that many people could identify a soldier's equipment, at least enough to appreciate the satirical imagery.

A soldier taking food for the march from his previous night's hosts would have had a limited choice in both variety and amount. This too would have to be divided amongst all the soldiers sharing the quarters. Oats and other bagged cereals might be taken by the troops for use in gruels or porridge, though carrying these would have added to a soldier's marching load. The greater likelihood, borne out from surviving complaints by civilians, is that soldiers instead took the food best suited to travel with them and that was also comparatively easy for almost anyone to prepare and to cook – livestock. An account from Redbourn parish in Hertfordshire lists '8 sheepe taken away by the Souldiers that quartered at St Albans' and '16 sheepe taken away by souldiers 14 of them nowe greate with lamb' while another resident was 'damnified by the free quarter of soldiers and sheepe stolen from him to the value of £18 2s. 8d.' in 1643.[96] Most of the rural population, and a large minority of urban dwellers, kept some range of livestock including pigs and poultry.[97] Smallholdings also held sheep and cows, though sheep were mostly kept for their wool.[98] The greater portion of a civilian's meat was bacon, beef, and fish.[99] However, for hungry soldiers, meat was meat. In the autumn of 1642 Parliamentarian soldiers happily stole, slaughtered, and ate the deer from the

---

95 John Barratt, 'The King's Irish': The Royalist Anglo-Irish Foot of the English Civil War (Warwick: Helion, 2019), pp.11–50.
96 Alan Thomson (ed.), The Impact of the First Civil War on Hertfordshire, 1642–47 (Hertford: Hertfordshire Record Society, Vol. 23, 2007), pp.119–120.
97 Peachey, The Soldier's Life in the English Civil War, p.134.
98 Peachey, The Soldier's Life in the English Civil War, p.134.
99 Peachey, The Soldier's Life in the English Civil War, pp.134–135.

parks of Royalist supporters.[100] Soldiers viewed the livestock which civilians kept for their produce, such as wool or eggs, simply as a source of food. This habit of taking the working livestock, perhaps even more than the imposed meals of bread and cheese, was heavily felt by the civilians. A pig that was meant to last the winter disappeared in a single night or a small flock of sheep kept for wool as income were driven off for food by soldiers. The Earl of Essex's army marched eastwards from Gloucester, after relieving the town in September 1643, driving with them 'about 1000 sheep and 60 head of Cattell, which were taken from Malignants and Papists in the Country for the maintenance of our army.'[101]

Officers and politicians were not insensible to the unreliable nature of feeding soldiers that quartering provided. Where possible officers sent foragers along and around the line of a march to locate and gather foodstuffs to supplement that which the soldiers might find in quarters. Nehemiah Wharton arrived in Byfield, Northamptonshire with the rest of Holles's regiment in August 1642 after a full day of marching, to find the village had no victuals of any kind available for them. Fortunately, in their case they were 'supplied with ten cart-loads of provision and beer from Banbury.'[102] As we shall see later, garrison troops could forage for their provisions, taking in supplies from surrounding villages to support their needs. The accounts of the town of Uttoxeter in Staffordshire detail regular amounts of victuals, most often bread, cheese, and oats, sent to the Royalist garrison at Tutbury from 1642–1646. However, in the spring of 1646, as the war developed and Parliamentarian forces closed in on Tutbury, Uttoxeter had to provide victuals to foragers of Sir William Brereton's Parliamentarian forces who were *en route* to besiege the Royalists at Tutbury Castle. In March, Uttoxeter provided 15s. 6d. for bread, cheese, and beer for soldiers marching to Tutbury, and again in April a further 7s. worth of 'bread cheese & drink' for soldiers from Leek who were also part of Brereton's forces.[103] Cavalry or dragoons, as mounted troops, would commonly be used for the task of foraging ahead of the main body of infantry, their mounted mobility allowing them to cover a wider area in less time.

The accounts from Uttoxeter reveal the distance that such foraging parties could travel as part of their duties. On 14 June 1644, Sir William Waller's army arrived at Stourbridge, 33 miles south-west of the town of Uttoxeter in Staffordshire, and 'lay 3 nights having some mutton, bread, cheese, and beere, sent to us out of the

---

100   *CSPD 1641–1643*, p.382, Aug. 30 [1642], Nehemiah Wharton to George Willingham; *CSPD 1641–1643*, p.384, Sept. 3 [1642], Nehemiah Wharton to George Willingham.
101   Foster, *A True and Exact Relation of the Marchings of the Two Regiments of the Trained-Bands of the City of London*, p.10.
102   *CSPD 1641–1643*, pp.379–380, Aug. 26 [1642], Nehemiah Wharton to George Willingham.
103   Cooper, 'The English Civil War in Staffordshire: The Experience of Uttoxeter', p.77.

Countrey.'[104] The accounts of Uttoxeter for 13 June 1644 show 'Sent to Sturbridge byt warr[ran]t to S[i]r W[illia]m Waller 25 dozen bread & an half, & 57 p[oun]d of bacon and & 67 p[oun]d of cheese.'[105] Thus foraging parties from Waller's army were travelling at least 30 miles away from his main line of march and if the dates on both sources are correct, collecting food for where they knew the army would be the next day. This example emphasises the importance of mounted men for an army, able to range far from the main line of march to secure supplies to supplement the army's quarters. It also supports the role of local garrisons in aiding the supply of marching armies as well. The Royalist garrison at Lichfield, and its patrols, lay quite close to the halfway point between Uttoxeter and Waller's Parliamentarian army at Stourbridge so the foragers, and their supplies secured at Uttoxeter, would have almost certainly have had to bypass this area, instead passing through areas patrolled by the Parliamentarians, possibly the garrison at Stafford. If more than one army was operating in the vicinity the demand for resources upon the local area would be high. In March 1644 the village of Upton had first Parliamentarian forces 'gathering victuals for the Parlement Army' as they besieged Royalist held Newark, and again within weeks Upton had to send at least four more carts of supplies, this time for the recently arrived Royalist forces under Prince Rupert who had arrived to relieve the garrison.[106]

Whether by cash or receipt, the reliance on quartering did not guarantee that a soldier would have enjoyed the necessary provisions. It is perhaps little wonder that quartering led to hungry and underfed soldiers, and it is also perhaps worth emphasising here that it was not only the civilians who suffered under the vagaries and unreliability of the quarter system. At the outbreak of the Civil Wars in 1642, both the King's and Parliament's forces were heavily reliant on quartering to feed their troops. We know from surviving contemporary sources that the supply of food for the marching armies leading up to Edgehill were intermittent at best because of this reliance on quartering and foraging. A regiment might eat well one day and then suffer from a shortage another. The letters of Nehemiah Wharton show that the Parliamentarian troops made extensive use of quartering in the 1642 Edgehill campaign. After marching into Buckinghamshire on 12 August 1642 'but wanting room for the regiment comming after us we were constrained to march four miles further unto Great Missenden, where we had noble entertainment from the whole town.'[107] Likewise at Aylesbury a day later, 'In this town our welcome

104 Richard Coe, *An Exact Diarie. Or a Breife Relation of the Progresse of Sir William Wallers Army Since the Joyning of the London Avxilliaries with His Forces* (London, 1644), p.4.
105 Cooper, 'The English Civil War in Staffordshire: The Experience of Uttoxeter', p.73.
106 Bennett, *A Nottinghamshire Village in War and Peace*, p.16.
107 *CSPD 1641–1643*, p.372, Aug. 15 [1642], Nehemiah Wharton to George Willingham.

is such that we want nothing.'[108] As the army began to concentrate, with more regiments marching in close proximity to one another, the ability of localities to support the larger numbers of troops began to wane, and the units late into towns or villages had neither food nor lodgings available for them. When Wharton and the rest of Holles's regiment marched into Byfield in Northamptonshire late at night they 'could get no quarter, neither meat, drink, nor lodging.'[109] Units of the army ahead in the order of march would have eaten all the available provender, and regiments arriving later then found that all the food and drink was gone. Likewise, when opposing armies were manoeuvring in close proximity to each other, enemy regiments could add to the pressures of supply. Such was the case when Wharton and his comrades 'marched two miles further to Aston Cantlow where we could get no quarter, neither bread nor drink, by reason of the Lord Compton's late being there.'[110] By early September, after a month of marching and being reinforced by other units, even regimental officers failed to secure lodgings and food with the common soldiers, if they were lucky, relying instead on animal pens for shelter from the elements.[111] Clarendon claimed that the Royalist army had no food for two days before the Battle of Edgehill.[112] These examples highlight the variable, and often insufficient, nature of quartering for marching troops as a means of provision, and reveal the imperfect nature of relying on quartering for shelter.

There exist many examples of soldiers on campaign having to make camp for extended periods without cover. Given the rural areas of the British Isles where most soldiers campaigned, limited shelter for elements of the army would not have been unusual. During October 1643, in Lincolnshire Captain Rich of the Eastern Association claimed 'The winter is already come, and our lying in the field hath lost us more men than have been taken way either by the sword or bullet.'[113] According to surviving parish accounts, in June 1645 soldiers of the New Model Army were 'lying in the feeldes' of Northamptonshire for want of sufficient shelter amongst local villages.[114] David Appleby claims that veteran soldiers were identifiably more weather beaten and worn than any civilian who worked outdoors as the latter at least had regular shelter.[115]

---

108 *CSPD 1641–1643*, p.372, Aug. 15 [1642], Nehemiah Wharton to George Willingham.
109 *CSPD 1641–1643*, p.379, Aug. 26 [1642], Nehemiah Wharton to George Willingham.
110 *CSPD 1641–1643*, p.392, Sep. 26 [1642], Nehemiah Wharton to George Willingham.
111 *CSPD 1641–1643*, p.384, Sep. 3 [1642], Nehemiah Wharton to George Willingham.
112 Hyde, *The History of the Rebellion and Civil Wars in England*, II, pp.359–360.
113 Quoted in Alfred Kingston, *East Anglia and the Great Civil War*, (London: E. Stock, 1897), p.147.
114 TNA SP 28/173, 'Harteton Boock' unfol.
115 David Appleby, 'The Third Army: Wandering Soldiers and the Negotiation of Parliamentary Authority, 1642–1654' in David Appleby and Andrew Hopper (eds), *Battle-*

The King's army in the Second Bishops' War was supposed to be accompanied by sufficient tents for shelter, following the lack of shelter troops suffered in the First Bishops' War where the idea of tents had been discarded because of the expense.[116] However, due to the problems with securing sufficient transportation in 1640 these did not accompany the regiments meaning the King's soldiers had to 'lye on the bare ground most of them without any straw under them and greene sodde under their head, and little or noe shelter.'[117] In February 1643 in preparation for that year's campaigning the Earl of Essex's army ordered 944 tents and 942 were delivered to the army the following month.[118] If these were the total number of tents for the army, they would have needed to be large to provide cover for all of the army's soldiers. Even six-man tents would only have provided enough shelter for 5,600 men, which was only a portion of Essex's perhaps 20 infantry regiments. Even if these regiments were at half strength at the time, there would have still been around 8,000 infantry in the army at this time, not including cavalry, dragoons, or artillery crews.[119] Instead these were perhaps intended to supplement the shelter the army obtained from quartering. At its formation in 1645, from the surviving contracts and receipts, the New Model Army does not appear to have placed orders for any tents either as new or as replacements.[120] It may have been that they had inherited enough tents from the three founding armies of Essex, Manchester, and Waller, but this seems unlikely given the number of extra pressed men the New Model Army needed in order to bring it up to establishment strength (see chapter three). Given the problems with securing sufficient transportation during this period, the three Parliamentarian forces, all understrength, would not have carried more tents than they needed. Add the influx of new recruits on top of this and no surviving evidence of contracts for tents suggests a standard issue of tents at the founding of the New Model Army is doubtful.

The situation regarding tents appears to have been different when planning for later campaigns of the army when outside of England. Oliver Cromwell's forces for Ireland were issued with tents as he wrote to Parliament stating that 'We keep

---

Scarred: Mortality, Medical Care and Military Welfare in the British Civil Wars (Manchester University Press, 2018), p.145.
116 TNA SP 16/412/136 Estimate for costs of supplying King's army. 7,500 tents were estimated to have cost £9,350.
117 Bodleian Rawlinson Ms B 210, f.41v.
118 Simon Marsh (ed.), *The Train of Artillery of the Earl of Essex: The Accounts of Sir Edward Peyto Lieutenant General of the Train of Artillery, October 1642–September 1643* (Romford: The Pike and Shot Society, 2016), pp.233–234.
119 Scott and Turton, *Hey for Old Robin!*, p.198.
120 Mungeam, 'Contracts for the Supply of Equipment', pp.53–115.

the field much; our tents sheltering us from the wet and cold.'[121] Why the New Model Army took tents to Ireland and not in the earlier campaigns is unclear, but it is possibly a recognition that relying on local shelter in Ireland, amidst a population presumed to be hostile and in territory heavily devastated by almost a decade of warfare, would not serve. The provision of tents for this army was possibly based on necessity when quartering amongst the population for extended periods was either insufficient or unviable. For the invasion of Scotland in 1650 the army was again issued with tents in time for winter for every six men 'a Tent, for their better quartering in the field'.[122] However, the earlier armies of Parliament remained dependent on quartering for victuals, and for billets where possible, for much of the English Civil Wars. By 1645 Parliament could only clarify the terms of quartering and how receipts for non-payment were to be issued, fixing the rates of quartering men and horses in the hopes of ending free quarter by ensuring it was affordable for the soldiers rather than stopping the use of quartering entirely.[123]

A concentrated army needed a large amount of food and, unless a regular supply of food was carried with the army, the speed of the army was partially dictated by the need to disperse its men into quarters and assemble them again. This dispersal was hazardous while campaigning when enemy proximity and activities could put elements of the army at risk if they were too dispersed and unable to support one another in the event of an attack.[124] Units of a marching army dispersed into quarters were extremely vulnerable to mobile and active enemy units, particularly if the enemy remained concentrated. Such was the case that the close proximity of a sufficiently large enemy force often demanded that an army did not disperse into quarters. For an army reliant on quartering to feed and shelter its men, this could have meant long periods of hunger, exhaustion, and even dehydration before a battle as the armies manoeuvred for position and had to remain concentrated in proximity to the enemy. Even foraging would have been limited as troops from both sides drew down the limited available mobile foodstuffs in the area. In early September 1643, elements of Essex's Parliamentary army, struggling to forage for supplies in the 'wasted country' in Gloucestershire, managed to surprise and

---

121 Oliver Cromwell to William Lenthall, Dublin, 17th September 1649, in Carlyle, *Oliver Cromwell's Letters and Speeches with Elucidations*, II, p.201.
122 Charles Terry, *The Life and Campaigns of Alexander Leslie, First Earl of Leven* (London: Longman, Green, and Co., 1899), pp.465–466.
123 *LJ*, VII, pp.376–379, Article 6, 16 May 1645, Instructions for the Commissioners Appointed to Reside with the Army.
124 Nusbacher, 'Civil Supply in the Civil War: Supply of Victuals to the New Model Army on the Naseby Campaign, 1–14 June 1645', pp.145–160.

capture a Royalist cavalry force at Cirencester along with '30 cart-loads of bread and cheese and other provisions'.[125]

Just before the Battle of Edgehill in October 1642 the Royalists had dispersed their forces following their concentration on the march to besiege Banbury. On the night of 22 October some of the Royalist army was still searching for and allocating billets in the nearby villages. The proximity of the Royalist and Parliamentarian armies to one another was only revealed when a Royalist quartermaster's detachment encountered their opposite number from the Earl of Essex's army at the village of Wormleighton engaged in the same business.[126] The revelation for both sides that the enemy was in such close proximity led to both armies rapidly concentrating their dispersed men again in preparation for battle.[127] The combination of marching, dispersal, and then a hurried concentration would have meant that many soldiers might not have been able to secure quarters, or at least not had enough time to secure a substantial meal. Under such circumstances, it is not surprising that Clarendon claimed that at the battle 'there were very many Companies of the Common Soldiers who had scarce eaten Bread in eight and forty hours'.[128] He was correct in stating that with the enemy in such close proximity the 'only way to cure this was a Victory', as the result of a substantial victory would have dispersed or driven off the enemy army and allowed elements of the victorious army the freedom to quarter and forage without risk of being attacked.[129] Edgehill was not the only time where armies were forced to survive without shelter or food because of the proximity of the enemy. In September 1643, while marching to relieve Gloucester, Henry Foster and the Red Regiment of the London Trained Bands were roused at the news that a Royalist force was nearby. They 'stood in the open field all night, having neither bread nor water to refresh our selves, having also marched the day before without any sustenance neither durst we kindle any fire though it was a very cold night.'[130]

---

125 Walter Money, *The First and Second Battles of Newbury and the Siege of Donnington Castle During the Civil War* (London, 1881), pp.5–6.
126 Scott, Turton, von Arni, *Edgehill, The Battle Reinterpreted*, pp.6–7.
127 Scott, Turton, von Arni, *Edgehill, The Battle Reinterpreted*, pp.7–8.
128 Hyde, *The History of the Rebellion and Civil Wars in England*, II, pp.359–360.
129 Hyde, *The History of the Rebellion and Civil Wars in England*, II, p.360.
130 Foster, *A True and Exact Relation of the Marchings of the Two Regiments of the Trained-Bands of the City of London*, p.5.

Magazines and Marching Supplies

Quartering was an inefficient system but one that could, under certain circumstances, provide victuals and billets to the soldiers of an army on campaign or to those in garrison. Its imperfections of relying too heavily on poorly paid troops to reimburse civilians who may not have had sufficient victuals or billets for them led to other attempts to either replace, or at least to supplement, quartering. In France and other European countries, systems of magazines were established within particular towns to support the army, providing storehouses, clothing, weapons, and victuals which supplied the soldiers garrisoning those towns, and acted as supply depots for allied armies campaigning nearby.[131] However, the British Isles, largely at peace internally for so long, had very few established garrisons at the outbreak of the British Civil Wars, and even fewer magazines. The lack of a standing army before the wars meant that there was no need for such depots of supplies, particularly as almost every regiment recruited in the preceding decades was for foreign service rather than internal security.[132]

However, the activities of Sir Jacob Astley in the autumn of 1638 highlight that there were officers in English service who understood the complexity of victualling an army and the necessity to plan as thoroughly as possible for it. Astley was a veteran soldier, having seen extensive service on the Continent in Dutch, Danish, Swedish, and German armies.[133] Astley's activities in the North of England in the winter of 1638–1639 as the officer charged with investigating and preparing the North for war produced a flurry of orders, plans, and recommendations designed to ensure that the regiments would have the necessary food for the forthcoming campaign. Every captain was to ensure his company had their own 'Waggon or Cart' and that every soldier was to be issued with a 'Knapsack wherein to carry certaine daies Victualls.'[134] Astley was not planning on relying on local quartering and foraging on the presumed march from Berwick-on-Tweed to Edinburgh, and the men would carry their own rations to ensure that they ate. While at Newcastle-upon-Tyne, Astley obtained prices for victuals at the local market in readiness for purchasing supplies. Interestingly, the industrious officer also identified specific locations along the River Tyne for 'Stages for the Supply of Victualls for sustayning of an Army.'[135] In other words, he was marking out locations for forward supply magazines. Not only was he planning for the troops to carry their own food, but he

---

131   See for example Lynn, 'Food, Funds, and Fortresses'.
132   Spring, *The First British Army*.
133   Barratt, *Cavalier Generals: King Charles I & his Commanders in the English Civil War*, pp.45–47.
134   TNA SP16/396, Council of War entry book, f.39.
135   TNA SP16/396, Council of War entry book, f.41.

was also planning for the purchase of victuals locally and laying the groundwork for the establishment of a series of European-style magazines of supplies to draw upon. As these staging areas which Astley identified lay along the river Tyne, upstream from the town, this suggests that he was planning for the supplies to be transported by river. They would then likely be stocked from products obtained at Newcastle market, hence his securing of prices, and from other material and supplies brought in through the port by sea. Sir Jacob Astley at least, as a veteran of warfare on the Continent, clearly recognised the risks inherent in an army relying solely on quartering. He appeared to have been doing his best to create a parallel, military type structure based on magazines and regimental supplies to run alongside the civilian infrastructure.

Unfortunately, not everyone had Astley's experience or appreciation for how long it took to prepare an efficient and reliable supply of provisions. We do not know why his recommendations were not acted upon, but we can reason that, given the problems Charles had in raising money for the war, there was simply neither credit nor coin available to meet the recommendations. England was struggling with buying even the more overt necessities of warfare such as arms, armour, and powder well into 1639.[136] The English attempts to feed their army in the First Bishops' War were a failure brought about by late planning and a poor appreciation of the complexities of victual supply, compounded by a shortness of ready money. The only magazines of serious size to be assembled were at Hull and Newcastle-upon-Tyne, both being supplied by sea rather than land. As mentioned above, the overall logistical organisation for this campaign appears to have been somewhat chaotic, with key personnel and planning forgotten or simply not implemented. As late as 1 April 1639, when the campaign was already underway and the English army in the north was struggling for food, there had been no provisioning officer employed in organising the cost of the men's rations from their pay: 'if victuals or clothes be allowed to soldiers whereof a defalcation must be made upon their pay, he desires an officer may be appointed to estimate the same, and set down how much is to be deducated per diem of the soldier's pay for the same.'[137]

Meanwhile the Covenanter forces, with a command structure heavily populated by veterans of Continental warfare, had made their own strenuous efforts to prepare for war. This included the removal of all sources of food from the border area to prevent the English army from foraging to supplement their provisions. On 23 April 1639, Edmund Rossingham claimed that '[The Scots] have withdrawn all their cattle and other goods and all forage 20 miles within the borders, that the King's army may find no more provisions for horse and man than they bring

---

136 Edwards, *Dealing in Death*, pp.185–187.
137 *CSPD 1639*, p.73, April 23, Edmund Rossingham to Edward Viscount Conway.

with them.'[138] This was a clear strategic move on the part of the Covenanters as in comparison the local civilians of both Scots and Borderers were more than happy to provide English soldiers with provisions, but only if the King's forces had cash to offer. Henry de Vic, writing from the English garrison at Berwick at around the same time, noted, 'The country hereabout, having taken notice of the good and ready payment we make for what we have, are beginning to come in with all the things that they think we want and these parts afford.'[139]

Whereas the rest of the border area had been devoid of English soldiers before their army marched north, allowing the Scots a free hand in clearing the area of forage, the border near to Berwick was likely left relatively untouched due to the proximity of the established English garrison there. As the King's army moved towards Berwick, these supplies proved insufficient to feed the larger numbers of men gathered in close concentration to one another. As previously noted, Astley had advised the establishment of several magazines along the planned line of march of the army, but instead supplies had been gathered only at two major coastal magazines at Newcastle and Hull. These were unfortunately many miles to the south and the lack of sufficient wagons for the campaign dramatically undermined any efforts to move provisions to the army. By 28 May, at a time when the English army was struggling with hunger in their camp around Berwick, the magazine at Newcastle around 60 miles away had

> many garners [stores or granaries] so filled with very good bread, cheese, and butter, with such mountains of rye, miscellane, and excellent oats, as was to be incredible but that I saw it. Besides the great store at Newcastle ready to supply this, and every day coming, Mr. Pinckney, the commissary for victuals, a very honest gent, tells me that there were 57 cartloads of good bread ready to have been brought to the army on the late want, but no carts could be got to bring it, so the fault was not his, but the country's who have not yet learned their lesson.[140]

Despite men like Astley trying to prepare for the supply of provisions as much as six months before the army marched north, the realities of implementing a complex logistical system outweighed their optimistic plans.

The political and social resistance to the King's efforts in raising and fielding forces in England for the Second Bishops' War is well documented elsewhere.[141]

---

138 *CSPD 1639*, p.73, April 23, Edmund Rossingham to Edward Viscount Conway.
139 *CSPD 1639*, p.66, April 21, Henry de Vic to Secretary Windebank.
140 *CSPD 1639*, p.250, Edward Norgate to Secretary Windebank, p.250.
141 See Fissel, *The Bishops' Wars: Charles I's campaigns against Scotland 1638–1640*.

However, the Covenanters' experience of supplying their army on campaign, and planning their strategic operations around the availability of food, stands in contrast to the King's attempts in 1639. Scotland lacked both the population and the arable productivity to support a large army indefinitely. Adding further to the challenges, Scottish military transportation rested primarily on packhorses rather than more efficient draught vehicles. Alexander Leslie, commander of the Covenanter army, had to navigate these difficulties while maintaining an army quartered in Scotland in a defensive array. Throughout July 1640 the Covenanters had assembled their army and, for political reasons, waited in Berwickshire.[142] In that time Leslie issued his *Articles and Ordinances of Warre* which was printed and read out to every company of the army. Article 10 made clear the punishment of any soldier in the Covenanting army who 'shall take by violence either horse, catell, goods, money, or any other thing' on the march in either England or Scotland.'[143] In preparation for the invasion of England, with the aim of capturing Newcastle, the army command wanted a full two weeks' worth of provisions with the army to maintain strategic mobility and to limit the chance of hungry troops imposing themselves on English civilians. Although 500 cattle and several thousand sheep were gathered for the march the supply officers 'could not gett a fourteen days provisions to the fore' nor 'horses to carrie it.'[144] Despite their efforts, the limited provisions that the Covenanters marched south with, combined with the restrictions on quartering, meant that by the end of August the victual situation was grim, with desertion on the rise as a result. These losses, coupled with the need to garrison English towns after the Battle of Newburn, caused Leslie to request 5,000 more men from Scotland.[145] The supply situation was not improved after the Scots capture of Newcastle, despite the stores held there.

On the march south the animals gathered had travelled in close proximity with the army and this food was able to be distributed quickly to the regiments. As the army dispersed into an army of garrison and occupation across the English countryside the ability to feed the army centrally was lost. As the English had found, having the large stockpile of supplies at Newcastle was unhelpful if there was no means of transporting it to the distant forces. It is important to note here that, although the stockpile at Newcastle was impressive the previous year,

---

142 Edward Furgol, 'Beating the Odds: Alexander Leslie's 1640 Campaign in England' in Steve Murdoch and Andrew Mackillop (eds), *Fighting for Identity: Scottish Military Experience c.1550–1900* (Leiden, Netherlands: Brill, 2002), p.42.
143 Alexander Leslie, *Articles and Ordinances of Warre for the Present Expedition of the Army of the Kingdome of Scotland. By the Committee of Estates, and his Excellence, the Lord Generall of the Army* (Edinburgh: 1640).
144 Baillie, *The Letters and Journals of Robert Baillie*, I, p.256.
145 Furgol, 'Beating the Odds: Alexander Leslie's 1640 Campaign in England', p.54.

after the Covenanter army occupied the town the stockpile was not replenished, and any amounts brought in would not have lasted long. As with the example of the Winchester garrison above, troops would have rapidly run down stores that were not regularly restocked. Magazines needed constant replenishment to function and Leslie's lightning campaign at Newburn was in part a response to the difficulties he had supplying his forces within Scotland. His supply officers had found it difficult, gathering less than the 14 weeks of supply he had wanted in Scotland, so replenishing the magazines at Newcastle and establishing others at the newly occupied English towns would have been beyond the ability of the Covenanters. Instead, as discussed in the section on taxation below, the newly dispersed army became more reliant on local quartering for its victuals.

Leslie was not the only general of the Civil Wars able to make use of herds of livestock to provide strategic mobility to his forces, although in Leslie's case this was necessarily brief. The Ulster Confederate rebels, supplied 'on the hoof' by huge numbers of cattle by native drovers, were able to hold the strategic initiative in Ulster as their more mobile supply lines allowed for greater flexibility of movement.[146] Meanwhile, the Scots army in Ulster had to abandon their 1642 offensive when supplies ran out, remaining on the defensive for the next four years.[147] The Ulster Confederates' experience suggests a similarity in freedom of movement to that of Leslie's Newburn campaign, but the smaller size of the Ulster army and the greater availability of livestock enhanced their mobility.

The reliance on livestock to supply an army on the march was not an option for all forces in the Civil Wars. The Irish reliance on the use of livestock to supply their marching armies is no surprise when one considers how important cattle and other livestock were to the Irish pre-war economy. According to a 1621 speech in Parliament there were '100,000 head of cattle brought every year out of Ireland.'[148] According to Ormond, an English House of Commons inquiry found that 'about sixty-one thousand head of great cattle' had been brought over in 1660.[149] Even in 1641, the first full year of the rebellion, perhaps 20,000 head of cattle were transported into England from Ireland.[150] This access to cattle as a form of supply was an important element of the Confederate supply lines. When the Cessation of Arms was signed in September 1643, the Confederates undertook to pay Ormond

---

146 Ohlmeyer, 'The Wars of Religion, 1603–1660', p.178.
147 Ohlmeyer, 'The Wars of Religion, 1603–1660', p.180.
148 William Cobbett (ed.), *The Parliamentary History of England, from the Earliest Period to the Year 1803: From Which Last-mentioned Epoch it is Continued Downwards in the Work Entitled "Hansard's Parliamentary Debates"* (London, 1806), p.1195.
149 Carte, *The Life of James, Duke of Ormond*, IV, p.234.
150 Donald Woodward, 'The Anglo-Irish Livestock Trade of the Seventeenth Century', *Irish Historical Studies* Vol. 18, No. 72 (Sep. 1973), p.493.

£30,000 'which by the articles of the cessation was to be paid, half in money, and the rest in beeves and ammunition.'[151] As seen in Scotland, Leslie was able to make use of it for less than a single campaigning season and the Irish Confederates in Ulster, with their smaller numbers and the largely defensive stance of their opponents, stretched this further. The use of livestock as an army-wide system of provision was problematic on a few levels but perhaps of most immediate concern was the amount of fodder which would have to be spread between a much greater number of animals. An army already needed large amounts of fresh fodder to feed the mounts of its cavalry and dragoon units, as well as large numbers of transportation animals supporting its train of artillery and other baggage. It is probably no coincidence that the armies which made extensive use of livestock supplies in the Civil Wars were also the two – Leslie's Army of the Covenant and the Ulster Irish – who lacked substantial wagons and teams of draught horses, large numbers of cavalry, and large numbers of heavy artillery pieces. Livestock also had minds of their own and feet, which made keeping them problematic, particularly when their escorts were distracted. After relieving Gloucester in September 1643, the Red Regiment of the London Trained Bands had 'eighty-seven sheep' allocated to them from those gathered locally 'for the maintenance' of the Earl of Essex's army, but they 'afterwards lost them all' when the regiment deployed for the First Battle of Newbury.[152]

Purchase

Outside of daily victuals the preference for supplying provisions for the soldiers, at least by the governing authority, appears to have been contracted purchase orders. Here the army and those in authority over them could place large, bulk orders amongst civilian contractors to supply its soldiers. This could be with funds allocated to the individual units, who then placed and purchased their necessities themselves. For example, in March 1647 when Colonel James Castle's regiment of foot was being dispatched for service in Ireland, and was to be granted 'money wherewith to buy shoes and other necessaries'.[153] It could also mean dealing with the suppliers directly and issuing them to the soldiers upon receipt of the goods, or through stores being gathered for that purpose, which was often the case for large, multi-regiment sized orders. £6,000 worth of provisions, primarily clothing, were to be dispatched to the Parliamentarian forces in Ireland in November 1647,

---

151 Carte, *The Life of James, Duke of Ormond*, III, p.234.
152 Foster, *A True and Exact Relation of the Marchings of the Two Regiments of the Trained-Bands of the City of London*, p.9.
153 *CSPI 1647–1660*, p.734, 4 March, Further Orders of the Same.

with the 'clothes supplied to be obtainable for ready money' and with itemised costs per item of clothing.[154] This bulk purchasing could be effective, particularly if the army was located in close proximity to the suppliers and could thus hold them to account for the quality of their work, as distance from suppliers could, and did, lead to the supply of poor quality products. This method of supplying bulk orders for the military was not without risk to the suppliers. In May 1639, while the King's army struggled to supply its regiments in the north, the Holt family was still seeking protection or repayment for more than £5,300 which the family had expended supplying victuals for the Royal attack on the Isle du Rhé over a decade previously.[155] In contrast, some units, particularly garrisons, could secure supplies themselves and not have to rely on a centralised distribution system as the field armies had to. In December 1643, the Staffordshire Parliamentary Committee bought 'fivescore and eighteen yards of gray cloth at 2s. the yd. for cotes for the soldiers' from Thomas Hanson although it was noted they had no ready cash to pay him.[156] In 1643, the Royalist garrison at Lichfield under the command of Colonel Richard Bagot not only assembled a corn mill and gunpowder production facilities, but Bagot was also able to order 'cloth for clothing divers' of the soldiers and caps for his infantry.[157]

Clothing for the Protestant forces designed to counter the rebellion in Ireland (before the outbreak of the English Civil War) provides the best example of how centralised supply and distribution was not necessarily the most efficient. In February 1642, the Lord Justices in Ireland had asked that funds be made available to them for Irish suppliers to make uniforms for the increased numbers of soldiers in Ireland, many of whom, having been hastily raised, were not fully equipped. These men fell 'sick daily through cold for want of clothes and shoes.'[158] They claimed that the Irish suppliers 'are resident here and may be called to account' if the clothing did not meet requirements, while they felt that the suppliers in England 'may be careless of what suits to send us over being out of our reach to question them.'[159] In that concern, the Lord Justices were to be proven correct. The 6,000 suits of clothing (with caps) which arrived in Dublin from England were described as being made from poor quality cloth and 'the suits ill and slightly made up, the cassock not lined, the lining of the breeches from very bad cloth,

---

154 *CSPI 1647–1660*, p.765, 12 Nov., Further Orders of the Same.
155 *CSPD 1639*, p.147, May 10, Order of Council.
156 Pennington and Roots, *The Committee at Stafford, 1643–1645*, p.25.
157 Atherton, 'The Accounts of the Royalist Garrison of Lichfield Close, 1643–5' pp.70–71.
158 HMC, *Calendar of the Manuscripts of the Marquess of Ormonde*, II, p.71.
159 HMC, *Calendar of the Manuscripts of the Marquess of Ormonde*, II p.76.

the caps to little as they cannot be useful for the soldiers and such of them as were brought to this board are so little as they can hardly come on the head of a child.'[160]

There were certainly concerns of corruption within the supply chain for uniforms. John Davies was an official whose job it was to find, buy, and dispatch clothing and other supplies for the soldiers in Ireland, including the materials to make them. Davies was suspected of buying poor quality materials and charging close to twice the true value to Parliament. Cloth believed to be worth eight shillings he sold for eighteen shillings, and for uniforms which were worth ten shillings he was charging seventeen shillings.[161] Those uniforms which he sent 'were found to be very Course shrinking Cloth, and most of the Sutes too little and unserviceable.'[162] It is estimated that Davies was able to extract over £12,000 from Parliament over the course of eight to nine months, with a sizeable proportion of that as illegal profit.[163] This was not an isolated event, as in 1645 Commissary George Wood found that the clothing in stores for which Parliament had been charged 17s a set, was actually only worth a little over half that amount at 9s 9½d on inspection. Apparently, Wood's major concern was that this difference was being borne by the 'poor soldiers' who would pay for the clothing in deductions from their wages.[164] Although not directly connected to the operational level of logistics and supply, this aside regarding corruption, cost inflation, and profiteering helps put into context the need to supplement work done on the financial aspects of logistics, such as the work undertaken by Wheeler, with the operational work this study is focused on.

It is worth highlighting that the term 'uniform coat' is a misnomer. There was no national homogenous uniform for the armies of the seventeenth century, although individual colonels attempted to have uniformity across their own regiment. Instead, the term 'uniform coat' as used here refers to a particular cut of coat which was issued to soldiers. A 'suit of clothes', on the few occasions this was issued, was (ideally) a full set including a coat, doublet, breeches, stockings,

---

160 HMC, *Calendar of the Manuscripts of the Marquess of Ormonde*, II p.196.
161 *The State of the Irish Affairs, for the Honourable Members of the Houses of Parliament; as They Lye Represented Before Them, from the Committee of Adventurers in London for Lands in Ireland, Sitting at Grocers-Hall for That Service* (London: 1645), p.26. If this was the same John Davis who had previously served as 'commissary at Carrickfergus in the kingdome of Ireland' then he may have had several years' experience in supplying soldiers in Ireland having been in that previous position this October 1642, see Bodleian Rawlinson Ms. A 110, f.47, Mr Thompson for salt delivered to Carickfergus, 22 March 1643.
162 *The State of the Irish Affairs, for the Honourable Members of the Houses of Parliament; as They Lye Represented Before Them...* p.26.
163 *The State of the Irish Affairs, for the Honourable Members of the Houses of Parliament; as They Lye Represented Before Them...*, p.3.
164 TNA SP 28/33/443, Specification of George Wood, Commissary Officer.

and perhaps headwear such as those issued to the troops for Ireland in 1642. The terms 'coat' and 'cassock' appear to refer to the same item of clothing as a 'uniform coat', being the half-length and sleeved overcoat that was the main item of clothing for a soldier. Despite a commonly held belief that the soldiers of the English Civil Wars fought primarily in civilian clothing, there is evidence that many such coats were made for the soldiers on both sides. Prior to the British Civil Wars, apart from being so important to a soldier's health and welfare, clothing was seen as a part of a soldier's enlistment with his 'coat and conduct money' mentioned in chapter three above. During Queen Elizabeth's and King James's reigns soldiers were meant to be issued with two suits of clothing a year: wool for winter, and linen for summer.[165] However, by the time of the British Civil Wars, and certainly by their end, it appears that a soldier was only issued with one per year, further adding to the wear and tear of any uniform he was issued with, as his clothing was now expected to last a year rather than six months. Presumably this could mean an increased risk of exposure to heat or cold if the one suit of clothing issued was not suitable for the time of year. With hindsight, while typhus, or 'camp fever', and its causes were not identified at the time, the lack of fresh clothing and the close confines of military life would have increased the chances of the soldiers catching and spreading the disease, which is spread by bites of body-lice which live in the seams of clothing.[166]

The uniform coats provided for the soldiers enlisted to fight the Irish rebels in 1641 and 1642 were of a type that Parliament would use more than once through the wars, with some of the coats ordered for the New Model Army being of a similar design. The coats ordered for Ireland in 1642 were 'to be made of good serviceable cloth faced before and on the sleeves with baize and fitted with tape strings at eight shillings and sixpence each coat.'[167] The Irish Lord Justices' complaints of 1642 about the small size of this clothing may well have inspired the inclusion in the 1645 order for coats for the New Model Army that the 'Cloth both of ye Coates and ye Breeches to be first shrunke in Cold water' beforehand.[168] This was to ensure that the cloth shrank before being cut to size and avoiding the new coats shrinking and becoming useless the first time they were exposed to water, such as a heavy rainfall. Presumably the New Model Army was issued with unlined coats as these were cheaper than the earlier lined designs. A year previously, in 1644, Parliament had ordered 7,400 broadcloth coats with undyed linen liners for supplying their

---

165 Spring, *The First British Army*, p.49.
166 Lenihan, *Fluxes, Fevers, and Fighting Men: War and Disease in Ancien Régime Europe 1648–1789*, pp.20–22.
167 'Minute Book of the Commissioners for Irish Affairs' in Snow and Young, *The Private Journals of the Long Parliament: 7 March to 1 June 1642*, p.443.
168 Mungeam, 'Contracts for the Supply of Equipment', p.68, f.27v. and f.28r, p.69.

Covenanter Scots allies, these coats cost at least 16 shillings each.[169] The combined cost of an unlined coat for the New Model Army, together *with* a pair of breeches was 16 shillings compared to the costs of the earlier lined coat *without* breeches.[170] Given the reduction to one issue a year it is likely that the unlined coats were, in addition to being cheaper to produce, less warm than the more expensive lined coats which would have made the cold months of the year that little bit more unpleasant for the serving soldier.

The Royalist army units in Oxford were supplied with fresh uniforms in the summer of 1643 having 'clothed all their foote soldiers in redd and blew having all of them monteroes, coates and briches' according to Parliamentary reports.[171] The Montero cap was a design popularly issued to soldiers and was possibly a design unique to the military as 'the fashion of the Montero [is] much differing from other mens hatts' and often worn by soldiers in Europe 'instead of Helmets'.[172] The production of uniforms for the Royalists had begun at Oxford in January 1643 at 'the Musicke Schoole, and in the Astronomy Schoole adjoyninge to it' when according to a resident eyewitness 'a great many of taylers', those in Oxford and those resident 'within ten miles', were 'set on work to cutt out these coates, to the number of 4000 or 5000'.[173] This habit of bulk orders would have produced a degree of uniformity across several regiments in various armies years before the red-coated New Model Army took to the field. However, the deterioration of clothes on campaign was inevitable and soldiers needed to find a replacement wherever they could. While the soldiers for Ireland were initially clothed in full, surviving evidence from the later British Civil Wars suggests that the focus was on the uniform coat alone. The Earl of Essex's forces were possibly equipped only with uniform coats at first, supplying the rest of their clothing themselves, or at least no surviving records indicate a centralised purchase or delivery of such clothing.

The system of purchasing was entirely reliant on the civilian suppliers' willingness and ability to meet the demand. Suppliers extending credit or accepting delayed payment for their products was a risky endeavour – as the Holt family could attest. Contractors also offered to provide clothing for the King's army including Mr Thomas Bushell who, in March of 1643

---

169 Peachey, *The Soldier's Life in the English Civil War*, pp.27–28.
170 Mungeam, 'Contracts for the Supply of Equipment', p.68, f.27v and p.69, f.28r.
171 Luke, *Journal of Sir Samuel Luke*, p.119.
172 Famiano Strada, and Robert Stapylton, *De Bello Belgico: The History of the Low-Countrey Warres* (London: 1650), p.56.
173 Andrew Clark (ed.), *The Life and Times of Anthony Wood, Antiquary of Oxford, 1632–1695, Described by Himself*, Vol. 1 (1632–1663) (Oxford: Oxford Historical Society, 1891), pp.83–84.

made his proposition this that he would procure for the King's Souldiers Cassocks, Breeches, Stockings & Capps at reasonable rates to be delivered at Oxford, and at the delivery to receyve ready money, or a bill of exchange to be payd at London, the choyce to be left to them who provide the clothes. And when one Loade of Clothes is brought, or in bringing, to go on with providing of a second Loade, and so from time to time till the Kings Army be all provided for, and payd for in such manner as before.[174]

The Protestant forces in Ireland throughout 1642 and 1643 lacked both the local suppliers capable of producing the required provisions and the credit to engage with them if they existed. Despite attempts by the Irish Government in 1641 to secure English money for establishing Irish-based suppliers, the initial forces sent to Ireland, along with the supplies bought and dispatched to Ireland for local forces there were instead provided primarily out of England. The commanders of the Protestant Irish forces subsequently struggled to keep their troops supplied when Parliament's attention turned to England and to prosecuting their war with the King. The Marquess of Ormond, commander of the King's forces in Ireland, suffered extreme difficulties in supplying his own troops with regular clothing. These problems are well illustrated by the letters that preceded his dispatch of Royalist troops back to England. In October 1643, Ormond warned of these soldiers' poor clothing in a letter to Orlando Bridgeman, the Royalist official dispatched from Oxford to Chester to prepare for the arrival of the regiments. Ormond's letter stated that:

> In these former despatches I expressed, as neat as words could do it, at least any of mine, the miserable wants the soldier had sustained here, and how absolutely necessary it would be to have provision in good measure made for them of victual, money, clothes, shoes, and stockings; without which they would not only be unserviceable, but very seduceable, by those doubtless will attempt to corrupt both them and officers from their allegiance. Which I inform you of, because I understand you are principally and deservedly trusted by his majesty in these parts: and to the end you may set the uttermost of your endeavours a work to prevent the danger the wants of the army when it shall arrive (if it so please God) on that side may bring upon his majesty's service[175]

---

174 Phillips, 'The Ottley Papers', II, p.273.
175 Carte, *The Life of James, Duke of Ormond*, V, pp.478–479.

Ormond again repeated his concerns in a letter that same month to the Archbishop of York, John Williams, stating 'the greatest danger I fear, when they are landed on the other side [in England], is that if provision of shoes, stockings, and clothes, and money be not instantly with them, it will be easy to seduce them with likely promises of having these wants supplied.'[176] Ormond was evidently concerned with the provision of clothing for his veterans and desperate to emphasise their need. This serves to underscore the issues Ormond himself must have been experiencing in supplying his own forces in Ireland at the time. As already mentioned, the lack of surviving sources in Ireland is frustrating, but the fact that Ormond seemed unable to provide for many of his troops' basic needs leads one to believe that his supply situation in Ireland must have been truly dire. That Ormond could not support these troops in either pay or supply strongly argues an inability to do so, although it could simply have been a case of priority. The fact that these men had stayed with their regiments under such circumstances as these suggests that they had little choice but to do so and that deserting was not seen as an option. In which case, it is possible that Ormond may have felt that his limited resources were better spent elsewhere than on the English troops. Ormond's fears over their loyalties on returning to England may very well have reflected this, rather than just concern for his soldiers, however, there is no way of knowing. Certainly, the men had been fighting for months without any pay, and the King promised Ormond that the veterans arriving in England would not only 'receive our pay in the same proportion and manner with the rest of our army heere', but that the soldiers would also receive their 'arreares that shall bee due to any of them.'[177]

In response to Ormond's concerns, Bridgeman assured him that he had secured 1,200 pairs of shoes and stockings 'and the rest were in the making' for the elements of the army dispatched to Chester.[178] He had 'gotten cloth and frize sufficient for them all, not yet made into apparel, but hastened it to Chester, where I hope to have it fitted up this weeke and the next.'[179] That Bridgeman, an experienced administrator, believed he could have 2,000 uniform coats made at Chester within a fortnight suggests that regional towns had the capacity for rapid clothing production if needed, since this was a production average of over 160 uniforms per day excluding the Sundays. Unfortunately, we do not know any more details than that – such as the cost of these coats or their pattern. Ormond's warning to Bridgeman, however, was not exaggerating the condition of the troops. When they arrived in Chester they were apparently so poorly clothed that Bridgeman had the

---

176 Carte, *The Life of James, Duke of Ormond*, V, pp.479–481.
177 Carte, *The Life of James, Duke of Ormond*, V, pp.465–467.
178 Carte, *The Life of James, Duke of Ormond*, V, p.526.
179 Carte, *The Life of James, Duke of Ormond*, V, p.526.

Mayor of Chester organise a collection of clothing from the residents of Chester, which provided enough civilian apparel for 300 of the soldiers until their uniforms were ready.[180] The outbreak of civil war in England and the subsequent sundering of supply lines to the forces in Ireland suggests that a year of campaigning without fresh supplies of clothing and money was sufficient to turn uniformed soldiers into men desperate for any sort of clothing. The situation in England at this time was not quite so dire. Despite his preparations for the arrival of these veterans while they were *en route*, that Bridgeman was still surprised at the state of the English veterans from Ireland upon their arrival suggests strongly that other English soldiers Bridgeman had seen previously in Oxford, Chester, and elsewhere in England were not reduced to such straits.

The efforts in providing clothing for soldiers throughout the English Civil Wars was focused on the coat as this functioned not only as clothing but also an identifier, and the concentration on production allowed for bulk orders to be delivered quicker than a full set of clothing. However, it meant that soldiers would have had to source the rest of their clothing themselves, as well as replacements when whatever clothing or uniforms they had, or were issued with, wore out. Some were issued through their commanders who made use of local traders, such as the cavalry troopers issued with replacement clothing at Ludlow in 1644 by Sir Michael Wodehouse.[181] Others appear to have seized clothing when they needed it, such as when troops under Prince Rupert and Prince Maurice seized clothes and provisions in Herefordshire, also in 1644.[182] However, others who were issued clothing from stores rather than those reliant on local purchase or plunder might have been lucky enough to gain access to a full suit of uniform clothing. An example would be the intended recipients of the stores George Wood investigated in 1645, discussed earlier.

The largest concern for generals appears to have been the provision of ready victuals for their troops rather than clothing. An intriguing letter from the siege of Tiverton Castle in October 1645 suggests that the New Model Army under General Sir Thomas Fairfax had found a new method of gathering provisions without the need for either magazines or quartering. The letter, written to the Speaker of the House of Commons, is signed by four members of the Houses of Parliament detailing the successful siege of the castle and numerous other aspects of the campaign. The important part follows a description on the state of the New Model Army soldiers at Tiverton after the Royalist garrison had surrendered:

---

180 John Barratt, *The Great Siege of Chester* (Stroud: The History Press, 2011), p.63.
181 SA LB7/2015, receipts of clothing from Owen Jones, tailor.
182 Ian Atherton, 'An Account of Herefordshire in the First Civil War', *Midland History*, Vol. 21, No. 1 (1996), p.147.

wee cannot but make it out request that mony may bee speeded to them, without which, it is much doubted how they will be supplied, the country where they advance not having in their quarters wherewith to supply them. But if money bee wanting to pay in the market which is appointed to follow the armie with provisions from our reare, the market will faile.[183]

This siege was part of the campaign into the South-West of England to extinguish the last remnants of Royalist forces there. A few points can be drawn out of this extract, including the note that without money soldiers would be reliant on quartering on the local civilians for food and that this would not work. Of key importance is the reference to the existence of a market following the army from which the soldiers could buy their provisions if, and only if, they had the money. Soldiers paying for their food with their own wages was nothing new in of itself, even when supplied out of magazines the soldiers' pay was stopped for the costs of the items provided. However, a moving market dependent on the soldiers' custom, following the soldiers who could buy their provisions from merchants directly, appears a new method of supplying the troops. This may have been solely for the push into the Devon and Cornwall peninsula, especially introduced to ensure that the New Model Army did not suffer the supply issues which had contributed to the Earl of Essex's defeat the previous year in the Lostwithiel campaign. However, Aryeh Nusbacher's article on the New Model's campaign at Naseby suggests that on that campaign the approach to provisioning was similar to that of the later South-West campaign. According to Nusbacher in June 1645, at the outset of the Naseby campaign, Fairfax complained to fellow officers that a reliance on foraging and quartering was negatively impacting his ability to gather sufficient provisions for his army. Nusbacher argues that Fairfax, with the support of Parliament, encouraged food traders and sutlers to follow the New Model Army wherever it marched and forbade his troops from plundering or threatening the merchants. In this way the merchants were able to feel safe in dealing with the soldiers and the merchants could themselves send out agents to source food which they could then resell, at a profit, to the soldiers in camp. Nusbacher believes that this mobile supply market was a major factor in the speed and prosecution of the campaign as Fairfax and his men gained mobility and strategic speed which was denied to their opponents.[184] Following the Naseby campaign, and the reduction of Royalist strongholds, there would have been a decreasing risk of skirmishes and raids

---

183 HMC, *Thirteenth Report, Appendix, The Manuscripts of his Grace the Duke of Portland*, I, pp.292–293.
184 Nusbacher, 'Civil Supply in the Civil War: Supply of Victuals to the New Model Army on the Naseby Campaign, 1–14 June 1645', pp.145–160.

from the Royalists as they withdrew westward. This in turn would have probably encouraged merchants to undertake the work of supplying the New Model Army for ready profit, knowing that the risk of being intercepted by Royalist foragers or patrols had been greatly lessened.

Detail of the New Model Army supply wagons on Streeter's engraving in *Anglia Rediviva*, Joshua Sprigge (London, 1647). As with the number of men shown in the regiments of horse and foot Streeter has simplified the engraving by reducing the number of horses shown for each wagon, although the wagons themselves are shown accurately. (Public Domain via Stephen Ede-Borrett collection)

Taxation

The details of Civil War financial taxation, its implementation and its administration, has been extensively studied by others.[185] Instead of considering taxation as a source of local or central government financing, this section focuses on taxation as a method of supplying food and provision at the operational level. As the lack of ready cash impacted an army's ability to provision their troops and without a supply of money, military officers had to find other methods of sustaining

---

185 See Holmes, *The Eastern Association in the English Civil War*, pp.117–180; Hutton, *The Royalist War Effort 1642–1646*, pp.89–108. Almost all county studies have considered taxation, however Hughes, *Politics, Society and Civil War in Warwickshire* and Gratton, *The Parliamentarian and Royalist War Effort in Lancashire* are the perhaps the best examples.

their troops. By 1 September 1640, only three days after their victory at the Battle of Newburn, the Scottish Covenanting army was running out of money to buy bread and beer in newly occupied Newcastle and as a result had to pay for the provisions, at least in part, with promissory notes.[186] Officers then began allowing their troops to plunder and loot houses 'if they [the Scots] find no dwellers' with the reasoning that if the owners had fled then the former occupants were enemies and therefore plunder was acceptable.[187] By the second week of September 1640, necessity demanded that the Covenanting army had to source more supplies for its maintenance and they began dispatching troops to surrounding English towns demanding food at rates dictated by the Scottish officers.[188] By the end of September the money for this food was no longer coming from Scotland, but from taxes imposed on the occupied English areas. While Leslie's army appears to have been able to be largely self-sustaining for the initial assembling, and the lightning campaign around Newburn in August, it could not continue in this way for more than six weeks from when the army gathered in mid-July to the beginning of September. After this point the army briefly relied on plunder and threat of pillaging to gather supplies but eventually had to increasingly rely on impositions on the occupied areas of England. Financial exactions began with those English in the area identified as either Roman Catholics or Episcopalians, but this was apparently insufficient and by the end of September the Scots began taxing the rest of the population in the areas they occupied, including their co-religionists.[189] The importance of this tax for the maintenance of the Covenanting army is highlighted by the fact that Scottish soldiers who plundered English taxpayers 'if they take an egg or a chicken from those who pay contribution' were hanged by the Covenanting army authorities.[190] Technically then, the Covenanting occupying forces were able to nominally avoid free quarter by paying for the provisions they drew from local civilians. However, the money used to pay for provisioning the army was raised by taxing these same occupied territories.

It is striking that even the most well-organised and trained army in the British Isles at the time was only able to campaign for a month and a half on its own supply systems before falling back on quartering on civilians. However, it is possible that the Covenanters were making less use of quartering than an English army would have, instead being reliant on markets and taxation for their victuals, but using

---

186 *CSPD 1639–1640*, pp.60–62, Sept. 14, Secretary Vane to Secretary Windebank and p.68, Sept 16, Secretary Vane to Secretary Windebank.
187 *CSPD 1639–1640*, Sept. 16, Secretary Vane to Secretary Windebank, p.68.
188 *CSPD 1639–1640*, Sept. 9, William Roane to [Sir John Lambe], p.35; Furgol, 'Beating the Odds: Alexander Leslie's 1640 Campaign in England', p.55.
189 *CSPD 1639–1640*, pp.68–69, Sept. 16, Secretary Vane to Secretary Windebank.
190 *CSPD 1639–1640*, p.35, Sept. 9, William Roane to [Sir John Lambe].

tents for their billets at least when marching out on campaign – wisely given the circumstances, as it stands in stark contrast to the English experience related above. In 1639, while encamped in Berwickshire, Covenanter officers, particularly senior ones, had tents with their 'sojours [soldiers] about all in hutts of tinder [wood], covered with divot [turf] or straw.'[191] For his campaign in 1640, Leslie had procured enough tents for them to be provided for his whole army, with one 'for every six soldiers'.[192] Robert Baillie claimed these had been manufactured by cloth and canvas donations from Scottish civilians.[193]

The role of local garrisons in securing local supplies during the English Civil War was not dissimilar to the Scottish methods during their occupation in 1640. Work on the experience of garrisons and their role in the wider war effort has been undertaken separately by Ian Atherton, Andrew Hopper, and Elias Kupfermann, revealing the development of garrison warfare, and importantly, their administration.[194] An effective garrison in the English Civil War was not one that plundered or raided the local population to support itself, such as the Parliamentary garrison at Edgbaston. Instead, successful garrisons which were effective enough to be at least partially self-reliant from central supply, were ones whose main source of income became the imposition of taxation on the local civilian population.[195] This allowed for the extraction of resources and not just coin, but often food and other provisions which the garrison could use to support itself. The Constable's Accounts of Uttoxeter are replete with examples of provisions sent to the Royalist garrison at Tutbury. In December 1643 these included '25 strikes of Oats that were sent for by Warrant to Tutbury.' On 7 May 1644 Uttoxeter sent approximately 17lbs of cheese and five pots of butter, in addition to the sum of £50 paid 'in money & Returns to Tutbury Castle' in August of the same year.[196] The village constables of Upton in Nottinghamshire recorded several occasions where garrison troops from Newark 'came for the Assessment' and needed to be provided with 'meat & drink' or other provisions.[197] By co-existing with the local civilian population rather than simply tyrannically occupying them, the garrisons

---

191 Baillie, *The Letters and Journals of Robert Baillie*, I, p.211.
192 Terry, *The Life and Campaigns of Alexander Leslie, First Earl of Leven*, p.106.
193 Baillie, *The Letters and Journals of Robert Baillie*, I, p.255.
194 Atherton, 'Royalist Finances in the English Civil War: The Case of Lichfield Garrison, 1643–5', pp.43–67; Andrew Hopper, '"Tinker" Fox and the Politics of Garrison Warfare in the West Midlands, 1643–50', *Midland History*, Vol. 24 (1999), pp.98–113; Kupfermann, 'The Role of Windsor Castle During the English Civil Wars'.
195 Atherton, 'Royalist Finances in the English Civil War: The Case of Lichfield Garrison, 1643–5', p.67.
196 Cooper, 'The English Civil War in Staffordshire: The Experience of Uttoxeter', pp.72–73 & 90.
197 For examples see Bennett, *A Nottinghamshire Village in War and Peace*, pp.12, 14, 17, 19.

could draw at least part of the resources necessary for their continued survival from a more cooperative civilian population rather than an utterly hostile one.

Plunder and Requisition

Plundering of local civilians by starving, unpaid or simply bored soldiers was not always a criminal act. On several occasions it, or the threat of it, was actively used by military authorities as a means of leverage. In early September 1640, Scottish officers in the occupied area of England cautioned local gentry that they needed to ensure prices remained reasonable otherwise the occupying Covenanter army's money would run out all the quicker. If this happened, the local worthies were told, then supplies would need to be taken unpaid and by force.[198] Prior to this extortion, it was reported that Scottish troops used plundering against Catholics in England with the tacit agreement of their officers – they 'pay for all they take unless they meet with a recusant, and them they plunder.'[199] That both the plunder and the threat of plunder occurred before the Scots had successfully implemented their taxation system in the occupied areas, upon which they later relied to pay for their quarters, suggests that these earlier actions were only used until a better solution was found. It was only after this taxation had begun that pillaging and plundering of any kind was actually punished by hanging. This is supported by the experience of the Royalist garrison at Lichfield in 1643 that, according to Atherton, used plunder as a temporary expedient until more efficient systems of resource gathering and taxation could be established.[200]

The dependency on quarter (or with pay arrears free quarter) could turn a civilian population of an area progressively resistant and hostile to an army and its leaders. Both sides recognised this, with Royalist and Parliamentarian commanders alike during the First Civil War threatening increasingly harsher treatment against soldiers who preyed on civilians – regardless of the plundering activities being forced on the soldiers by the commanders' inability to pay or even supply their own troops. Jonathon Worton argues that for ordinary civilians there was little to differentiate between 'requisitioning by warrant, commandeering or outright looting.'[201] In the immediate sense this was true as they all meant the loss of property without repayment and only with hindsight can it be argued that some may have been able to gain restitution and/or repayment by a victorious

---

198 Furgol, 'Beating the Odds: Alexander Leslie's 1640 Campaign in England', p.55.
199 CSPD 1640–1641, Aug. 28, Secretary Vane to Secretary Windebank, p.642.
200 For use of plunder as temporary expedient under more efficient systems see Atherton, 'Royalist Finances in the English Civil War: The Case of Lichfield Garrison, 1643-5', p.67.
201 Worton, *To Settle the Crown*, p.160.

Parliament after 1646. However, the military authorities certainly saw a difference and made efforts to limit unauthorised plundering, particularly on civilians in areas that they controlled and who they relied upon for supplies and taxation. Colonel Van Geyrish's troopers' looting in Shropshire was extensive enough that the commander of Ludlow, Sir Michael Woodhouse, complained to Prince Rupert in the autumn of 1644 that these men were 'quartered to destroy and not advance the service.'[202] Van Geyrish's regiment was not only quartered at Ludlow but also issued clothing, shoes, boots, and equipment from various traders in the town. Sir Michael clearly felt that their plundering was excessive under these circumstances and took the side of the civilians.[203] This contrasts with the authorised requisitions in Ludlow itself where the soldiers of Sir Michael's garrison served warrants to townspeople before appropriating bedding and linens for their quarters in the castle above the town. How Sir Michael and other commanders decided what necessary requisitions were and what was unnecessary looting, we can only infer. In the case of Van Geyrish's troopers, having been issued with the necessary provisions and quartered at Ludlow, Sir Michael saw no forgivable reason for them to plunder civilians as, in his mind, their needs had been met.

The few surviving sources regarding the supply of troops in Ireland paint a bleaker picture than elsewhere in the British Isles. Dublin-based Protestant forces totalling 3,000 infantry and 500 cavalry were sent into the rebel-held Pale in 1642, not as part of a campaign of reconquest but in 'hope to hold them in heart with pillage amongst the rebels'.[204] In March 1642 the Protestant forces sent to relieve Drogheda were ordered to

> Wound, kill, slay, and destroy, by all the ways and means [you] may, all the said rebels, their adherents and relievers, to burn, spoil, waste, consume, destroy and demolish all the places, towns, and houses where the said rebels are, or have been relieved and harboured, and all the corn and hay there, and kill and destroy all the men there inhabiting able to bear arms.[205]

For much of the Confederate Wars, the larger part of Ireland, including the majority of Ireland's food producing territory, was occupied by the rebels. In 1642 the Irish Protestant government still assumed there would be regular supplies and reinforcements from England and Scotland to support any counter-rebellion

---

202 Worton, *To Settle the Crown*, p.161.
203 For quartering bill see SA, LB7/2066; For issues of clothing and equipment see SA, LB7/2015; SA, LB7/2081.
204 HMC, *Calendar of the Manuscripts of the Marquess of Ormonde*, II, p.86.
205 HMC, *Calendar of the Manuscripts of the Marquess of Ormonde*, II, p.86.

campaigns. Given those circumstances it is not unreasonable that a scorched earth response to the rebellion was seen as a viable military strategy. However, this destructive approach to the food production that the Protestant forces could achieve, and the slump in English materiel support due to the worsening tensions between King and Parliament, led to a dramatic rise in local food prices. The cost of wheat, necessary for the production of those most basic of military rations – bread and biscuit, rose throughout 1642, from around 10 shillings per barrel in October 1641 to 18 shillings in July 1642 and then rising to 22 shillings in December 1642, more than doubling the price from a little over a year earlier.[206] Prices would continue to fluctuate on an upward trend and reach 30 shillings per barrel of wheat by July 1644.[207] The resulting limits on food purchasing that this shortage produced dramatically hampered the ability of the Protestant forces to reconquer Ireland.

Here we see a different use of plunder. The orders for the Protestants sent to relieve Drogheda might be considered part of a punitive expedition – wanton spoilage and destruction to punish the civilian population for supporting the rebels – rather than a means of obtaining supplies. However, I would suggest that at least part of the reasoning was in fact a form of supply denial. As we have seen, militaries were incredibly reliant on civilian populations to provide them with provisions and other means. If you were to destroy this civilian infrastructure – to 'burn, spoil, waste, consume, destroy and demolish all the places, towns, and houses' in the area from where you knew your enemy drew supply, as well as all of the crops and fodder in the area – it would be a powerful attack against the ability of the enemy to draw supplies, particularly if you are in no position to occupy it yourself, as was the case with the territory under discussion. It is worth remembering as well, that in March 1642 the Protestant forces in Ireland were still confident of receiving provision and supply from England, from where men, supplies, and funds were still being delivered, and so wreaking such havoc on the enemy supply system made military sense. Throughout this study it has been shown how dependent the military was on civilians for supplying a myriad of transportation, food, shelter, and manpower needs. If that is the case, then an argument could be made that destroying civilian infrastructure, crops, and dwellings is also denying them to the enemy forces. If the military and civilian are so intertwined in terms of logistics and supply, it is a question as to what point

---

206 Bodleian Rawlinson, Ms A 110, f.3v, *Corne, etc., delivered in Ireland.*; Bodleian Rawlinson, Ms A 110, f.22v, *Brown, Crone and Beard for wheate;* Lenihan, *Confederate Catholics at War*, p.58.
207 Lenihan, *Confederate Catholics at War*, p.58.

can you reasonably separate the two when it comes to attacking the enemy supply system.

Conclusion

The supplying of regular provisions in the necessary amounts to early modern armies was predominantly an insurmountable task hampered by transportation, technology levels, suitable food preservation, and ready money. Every attempt during the British Civil Wars to supply the various armies was never sufficient in and of itself to support the needs of the soldiers. The most common method – quartering – could work in theory, but only if there were enough households locally to support the armies, with enough readily available food and shelter to spare for the soldiers, and enemy forces were not close enough to threaten the army if it was dispersed. If any of these factors, which military officers generally had no control over, were not met then finding sufficient supply and shelter for their men was not possible. The other systems used appear to be largely supplementary to quartering rather than replacement systems – these being purchase, pillaging, taxation, and requisition. The purchase of supplies or shelter was only possible if the goods were readily available, if the army had the means to store them, and if the army was able to transport the goods to the soldiers in the field. The movement of an army, which rapidly consumed what resources were readily available, led the soldiers to take whatever was accessible and this was often at a substantial cost to local civilians. It is worth reiterating how reliant the soldiers were on civilians, either directly as householders quartering them or as the taxpayers and producers that supplied their needs through other systems. Plundering too was reliant on civilians, but as this seems to have been used primarily out of desperation, as a threat, or a strategic choice, it was preferred, by both military and civilians, that it was supplanted by other systems.

Despite the impact that the supply of provisions had on both strategic and tactical planning, the importance of provisions remains absent in the work of most historians. An example here will serve to highlight this point. Ian Roy sought to answer one of the most debated topics of the military history of the British Civil Wars in his article 'Why did Prince Rupert Fight at Marston Moor?'[208] Why did the Prince, who had marched north to relieve the embattled Earl of Newcastle's Royalist army, decide to launch an attack against a force composed of three enemy armies which certainly outnumbered his own perhaps by as much as two to one? And with a force partly composed of men who, as we saw, were reportedly near

---

208 Ian Roy, 'Why did Prince Rupert Fight at Marston Moor?' *Journal of the Society for Army Historical Research*, 86 (347), Autumn 2008, pp.236–257.

mutiny over their lack of pay. In his article Roy outlines all of the possible theories historians and contemporaries have proposed, including: Rupert's arrogance in his belief regarding his own military capabilities, the King's letter demanding action, Rupert's personal animosity to the Scots and to rebels, desire of a victory to weaken his enemies who sat on the Royalist Council of War, or his belief in the desperation of the Royalist cause. Looking at the question through the lens of the supply of provisions makes the answer much, much simpler.

On his march north Rupert would have stripped the land of all easily accessible food to feed his men through quartering and foraging. This would have removed all of the surplus available food within perhaps a 30 mile range of the army's line of march. Once at York, in an area already foraged and quartered over by four other armies – three enemy, and the Royalist Earl of Newcastle's who Rupert was sent to aid – he had no choice but to fight. Withdrawing so soon after arriving, possibly with the addition of the bulk of Newcastle's unpaid men, would have necessitated dispersing his army over a wider area in order to find the supplies of food necessary to feed them, which he could not have done with three enemy armies in such close proximity. His dispersed army would have been destroyed in detail as the enemy brought their already superior numbers to bear on his divided and scattered units. His foragers too would have struggled to bring in any significant food supplies in the face of numerous enemy cavalry patrols.

Alternatively, he could perhaps have attempted to march away keeping his army concentrated in the withdrawal back towards friendly territory through the area he had recently marched through, which would have been bare of supplies. With an enemy in pursuit and no immediate food supplies his starving men would have deserted in their desperation to find food. Rupert would have seen his regiments melt away even before the enemy attacked his forces. Rupert's choices at Marston Moor, based solely on the realities of supply, were either to withdraw (facing an inevitable destruction through dispersal and destruction of his forces or through desertion) or to fight. Why did Prince Rupert fight at Marston Moor? Because the methods available to him for supplying and feeding his army at that time meant that he simply had no other choice.

Conclusion

In the introduction of this book, I showed how the military logistics and supply systems during the British Civil Wars have been largely understudied, particularly at the operational level. Indeed, it was clear that the value of research into military logistics and supply across history more broadly has been generally under appreciated. To quote Luttwak again, 'whatever is dramatic easily displaces what is merely important'.[1] The need to attract and engage audiences, and to attempt to answer historical questions concisely, are understandable drivers in current historical study. The limited surviving source material has perhaps been another factor for historians, however by careful application of a broad range of both civilian and military sources a much clearer picture of what these logistic and supply systems might have looked like during the British Civil Wars and how they operated can be gained. This holds value in contributing to filling the yawning gap in the considerations around early modern military operations, certainly from the perspective of the British Isles as outlined in the introduction.

By sidestepping operational logistics and supply, leaving it largely unexplored, there are questions about the history of warfare and society which have gone unanswered, indeed unasked, for too long. From new perspectives on tactical successes, strategic choices, and the societal impacts of warfare, an analysis of logistics and supply paves the way to a greater understanding of the whys and hows. One of the major overarching conclusions of this work, shown to have held true for all aspects of logistics and supply, is that the military during the British Civil Wars was incredibly reliant on both the existing civilian infrastructure and the continual interaction with civilians throughout the wars. Without engaging with the civilian populace, the military would not have been able to obtain the food to eat, the soldiers to fight with, the clothes for them to wear, or the transportation to move it all to where it needed to be. At this point in the study, it is perhaps not

---

1 Edward Luttwak, 'Logistics and the Aristocratic Idea of War' in *Feeding Mars: Logistics in Western Warfare from the Middle Ages to the Present*, edited by John A. Lynn (Boulder: Westview Press, 1993), p.4.

unreasonable to point out that without any effective interaction or cooperation between the military and civilian it is difficult to see how the wars could have been fought at all.

This study was written with the intent of showing how the military logistic and supply systems of the British Civil Wars operated, and to highlight that they were heavily reliant on civilian interactions in order to function, based as these systems were on the pre-existing civilian methods and infrastructure. Establishing the military systems on civilian structures and vehicles was a natural response to the outbreak of war after decades of internal peace. There was little pre-existing military infrastructure in place and for limited periods and expectations the civilian transport network could operate to military needs rather well – the English response to the Irish rebellion stands out here as an example. Here military supplies were shipped westward along the roads using the civilian carrier network. These carriers were sometimes impressed but, as seems to have been the case for men like George Wood and William Pennoyer, they often appear to have been paid to transport goods along with their usual routes.

However, this reliance on civilian methods, developed for civilian needs in time of peace, struggled to adapt to military needs, or perhaps it is more correct to say the military struggled to adapt the civilian methods to their specific military needs. For campaigns in the North of England, veteran soldiers, such as Sir Jacob Astley, had advised the making of large numbers of supply dumps in preparation for fielding an army in an area that would otherwise struggle to feed large numbers of troops. This advice was not implemented, much to the detriment of the army, although a limited number of dumps were built in the east coast cities of England. The wagons preferred by the English military were also few and far between in the North of England, and the speed of construction of new ones was insufficient to meet the army's needs. This forced the English forces in 1639 and 1640 to try and secure sufficient wagons from the whole of England. However, because of the pre-existing civilian preferences born out of the suitability for the local topography, many areas only had carts to send and even when they arrived the vehicles appear to have come equipped with civilian size horse teams. Attempts to adapt these vehicles to the needs of the military required more horses and as a result also needed more harness for the extra animals, with the latter an element completely unforeseen by anyone in the military administration.

In contrast, the Scottish forces in the Bishops' Wars, planned their military operations around the forms of transport available to them, and around their known limitations. Without access to numbers of draught animals or of vehicles, Leslie made use of lighter artillery, a moving supply of livestock, and a streamlined baggage train composed of packhorses which were able to travel quicker, but carry comparatively less, than wagons. In 1640, these considerations allowed him to

Artillery of Spanish garrison leaving Maastricht in 1632. Jan van de Velde (II), after Jan Martszen the Younger, 1632 (Rijksmuseum).

plan a swift campaign into England in order to place the burden of supporting his troops onto England. This, combined with a recruitment system providing a better quality of soldier, ensured the Scottish success in 1640.

When logistical plans failed, strategic plans had to change. In Ireland the Protestant forces planned for reinforcement and logistical support from England and pursued a scorched earth policy in the nearby areas, confident that this would deny supply to the rebellion. However, with the outbreak of civil war in England, this severing of the supply lines from England meant Irish Protestants had then to try to draw supply from areas they themselves had devastated, turning their plans of reconquest into defensive postures.

Regional variation amongst civilian practices also heavily impacted the military supply systems as demonstrated throughout this work. The economic dispersal of vehicles meant that Parliamentarian armies would be able to base most of their land transport on the large and efficient wagon, and by sea on the heavier coastal transportation of the east coast collier. This latter method would have remarkable results when Parliament invaded Ireland and Scotland in the later stages of the war, also being the lynchpin of supporting a larger and more successful invasion of Scotland in 1650 than Charles I ever came close to achieving in 1640. In comparison, the Royalists were often forced to rely on the less substantial carts for most of their transport vehicles - and sometimes even packhorses – which, although providing them with perhaps a degree more speed over rugged terrain, were less efficient overall

The rivers of England played a key role in supplying forces as well, and in fact one so important that they had a pronounced impact on strategic planning as both Royalists and Parliamentarians attempted to gain absolute control of the major rivers. The desire to secure the efficient and significant river transportation opportunities of the River Severn was probably the main aim of the Royalist siege of Gloucester, which itself led to the First Battle of Newbury in 1643. Again, logistics and supply were crucial in shaping campaign strategy, and the reason many historians have puzzled over the decisions to attack Gloucester is because of an absence of interest in, or a lack of appreciation of, these particular factors. It is difficult to fully understand strategic reasoning without an appreciation of logistics and supply.

The reliance on civilian interaction was not simply one of imposition. Without active civilian engagement supplies were harder to come by and logistical challenges were made that much greater. This is exemplified in the supply of manpower, where the reliance on parish instruments to gather local men for service in the armies was hampered by the determination of civilians to place their own local needs first. The men first sent to war were those seen as the greatest burden on the parish, as these were the most easily spared. Interestingly, as demonstrated by the example of the Royalist impressment docket, the military recognised this and there appears to have been a compromise made between military needs and what the parish was willing, or able, to supply in terms of manpower. However, greater numbers of men were required in England to refill the armies of the Royalists and the Parliamentarian forces than the parish system could readily supply. Here the military demand for fresh manpower was too great for the civilians to easily or willingly meet, and the problems of recruit desertion and limited manpower continued.

A prime example of the military struggling in the face of the simple realities of civilian life is best exemplified by the provision of food on campaign. Here the reality of relying on quartering was far from what was preferred by the generals, but it was often forced upon them, and their men, by the lack of anything better.

Remember, the difficulties of providing enough transportation meant that consistent, daily supplies of food were unrealistic, and that said supplies had to be sourced as close as possible to the soldier. As a result, supplying troops on campaign with victuals was intermittent and dependent on what food was available from civilians nearby or within foraging range. It appears that the New Model Army found a way around this in their later campaigns in England when they attempted new systems of moving markets to supply men on campaign, but the New Model appears, again, to have relied on civilians, although in this case civilian sutlers and merchants willing to follow the army and provide food – for a profit.

Even something as simple and necessary as the provision of food, and shelter, held weighty consequences for strategic realities. This was not just for keeping men in the field but being pivotal to a general's decision to fight. The surprise proximity of the armies to one another near Edgehill, and the necessity to defeat the enemy to secure local resources, may have directly led to the timing and place of the first major battle of the British Civil War. The realities of supply impacting the strategic front is supported by the decision by the Royalists to attack Gloucester, but it is most obvious in the example of Marston Moor where an understanding of the realities of operational logistics and supply have now, as I have argued, provided a clear explanation as to why Prince Rupert chose to fight there – because in the face of logistical realities the decision was made for him. Fight or flee, the Royalist force's only chance was in a battlefield victory, and nothing less could save the combined Royalist armies.

While this study of logistics and supply does not answer all the questions of the British Civil Wars, it does hopefully contribute to the debate on some of them and even challenges some existing preconceptions. For the former, while it does not answer how, or why, Parliament ended up as overall victor of the Wars, it is interesting that the faction which did was also the only one with control of the east coast colliers and the one also able to make extensive use of the four-wheeled wagon. These gave Parliament the capabilities of fielding carriers on both land and sea which were far superior in terms of capacity and efficiency than anything their opponents could utilise. Leslie's aggressiveness in the Second Bishops' War and the Protestant forces in Ireland's difficulties in reconquest also take on extra meaning when looked at through the lens of logistics and supply. Perhaps most interestingly of all are the necessities of replenishment of manpower while on campaign, which meant that armies were recruited locally wherever they could be, including former Royalists into the New Model and Scottish armies, and most curiously, native Irish Catholics into Cromwell's forces in Ireland.

This study has also tied into existing work on the period more broadly, with the dependence on civilian interactions reinforcing the importance of studies in administration and it has also perhaps challenged the idea that the military were solely imposed upon civilians, suggesting a closer relationship between early modern soldiers and civilians. If you were to draw a line from almost any aspects of logistics and supply, be that food, manpower, clothing, or transportation during the British Civil Wars, at the other end of that line at its source would ultimately be a civilian. It is, then, worthwhile considering what further studies of this topic would reveal.

Ultimately, the role of logistics and supply in overall strategy, in operational and tactical decisions, and how logistics and supply was eventually undertaken, directly influenced the planning of battles and of campaigns themselves as well as having had an impact on their outcome. Both were heavily ingrained within the events of the British Civil Wars and cascaded through all aspects of the conflicts. Vertically, they affected every level from tactics to grand strategy, where the realities of supply dictated the behaviour of troops, the movement of armies, and the choice of campaigning targets. Horizontally, at each level soldiers were tied into a broader, non-combat military infrastructure, and from there into a sometimes willing, though often over-stressed, civilian infrastructure that was vital to the survival, movement, and effective deployment of the armies. The necessary reliance upon pre-existing civilian infrastructure, built without consideration of possible military realities and a foresight of what was to come, would only have deepened the consequences of the strength of this relationship. Even activities previously seen as entirely to the benefit of an army, such as free quarter, serve to illustrate both the realities of this reliance and the harsh operational consequences it forced upon both soldiers and generals as well as the civilians.

The preceding chapters outlined how armies operated their logistics and supply systems, and while there were regional variations in animals, vehicles, ships, and recruitment, the civilian interaction was essential. Whether it was as impressed drivers, builders of carts, operators of barges, merchant seamen, or the overworked parish constable, the foundations of an early modern military logistic and supply line rested, often reluctantly, upon civilians. Logistics and supply show us how closely civilians were connected to the war efforts of armies in this period, and even challenges the idea of being able to treat them as separate to military affairs when viewed through this lens – certainly, contemporaries did not do so. As much as this book, and the study of logistics and supply more broadly, contributes towards our understanding and expansion of those areas seen as traditional military history, the overarching conclusion is the value of applying the lens of logistics and supply towards the study of 'war and society'. Or perhaps, in the case of the military logistic and supply systems of the British Civil Wars, we should say warfare entwined with society.

Bibliography

Primary Sources

British Library, London
Harley Ms 6852, ff.175–178, Papers of the Secretary of the Royalist Council of War, 17 August 1643
Add. Ms 18979, f.204
Add Ms 26781, f.73, Sir Edward Dering's Lieutenancy Book, 1630–1640

Bodleian Library, Oxford
Carte Ms 1, ff.214r–215v, William St Leger to Ormonde, 21 July 1640
Carte Ms 10, f.718.
Carte Ms 26, f.263, 3 August 1650, Ormond to Clanricarde
Rawlinson Ms A 110, f.3v, *Corne, etc., delivered in Ireland*
Rawlinson Ms A 110, f.8, *Mr Pennoyer for wagons to carry powder and match to Bristoll.*
Rawlinson Ms A 110, f.13, *Provisions for Athlone.*
Rawlinson Ms A 110, f.22v, *Brown, Crone and Beard for wheate*
Rawlinson Ms A 110, ff.44, 45v, Wood £214 13s 7p for sending away of provisions
Rawlinson Ms A 110, f.47, Mr Thompson for salt delivered to *Carickfergus*, 22 March 1643
Rawlinson Ms B 210, f.41v
Rawlinson Ms D 395, ff.208–9, Trayne of Artillery
Tanner Ms 57, f.67
Tanner Ms 61, f.149

National Records of Scotland, Edinburgh
GD 406/1, Hamilton Papers

The National Archives, Kew
E 190, Exchequer: King's Remembrancer: Port Books
SP 16, Secretaries of State: State Papers Domestic, Charles I
SP 28, Commonwealth Exchequer Papers

WO 49, Ordnance Office: Various Accounts
WO 55, Ordnance Office and War Office: Miscellaneous Entry Books and Papers

Shropshire Archives, Shrewsbury
X6000, Manuscript Collection (Deeds)
LB7, Ludlow Borough Collection

Staffordshire Record Office, Stafford
D3712/4/1, Mavesyn Ridware Parish Book, 1642–1698

William Salt Library, Stafford
SMS 479–600, Autograph Letters: Civil War

Published Primary Sources

i) Tracts, Letters, and Pamphlets
A Briefe Relation of Some Affaires and Transactions, Civill and Military, Both Forraigne and Domestique, 48 (16–23 July 1650)
A Continuation of the Late Proceedings of His Majesties Army at Shrewsbury, Bridge-North, and Manchester London: 12 October 1642)
A Perfect and Particular Relation of the Several Marches and Proceedings of the Armies of Ireland from the Taking of Drogheda to this Present (London: 1649)
A Relation of the Battel fought between Keynton and Edgehill, by His Majesty's Army and That of the Rebels (Oxford: 1642)
A Relation Touching the Present State and Condition of Ireland. Collected by a Committee of the House of Commons (London: 1642)
Articles and Ordinances of Warre: for the Present Expedition of the Army of the Kingdome of Scotland. (London: 1644)
Certaine Informations from Severall Parts of the Kingdome, Issue 13, April 10 (London: 1643)
Charles I, 'The Commission to the Lords and others of the privy Counsell concerning the present raising of money' in Thomas Fuller (ed.) *The sovereigns prerogative and the subjects priviledge...* (London, 1657), pp.229–231
Coe, Richard, *An Exact Diarie. Or a Breife Relation of the Progresse of Sir William Wallers Army...* (London: 1644)
Fairfax, Thomas and Cromwell, Oliver, *Three Letters, from the Right Honourable Sir Thomas Fairfax, Lieut. Gen. Crumwell and the Committee Residing in the Army.* (London: 1645)
Fiennes, Nathaniel, *A Relation Made in the House of Commons by Col. Nathaniel Fiennes Concerning the Surrender of the City and Castle of Bristoll... etc.* (London: 1643)

Foster, Henry, *A True and Exact Relation of the Marchings of the Two Regiments of the Trained-Bands of the City of London Being the Red & Blew Regiments... etc.* (London: 1643)

Holme, Randle, *The Academy of Armory, or, A Storehouse of Armory and Blazon Containing the Several Variety of Created Beings... etc.* (London: 1688)

Hulls Managing of the Kingdoms Cause: Or, A brief Historicall Relation Of The Severall Plots and Attempts Against Kingston upon Hull... etc. (London: 1644)

Jones, Michael, *Lieut-General Jones's Letter to the Councel of State, of a Great Victory Which it Hath Pleased God to Give the Forces in the City of Dublin... etc.* (London: 1649)

Kightley, Edward, *A Full and True Relation of the Great Battle Fought Between the Kings Army, and his Excellency, the Earle of Essex, upon the 23. of October Last Past* (London: 1642)

Laws and Ordinances of Warre, Established for the Better Conduct Of The Army, By His Excellency the Earl of Essex... etc. (London: 1643)

Leslie, Alexander, *Articles and Ordinances of Warre for the Present Expedition of the Army... etc.* (Edinburgh: 1640)

Mercurius Aulicus .... The Eighteenth Weeke, Ending May 4 1644 (Oxford: 1644)

Military Orders and Articles Established by His Majesty for the Better Ordering and Government of His Majesties Army ... etc. (London: 1648)

The English Irish Souldier with His New Discipline, New Armes, Old Stomacke, and New Taken Pillage: Who Had Rather Eate Than Fight (London: 1642)

The Parliament Scout Communicating his Intelligence to the Kingdome, 16 (October 6, 1643)

The State of the Irish Affairs... etc. (London: 1645)

Topsell, Edward, *The Historie of Foure-Footed Beastes Describing the True and Liuely Figure of Euery Beast... etc.* (London: 1607)

True Intelligence from the Head-Quarters, or, The Daily Motions and Proceedings of the Parliaments Army... 2 (23–30 July 1650)

Vicars, John, *Gods Arke Overtopping the Worlds Waves, or the Third Part of the Parliamentary Chronicle* (London: 1646)

ii) Books

Borlas, Edmund, *The History of the Execrable Irish Rebellion Trac'd from .... the 23 of October, 1641, and Thence Pursued to the Act of Settlement* (London: 1680)

Boteler, Nathaniel, *Six Dialogues About Sea-Services Between a High-Admiral and a Captain at Sea* (London: 1685)

Boyle, Roger, *A Treatise of the Art of War: Dedicated to the Kings Most Excellent Majesty* (London 1677)

Delaune, Thomas, *The Present State of London: or, Memorials Comprehending a Full and Succinct Account of the Ancient and Modern State Thereof* (London: 1681)

Fuller, Thomas (ed.), *The Sovereigns Prerogative and the Subjects Priviledge Discussed... etc.* (London: 1657)

Hexham, Henry, *The First Part of the Principles of the Art Military Practiced in the Warres of the United Netherlands... etc.* (Delft, The Netherlands: 1642)
Hexham, Henry, *The Second Part of the Principles of Art Military, Practised in the Warres of the United Provinces... etc.* (Delft, The Netherlands: 1642)
Leslie, David, *Generall Lessley's Direction and Order for the Exercising of Horse and Foot... etc.* (London: 1642)
Loggan, David, *Oxonia Illustrata* (Oxford: 1675)
Markham, Francis, *Five Decades of Epistles of Warre* (London: 1622)
Markham, Gervase, *The Complete Farriar, or the Kings High-Way to Horsemanship* (London: 1639)
Markham, Gervase, *The Second Part of the Soldiers Grammar... etc.* (London: 1627)
Monck, George, *Observations upon Military & Political Affairs* (London: 1671)
Money, Walter, *The First and Second battles of Newbury and the Siege of Donnington Castle During the Civil War* (London, 1881)
Sprigg, Joshua, *Anglia Rediviva Englands Recovery...* (London: 1647)
Taylor, John, *The Carriers Cosmographie or A Briefe Relation, of the Innes, Ordinaries, Hosteries, and Other Lodgings In, and Neere London... etc.* (London: 1637)
Strada, Famiano, and Stapylton, Robert, *De Bello Belgico: The History of the Low-Countrey Warres* (London: 1650)
Turner, James, *Pallas Armata: Military Essayes of the Ancient Grecian, Roman, and Modern Art of War* (London: 1683)
Vicars, John, *Magnalia Dei Anglicana. Or, Englands Parliamentary Chronicle... etc.* (London: 1646)

Primary Sources Published Since 1700

Atherton, Ian, 'An Account of Herefordshire in the First Civil War', *Midland History*, vol.21, no.1 (1996), pp.136–155
Atherton, Ian, 'The Accounts of the Royalist Garrison of Lichfield Close, 1643–1645', *Staffordshire Studies*, vol.18 (2007), pp.63–96
Atherton, Ian, and Carr, Ivor (eds), *The Civil War in Staffordshire in the Spring of 1646: Sir William Brereton's Letter Book, April–May 1646* (Staffordshire Record Society, Collections for a History of Staffordshire, 4th Series, vol.21, 2007)
Baillie, Robert, *The Letters and Journals of Robert Baillie, 1637–1662* (ed.) David Laing, 3 volumes (Edinburgh: Bannatyne Club, 1841–1842)
Bennett, Martyn (ed.), *A Nottinghamshire Village in War and Peace: The Accounts of the Constables of Upton, 1640–1666* (Nottingham: The Thoroton Society of Nottinghamshire, vol.39, 1995)
Birch, Thomas (ed.), *The History of the Royal Society*, vol.3 (London: 1756)
Bothelho, Lynn A. (ed.), *Churchwardens Accounts of Cratfield* (Suffolk Records Society, vol.42, 1999)
Brereton, William, *Travels in Holland, the United Provinces, England, Scotland, and Ireland, 1634–1635* (ed.) E. Hawkins (London: Chetham Society, 1844)

Brown, Peter H. (ed.), *Register of the Privy Council of Scotland, 2nd Series, vol.7, 1638-1643* (Edinburgh: H.M. General Register House, 1906)

Buck, Samuel, and Buck, Nathaniel, *Buck's Antiquities; or Venerable Remains of Above Four Hundred Castles, Monasteries, Palaces, &c. &c. in England and Wales*, vol.1 (London, 1774)

Calendar of State Papers, Domestic Series, 1625-1651, 26 volumes (London: HMSO, 1858-97)

Calendar of State Papers, Relating to Ireland, 1633-1660, 2 volumes (London: HMSO, 1901 & 1908)

Calendar of State Papers, Venetian, 1640-1647, 3 volumes (London: HMSO, 1924-1926)

Carlyle, Thomas (ed.), *Oliver Cromwell's Letters and Speeches with Elucidations*, vol.2 (London, 1850)

Carte, Thomas (ed.), *A Collection of Original Letters and Papers, Concerning the Affairs of England, from the Year 1641 to 1660.* 2 volumes (London, 1739)

Carte, Thomas (ed.), *The Life of James, Duke of Ormond,* 6 volumes. (Oxford: Oxford University Press, 1851)

Clark, Andrew (ed.), *The Life and Times of Anthony Wood, antiquary of Oxford, 1632-1695, Described by Himself, vol.1 (1632-1663)* (Oxford: Oxford Historical Society, 1891)

Coates, Wilson H., Young, Anne S., and Snow, Vernon, F. (eds) *The Private Journals of the Long Parliament: 3 January to 5 March 1642* (New Haven: Yale University Press, 1992)

Cobbett, William (ed.), *The Parliamentary History of England, from the Earliest Period to the Year 1803* (London, 1806)

Cooper, David (ed.) 'The English Civil War in Staffordshire: The Experience of Uttoxeter', *Staffordshire Studies,* vol.19 (2008), pp.61-100

Day, William A. (ed.), *The Pythouse Papers: Correspondence Concerning the Civil War, the Popish Plot, and a Contested Election in 1680.* (London: Bickers, 1879)

Deering, Charles, *Nottinghamia Vetus Et Nova: or An Historical Account of the Ancient and Present State of the Town of Nottingham* (London, 1751)

Earwaker, John P. (ed.), *The Constables' Accounts of the Manor of Manchester from the Year 1612 to the Year 1647, and from the Year 1743 to the Year 1776,* Vol. 2 (Manchester, J.E. Cornish, 1892)

Dore, Robert N. (ed.) *The Letter Books of Sir William Brereton*, vol.1 (Gloucester: Lancashire and Cheshire Record Society, vol.123, 1984)

Fiennes, Celia, *Through England on a Side Saddle in the Time of William and Mary, Being the Diary of Celia Fiennes* (ed.) E. Griffiths (London: The Leadenhall Press, 1888)

Firth, Charles H., *The Memoirs of Edmund Ludlow Lieutenant-General of the House in the Army of the Commonwealth of England, 1625-1672,* 2 volumes (Oxford: Clarendon Press, 1894)

Firth, Charles H., and Rait, Robert S., *Acts and Ordinances of the Interregnum, 1642-1660*, vol.1 (London: His Majesty's Stationery Office, 1911)

Gilbert, John T. (ed.), *History of the Irish Confederation,* vol.1 (Dublin: M.H. Gill & Son, 1882)

Gough, Richard, *Antiquities & Memoirs of the Parish of Myddle County of Salop* (Shrewsbury: Adnitt & Naunton, 1875)

Historical Manuscripts Commission Reports:
Fifth Report, Part I: Report and Appendix (London: HMSO, 1876)

Twelfth Report, Appendix Part II, The Manuscripts of the Earl Cowper, K.G. Preserved at Melbourne Hall, Derbyshire, vol.2 (London: HMSO, 1888)

Thirteenth Report, Appendix, The Manuscripts of his Grace the Duke of Portland, Preserved at Welback Abbey, 2 volumes. (London: HMSO, 1891 & 1893)

Calendar of the Manuscripts of the Marquess of Ormonde, K. P., Preserved at Kilkenny Castle, volumes 1-2 (London: HMSO, 1895 & 1903)

Calendar of the Manuscripts of the Most Hon. The Marquess of Salisbury, KG., etc, Preserved at Hatfield House, vol.15 (London: HMSO, 1930)

Manuscripts of the Duke of Buccleuch and Queensberry, preserved at Montagu House, vol.1 (London: HMSO, 1899)

Report on the Manuscripts of the Late Reginald Rawdon Hastings, Esq. Of the Manor House, Ashby-de-la-Zouch, vol.2 (London: HMSO, 1930)

Hogan, James. (ed.), *Letters and Papers Relating to the Irish Rebellion Between 1642-46* (Dublin: Dublin Stationery Office, 1936)

Hopton, Ralph (C. Chadwyck-Healey ed.), *Bellum Civile: Hopton's Narrative of his Campaign in the West (1642-1644) and Other Papers* (Taunton: Somerset Record Society, 1902)

Clarendon, Edward, Earl of, *The History of the Rebellion and Civil Wars in England* (ed.) W.D. Macray, 6 volumes (Oxford: Clarendon Press, 1826)

Journals of the House of Commons, volumes 2-4, 1640-1646 (London: HMSO, 1802)

Journals of the House of Lords, volumes 4-9, 1629-1648 (London: HMSO, 1767-1830)

Larkin, James F., and Hughes, Paul L. (eds), *Stuart Royal Proclamations, vol.1: Royal Proclamations of King James I, 1603-1625* (Oxford: Oxford University Press, 1973)

Larkin, James F. (ed.), *Stuart Royal Proclamations. vol.2. Royal Proclamations of King Charles I, 1625-1646* (Oxford University Press, 1983)

Luke, Samuel, *Journal of Sir Samuel Luke: Scoutmaster to the Earl of Essex, 1642-1644*, I. G. Philip (ed.), 3 parts (Oxfordshire Record Society, 1950-1953)

Lyle, J. V. (ed.), *Acts of the Privy Council of England, 1627,* vol.42 (London: HMSO, 1938)

Malbon, Thomas, *Memorials of the Civil War in Cheshire and the Adjacent Counties* (ed.) J. Hall (Record Society of Lancashire and Cheshire, 1889)

Marsh, Simon (ed.), *The Train of Artillery of the Earl of Essex: The Accounts of Sir Edward Peyto Lieutenant General of the Train of Artillery, October 1642-September 1643* (Romford: The Pike and Shot Society, 2016)

Masson, David (ed.), *Register of the Privy Council of Scotland, 2nd Series, vol.1, 1625-1627* (Edinburgh: HM General Register House, 1899)

Masson, David (ed.), *The Quarrel Between the Earl of Manchester and Oliver Cromwell: An Episode of the English Civil War* (Camden Society, New Series, vol.12, 1875)

Nicholson, J. (ed.), *Minute Book of the War Committee of the Covenanters in the Stewartry of Kirkcudbright, 1640 and 1641* (Kirkcudbright, J. Nicholson, 1855)

Peacock, Edward (ed.), *The Army Lists of the Roundheads and Cavaliers, Containing the Names of the Officers in the Royal and Parliamentary Armies of 1642* (London: J.C. Hotten, 1863)

Pennington, Donald H., and Roots, Ivan A. (eds), *The Committee at Stafford, 1643–1645: The Order Book of the Staffordshire County Committee* (Manchester: Manchester University Press, 1957)

Phillips, W. (ed.), 'The Ottley Papers Relating to the Civil War', *Transactions of the Shropshire Archaeological and Natural History Society*, 2nd Series, vols.6 (1894)

Phillips, W. (ed.), 'The Ottley Papers relating to the Civil War', II, *Transactions of the Shropshire Archaeological and Natural History Society*, 2nd Series, vol.7 (1895)

Raithby, John (ed.), *Statutes of the Realm: vol.5, 1628–80* (London: Great Britain Record Commission, 1819)

Raithby, John (ed.), *Statutes of the Realm: vol.6, 1685–94* (London: Great Britain Record Commission, 1819)

Roy, Ian. (ed.), *The Royalist Ordnance Papers, 1642–1646*, 2 volumes. (Oxford: Oxfordshire Record Society, 1963 & 1975)

Rushworth, John (ed.), *Historical Collections of Private Passages of State: vol.3, 1639–40* (London, 1721)

Rushworth, John (ed.), *Historical Collections of Private Passages of State: vol.4, 1640–42* (London, 1721)

Rushworth, John (ed.), *Historical Collections of Private Passages of State: vol.6, 1645–47* (London, 1722)

Snow, Vernon F., and Young, Anne S. (eds), *Private Journals of the Long Parliament, 2 June to 17 September 1642* (New Haven: Yale University Press, 1987)

Snow, Vernon F., and Young, Anne S. (eds), *The Private Journals of the Long Parliament: 7 March to 1 June 1642* (New Haven: Yale University Press, 1992)

Stevenson, David. (ed.), *The Government of Scotland Under the Covenanters, 1637–1651* (Edinburgh: Scottish History Society, 1981)

Stukeley, William, *Itinerarium Curiosum, or, An Account of the Antiquities, and Remarkable Curiosities in Nature or Art, Observed in Travels Through Great Britain* (London, 1776)

Symonds, Richard, *Diary of the Marches of the Royal Army* (eds) C. E. Long and I. Roy (Cambridge: Cambridge University Press, 1997, first pub. 1859)

Terry, Charles S. (ed.), *Papers Relating to the Army of the Solemn League and Covenant, 1643–1647*, 2 volumes. (Edinburgh: Edinburgh University Press for the Scottish History Society, 1917)

Thomson, Alan (ed.), *The Impact of the First Civil War on Hertfordshire, 1642–47* (Hertford: Hertfordshire Record Society, vol.23, 2007)

Townsend, Henry, *Diary of Henry Townshend of Elmley Lovett, 1640–1663* (ed.) J. W. Willis Bund (London: Worcestershire Historical Society, 1920)

Townshend, Dorothea (ed.), *The Life and Letters of the Great Earl of Cork* (New York: E.R. Dutton, 1904)

Toynbee, Margaret (ed.), *The Papers of Captain Henry Stevens Waggon-Master-General to King Charles I* (Oxford: Oxfordshire Record Society, 1962)

Warburton, Elliot, *Memoirs of Prince Rupert, and the Cavaliers: Including Their Private Correspondence, Now First Published from the Original MSS*, 3 volumes. (London: R. Bentley, 1849)

Warwick, Philip, *Memoires of the Reign of King Charles I* (London, 1702)

Secondary Sources

Books

Abram, Andrew, *More Like Lions Than Men: Sir William Brereton and the Cheshire Army of Parliament, 1642–1660* (Warwick: Helion, 2020)

Aldcroft, Derek, and Freeman, Michael (eds), *Transport in the Industrial Revolution* (Manchester: Manchester University Press, 1983)

Appleby, David J., and Hopper, Andrew (eds), *Battle-scarred: Mortality, Medical Care and Military Welfare in the British Civil Wars* (Manchester: Manchester University Press, 2018)

Barker, Rosalin, *The Rise of an Early Modern Shipping Industry, Whitby's Golden Fleet, 1620–1750* (Woodbridge: Boydell & Brewer, 2011)

Barnes, Thomas G., *Somerset, 1625–1642: A County's Government During the 'Personal Rule'* (Oxford: Oxford University Press, 1961)

Barratt, John, *'Better Begging than Fighting': The Royalist Army in Exile in the War Against Cromwell 1656–1660* (Solihull: Helion, 2016)

Barratt, John, *Cavalier Capital: Oxford in the English Civil War, 1642–1646* (Solihull: Helion, 2015)

Barratt, John, *Cavalier Generals: King Charles I and His Commanders in the English Civil War, 1642–46* (Barnsley: Pen & Sword Military, 2004)

Barratt, John, *Cavaliers: The Royalist Army at War, 1642–1646* (Stroud: Sutton Publishing, 2000)

Barratt, John, *The Great Siege of Chester* (Stroud: The History Press, 2011)

Barratt, John, *'The King's Irish': The Royalist Anglo-Irish Foot of the English Civil War* (Warwick: Helion, 2019)

Bartlett, Thomas, and Jeffrey, Keith (eds), *A Military History of Ireland* (Cambridge: Cambridge University Press, 1996)

Bence-Jones, Mark, *The Cavaliers* (London: Constable, 1976)

Bennett, Martyn, *Cromwell at War: The Lord General and his Military Revolution* (London: I.B.Taurus, 2017)

Bennett, Martyn, *The Civil Wars Experienced: Britain and Ireland, 1638–1661* (London: Routledge, 2000)
Bennett, Martyn, *The Civil Wars in Britain & Ireland, 1638–1651* (Oxford: Blackwell, 1997)
Black, Jeremy, *A Military Revolution? Military Change and European Society, 1550–1800* (London: Palgrave, 1991)
Blackmore, David, *Destructive and Formidable: British Infantry Firepower, 1642–1765* (London: Frontline Books, 2014)
Blakemore, Richard J., and Murphy, Elaine, *The British Civil Wars at Sea, 1638–1653* (Woodbridge: Boydell & Brewer, 2018)
Boynton, Lindsay, *The Elizabeth Militia, 1558–1638* (London: Routledge & Kegan Paul, 1967)
Brewer, John, *The Sinews of Power: War, Money, and the English State, 1688–1783* (London: Unwin Hyman, 1989)
Brown, Ian M., *British Logistics on the Western Front* (Wesport, Connecticut: Praeger Publishers, 1998)
Bull, Stephen, *The Furie of the Ordnance: Artillery in the English Civil Wars* (Woodbridge: The Boydell Press, 2008)
Burne, Alfred H., and Young, Peter, *The Great Civil War: A Military History of the First Civil War, 1642–1646* (Moreton-in-Marsh: Windrush Press, 1998)
Carlton, Charles, *Going to the Wars: The Experience of the British Civil Wars, 1638–1651* (London: Routledge, 1992)
Carlton, Charles, *This Seat of Mars: War and the British Isles, 1485–1746* (London: Yale University Press, 2011)
Capp, Bernard, *Cromwell's Navy: The Fleet and the English Revolution, 1648–1660* (Oxford: Clarendon Press, 1992)
Chartres, John A., *Internal Trade in England, 1500–1700* (London: Macmillan, 1977)
Clark, Colin, and Haswell, Margaret, *The Economics of Subsistence Agriculture* (London: Macmillan, 1964)
Clark, Peter (ed.), *The Cambridge Urban History of Britain Vol. 2, 1540–1840* (Cambridge: Cambridge University Press, 2000)
Crofts, John, *Packhorse, Waggon, and Post: Land Carriage and Communications under the Tudors and Stuarts* (London: Routledge, 1967)
Cruickshank, Charles G., *Elizabeth's Army* (Oxford: Oxford University Press, 1966)
Day, Jon, *Gloucester & Newbury 1643: The Turning Point of the Civil War* (Barnsley: Pen & Sword Books, 2007)
Donagan, Barbara, *War in England, 1642–1649* (Oxford: Oxford University Press, 2010)
Edwards, Peter, *Dealing in Death: The Arms Trade and the British Civil Wars, 1638–52* (Stroud: Sutton Publishing, 2000)
Edwards, Peter, *Horse and Man in Early Modern England* (London: Continuum, 2007)
Everitt, Alan, *The Community of Kent and the Great Rebellion, 1640–60* (Leicester: Leicester University Press, 1966)

Foxton, P.D., *Powering War: Modern Land Force Logistics* (London: Brassey's, 1994)
Firth, Charles, *Cromwell's Army: A History of the English Soldier During the Civil Wars, the Commonwealth and the Protectorate* (London: Methuen, 1902)
Fissel, Mark C., *English Warfare 1511–1642* (London: Routledge, 2001)
Fissel, Mark C., *The Bishops' Wars: Charles I's Campaigns Against Scotland, 1638–1640* (Cambridge: Cambridge University Press, 1994)
Fletcher, Anthony J., *A County Community in Peace and War: Sussex, 1600–1660* (London: Longman, 1975)
Flintham, David, *Civil War London: A Military History of London under Charles I and Oliver Cromwell* (Solihull: Helion, 2017)
Freedman, Lawrence, *Strategy: A History* (Oxford: Oxford University Press, 2013)
Furgol, Edward M., *A Regimental History of the Covenanting Armies, 1639–1651* (Edinburgh: John Donald Publishers, 1990)
Gardner, Samuel R., *History of the Great Civil War*, 4 vols. (London: The Windrush Press, 1987)
Gentles, Ian, *The New Model Army in England, Ireland, and Scotland, 1645–1653* (Oxford: Blackwell, 1992)
Gerhold, Dorian, *Carriers & Coachmasters: Trade and Travel Before the Turnpikes* (Chichester: Phillimore, 2005)
Glozier, Matthew, *Scottish Soldiers in France in the Reign of the Sun King: Nursery for Men of Honour* (Leiden: Brill, 2004)
Gratton, James M., *The Parliamentarian and Royalist War Effort in Lancashire, 1642–1651* (Manchester: The Chetham Society Series III Vol. 48, 2010)
Haythornthwaite, Philip J., *British Infantry of the Napoleonic Wars* (London: Arms and Armour Press, 1987)
Heidler, David S., and Heilder, Jeanne T., *Encyclopaedia of the American Civil War: A Political, Social, and Military History* (W. W. Norton, 2002)
Hess, Earl, *Civil War Logistics: A Study of Military Transportation* (Baton Rouge: Louisiana State University Press, 2017)
Holmes, Clive, *The Eastern Association in the English Civil War* (London: Cambridge University Press, 1974)
Hopper, Andrew, *Turncoats and Renegadoes: Changing Sides During the English Civil Wars* (Oxford: Oxford University Press, 2014)
Hughes, Ann, *Politics, Society, and Civil War in Warwickshire, 1620–1660* (Cambridge University Press, 1997)
Hughes, Ann, *The Causes of the English Civil War* (London: Palgrave, 1998)
Huston, James A., *The Sinews of War: Army Logistics, 1775–1953* (Washington D.C.: Office of the Chief of Military History, United States Army, 1966)
Hutton, Ronald, *The Royalist War Effort, 1642–1646*, 2nd Edition (Abingdon: Routledge, 2003)
Jomini, Antoine-Henri, *The Art of War* (ed.) C. Messenger (London: Greenhill, 1992)
Keeler, Mary F., *The Long Parliament, 1640–1641: A Biographical Study of its Members* (Philadelphia: American Philosophical Society, 1954)

Kenyon, John and Ohlmeyer, Jane (eds), *The Civil Wars: A Military History of England Scotland and Ireland, 1638-1660* (Oxford: Oxford University Press, 1998)

Kingston, Alfred, *East Anglia and the Great Civil War: The Rising of Cromwell's Ironsides in the Associated Counties of Cambridge, Huntingdon, Lincoln, Norfolk, Suffolk, Essex, and Hertford* (London: E. Stock, 1897)

Kishlansky, Mark A., *The Rise of the New Model Army* (Cambridge University Press, 1979)

Langdon, John, *Horses, Oxen and Technological Innovation: The Use of Draught Animals in English Farming from 1066 to 1500* (Cambridge: Cambridge University Press, 1986)

Leadbetter, Peter, *The Perfect Militia: The Stuart Trained Bands of England and Wales 1603–1642* (Warwick: Helion, 2021)

Lenihan, Pádraig, *Confederate Catholics at War, 1641-1649* (Cork: Cork University Press, 2001)

Lenihan, Pádraig (ed.), *Conquest and Resistance: War in Seventeenth-Century Ireland* (Leiden: Brill, 2001)

Lenihan, Pádraig, *Fluxes, Fevers, and Fighting Men: War and Disease in Ancien Régime Europe, 1648–1789* (Warwick: Helion, 2019)

Lipscombe, Nick, *The English Civil War: An Atlas and Concise History of the Wars of the Three Kingdoms, 1639–51* (Oxford: Osprey, 2020)

Louth, Warwick, *The Arte Militaire: The Application of 17th Century Military Manuals to Conflict Archaeology* (Solihull: Helion, 2016)

Lynch, John, *Bristol and the Civil War: For King and Parliament* (Stroud: Sutton, 1999)

Lynn, John A. (ed.), *Feeding Mars: Logistics in Western Warfare from The Middle Ages to The Present* (Boulder, Colorado: Westview Press, 1994)

Macinnes, Allan I., *The British Revolution, 1629–1660* (Basingstoke: Palgrave Macmillan, 2005)

Malcolm, Joyce L., *Caesar's Due: Loyalty and King Charles, 1642–1646* (London: Swift, 1983)

McGrath, Patrick. (ed.), *Merchants and Merchandise in Seventeenth-Century Bristol* (Bristol: Bristol Record Society, 1955)

Morrill, John, *Cheshire 1630–1660: County Government and Society During the 'English Revolution'* (Oxford: Oxford University Press, 1974)

Morrill, John, *The Revolt of the Provinces: Conservatives and Radicals in the English Civil War, 1630–1650* (London: Longman, 1980)

Morrill, John (ed.), *The Scottish National Covenant in its British Context* (Edinburgh: Edinburgh University Press, 1990)

Morris, Robert, *Public Transport in England and Wales, 1580–1642* (Bristol, Stuart Press, 2010)

Murdoch, Steve (ed.), *Scotland and the Thirty Years' War, 1618–1648* (Leiden: Brill, 2001)

Murdoch, Steve and Grosjean, Alexia, *Alexander Leslie and the Scottish Generals of the Thirty Years' War, 1618–1648* (London: Pickering & Chatto, 2014)

Murdoch, Steve and Mackillop, Andrew (eds), *Fighting for Identity, Scottish Military Experience c.1550–1990* (Leiden: Brill, 2002)

Murphy, Elaine, *Ireland and the War at Sea, 1642–1653* (Woodbridge, Boydell & Brewer, 2012)

Nef, John, *The Rise of the British Coal Industry*, vol.1 (Oxford: Frank Cass, 1932)

Newman, Peter R., *Atlas of the English Civil War* (London: Routledge, 1998)

Nolan, Cathal J., *The Allure of Battle: A History of How Wars Have Been Won and Lost* (Oxford: Oxford University Press, 2017)

Parker, Geoffrey, *The Army of Flanders and the Spanish Road 1567–1659: The Logistics of Spanish Victory and Defeat in the Low Countries' Wars,* 2nd Edition (Cambridge University Press, 2004)

Parker, Geoffrey, *The Military Revolution: Military Innovation and the Rise of the West, 1500–1800,* 2nd Edition (Cambridge: Cambridge University Press, 2006)

Parkes, Joan, *Travel in England in the Seventeenth Century* (London: Oxford University Press, 1925)

Parrott, David, *Richelieu's Army: War, Government and Society in France, 1624–42* (Cambridge: Cambridge University Press, 2008)

Parrott, David, *The Business of War. Military Enterprise and Military Revolution in Early Modern Europe* (Cambridge: Cambridge University Press, 2012)

Pawson, Eric, *Transport and Economy: the Turnpike Roads of Eighteenth Century England* (London: Academic Press, 1977)

Peachey, Stuart, *The Soldier's Life in the English Civil War: Organisation, Food, Clothing, Weapons, and Combat* (Bristol: Stuart Press, 2016)

Pocock, John G.A., *The Discovery of Islands* (Cambridge: Cambridge University Press, 2006)

Powell, John R., *The Navy in the English Civil War* (London: Archon Books, 1962)

Prendergast, John P., *The Cromwellian Settlement of Ireland* (New York: P.M. Haverty, 1868)

Reece, Henry, *The Army in Cromwellian England, 1649–1660* (Oxford: Oxford University Press, 2013)

Reese, Peter, *Cromwell's Masterstroke: The Battle of Dunbar, 1650* (Barnsley: Pen & Sword, 2006)

Reid, Donald, *English Civil War Firearms* (Leigh-on-Sea: Partizan Press, 1989)

Reid, Stuart, *Dunbar 1650: Cromwell's Most Famous Victory* (Oxford: Osprey, 2008)

Reid, Stuart, *All the King's Armies: A Military History of the English Civil War, 1642–1651* (Staplehurst: Spellmount, 1998)

Reid, Stuart, *Crown, Covenant, and Cromwell: The Civil Wars in Scotland, 1639–1651* (Barnsley: Frontline Books, 2012)

Roberts, Keith, *Cromwell's War Machine: The New Model Army, 1645–1660* (Barnsley: Pen & Sword Military, 2009)

Robinson, Gavin, *Horses, People and Parliament in the English Civil War: Extracting Resources and Constructing Allegiance* (Farnham: Ashgate Publishing, 2012)

Rodger, Nicholas A.M., *The Safeguard of the Sea: A Naval History of Britain, Vol.1, 1660–1649* (London: Harper Collins, 1997)
Rodger, Nicholas A.M., *The Command of the Ocean: A Naval History of Britain, 1649–1815* (London: Penguin Group, 2004)
Rogers, Clifford J. (ed.), *The Military Revolution Debate, Readings on the Military Transformation of Early Modern Europe* (Boulder, Colorado: Westview, 1995)
Royle, Trevor, *Civil War: The Wars of the Three Kingdoms, 1638–1660* (London: Abacus, 2005)
Ruppenthal, Roland G., *Logistical Support of the Armies*, 2 volumes. (Washington D.C.: Office of the Chief of Military History, United States Army, 1959)
Ryder, Ian, *An English Army for Ireland* (Newthorpe: Partizan Press, 1987)
Scott, Christopher, and Turton, Alan, *Hey For Old Robin! The Campaigns and Armies of the Earl of Essex During the First Civil War, 1642-44* (Solihull: Helion, 2017)
Scott, Christopher L., Turton, Alan, and von Arni, Eric G., *Edgehill, The Battle Reinterpreted* (Barnsley: Pen & Sword, 2005)
Seyer, Samuel, *Memoirs Historical and Topographical of Bristol and its Neighbourhood, from the Earliest Period Down to the Present Time* (Bristol: J.M. Gutch, 1823)
Shearwood, Mark W., *The Perfection of Military Discipline: The Plug Bayonet and the English Army, 1660–1705* (Warwick: Helion, 2020)
Sheffield, Gary, *Forgotten Victory: The First World War: Myths and Realities* (Sharpe Books, 2018)
Sherwood, Roy, *The Civil War in the Midlands, 1642–1651*, 2nd Edition (Stroud: Alan Sutton, 1997)
Singleton, Charles, *'Famous By My Sword': The Army of Montrose and the Military Revolution* (Solihull: Helion, 2014)
Spring, Laurence, *In the Emperor's Service: Wallenstein's Army, 1625–1634* (Warwick, Helion, 2019)
Spring, Laurence, *The Armies of Sir Ralph Hopton: The Royalist Armies of the West, 1642–46* (Warwick, Helion, 2020)
Spring, Laurence, *The Campaigns of Sir William Waller, 1642–1645* (Warwick, Helion, 2019)
Spring, Laurence, *The First British Army, 1624–1628: The Army of the Duke of Buckingham* (Solihull, Helion, 2016)
Stater, Victor L., *Noble Government: The Stuart Lord Lieutenancy and the Transformation of English Politics* (Athens, Ga: University of Georgia Press, 1994)
Stevenson, David, *Scottish Covenanters and Irish Confederates: Scottish-Irish Relations in the Mid-Seventeenth Century* (Belfast: Ulster Historical Foundation, 1981)
Stoyle, Mark, *Loyalty and Locality: Popular Allegiance in Devon During the English Civil War* (Exeter: Exeter University Press, 1994)
Stoyle, Mark, *Soldiers & Strangers: An Ethnic History of the English Civil War* (New Haven: Yale University Press, 2005)
Stuart, Robert, *Wagons, Carts, and Pack Animals, 1580–1660* (Bristol: Stuart Press, 1996)

Summerhays, Reginald S., *The Observer's Book of Horses and Ponies* (London: Frederick Warne, 1974)
Terry, Charles S., *The Life and Campaigns of Alexander Leslie, First Earl of Leven* (London: Longman, Green, and Co., 1899)
Thirsk, Joan, *The Agrarian History of England and Wales, Volume 5 Part 1: Regional Farming Systems* (Cambridge: Cambridge University Press, 1984)
Thompson, Julian, *Lifeblood of War: Logistics in Armed Conflict* (London: Brassey's, 1998)
Tzu, Sun, *The Art of War* (Minneapolis: Filiquarian Publishing, 2006)
Underdown, David, *Somerset in the Civil War and Interregnum* (Newton Abbot: David and Charles, 1973)
van Creveld, Martin, *Supplying War: Logistics from Wallenstein to Patton*, 2nd Edition (Cambridge: Cambridge University Press, 2004)
von Arni, Eric G., *Justice to the Maimed Soldier: Nursing, Medical Care and Welfare for Sick and Wounded Soldiers and their Families during the English Civil Wars and Interregnum, 1642–1660* (Aldershot: Ashgate, 2001)
von Clausewitz, Carl, *On War* (ed.) M. Howard and P. Paret (Princeton: Princeton University Press, 1984)
Wanklyn, Malcolm, *Reconstructing the New Model Army: vol.1, Regimental Lists April 1645 to May 1649* (Solihull: Helion, 2015)
Wanklyn, Malcolm, *Reconstructing the New Model Army: vol.2, Regimental Lists 1649 to 1663* (Solihull: Helion, 2016)
Wanklyn, Malcolm, *The Army of Occupation in Ireland 1603–42: Defending the Protestant Hegemony* (Warwick: Helion, 2022)
Wanklyn, Malcolm, and Jones, Frank, *A Military History of the English Civil War: Strategy and Tactics* (Harlow: Pearson Education, 2005)
Waylen, James, *A History Military and Municipal of the Town (Otherwise Called the City) of Marlborough and more Generally of the Entire Hundred of Selkley* (London: John Russel Smith, 1854)
Wheeler, James S., *Cromwell in Ireland* (Dublin: Gill & Macmillan, 1999)
Wheeler, James S., *The Irish and British Wars 1637–1654: Triumph, Tragedy, and Failure* (London: Routledge, 2002)
Wheeler, James S., *The Making of a World Power: War and Revolution in Seventeenth Century England* (Stroud: Sutton Publishing, 1999)
Willan, Thomas S., *River Navigation in England, 1600–1750* (London: Oxford University Press, 1936)
Willan, Thomas S., *The English Coasting Trade, 1600–1750* (Manchester: Manchester University Press, 1938)
Willan, Thomas S., *The Inland Trade: Studies in English internal trade in the sixteenth and seventeenth centuries* (Manchester: Manchester University Press, 1976)
Wilson, Charles H., *England's Apprenticeship, 1603–1769* (London: Longman, 1965)
Worthington, David, *Scots in the Habsburg Service, 1618–1648* (Leiden: Brill, 2004)

Worton, Jonathan, *To Settle the Crown: Waging Civil War in Shropshire, 1642–1648* (Solihull: Helion, 2016)
Wroughton, John, *An Unhappy Civil War: The Experiences of Ordinary People in Gloucestershire, Somerset and Wiltshire, 1642–1646* (Bath: The Lansdown Press, 1999)
Young, Peter, *Edgehill 1642* (Witney, Windrush Press, 1997)
Young, Peter, and Emberton, Wilfred, *The Cavalier Army: Its Organisation and Everyday Life* (London: George Allen & Unwin, 1974)
Young, Peter, and Holmes, Richard, *The English Civil War* (Ware: Wordsworth Editions, 2000)

Journal Articles and Chapters in Edited Volumes
Appleby, David J., 'The Third Army: Wandering Soldiers and the Negotiation of Parliamentary Authority, 1642-1654' in Appleby, D. J., and Hopper, A. (eds), *Battle-Scarred: Mortality, Medical Care and Military Welfare in the British Civil Wars* (Manchester University Press, 2018), pp.137–155
Armstrong, John, and Bagwell, Philip S., 'Coastal Shipping,' in Aldcroft, D., and Freeman, M. (eds), *Transport in the Industrial Revolution* (Manchester University Press, 1983), pp.142–176
Armstrong, Robert, 'The Long Parliament Goes to War: The Irish Campaigns, 1641-3', *Historical Research*, Vol.80, No.207 (February 2007), pp.73–99
Atherton, Ian, 'Battlefield, Burials and the English Civil Wars' in Appleby, D. J., and Hopper, A. (eds), *Battle-Scarred: Mortality, Medical Care and Military Welfare in the British Civil Wars* (Manchester: Manchester University Press, 2018), pp.23–39
Atherton, Ian, 'Royalist Finances in the English Civil War: The Case of the Lichfield Garrison, 1643–5', *Midland History*, Vol.33, No.1 (2008), pp.43–67
Ball, R.M., 'After Edgehill Fight', *Historical Research*, Vol.67, No.162 (1994), pp.111–116
Beaumont, H., 'Events in Shropshire at the Commencement of the Great Civil War', *Transactions of the Shropshire Archaeological Society*, Vol.51, No.1 (1941), pp.11–42
Bennett, Martyn, 'Henry Hastings and the Flying Army of Ashby-de-la-Zouch', *Transactions of the Leicestershire Archaeological and Historical Society*, Vol.56 (1980–81), pp.62–70
Bogart, D., Dunn, O., Alvarez-Palau, E. J., and Shaw-Taylor, L., 'Speedier Delivery: Coastal Shipping Times and Speeds During the Age of Sail', *The Economic History Review Website*, <https://onlinelibrary.wiley.com/doi/abs/10.1111/ehr.13004≥ Accessed 16 August 2020
Carter, D.P., 'The Exact Militia in Lancashire, 1625-1649', *Northern History*, Vol.11 (1976), pp.87–106
Chartres, John A., 'Road Carrying in England in the Seventeenth Century: Myth and Reality' *The Economic History Review*, Vol.30, No.1 (February 1977), pp.73–94
Clark, A., 'The Essex Territorial Force, 1625-1638', *Essex Review*, Vol.18, No.70 (1909), pp.65–74

Cook, Bronwen, '"A True, Faire, and Just Account": Charles Huggett and the Content of Maldon in the English Coastal Shipping Trade, 1679–1684', *The Journal of Transport History*, Vol.26, No.1 (2005), pp.1–18

Croxton, Derek, 'A Territorial Imperative? The Military Revolution, Strategy and Peacemaking in the Thirty Years War', *War in History*, Vol.5, No.3 (1998), pp.253–279

Davie, Hugh G.W., 'The Economics and Logistics of Horse-drawn Armies', *British Journal for Military History*, Vol.7.1 (2021), pp.21–45.

Davies, Godfrey, 'The Formation of the New Model Army', *The English Historical Review* Vol.56, No.221 (Jan 1941), pp.103–105

Davies, Godfrey, 'The Parliamentary Army under the Earl of Essex, 1642–5', *The English Historical Review*, Vol.49, No.193 (January 1934), pp.32–54

Dunn, Oliver, 'A Sea of Troubles? Journey Times and Coastal Shipping Routes in Seventeenth Century England and Wales', *The Journal of Transport History*, Vol.41, No.2 (January 2020), pp.184–207

Edwards, Peter, 'The Supply of Horses to the Parliamentarian and Royalist Armies in the English Civil War', *Historical Research*, Vol.68. No.165 (February 1995), pp.121–140

Edwards, Peter, 'Turning Ploughshares into Swords: The Arms and Military Equipment Industries in Staffordshire in the First Civil War, 1642–1646', *Midland History*, Vol.27, No.1 (2002), pp.52–79

Furgol, Edward, 'Beating the Odds: Alexander Leslie's 1640 Campaign in England' in Murdoch, Steve and Mackillop, Andrew (eds), *Fighting for Identity: Scottish Military Experience c.1550–1900* (Leiden, Netherlands: Brill, 2002), pp.33–60

Furgol, Edward M., 'Scotland Turned Sweden: The Scottish Covenanters and the Military Revolution, 1638–1651,' in Morrill, J. (ed.), *The Scottish National Covenant in its British Context* (Edinburgh: Edinburgh University Press, 1990), pp.134–154

Gentles, Ian, 'The Arrears of Pay of the Parliamentary Army at the End of the First Civil War', *Bulletin of the Institute of Historical Research*, Vol.48, No.117 (May 1975), pp.52–63

Gentles, Ian, 'The Choosing of Officers for the New Model Army', *Historical Research*, Vol. 67 (1994), pp.264–285

Gerhold, Dorian, 'The Growth of the London Carrying Trade, 1681–1838', *The Economic History Review*, Vol.41, No.3 (August 1988), pp.392–410

Gerhold, Dorian, 'Pack Horses and Wheeled Vehicles in England, 1550–1800', *The Journal of Transport History*, Vol.14, No.1 (March 1993), pp.1–26

Graham, Aaron, 'The Earl of Essex and Parliament's Army at the Battle of Edgehill: A Reassessment', *War in History*, Vol.17, No.3 (2010), pp.276–293

Hardacre, P.H., 'Patronage and Purchase in the Irish Standing Army Under Thomas Wentworth, Earl of Strafford, 1632–1640 (Continued)', *Journal for the Society of Army Historical Research*, Vol.67, No.270 (Summer 1989), pp.94–104

Hopper, Andrew, '"Tinker" Fox and the Politics of Garrison Warfare in the West Midlands, 1643–50', *Midland History*, Vol. 24 (1999), pp.98–113

Hutton, Ronald, and Reeves, Wylie, 'Sieges and Fortifications' in Kenyon, John and Ohlmeyer, Jane (eds), *The Civil Wars: A Military History of England Scotland and Ireland, 1638-1660* (Oxford: Oxford University Press, 1998), pp.195-233

Kent, Joan, 'The English Village Constable, 1580-1642: The Nature and Dilemmas of the Office', *Journal of British Studies*, Vol. 20, No. 2 (Spring, 1981), pp.26-49

Kishlanksy, Mark, 'The Case of the Army Truly Stated: the Creation of the New Model Army', *Past and Present*, Vol.81 (1978), pp.64-69

Lowe, John, 'The Campaign of the Irish Royalist Army in Cheshire, November 1643-January 1644', *The Historic Society of Lancashire & Cheshire* Vol. 3 (1959), pp.47-76

Lloyd, W.V., 'Montgomeryshire Horses, Cobs, and Ponies', *Collections Historical & Archaeological Relating to Montgomeryshire and its Borders*, Vol.22 (1888), pp.17-34

Luttwak, Edward N., 'Logistics and the Aristocratic Idea of War', in Lynn, J. (ed.), *Feeding Mars: Logistics in Western Warfare from the Middle Ages to the Present* (Boulder: Westview Press, 1993), pp.3-6

Lynn, John A., 'Food, Funds, and Fortresses: Resource Mobilization and Positional Warfare in the Campaigns of Louis XIV', in Lynn, J. (ed.), *Feeding Mars: Logistics in Western Warfare from the Middle Ages to the Present* (Boulder, Colorado: Westview Press, 1993), pp.137-160

Lynn, John A., 'The Embattled Future of Academic Military History', *Journal of Military History*, Vol.61, No.4 (1997), pp.777-789

Malcolm, Joyce L., 'A King in Search of Soldiers: Charles I in 1642', *Historical Journal*, Vol.21 (1978), pp.251-273

Matthews, Mark, 'Shipping and Local Enterprise in the Early Eighteenth Century', *Journal of Transport History*, Vol.24, No.2 (2003), pp.139-153

Moyar, Mark, 'The Current State of Military History', *The Historical Journal*, Vol.50, No.1 (2007), pp.225-240

Mungeam, Gerald I. (ed.), 'Contracts for the Supply of Equipment to the "New Model" Army in 1645', *The Journal of The Arms & Armour Society*, Vol.6, No.3 (September 1968), pp.53-115

Murdoch, Steve, Grosjean, Alexia, and Talbott, Siobhan, 'Drummer Major James Spens: Letters from a Common Soldier Abroad, 1617-1632', *Northern Studies*, Vol.47 (2015), pp.76-101

Murphy, Elaine, 'Atrocities at Sea and the Treatment of Prisoners of War by the Parliamentary Navy in Ireland, 1641-1649', *The Historical Journal*, Vol.53, No.1 (March 2010), pp.21-37

Nusbacher, Aryeh J.S., 'Civil Supply in the Civil War: Supply of Victuals to the New Model Army on the Naseby Campaign, 1-14 June 1645', *The English Historical Review*, Vol.115, No.460 (February 2000), pp.145-160

Oestmann, Anne, 'Billeting in England During the Reign of Charles I, 1625-1649: The Case of Tickhill/Yorkshire', *Arbeitskreis Militär und Gesellschaft in der Frühen Neuzeit e.V.*, Vol.10, No.1 (2006), pp.74-90

Ohlmeyer, Jane H., 'The Antrim Plot of 1641: A Rejoinder' *The Historical Journal*, Vol.37, No.2 (1994), pp.431–437

Ohlmeyer, Jane, 'The Wars of Religion, 1603–1660' in Bartlett, T., and Jeffrey, K. (eds), *A Military History of Ireland* (Cambridge: Cambridge University Press, 1996), pp.160–187

Parker, Geoffrey, 'The "Military Revolution," 1560–1660–A Myth?', *The Journal of Modern History*, Vol.48, No.2 (1976), pp.195–214

Parrott, David, 'Strategy and Tactics in the Thirty Years' War: The "Military Revolution"', *Militärgeschichtliche Mitteilungen*, Vol.18 (1985), pp.7–25

Perceval-Maxwell, Michael, 'The "Antrim plot" of 1641–A Myth? A Response', *The Historical Journal*, Vol.37, No.2 (1994), pp.421–430

Perjes, Géza, 'Army Provisioning, Logistics, and Strategy in the Second Half of the 17th Century', *Acta Historica Academiae Scientiarum Hungaricae*, Vol.16, No.1/2 (1970), pp.1–52

Porter, Stephen, 'Farm Transport in Huntingdonshire, 1610–1749', *The Journal of Transport History*, Vol.3, No.1 (March 1982), pp.35–46

Powell, John R., 'Blake and the Defence of Lyme Regis', *The Mariner's Mirror*, Vol.20, No.4 (1934), pp.448–474

Roberts, Michael, 'The Military Revolution, 1560–1660', in Rogers, C. J. (ed.), *The Military Revolution Debate, Readings on the Military Transformation of Early Modern Europe* (Boulder, Colorado: Westview, 1995), pp.13–35

Robinson, Gavin, 'Horse Supply and the Development of the New Model Army, 1642–1646', *War in History*, Vol.15, No.2 (2008), pp.121–140

Rogers, Clifford J., 'The Military Revolutions of the Hundred Years' War', *The Journal of Military History*, Vol.57, No.2 (1993), pp.241–278

Roy, Ian, 'England Turned Germany? The Aftermath of the Civil War in Its European Context', *Transactions of the Royal Historical Society*, 5th Series, Vol.28 (1978), pp.127–144

Roy, Ian, 'Why did Prince Rupert Fight at Marston Moor?', *Journal of the Society for Army Historical Research*, Vol.86, No. 347 (Autumn 2008), pp.236–257

Rutherford, Stephen M., 'A New Kind of Surgery for a New Kind of War: Gunshot Wounds and Their Treatment in the British Civil Wars' in Appleby, D. J., and Hopper, A. (eds), *Battle-Scarred: Mortality, Medical Care and Military Welfare in the British Civil Wars* (Manchester: Manchester University Press, 2018), pp.57–77

Sacks, David H., and Lynch, Michael, 'Ports 1540–1700' in Clark, P. (ed.), *The Cambridge Urban History of Britain Vol.2, 1540–1840* (Cambridge: Cambridge University Press, 2000), pp.377–424

Schwoerer, Lois G., '"The Fittest Subject for a King's Quarrel": An Essay on the Militia Controversy, 1641–1642', *Journal of British studies*, Vol.11, No.1 (November 1971), pp.45–76

Skidmore, Peter, 'Vessels and Networks: Shipowning in North-West England's Coasting Trade in the Late Eighteenth and Early Nineteenth Centuries', *The Mariner's Mirror*, Vol.99, No.2 (April 2013), pp.153–170

Stater, Victor L., 'The Lord Lieutenancy on the Eve of the Civil Wars: The Impressment of George Plowright', *The Historical Journal,* Vol.29, No.2 (June 1986), pp.279-296
Stearns, Stephen J., 'Conscription and English Society', *Journal of British Studies*, Vol.11, No.2 (May 1972), pp.1-23
Stewart, Laura A.M., 'Military Power and the Scottish Burghs, 1625-1651', *Journal of Early Modern History,* Vol.15 (2011), pp.59-82
Stoyle, Mark, 'The Old Cornish Regiments, 1643-44', *Cornish Studies*, Vol.16 (2008), pp.26-47
Stoyle, Mark 'The Road to Farndon Field: Explaining the Massacre of the Royalist Women at Naseby', *The English Historical Review,* Vol.123, No.503 (2008), pp.895-923
Temple, Robert, 'The Original Officer List of the New Model Army', *Bulletin of the Institute of Historical Research*, Vol.59 (1986), pp.50-77
Wanklyn, Malcolm, 'Choosing Officers for the New Model Army, February to April 1645', *Journal of the Society for Army Historical Research*, Vol.92 (2014), pp.109-125
Wanklyn, Malcolm, 'Cromwell's Generalship and the Conquest of Scotland, 1650-1651', *Cromwelliana* Vol.3, No.4 (2015), pp.36-50
Wanklyn, Malcolm, 'The Impact of Water Transport Facilities on the Economies of English River Ports, c.1660-c.1760', *The Economic History Review,* Vol.49, No.1 (1996), pp.20-34
Wanklyn, Malcolm D.G., 'The Severn Navigation in the Seventeenth Century: Long-Distance Trade of Shrewsbury Boats', *Midland History,* Vol.13, No.1 (1988), pp.34-58
Wanklyn, Malcolm, and Young, Peter, 'A King in Search of Soldiers: Charles I in 1642. A Rejoinder', *Historical Journal,* Vol.24 (1981), pp.147-154
Wheeler, James S., 'The Logistics of Conquest', in Lenihan, P. (ed.), *Conquest and Resistance: War in Seventeenth-Century Ireland* (Leiden: Brill, 2001), pp.177-210
Wheeler, James S., 'The Logistics of the Cromwellian Conquest of Scotland 1650-1651', *War & Society* Vol.10, No.1 (May 1992), pp.1-18
Willan, Thomas S., 'The River Navigation and Trade of the Severn Valley, 1600-1750', *The Economic History Review,* Vol.8, No.1 (November 1937), pp.68-79
Woodward, Donald, 'The Anglo-Irish Livestock Trade of the Seventeenth Century', *Irish Historical Studies,* Vol.18, No.72 (September 1973), pp.489-523

Unpublished Theses
Bennet, Martyn, 'The Royalist War Effort in the North Midlands, 1642-1646', PhD Thesis (University of Loughborough, 1986)
Coates, Ben, 'The Impact of the English Civil War on the Economy of London, 1642-1650', PhD Thesis (University of Leicester, 1997)
Furgol, Edward, 'The Religious Aspects of the Scottish Covenanting Armies, 1639-1651', DPhil Thesis (University of Oxford, 1983)

Greenhall, Matthew, 'The Evolution of the British Economy: Anglo-Scottish Trade and Political Union, an Inter-regional Perspective, 1580–1750', PhD Thesis (University of Durham, 2011)

Harrison, George, 'Royalist Organisation in Wiltshire, 1642–1646', PhD Thesis (Royal Holloway, University of London, 1963)

Hutton, Gillian M., 'Roads and Routeways in County Durham: 1530–1730', PhD Thesis (University of Durham, 2011)

Kupfermann, Elias, 'The Role of Windsor Castle During the English Civil Wars, 1642–1650', MPhil Diss. (University of Leicester, 2019).

Robinson, Gavin, 'Horse Supply in the English Civil War, 1642–1646', PhD Thesis (University of Reading, 2001)

Websites

'1641 Depositions, Trinity College Dublin', <1641.tcd.ie>

'Civil War Petitions', <www.civilwarpetitions.ac.uk>

'England', topographic-map.com, <https://en-gb.topographic-map.com/maps/b9/England/> Accessed 18 August 2020

'Oxford Dictionary of National Biography', <https://www.oxforddnb.com/>

'National Covenant, solemn agreement inaugurated by Scottish churchmen on Feb. 28, 1638, in the Greyfriars' churchyard, Edinburgh (1638)', Reformation History, <http://reformationhistory.org/nationalcovenant.html> Accessed 12 March 2020

'The Petition of Right', UK Parliament Digital Archive, <https://digitalarchive.parliament.uk/HL/PO/PU/1/1627/3C1n2> Accessed 28 September 2021

'Theses in progress (UK)', listed in *History Online*, website of the Institute of Historical Research, <www.history.ac.uk/history-online≥, Accessed 31 June 2019

'United Kingdom Topographic Map', PhysicalMap.org, <https://physicalmap.org/node/45> Accessed 7 July 2021

About the author

Glenn W. Price is a professional researcher and analyst with a lifelong passion for history, particularly military and political history, wargaming, and writing. Entering academia as a mature student he successfully achieved a BA in both History and International Relations, an MRes in Medieval Military and Political History, and has subsequently been awarded a doctorate in history for his research on the military logistics and supply systems of the British Civil Wars.

Other titles in the Century of the Soldier series

No 1 *'Famous by my Sword'*: *The Army of Montrose and the Military Revolution*
No 2 *Marlborough's Other Army*: *The British Army and the Campaigns of the First Peninsular War, 1702–1712*
No 3 *Cavalier Capital: Oxford in the English Civil War 1642–1646*
No 4 *Reconstructing the New Model Army: Vol 1: Regimental Lists April 1645 to May 1649*
No 5 *To Settle the Crown: Waging Civil War in Shropshire, 1642–1648*
No 6 *The First British Army, 1624–1628: The Army of the Duke of Buckingham*
No 7 *Better Begging Than Fighting: The Royalist Army in Exile in the War against Cromwell 1656–1660*
No 8 *Reconstructing the New Model Army: Vol 2: Regimental Lists April 1649 to May 1663*
No 9 *The Battle of Montgomery 1644: The English Civil War in the Welsh Borderlands*
No 10 *The Arte Militaire: The Application of 17th Century Military Manuals to Conflict Archaeology*
No 11 *No Armour But Courage: Colonel Sir George Lisle, 1615–1648*
No 12 *Cromwell's Buffoon: The Life and Career of the Regicide, Thomas Pride*
No 14 *Hey for Old Robin! The Campaigns and Armies of the Earl of Essex During the First Civil War, 1642–44*
No 15 *The Bavarian Army during the Thirty Years War*
No 16 *The Army of James II, 1685-1688: The Birth of the British Army*
No 17 *Civil War London: A Military History of London under Charles I and Oliver Cromwell*
No 18 *The Other Norfolk Admirals: Myngs, Narbrough and Shovell*
No 19 *A New Way of Fighting: Professionalism in the English Civil War*
No 20 *Crucible of the Jacobite '15: The Battle of Sheriffmuir 1715*
No 21 *'A Rabble of Gentility': The Royalist Northern Horse, 1644–45*
No 22 *Peter the Great Humbled: The Russo-Ottoman War of 1711*
No 23 *The Russian Army In The Great Northern War 1700–21: Organisation, Matériel, Training, Combat Experience and Uniforms*
No 24 *The Last Army: The Battle of Stow-on-the-Wold and the End of the Civil War in the Welsh Marches, 1646*
No 25 *The Battle of the White Mountain 1620 and the Bohemian Revolt, 1618–22*
No 26 *The Swedish Army in the Great Northern War 1700–21: Organisation, Equipment, Campaigns and Uniforms*

No 27 *St. Ruth's Fatal Gamble: The Battle of Aughrim 1691 and the Fall Of Jacobite Ireland*
No 28 *Muscovy's Soldiers: The Emergence of the Russian Army 1462–1689*
No 29 *Home and Away: The British Experience of War 1618–1721*
No 30 *From Solebay to the Texel: The Third Anglo-Dutch War, 1672–1674*
No 31 *The Battle of Killiecrankie: The First Jacobite Campaign, 1689–1691*
No 32 *The Most Heavy Stroke: The Battle of Roundway Down 1643*
No 33 *The Cretan War (1645–1671): The Venetian-Ottoman Struggle in the Mediterranean*
No 34 *Peter the Great's Revenge: The Russian Siege of Narva in 1704*
No 35 *The Battle Of Glenshiel: The Jacobite Rising in 1719*
No 36 *Armies And Enemies Of Louis XIV: Volume 1 - Western Europe 1688–1714: France, Britain, Holland*
No 37 *William III's Italian Ally: Piedmont and the War of the League of Augsburg 1683–1697*
No 38 *Wars and Soldiers in the Early Reign of Louis XIV: Volume 1 - The Army of the United Provinces of the Netherlands, 1660–1687*
No 39 *In The Emperor's Service: Wallenstein's Army, 1625–1634*
No 40 *Charles XI's War: The Scanian War Between Sweden and Denmark, 1675–1679*
No 41 *The Armies and Wars of The Sun King 1643-1715: Volume 1: The Guard of Louis XIV*
No 42 *The Armies Of Philip IV Of Spain 1621–1665: The Fight For European Supremacy*
No 43 *Marlborough's Other Army: The British Army and the Campaigns of the First Peninsular War, 1702–1712*
No 44 *The Last Spanish Armada: Britain And The War Of The Quadruple Alliance, 1718–1720*
No 45 *Essential Agony: The Battle of Dunbar 1650*
No 46 *The Campaigns of Sir William Waller*
No 47 *Wars and Soldiers in the Early Reign of Louis XIV: Volume 2 - The Imperial Army, 1660–1689*
No 48 *The Saxon Mars and His Force: The Saxon Army During The Reign Of John George III 1680–1691*
No 49 *The King's Irish: The Royalist Anglo-Irish Foot of the English Civil War*
No 50 *The Armies and Wars of the Sun King 1643-1715: Volume 2: The Infantry of Louis XIV*

No 51 *More Like Lions Than Men: Sir William Brereton and the Cheshire Army of Parliament, 1642–46*
No 52 *I Am Minded to Rise: The Clothing, Weapons and Accoutrements of the Jacobites from 1689 to 1719*
No 53 *The Perfection of Military Discipline: The Plug Bayonet and the English Army 1660–1705*
No 54 *The Lion From the North: The Swedish Army During the Thirty Years War: Volume 1, 1618–1632*
No 55 *Wars and Soldiers in the Early Reign of Louis XIV: Volume 3 - The Armies of the Ottoman Empire 1645–1718*
No 56 *St. Ruth's Fatal Gamble: The Battle of Aughrim 1691 and the Fall Of Jacobite Ireland*
No 57 *Fighting for Liberty: Argyll & Monmouth's Military Campaigns against the Government of King James, 1685*
No 58 *The Armies and Wars of the Sun King 1643-1715: Volume 3: The Cavalry of Louis XIV*
No 59 *The Lion From the North: The Swedish Army During the Thirty Years War: Volume 2, 1632–1648*
No 60 *By Defeating My Enemies: Charles XII of Sweden and the Great Northern War 1682–1721*
No 61 *Despite Destruction, Misery and Privations..: The Polish Army in Prussia during the war against Sweden 1626–1629*
No 62 *The Armies of Sir Ralph Hopton: The Royalist Armies of the West 1642–46*
No 63 *Italy, Piedmont, and the War of the Spanish Succession 1701–1712*
No 64 *'Cannon played from the great fort': Sieges in the Severn Valley during the English Civil War 1642–1646*
No 65 *Carl Gustav Armfelt and the Struggle for Finland During the Great Northern War*
No 66 *In the Midst of the Kingdom: The Royalist War Effort in the North Midlands 1642–1646*
No 67 *The Anglo-Spanish War 1655–1660: Volume 1: The War in the West Indies*
No 68 *For a Parliament Freely Chosen: The Rebellion of Sir George Booth, 1659*
No 69 *The Bavarian Army During the Thirty Years War 1618–1648: The Backbone of the Catholic League (revised second edition)*
No 70 *The Armies and Wars of the Sun King 1643-1715: Volume 4: The War of the Spanish Succession, Artillery, Engineers and Militias*
No 71 *No Armour But Courage: Colonel Sir George Lisle, 1615–1648 (Paperback reprint)*

No 72 *The New Knights:* The Development of Cavalry in Western Europe, 1562–1700

No 73 *Cavalier Capital:* Oxford in the English Civil War 1642–1646 (Paperback reprint)

No 74 *The Anglo-Spanish War 1655–1660:* Volume 2: War in Jamaica

No 75 *The Perfect Militia:* The Stuart Trained Bands of England and Wales 1603–1642

No 76 *Wars and Soldiers in the Early Reign of Louis XIV:* Volume 4 - The Armies of Spain 1659–1688

No 77 *The Battle of Nördlingen 1634:* The Bloody Fight Between Tercios and Brigades

No 78 *Wars and Soldiers in the Early Reign of Louis XIV:* Volume 5 - The Portuguese Army 1659–1690

No 79 *We Came, We Saw, God Conquered:* The Polish-Lithuanian Commonwealth's military effort in the relief of Vienna, 1683

No 80 *Charles X's Wars:* Volume 1 - Armies of the Swedish Deluge, 1655–1660

No 81 *Cromwell's Buffoon:* The Life and Career of the Regicide, Thomas Pride (Paperback reprint)

No 82 *The Colonial Ironsides:* English Expeditions under the Commonwealth and Protectorate, 1650–1660

No 83 *The English Garrison of Tangier:* Charles II's Colonial Venture in the Mediterranean, 1661–1684

No 84 *The Second Battle of Preston, 1715:* The Last Battle on English Soil

No 85 *To Settle the Crown:* Waging Civil War in Shropshire, 1642–1648 (Paperback reprint)

No 86 *A Very Gallant Gentleman:* Colonel Francis Thornhagh (1617–1648) and the Nottinghamshire Horse

No 87 *Charles X's Wars:* Volume 2 - The Wars in the East, 1655–1657

No 88 *The Shōgun's Soldiers:* The Daily Life of Samurai and Soldiers in Edo Period Japan, 1603–1721 Volume 1

No 89 *Campaigns of the Eastern Association:* The Rise of Oliver Cromwell, 1642–1645

No 90 *The Army of Occupation in Ireland 1603–42:* Defending the Protestant Hegemony

No 91 *The Armies and Wars of the Sun King 1643–1715:* Volume 5: Buccaneers and Soldiers in the Americas

No 92 *New Worlds, Old Wars:* The Anglo-American Indian Wars 1607–1678

No 93 *Against the Deluge:* Polish and Lithuanian Armies During the War Against Sweden 1655–1660

No 94 *The Battle of Rocroi:* The Battle, the Myth and the Success of Propaganda

No 95 *The Shōgun's Soldiers:* The Daily Life of Samurai and Soldiers in Edo Period Japan, 1603–1721 Volume 2

No 96 *Science of Arms: the Art of War in the Century of the Soldier 1672–1699:* Volume 1: Preparation for War and the Infantry

No 97 *Charles X's Wars:* Volume 3 - The Danish Wars 1657–1660

No 98 *Wars and Soldiers in the Early Reign of Louis XIV:* Volume 6 - Armies of the Italian States 1660–1690 Part 1

No 99 *Dragoons and Dragoon Operations in the British Civil Wars, 1638–1653*

No 100 *Wars and Soldiers in the Early Reign of Louis XIV:* Volume 6 - Armies of the Italian States 1660–1690 Part 2

No 101 *1648 and All That:* The Scottish Invasions of England, 1648 and 1651: Proceedings of the 2022 Helion and Company 'Century of the Soldier' Conference

No 102 *John Hampden and the Battle of Chalgrove:* The Political and Military Life of Hampden and his Legacy

No 103 *The City Horse:* London's militia cavalry during the English Civil War, 1642–1660

No 104 *The Battle of Lützen 1632:* A Reassessment

No 105 *Monmouth's First Rebellion:* The Later Covenanter Risings, 1660–1685

No 106 *Raw Generals and Green Soldiers:* Catholic Armies in Ireland 1641–1643

No 107 *The Khotyn Campaign:* Polish, Lithuanian and Cossack armies versus the might of the Ottoman Empire

No 108 *Soldiers and Civilians, Transport and Provisions:* Early Modern Military Logistics and Supply Systems During The British Civil Wars, 1638-1653

SERIES SPECIALS:

No 1 *Charles XII's Karoliners:* Volume 1: The Swedish Infantry & Artillery of the Great Northern War 1700–1721